The Qur'an
The Noble Reading

PLEASE NOTE:
THE ORIGINAL TEXT IS IN
ARABIC.

OutReach (Da'wah) Coordinator
Central Illinois Mosque and
Islamic Center (CIMIC)
106 S. Lincoln, Urbana, IL 61801
Ph: 217-344-1555
Cimic@prairienet.org
http://www.prairienet.org/cimic/

The Qur'an
The Noble Reading

Second Revised Edition

TRANSLATION BY
T.B. IRVING
(AL-HAJJ TA'LIM 'ALI)

The Mother Mosque Foundation
Cedar Rapids, Iowa
1993

COVER PHOTO:
Dome over the Prayer Niche or *Miḥrab* of
the Great Umayyad Mosque of Cordoba

Published By
THE MOTHER MOSQUE FOUNDATION
P.O. Box 1852
Cedar Rapids, IA 52406-1852
Library of Congress Catalog No. 92-83748

ISBN No. 0-911119-52-3

PRINTED IN THE UNITED STATES OF AMERICA

Dedicated to
my Children
and Grandchildren

TABLE OF CONTENTS

Explained; ix Who are Muslims; What is Islām; Renegades OR Turncoats;   //PART FOUR//   x Virtue; Food; Pilgrimage; xi Who are True Muslims; xii the Bitter Wind; xiii the Battle of Uḥud; xiv the Loan Business; the Pious OR Heedful; xv; xvi the Battle of Uḥud again; xvii Reliance on God; Martyrs; xviii; xix; xx Creation; the Town Crier; Refugees

i Orphans and Marriage; Inheritance; ii Inheritance (cont'd); iii Sexual Offences; Repentance; Marriage; iv   //PART FIVE//   iv (cont'd) Marriage and Divorce; v Controlling Passion; vi A Man's Responsibility; Matrimonial Rifts; Association; Kindness; vii Conditions for Prayer; Association Again; viii Obeying Authority; Trusts and Ownership; ix; x Striving for God; the Qurʾān; xi Good and Evil, the Qurʾān; Handling Rumors; Etiquette or Politeness; xii Agitators; xiii Manslaughter; Murder; Public Service; xiv Refugees; xv Prayers During Warfare; Prayer in General; xvi; xvii; xviii Association; the Worst Sin; Satan and Pagan Practices; Those Who go to Paradise; xix Orphans; Marriage Difficulties; xx Oaths and Evidence; Courtroom Procedure; Belief; Wavering; Lackeys OR Yesmen; xxi   //PART SIX//   xxi (cont'd) Saints' Worship; xxii Jews; Jesus; xxiii Other Prophets; Jesus Again; the Trinity; xxiv Inheritance

i Conduct and Food during Pilgrimage; Food Again; Marriage; ii Washing Before Prayer; iii the Children of Israel; Christians; Christ is not God; iv Moses; v Murder (Cain and Abel); Handling Sedition; vi Theft; Consolation, with Intrigue; Judicial Procedure; vii Mosaic Law; Jesus' Role; the Diversity of Human Life; viii; ix War; x Other Believers; Christians; the Trinity (again); Christ; xi Jews Again; Christians are Closer to Islām;   //PART SEVEN//   xi Christians (cont'd); xii Food; Oaths (Perjury); Liquor and Gambling; xiii Pilgrimage; Seafood; Good and Evil; xiv How to Believe; Pagan practices; Personal Responsibility; Wills; xv Jesus' Miracles; xvi Jesus Himself Rejects Godhood

i; ii God is One; iii Association is Wrong; iv; v; vi Tolerance; Good Manners; vii Keys to the Unseen; viii More on God; Handling Discussions; ix God's Guidance; Abraham's Search for God; x Other Prophets; xi; xii Proof of God; xiii God; the Creator of Everything; the Limits of Responsibility; Tolerance;   //PART EIGHT//   xiv Saying Grace over Food; xv; xvi Association is Deceitful; Infanticide Forbidden;

Pagan Practices; xvii, xviii Dietary Restrictions; Associators; xix Ten Commandments; the Straight Road; xx Sectarian Divisions; Abraham; Individual Responsibility; Collective Responsibility

i; ii the Devil with Adam; the Tree of Good and Evil; iii Sexual Misconduct; Etiquette; iv More Do Not's; Philosophy of History; v Heaven and Hell; vi; vii Creation; the Winds; viii Noah's Mission; ix ʿĀd and their Prophet Hūd; x Thāmūd and their Messenger [Methu-]Ṣāliḥ; Lot; xi Midian and their Prophet Shuʿayb;   //PART NINE//   xi (cont'd); xii Prosperity and Depression; xiii Moses; xiv; xv; xvi; xvii Moses on Mt. Sinai; Modesty and Good Conduct; xviii the Golden Calf; xix the Unlettered Prophet; xx; xxi the Sabbath Breakers; Imperfect Messages; xxii the Islamic Covenant; the Dog; the Losers; xxiii; xxiv Man's Reproduction; Association; Idol Worship; How to Listen to the Qurʾān   /BOW DOWN HERE/

i True Believers; ii Battle Tactics; iii; iv; v   //PART TEN//   v (cont'd) the Battle Scene at Badr; vi Facing Aggression; vii Philosophy of History; Handling Treachery; viii; ix Quality Overcomes Quantity; x Refugees

i Treaty Rights; ii Self-Defence; iii Associators Should Not Visit Mosques; the Use of Property and Wealth; iv Fighting; v God Has no Son; Clergy are Branded; the *Hijra* or Sacred Year; vi Draft Dodging; vii Agitators; Charity; viii Charity (cont'd); Hypocrites; Turncoats; ix; x; xi Shirkers Again; xii Nomads;   //PART ELEVEN//   xii (cont'd); xiii Always Build Firmly; xiv the Believers' Reward; xv; xvi

i Creation OR Cosmogony; ii the Arrogant Ones; Facing Trouble; Skeptics; Association as a Sin; iii Rain from Heaven; the Final Judgment; Associates Will Renounce Their Own Worship; iv God Alone; Truth; the Qurʾān; v Personal Responsibility; Nations; vi; vii God Needs no Son; viii Noah; Moses and Aaron; the Tournament of Magic; ix; x Freewill; Tolerance; xi God's Role Explained

i   //PART TWELVE//   ii; iii Noah; iv Noah's Embarkation Prayer; the Unseen; v Hūd Himself; vi Ṣāliḥ; vii Abraham; Isaac his Second Son; Lot's Story; viii Shuʿayb with Midian; ix Moses; Doomsday; x Prayer

Control; Correct Religion; v; vi The Final Hour

Introduction to
The Noble Reading

T. B. IRVING

THE QUR›ĀN IS A magnificent document that has been known for fourteen centuries because of its matchlessness or inimitability, its essential *iᶜjāz* (10:IV), to use the Qur›ānic term. A clear strain runs through its message, and the intent of this translation is to permit everyone, Muslim or non-Muslim alike, to understand the sacred document itself, even though they do not understand Arabic.

There is a necessity, almost an urgency now for an American version in contemporary English. Our holy Book should be recited on solemn occasions, both public and private, for comfort, morality and guidance. This process must begin in childhood in order for it to become familiar, for it is every Muslim's duty to read the Qur›ān and try to understand it. However, the duty has become a problem for those who no longer know any Arabic. A new generation of English-speaking Muslims has grown up in North America which must use our scripture differently than their fathers would have done. Their thinking roots have become distinct on a new continent without the familiar use of our holy tongue, and a great difference has developed between their customs and their ancestral faith.

American Muslims face many problems, and the younger ones face more than the usual group of teenagers; many now have reached the second and third generation when the use of Arabic is being forgotten in the home. It has rarely been taught as a formal subject of instruction, nor has the intellectual content of the Qur›ān been studied. The practice which has grown up around the traditional faith has been gravely weakened. Muslims do not have to dance the *dabka*, wear a fez, eat Arab-style bread or *shish kabob* in order to be good Muslims. You can have soft drinks, but it is harder to handle stronger beverages and remain faithful to Islam.

In the first place, any accurate version is really a *tafsīr* or commentary written in the target language, and it is important for us to have a trustworthy one with Islamic views. The Qur›ān itself says that any divine message should be presented in a people's own tongue: "We have not sent any messenger unless he was to explain to them in his folk's own tongue" (**Abraham** 14:4). Later on some poetic spirit may bring us the noble paraphrase that we likewise need; I have attempted no such paraphrase myself, because I might feel inclined to take too many liberties with it. Right now the message must simply be accurate, and clear enough so that it will convince even a child. It should be a document one can read, as well as offer a basis for research, a useful whole. Centuries of research have in fact been spent on it, by Muslims and non-Muslims alike. I am not concerned with later development and exegesis here, but merely with the statement or restatement of the initial message.

The Bible as we know it, and as the Jews and Christians have known it, and especially knew it in the Prophet's day, is not as reliable as the Qur'ān, and has led to constant variation, especially in its interpretation. Thus despite the difficult relations that exist between the West and the Islamic Middle East at present, the basic document for all sides to understand the latter area is the Qur'ān, no matter how social scientists or theologians may try to interpret that part of the world after their own fashion.

Religion leads people to predictable action or reaction when its principles govern the outlook of its followers. Thus the Qur'ān is shunned or favored insofar as its principles lend themselves to controlling human behavior according to the morality or whims of those in power. Sacred symbols offer a way by which people can look at the Universe, give them a life style which tells them how things are and how they should be. The Orientalists who worked for London, Paris, the Hague or Lisbon wanted to control Islam for their own purposes, and they decreed that the word Islam means "submission." How far they strayed is now apparent, as the Islamic lands throw off their yokes and try to regain their ancient principles.

However, translations by Muslims are not always acceptable. Muḥammad 'Alī's is clear but his commentary and at times the English text can be affected by his sectarian tendency. Besides he has used the Havas Arabic dictionary and this is risky because of its hindthoughts carried over from Catholicism. A. Yūsuf 'Alī's is more satisfactory as a commentary but his English is overladen with extra words which neither explain the text nor embellish the meaning. True embellishment is the simple telling word which does not detract, but carries the mind directly to the meaning. Marmaduke Pickthall accomplished his labor in the East, and therefore his translation is in heavy Jacobean English laid upon a superstructure of Eastern preoccupations. *The Koran* by N. J. Dawood which is published in the Penguin series of World Classics is better than most, but it often becomes merely a prosaic paraphrase. 'Abd al-Mājid Daryābādī is clear, but hard to work with because of its arrangement, especially in the naming and numbering of chapters. Egyptian and Pakistani interpreters often show that they have not been talking to anyone outside of their own circle, and this lack has hurt even their political propaganda. Mercier unfortunately was translated into English from his French version, just as de Ryer and Sale came to us more from previous translations into Latin than directly from the Arabic. Likewise the new Japanese translation was made from the English, as the modern Spanish is from French and German. Andalusia has forgotten its glory!

Since studies like Nöldeke's and Bell's exist for those who need a barren type of criticism, it is not my purpose to follow in that line of research, but rather just as painstaking a one in trying to lay before the English-speaking world at the end of the twentieth century of their era, or the beginning of the fifteenth century of the Hijra, the message of the Qur'ān in reverent yet contemporary English. My purpose is not to enter into theological controversy, nor to test the ancestry of ideas that can be found elsewhere; I will not indulge in refutation, especially of old chestnuts, but let the text and the message stand for themselves. This is a long and dignified tradition which should be made part of the world heritage in a universal age.

As with the Spanish poet Alonso de Ercilla in sixteenth century Chile, the Qurɔān was written down on whatever writing material was available: paper, leather, parchment, stones, wooden tablets, the shoulder blades of oxen, and the "breasts of men." Where did they secure such a quantity of paper or parchment which was needed to make the final copies of ɔUthmān's version?

The present and traditional order is not chronological, but arranged topically, as an editor has a right to do with any book in his hands. How to split up the corpus has always been a problem, especially for Western critics, but changing the order of the text has not bred believers in the West. The vaunted scientific method of investigating texts at first hand is not practised by Western experts when dealing with Islam. However, the urge to revise has worried Western critics and Orientalists like Rodwell, Bell and Dawood, as well as many others.

The Book itself consists of 114 chapters of varying size which are arranged roughly according to their order of length. Its paragraphs and sections have a very traditional order that is easily followed and by which the verses can be located. The present order in the Qur'an was achieved before the Prophet's death. The third caliph 'Uthman ibn-'Affan (644–656) appointed a committee to collect an authorized version of the Qur'anic text in one volume. 'Uthman's committee was set up to publish the Qur'an in a standard version, and the members naturally showed great conscientiousness in this respect. This committee fulfilled its task well, and so within a score of years after the Prophet's death, a splendid job was accomplished.

If we follow the traditional order, then we receive the Prophet's essential message; while if we use a revised order, then we follow his historical mission. I prefer to follow the traditional order, and state the message so that Muslim scholars can follow this without effort, and on this order I have elaborated the present work for contemporary English-speaking readers. Within Islamic circles we cannot now produce a good English prayerbook until this is based upon a reliable English version of the Qurɔān.[1]

The message of Islam does not come through in most contemporary textbooks used in our schools. Very few have been written by sincere Muslims, so that Islam is derided, and kept at a distance, when we need a clear explanation in our own language, devoid of strained syntax and one which can be read meaningfully and reverently in public. Thousands of Westerners who are now living in or visiting the countries of the Middle East as well as others who never expect to live or visit there, need nonetheless to understand the ethical system which prevails in the Islamic world. The crisis in Iran has shown that.

The present volume (i.e. the English translation) has been planned as an advance edition only. What has been accomplished till now has been done mostly with my own resources. Thanks to the generous help of the Aossey brothers of Cedar Rapids, and the Canadian Muslims, especially those living around Niagara Falls, I was able to accomplish this task because they have indeed helped me financially. So have my friends in Qatar and the Arabian Gulf. God will bless their efforts and kindness, their essential *iḥsān* and *ṣadaqa*—in other words, true charity.

Nevertheless this translation is not the sacred canon but merely a thread of thought plus some inspiration which appear in the pages I have been preparing. Translation is literally impossible because interpretation in another language is an on-going process, especially with a document that must be used constantly. Almost every day I learn a new rendering for a word or phrase; then I must run this new thread of meaning through other passages. The Qurʾān is a living Book. We must respect yet find a way to interpret this sacred text, and not deform its meaning. The refrain running through Chapter 54 on **The Moon** tells us: "We have made the Qurʾān easy to memorize; yet will anyone memorize it?" (54:22). As it claims, the Qurʾānic message is easy to learn. It is divided up so that it can be read in sittings, or read straight through (17:xII). This is clear from the canon itself.

The Qurʾān is not a missionary manual but a record of experience. It forms both a message or *risāla*, an "ideology" carried by a *rasūl* or 'messenger'; and it is also a Book or scripture (*kitāb*) sent specifically via the Messenger Muhammad (*rasūl Allāh* or 'God's messenger')—may God accept his prayers and grant him peace! However the Qurʾān does not offer minute details about everything such as is found in many other scriptures; it is an existentialist document telling about the Prophet's experience during his mission to the Arabs and the world. It is the Noble Reading (56:III); it is a consecrated Text.[2]

In this new translation, I have attempted to accomplish what the West has generally failed to do with Islam: to study it from within and in the light of its own texts. The Qurʾān is obviously the best preparation for such an attempt. Moreover this book gives the young Muslim something to hold on to in this day when most authority on moral matters is being abdicated. The doctrinal and ethical superstructure raised on the Five Pillars and other beliefs does not belong in this Introduction, which has been presented merely as a means of helping understand the message.

I have tried to find the simplest word so that the Muslim child can understand it easily, and feel strengthened thereby. It is also intended for the pious non-Muslim who is not already tied up in theology of some other sort: we must be able to discuss Islam on our own terms, terms which have been made up through our own knowledge and our own use of the English language. This present volume has been prepared in order to spread greater understanding of the Islamic religion and to present the English-speaking world with a clear rendition of the original Arabic into intelligible modern English. Even in English, the tendency with the Bible now is away from the seventeenth-century language which sounds too much like Pickthall, into the English of present-day speakers.[3]

The Islamic community in the United States and Canada has in certain fashion commissioned me with this task, and I must thank my good friends of Cedar Rapids, Iowa especially for their constant encouragement in the venture, because the whole project has grown into a massive undertaking directed also to those non-Muslims who need an introduction to the basic scripture of Islam. I also would like to thank the many people whose enquiries and requests for information and material have kept me working at the job. I hope that in this new translation I have in some small measure achieved a version of the Noble Reading, *al-Qurʾān al Karīm*, which can open up its treasures and lay the basis for Islamic piety within the English language and throughout the English-speaking world. Thus for over twenty-three years, I have been reading the Qurʾān carefully in Arabic "at daybreak" (17:IX), with the aim of presenting it in a form which will live for a few decades longer, God willing, or at least until some more gifted worker takes up the challenge and improves on this version.

Grammar and Syntax

A translation from one language to another requires that the translator have the "feel" of both languages he is working with, that of the textual one which is being translated, and that of the target language. Many Qurʾānic translators, however, have been fluent even in a third tongue which has ended by confusing them; a close attachment to Latin, Urdu or French can hinder the smooth flow of Arabic words and phrases into English. Several previous translations of the Qurʾān have likewise been rendered grotesque by relying on antiquated grammar and twisted syntax, without mentioning other problems like terminology or the correct rendering of individual words. There is no reason why our holy Book must be quoted in awkward English: if the Arabic is clear (16:XIV, 26:XI) then why do we need to worry about it?

My aim has been to remain scrupulously faithful to the Arabic text, and still create a version which represents good American English prose and can be used confidently by English-speaking people. Arabic is paratactic in its structure while English syntax involves more clauses and phrases, although it does not approach the complexity of either Latin or German to which it is related.

Conjunctions and connectives pose one of our first problems, for one cannot turn English into parataxis and begin each sentence or phrase with a series of "and's" as is done in Arabic and Hebrew. Arabic actually has two common words for our single "and"; *wāw* (which is a prefix in Semitic) refers to the simultaneous "and", while *fā* (also a prefix) expresses the consecutive connector. The letter *fā*, can be rendered at times by 'then', 'next' and 'so', or even by the interjection 'why...!' as a further possibility. In English we use "so", "thus", "well", "then", "as well as" to connect sentences and thought groups in the same manner; we use "so" and "plus" constantly in this fashion in normal speech. On the other hand the simultaneous *wāw-* can be 'while' with following or linking verbs and 'as well as' with long lists of nouns, especially for the final one at the end of a list which needs to be included and have attention focused on it: "to Heaven and Earth, and to the mountains..." (33:IX). The common Semitic paratactic sentence is deadly in dealing with these long lists if it is not handled judiciously in translation. Conjunctions should bind the late-coming concept into the body of the main thought, and not just let ideas go on and on. Moreover neither of these particles *wāw* or *fā* need always be rendered into English.

Some confusion in translation stems at times from the inability to distinguish between noun and verbal sentences, as occurs in other Semitic languages too: "Verily, I say unto you..." OR "Verily I, say unto you..." as it should be punctuated, occurs in the New Testament in John 1:51 in the King James version, as well as other places, where the Aramaic dialect shines through the bad Greek. It is really, in contemporary English: "As for me, I tell you..." In the great hymn to "Light" we have the sentence "*Wa-alladhīna kafarū a‹mālu-hum ka-sarāb^{in} bi-qī‹at^{in}*" (24:v). This begins with a noun clause, and the resulting nominal sentence should be: "Those who disbelieve [will find] their deeds are like a mirage on a desert..." (**Light** 24:39). The need to put the subject first in English often leads us to use the passive.

The disjunctive pronoun precedes the common Spanish phrase: *A mï me gusta...* meaning 'I like...'; somewhat similar to *Le voici* for 'Here it is...' in French. In **The Opening** chapter (*al-Fātiḥa*) we find this construction used in the fourth line: "You do we worship and You do we call on for help" (1:15). There is no "only" in this sentence, as some translators insert; the disjunctive position itself gives the needed emphasis they are trying to find.

Verbs cause some difficulty too since they can vary in their usage. The English verbs "to be" and "to have" are generally expressed in Arabic only by means of the syntax governing pronouns and prepositions. How things exist, and how they should be or how we would like to have them, yields a different quality in Semitic speech; the tone of its ethos has other distinct roots. "Act" and "mean" in my translation are not always placed between brackets since, similar to "to be" and "to have", they are implied as active, mental verbs: "Your Lord *acts* as an Observer" (34:II (end). The verb "acted [honorably OR charitably]" in 2:VIII gives more force to the verbal quality.

"Giving" and "saying" are often not expressed clearly to a Western reader in other translations, and need to be assumed from the context and their prepositions. "Belongs" and "belonged to" are English verbs which sometimes must be inserted, as in "to God [belongs] the Unseen"— *li'Llāh^{i}* ... (16:XI); or "He owns whatever is in front of us, and whatever is behind us" in 19:IV. "Owns" is another verb that can be inserted for the prepositional phrase *la-hu* 'to him [is]', and at times is clearer than 'he has' (70:3).

Tense and conditional moods must be expressed with care, especially with the absent verb "to be"; *Lā ikrāh fī al-dīn* should be '[Let there be] no compulsion in religion' (**The Cow** 2:XXXIV). The softened imperative here expresses the difference between how things exist and how they should be, or how we would like to have them.

Collective nouns are generally considered as abstract feminines in Arabic, exactly what we find in the English words "cattle", "opera", "people". Plurals in Arabic which do not refer to human beings become abstract feminines, and take their adjectives in the feminine singular.

The partitive construction may be known to some educated speakers of English from their study of French; yet this knowledge has rarely been used by other translators from the Arabic: "seek *some of* his bounty..." we are enjoined in 17:vii; and *kulū min ṭayyibāt-i mā razaqnā-kum* 'eat the wholesome things we have provided you with' (20:iv); also "*some* of those We transported along with Noah" (19:iv); and "so We may show you [Moses] *some of* our greatest signs" (20:i). These examples provide a random sample.

The superlative absolute presents another problem. It appears as 'quite Aware' for God's quality as the *Aʿlam* (17:v); 'quite Observant' for *Abṣar*, and 'quite Alert' for *Asmaʿ* in 18:iv.

Translating into English has still other problems. For example, English is very deficient when it comes to 2nd-person pronouns, which nowadays are found only as "you", "your" and "yours". The old "ye", "thou" and "thee" as well as their respective possessive pronouns are obsolete, especially when teaching our children, even though they appear in the King James version of the Bible and the translation of *The Glorious Koran* as this has been rendered by Marmaduke Pickthall. His archaic quality cannot live on. The situation is further complicated by the use of the indefinite "you" referring to "anybody" or "everybody" as in the colloquial expression "You should do that!" Occasionally I indicate the singular and plural of this pronoun (as these may occur in Arabic), especially when the Prophet is addressed; at other times the message is directed to his audience or to believers. "You all" or "you (all)" is more natural than "ye" in North American English, and I have occasionally used this neutral though dialectal plural with discretion where one must show the difference between the singular and the plural pronoun of Arabic. It sounds more natural even outside of the Deep South, than the obsolete "ye" which few North Americans can use effectively any more. The vocative particle *yā...* is usually translated as 'O...!'; but it is usually omitted in contemporary English. Moses addresses his brother Aaron simply as "Son of my mother!" in 7:xviii.

English is also defective in the meanings for "man", both as this word is opposed sexually to "woman", and generically to the animal kingdom in general, and also to sprites. The singular *insān* means '(every) man' in 17:ii and 19:v, almost in the spirit of the medieval European mysteries; and in the Chapter *Al-ʿAṣr* we meet him "At eventide, everyman/[feels] at a loss..." (103:1-2).

"Man(kind)" and "people" are other defective expressions in English. The 'folk' meant by *qawm* are literally those who "stand up" alongside you to defend your common interests. *Ahl*, on the other hand, means those people from one's own tent group, "living down the street" or in the same apartment house, as we would express this in modern urban society. "Adam" is a symbol for original man, mentioned in the Qurʾān, but only referred to as the common ancestor of humanity: *Banū Ādam*. The name is derived from 'red earth' in Arabic referring to the clay God used in fashioning him.

The Arabic pronominal conjunction *man* is archaic when this is translated as 'whosoever' or even 'he who', and this usage confuses younger readers; generally I use 'anyone who' and only occasionally 'he who' for this pronoun.

On the English side, our word "day" shows lexical deficiencies, for the word can be contrasted first with the concept of "night" (*layl* vs. *nahār*), then with the sidereal day as this is found in calendar dates, in contrast to weeks and months (which is *yawm*). I use 'daytime' or 'daylight' for *nahār*; but 'day' only for the broader twenty-four hour period.

The simple possessive case occasionally seems to be difficult to translate properly into English, especially the form with the apostrophe. The Arabic word order induces this syntactic error since it apparently follows French or Romance style, especially for Western theological students who have studied Latin first; but it really is similar to elementary Germanic syntax, even to the omission of the article in the possessing element. However, since the sequence in Arabic is possessed-possessor, the opposite of English, it seems superficially to resemble French. If you write one under the other, however, then the reverse word order shows up the affinity, a trick I have used successfully on the blackboard with attentive students in my classes in Arabic.

These examples in short are some of the textual difficulties which the translator faces in handling the Qurʾān. It has been a challenging task, but always rewarding.

Handling Dualism and Pairs

The dichotomy of life has always intrigued and puzzled people. They have tried to explain this phenomenon by saying the world is made up from pairs, just as they were born from a father and a mother, and themselves expect to marry. Some examples of these associated pairs are Heaven and Hell, Hell and Hades (or *Jahannam* and *Jaḥīm* in Arabic, by some alliterative coincidence), Heaven and Earth, night and day, heat and cold, light and dark.

Ḥalāl and ḥarām are alliterated twin principles too that appear in 5:3 and other places in the Qurʾān; dividing things into the permitted and forbidden is common for mnemonic purposes. The 'hallowed' or *ḥarām* is almost like the concept of taboo which the West borrowed from the Polynesians following the voyages of Captain Cook to the Pacific in the late eighteenth century. The 'sacred' or *muqaddas* is a similar state: Jerusalem is *al-Quds al-Sharīf* or 'the Eminent Sanctuary' which Muslims can no longer visit freely or without sorrow.

Consciousness and the Unseen give us dualistic principles for knowledge as well. Bodily pains contrasted with physical pleasures form another duality linked to Heaven and Hell in our minds. So good and evil form another pair (4:xi) as we find them throughout God's creation; they both come ultimately from God, but are not co-equal (5:xviii). We need to turn evil into good (7:xii) since they all derive from God (5:xiii). God may have permitted the presence of evil, but He did not command its existence.

"Where is night when the day arrives?" asked the Prophet rhetorically when he was questioned on this matter of good and evil. We also hear:

> The blind and the sighted are not equal
> nor are darkness and light
> nor a shady nook and a heatwave.
> The living and the dead are not alike,
> God lets anyone He wishes listen, while you
> will not make those in their graves hear.
> (*Originator* 35:19-22).

> If there were other gods
> in either [Heaven or Earth]
> besides God [Alone],
> they would both dissolve in chaos.
> (*Prophets* 21:22)

This concern for twin principles led to the so-called "Persian error" which the Albigensians practised in southern France until one of the first crusades wiped them out in the twelfth century, the onset of the great pogroms of Europe, as that continent flexed its muscles to practise genocide. Manicheism, as it is called formally, had been brought to western Europe by Roman soldiers before the fall of their empire, if it had not been a remnant from ancient Indo-European folk religion, and a sister of Celtic Druidism. The Bogomils in the Balkans formed another dualistic cult like it; in the fourteenth century they welcomed the Turks and became Muslims to escape the political and religious tyranny of both Rome and Byzantium as represented in the Catholic and Greek Orthodox churches respectively. In this case Islam benefited from the industrious Slavs and Albanians who joined Islam, and who contributed statesmen and architects to the Ottoman empire.

In Islam the sin of dualism is part of Association or *shirk*, and thus is unpardonable (4:48, 116). This "Persian error" considers the presence of evil to be necessary, as are the other pairs like Light and Darkness, Night and Daylight: *al-layl wa al-nahār* of 2:164 etc. There has been overmuch study of Jewish and Christian sources for the antecedents of Islam, but little of Manicheism and Zarathustrianism.

How to be both artistic and correct with the dual in Arabic becomes a syntactic problem when it comes to translation into English. A dual of sorts is found in the English words "either" and "both", but English has no adequate inflections for expressions like "both of them", "the *two*" etc., except with parents and other married couples, such as with Adam and Eve (7:II). However 'both' is generally the best distinguishing word in English, with verbs and nouns as well. Its use occurs with Moses and Aaron in 20:II ("they *both* said"); also 10:VIII and 26:II, and with David and Solomon (21:VI, 27:II).

A concern for light comes up, as this is contrasted with darkness (2:XXXIV): "God ... brings out of darkness into Light" (2:XXXIV, 13:I and especially 24:V). Bitter cold and darkness make the night seem hideous;

though night can also comfort, since it acts as a "garment" (25:v). So do good and evil as we find them throughout God's creation, we have noticed.

Sex of course is based on dualism: "He has placed two pairs for every kind of fruit on it" (13:ɪ).

Terminology

The fascinating matter of root meanings in Arabic is a linguistic matter which I will now deal with in this section on terminology. As soon as one begins to use our current Arabic dictionaries, it becomes evident that they have not been compiled by believers. One can tell this by the approximation of many otherwise clear Islamic terms, as well as the prejudice or worry shown by outsiders, even in Wehr, which in any case was translated from the German. These modern lexicographers have never sat in a mosque, so concerned are they with Christian ceremonies and festivals. Penrice's dictionary and glossary of Qurʾānic terms is helpful, but it too must be used with caution, for it is overladen with nineteenth-century missionary terms. Havas is clearly Catholic, and at times abysmal in its ignorance of Islam. Professor Izutsu of Tokyo has best shown why it is so difficult to translate each term adequately. He is to be commended for this, but then he is not a Westerner, full of their ingrained prejudices.

Let us discuss some terms in more detail. For instance, with the shades of meaning in the root $\sqrt{\text{dh k r}}$ to 'remember', 'recall', and also, perhaps surprisingly, 'male'; in the II or causative form "*dh kk r*" it means to 'remind'; and in the V, which is the reflexive of II or the causitive, to 'reflect', 'bear in mind' (for one's own benefit). The root $\sqrt{\text{s l m}}$ gives us *as-salām* meaning 'peace' as a greeting to persons; *al-Islām* for 'surrender' and 'submission' for the colonialist non-believer (infidel is how he would call himself elsewhere), but for us, 'commitment' to God Alone; and *Muslim* as the one 'who has so surrendered' or 'committed himself' to the Deity, the man who lives 'at peace.' For Islam, the word 'commitment' is more positive, active and responsible than are 'surrender" or 'submission" which the Orientalists and missionaries use; we Muslims have a right to choose our own terminology in English. We must forge our own words for our terms and parables like those about Satan, Ishmael, Jesus, Diabolis etc.

The majestic figure of God Alone or *Allāh* forms the capstone of Islamic worship and thought. He is *aṣ-Ṣamad* of Chapter 112:2, the 'Focus' and 'Source' for everything. How should reverent Muslims name Him? God has a Hundred of the "Finest Names" (59:end). The names and attributes for God are many: "All-Knowing" in our Germanic roots becomes the "Omniscient" in European Latinized parlance, which has given us other terms like "circumnambulation", "genuflexion", "ablution", as well as "submission" and "surrender" as meanings for Islam.

Training for this purpose will come through study and spiritual exercise. Let us therefore discuss some secular virtues. I use the word 'achievement' rather than the more old-fashioned term 'triumph' for *fawz*. The virtues themselves are: first of all, *birr*, as the basic one which we meet in 2:xxɪɪ for the first time; 'righteousness' sounds too old-fashioned now. *Muḥsin* is 'kindly', a concept that comes from the heart. It might be 'beneficient' in Latinized jargon, for *bene-* means 'good' or 'well' that is similar to *khayr*; while *-ficent* means 'doing [it]'. The abstract noun in the causative IV form is *iḥsān* or 'kindness' and parallel in morphological pattern (IV vn.) to *Islām*, and *īmān* ('faith' or 'belief'). The ideal was static. Reverence calls for restraint before things holy, giving sanctity to attitudes. *Rushd* or *rashad* is the social ideal of 'common sense' or 'normal behavior'. We find it in the name of the twelfth-century Spanish Arab philosopher Ibn-Rushd, who prepared the text of Aristotle for the scholastic teachers in the rising European universities of the following century.

Similarly *kufr* is 'disbelief', 'ingratitude' and a *kāfir* is a 'disbeliever'; *shirk* means 'associating [someone else with God],' and a *mushrik* is such an 'associator'; *ṭāghūt* are those 'arrogant' persons who deliberately come between man and his God. *Al-muttaqīn* are 'the heedful', 'those who do their duty', while *taqwà* is the quality of 'heeding [God's decrees]', or 'heedfulness', 'piety', just plain 'doing one's duty' before God and man. The moral basis of the new state in Madina is seen in the 'realm' or *mulk* in what we now know as 'control' today, and this can be used both as a noun and a verb: "O God, Holder of Control!" (3:26)

The passage *Laysa al-birr . . .*, is rendered "It is not virtue . . ."; 'virtue' rather than 'piety' for this concept seems in order. *Al-fāsiqūn* are 'perverse', 'corrupt' or 'immoral' people (2:XII). We should notice how the terms Heaven and Hell are alliterative in both English and Arabic (*al-janna* and *al-jahannam*), to which we might add *jaḥīm* which I have rendered 'Hades' to maintain the poetical effect. I also want to keep *ad-dunyā* and *al-ʿālamīn* separate as this 'nearer [world]' and 'the (greater) Universe' respectively, so they can be separate in the text and in the reader's mind. The latter is really a plural in Arabic, but I have unified this concept in English. *Jinn* and *Rūḥ* are two terms for 'sprite(s)' and 'Spirit' respectively. *Jinn* is often rendered as 'spirit' too, although these are really separate concepts; I am rendering the former 'sprite(s)' and leaving the second as 'Spirit' or 'Breath' for *Rūḥ* as we see in 17:X (beginning). Sprites or *jinn*, as a term, is handled wretchedly by most commentators, because it represents a plural in itself, while *jinni* is the proper singular. *Jinn* are what are called elves or fairies in English folklore, and mean the personified powers of the supernatural which are vaguely sensed by less sophisticated people, whose forces we meet in Robert Frost's "Mending Wall". These sprites found in the title of Chapter 72, were made from the glow in fire (55:I), like the angels or Diabolis (7:II).

There are foreign-based words like *mīl*, the Roman 'mile' or a "thousand" paces; the *ṣīrāt* from Latin *strata* meaning 'street', its English-derived descendant; *qaṣr* from *castrum* which is Latin too, which *via* the Arabic, gives Spanish its *alcázar* (as well as *Castro*); *thawr* or 'bull' has its memories of the Minotaur in Crete, and *los toros* in Spain; *arḍ* or 'earth' reveal this kinship, especially in terms connected with ancient agriculture; *Burg* in Germanic is linked with the title of Chapter 85 or *Al-Burūj* meaning *Constellations*, those 'castles' that we see in the night sky—which give us 'borough' in English and "bourgeois" in European sociology and politics.

Many expressions are given an ironic cast in some translations like "grand vizier" for the Turkish prime minister, when a simpler term like 'prime minister' or 'premier' would take it out of the Arabian Nights and make it sound more appropriate and fitting for statecraft. "No burdened [soul] shall bear another's burden" (6:xx etc.) shows what a cabinet minister carries in his portfolio. Other Turkish or Anglo-Indian forms are "muezzin" and "kismet". Crusading terms like "infidel" for the non-believer or misbeliever, one who flashes "scimitars" instead of waving swords. Spellings of this sort are "Kaaba" and Port "Said" as if this latter were the past participle of our verb to "say"; they should read instead: "Kaʿba" and "Saʿīd".

The etymology of the word "worship" in English should be borne in mind, as an exercise giving 'value' or 'worth' to superior beings, what we might call reverence, and thus linking it to ʿibāda in Arabic. The true worshipper or ʿabd (96:1) we meet in many Islamic names (and which is reduced to the ironic "Abdul" or 'servant of the...' in Orientalist jargon exactly like "admiral" who is literally 'prince of the ...', we must presume "of the sea").

There is also much prejudice in many of the Orientalist weasel words such as the term "Moorish" in connection with Spanish Islam or the French Foreign Legion. *Jinete* meaning 'horseman' or 'rider' and *zanahoria* for 'carrot' are the only truly Moorish or Berber words in the common Spanish lexicon, while true Arabic ones occur there frequently; yet they are all called "Moorish". What does the term Moorish mean? Who invented the name "Mauretania" in this century to describe the region south of Morocco which really should be Shinqīt, as its inhabitants call it. Mauretania lay north of the Atlas Mountains in Roman times, and is probably derived from a Phoenician cognate with the modern *Maghrib* or 'place where the sun sets' or "West".

Spelling and Phonetics

Throughout this translation I have consistently used the Library of Congress system of transliteration. This is essentially the same as that employed by the Royal Asiatic Society of London and the Board of Geographic Names in Washington, which ran into much incongruity during its survey of the Middle East and North Africa.

A standardization of Arabic nomenclature is needed for the countries which were under different colonial rule. *Shaṭṭ al-ʿArab* formed by the confluence of the Tigris and the Euphrates upstream from Baṣra in southern Iraq becomes *Chott al-Jarīd* in Tunisia and *Chott ach-Charqui* in Algeria. The word for 'mountain' *jabal*, has half a dozen spellings as it crosses the map of the Arab world. Besides the colonial styles used by the European occupiers in their former colonies, we run into Egyptian and Pakistani spellings of Arabic words, neither of which are standard Arabic. The Spanish-style "Tetuán" in the former Spanish zone of northern Morocco has recently become "Tétouan" because King Ḥasan or "Hassan" speaks French. This is pure verbal baroque, as French Orientalism too often is.

The spellings of "Moslem", "Kaaba" (for Ka‹ba) have a true beginning in ignorance, but they never seem to point any way to salvation. The spelling "Koran" is often used by non-Muslims and western-trained Muslims, the same people as use the spelling "Moslems", as the late Professor Hitti did in his book *Islam* in his incredible quotation: "An old-fashioned *Moslem (sic)* goes through the legal ablutions before he opens the book" (pp. 26-27)! What sort of Muslim did he get his information from? When this is pronounced with a voiced "s", it gives us "Mozlum", which means the exact opposite of a man of peace, for *ḍhulm* or *ẓulm* is 'harm', 'evil' etc. A "Moslem" thus means a 'cruel' individual like any Oriental tyrant.

Fortunately Arabic itself has a standard orthography and has had one for 1400 years; it is only the ear of the former colonial master or the present glib newspaper or television reporter which needs training—or to be eliminated altogether. English moreover is a deficient language in its use of the Roman alphabet, while French is even worse, or perverse. Some aspects of Arabic spelling should be indicated clearly, and not confused, especially with long vowels and emphatic or velarized consonants: ṭ, ḍ, ḍh (or ẓ), ṣ and the occasional ḷ. These consonants all express phonemic and semantic differentiation, and so they should be indicated clearly in some fashion.

Similar needs exist in phonetics. The sounds of *hamza* (›) and *‹ayn* (‹) are two difficult letters to transcribe consistently, as well as to explain to the uninitiated. The first or *hamza* is the glottal stop which gives English the need of its alternate indefinite article "an" in order to avoid this between words that begin with a vowel (as we hear in the childish form of "I want *a apple*"). The *‹ayn* is the voiced pharyngeal fricative, and historically has given us the capital "E" in the Roman alphabet, which represented this originally in Phoenician; and this might be used to express this sound, except that it would lead to confusion, especially among the uninitiated. These two important letters in the Arabic and other Semitic alphabets are not usually indicated in the Roman transliteration that many people use; nevertheless they require some representation, especially so students may learn more easily. The words Sa‹ūdi Arabia and Port Sa‹īd are two common examples of this confusion; many people pronounce the common "Saudi" as two syllables only, even newscasters who might know better, while "*sa‹īd*" is not the past participle of the English verb to "say". In the name of the Prophet's youngest wife 'Ā›isha both *‹ayn* and *hamza* appear together within the same word which is known fairly commonly but almost always spelled merely approximately (it is the feminine present participle of the verb *‹āsh*, to 'live', and thus means a 'living' woman).

Long and short vowels moreover should be indicated clearly and not confused; these distinctions are basic to Arabic prosody and especially for proper Qur›ānic diction. I use the grave accent of French "`" to show the *alif maqṣūra*, or the long *à* representing a hidden *i* or *y* in the root as in the names Mūsà or ‹Īsà. The digraph "ou" is a hopeless representation because it cannot show whether the Arabic vowel is long or short. Emphatic or velarized consonants all have phonemic and semantic differentiation, and so they should also be expressed clearly. Perhaps capital letters might be used for typewriters without any symbols for such foreign accents. Many booksellers, for instance, do so.

Are Eastern non-Arab Muslims able to explain these sounds to speakers of English, especially to North American children whose educational system has little contact with the Middle East or with foreign language instruction? Do Pakistanis hear these sounds clearly, or can Egyptians explain them to young Americans or Canadians? It is likewise grotesque for English-speaking persons to be advised to say a "z" or "s" for the voiced "dh" (ذ) or the voiceless "th" (ث) which they already say in "*they*" and "*other*", or in "*th*ink" and "wi*th*". English speakers have enough difficulties already in learning a foreign language without having an unnecessary one thrust upon them.

Thus we come to

Style and Mood

I have felt a need to break away from the usual type of commentary, Christian, Orientalist and even some Muslim ones at times, in order to provide a fresh outlook on the Qurʾān—to move it out into the English-speaking consciousness. I am interested only in stating the Qurʾānic message in clear contemporary English. This task has thus been tackled gradually as I read the Arabic text over and over for more than two decades, trying to find an English cadence for it. This must not falsify the message but should allow fresh words and concepts to enter the English-speaking mind and emotions.

The English-speaking world already has a great tradition of reading scripture. We have had a long tradition of Psalm and Gospel reading in our Protestant communities which can lead us along the way, and give us a sense of direction or manner. Some Qurʾānic translators have tried to match this mood by making their versions archaic or Jacobean, although this is not the means to achieve reverence in our youth, who must understand what they are hearing or reciting. They need comprehensible yet reverent English which will be respected by future generations. I should like to duplicate the terse yet vibrant quality of the original Qurʾānic message. We must make our message simple and go back to the primitive Arabic meaning wherever this is possible; but the whole vocabulary will have to be made over in painstaking fashion. We need to take a fresh look at the original text and explore it for new content and present-day application.

Matters of style thus come up. There is as much use of the word *abadan* or 'never' in the chapter on **Light** (*an-Nūr*) 24 as there is in Poe's *The Raven*. "Among his signs are..." begins in 30:III and gives us an introductory refrain to each section of that chapter. There is a narrative quality to **The Ants** (*an-Namal*) 27 which is succinct, especially in Lot's story following verse 57. A phrase is repeated at the end of each section in this chapter: "Your Lord is the Powerful, the Merciful", as well as in **[Drawn up in] Ranks** (*al-Ṣāfāt*) 37. In 16:XIV, the style becomes rapid, as if one were being spoken to, as well as in chapter 28 (*al-Qaṣaṣ*) when Moses sees the Burning Bush. We have similar narrative at times in 25 **The**

Standard (OR **Criterion**) (*al-Furqān*) and 26 **Poets** (*ash-Shuʿarāʾ*) telling about Moses' visit to Pharaoh's court. The style throughout this chapter (cf. VIII) is rapid, and the passages are almost the same as they describe each prophet in turn, since these are examples to show how each separate messenger had been called a poet when he was literally inspired. The allegorical or analogous verses mentioned in 3:I and the parables in 2:XXXV are important. The style in 20:II reminds us that the Qurʾān is narrated by the Deity, and has been received directly through inspiration.

Style creates mood: rhymed prose meets the ear, to offer us diction. As a corollary, this edition is arranged in paragraphs, verses or lines so the reader, in both public and private, is guided to the rhythm and movement of the passage. *Sajʿ* (rhymed prose) is ancient, oral punctuation; it tells the reader where to pause during his recitation so that his listeners can hear the message reverently, and understand it more easily. Non-English speakers often read English translations without realizing where to make the proper pauses needed for reverent attention. We find this rhythm in Chapters **This Land** (*al-Balad*) 90 and **Morning Bright** (*aḍ-Ḍuḥā*) 93 as well as in the two final ones, **Dawn** (*al-Falaq*) 113 and **Mankind** (*an-Nās*) 114, which I have not attempted to reproduce. The contrasting English words "night" and "daylight" rhyme, while Heaven and Hell or Hades alliterate; but these must not become cacophonic or a jingle, because such is not within the spirit of the Qurʾān.

The present version has been arranged either in prose form or as rhythmic free verse, depending on the nature of the Arabic original. I have laid the more lyric sections in the form of free verse and rough stanzas. An ecstatic quality is found in the early Meccan chapters towards the end of our canonical text (but actually at the start of the primitive prophetic message). Here is seventh-century Arabia speaking to North Americans in the closing years of the twentieth century, or perhaps we should now say, to mark the opening of the new fifteenth century of the Hijra era.

Giving cadence and rhythm form part of ritual through visual and auditory formulae. Through rhythm we achieve a glimpse of reality and thereby become more familiar with the Universe and how it functions. Ritual leads us through initiation and passage, especially for the adolescent who needs it; in this fashion young people begin to participate in the collective advance whereby mankind achieves its vision of reality.

What is reality, we ask again? What is that central focus for life on which everything depends, that we hear about in "God is the Source [for everything]" (112:2 **Sincerity**)? Through reverence and restraint we achieve its image, a visual or verbal formula, but without setting up any idols.

I hope that these ideas can bring the reader closer to reality, to the Unseen, that mystery of the world and life. The way we respond to the call of reality, gives us visual and auditory cadence and rhythm. Narrated style is what we hear, as this is related by the Deity Himself: "Do not fear; I am with you both. I both hear and see." (20:26). God is Omnipresent.

The Sleepers in **The Cave** (*al-Kahaf*) (18:I-IV) has been one of the most difficult stories to translate into flowing and convincing English; likewise, Moses' Mystic Journey in the same chapter (IX-X), and the tale of Double Horns or Alexander the Great that follows it (XI). At 20:IV we learn how

Pharaoh was overwhelmed; while in 53:1 we see "the Hawthorn on the Boundary / alongside the Garden of Repose" covered with its wonderful golden moths or blossoms. The poetic chapters towards the end of our Book, plus passages throughout the sacred Text require talent and artistry, the use of the telling word wherever one can find one. The fascination rises towards the end of the Book, mounting in real rhythm: great verses require vivid concepts. I have continually sought the choice poetic figure which we can all enjoy, plus some word magic if this can be achieved.

The present work has been a long story, undertaken in many cities and regions, in Baghdad on the Tigris initially, then in Minneapolis on the Mississippi, in sight of the volcanoes of Guatemala, in a Chicago suburb, at home once again in Canada, and finally in the mountains of Tennessee; but the end is here at last.

The first attempt for my original presentation was the well-known Cedar Rapids edition called *Selections from the Noble Reading*. That slender yet beautiful volume was edited over a decade ago, and slowly it has received recognition, especially in North American Islamic circles and to some extent abroad. A second, revised edition has appeared in Lagos, Nigeria for school children and travellers in English-speaking West Africa. In the dozen years that have passed since the Cedar Rapids edition first appeared, I have kept polishing my text, comparing it with other versions, and bringing the religious concepts into focus more clearly. The task will never cease for as one generation grows and changes, so does its language and method of response. Only the Arabic is eternal, and the present work is merely an attempt to give the present generation of Muslims in North America an idea of their *Noble Reading*, where God speaks at times in His plural of majesty.

Chanting and Recitation

"Cantillation" is a quaint word that has crept into Orientalist studies on Islam to describe the traditional manner of reciting the Qurʾān for public worship. Others of this sort are "circumambulation" for walking around the Kaʿba, "submission" or "surrender" for the believer's commitment to live 'in peace'; "genuflection" for kneeling in prayer, and "ablution" for washing before it. Those who use the terms must never have sat quietly in a mosque waiting for divine service to begin; or if they did so, it must have seemed unusual to them. Yet English has a long tradition in this field with Gospel reading and the responsive recital of the Psalms.

The Qurʾān was called the divine "Reading" of Islam and it exists precisely for that purpose. It was generally read out loud and most frequently from memory after thorough training, the usual method of reproducing sacred books which is still in use today. One Part or *juzʾ* a day can be recited during Ramaḍān, which lasts thirty days in all; these thirty Parts are indicated with capital Roman numerals in the upper left-hand corner on each page of this edition.

As it claims, the Qurʾān is easy to memorize, and is divided up so that it can be read in sittings, or it can be read straight through (17:106). This is clear from the canon itself. Mercier and Arberry are the only non-Muslim

Western scholars who have approached this matter of Qurɔānic recital, and we refer you to them for the time being; the late Professor Mercier's liturgical preface on prosody to his anthology in some ways is better than Arberry's which is expressed in the Introduction to his first or shorter version, *The Koran*.

In pre-literary times, and especially before the invention of the printing press, public recitation was the way most scriptures were taught and memorized. Chanting was performed in a printless culture so that others could hear the sacred text, and thus participate in "reading" it. We should try to capture this effect again. Before the invention of the electric light, the motion picture and other mechanical contrivances which entertain us today, novels and scriptures were read in North America and other Western countries by families, especially on long winter nights. In the same way a tradition of recitation and schools to teach this method grew up within Islam and other religions. The *ḥāfiḍ*h and the *qāriɔ* who memorize and recite the Qurɔān belong to an honorable profession in Islamic countries, and today phonograph records and cassettes are made of their art. As the liturgy was worked out, the chant developed just as the Gregorian chant did in Catholic countries. This had probably been worked out originally in the cities of Mecca and Madīna, the twin *Ḥaramayn* of Islam.

Few musical instruments are mentioned in the Qurɔān, only the trumpet (*aṣ-ṣūr*) in 18:99 and bugle (*an-nāqūr*) in 74:8. None are rhythmic or percussive although some drums may have existed, and they are easy to improvise. Much rhythm in the Middle East is maintained by handclapping anyhow. The Ṣūfī orders later on and the craft guilds which supported them, eventually gave us the so-called "whirling dervishes" who sought to find God and recall Him in their ecstasy.

The lilt of the Qurɔānic style makes it easy to read and recite: "We have made the Qurɔān easy to memorize" (54:17 ff). Rhymed prose meets the ear just as paragraphs, lines of verse and punctuation marks meet the eye in reading the printed page. In divine worship these indications become a part of ritual; the image or visual formulae are thus important. Worship means devotion, as this is seen in the verb to 'devote' oneself, to give a *vow* to, for it means to render the sort of 'service' which we find outlined in **The Opening** chapter of the Qurɔān itself, the *Fātiḥa* (1:5): "*You* do we worship and *You* do we call on for help". The Universe moves on rhythm, which is part of its reality. Consciousness and the Unseen show that God is ineffable Intelligence, *al-ʿAql*: "Whenever We do read it, follow in its reading," we are told in 75:18, for the Qur'an has reached us in clear Arabic (12:2–3, 43:2–3 etc.).

The poetry of the early Muslims came from the *Badū* or Beduin, who had little formal culture or education; they preserved what their ancestors had taught them to remember in their great odes, even though the Prophet himself was declared not to be a poet, and rejected the term (52:29 and 69:41). Cadence and rhythm mold the phrase and sentence; God's hovering spirit can thus be sensed. Phonograph records, tapes or cassettes now help in learning to chant, either for listening or in order to learn the passage by heart; they provide the best contemporary way for the uninitiated to hear this art.

Any new reader, especially a fresh convert, needs to find the cadence when he is meeting this for the first time. For this reason, my translation has not been designed for memorizing but rather for reading from the printed page. The Qurʾān is literally untranslatable: each time one returns to it, he finds new meanings and fresh ways of interpreting it; the messages are endless for it is a living Book.

If this is the first time that you are reading the Qurʾān, then you may look for special passages to begin with. For instance, the first call to Muḥammad comes in the chapter 96 called *Al-ʿAlaq* **The Clot** (OR **Read!**). Here we find the beginning of that respect for reading and learning on which the later Islamic commonwealth was built up. His second call comes at the beginning of *al-Mudaththir* **The Man Wearing a Cloak** 74, and is confirmed in *al-Inshirāḥ,* **Consolation** 94: "Did We not relieve your breast for you?" These are the first thrilling words which God the Merciful spoke directly to His chosen messenger Muḥammad. Then followed the commission heard in *al-Aʿlà* **Glory to your Lord in the Highest!** 87. There is comfort for the Prophet during his trials in *aḍ-Duḥa* **Morning Bright!** 93, and more consolation in *al-Kawthar* **Plenty** 108. Two of Muḥammad's visions appear at the beginning of *an-Najm* **The Star** 53. He is told to reject *al-Kāfirūn* **Disbelievers** (OR **Atheists**) in 109, and rebuttal of the charge of being a poet is found in 52:29. Muḥammad clearly understood he was not one (36:69), although prophets are compared with *ash-Shuʿarāʾ* **Poets** 26 in the chapter by that name, because of the inspiration which both receive.

Muslims do not need to "cantillate", but to read the Qurʾān reverently. A traditional method of reading our holy Book has been built up for this purpose in Islamic countries; in North America we will have to work out a manner of our own. In the East, the Book is intoned or chanted somewhat like the Gregorian chant or the method of reciting the Psalms or Beatitudes in some churches. In divine worship this becomes the full *dhikr* or liturgic 'Mention' of God's names and attributes: "Whenever We read it, follow in its reading", we are told in 75:18, for the Qurʾān has reached us in "clear Arabic" (16:103). A true ecstatic quality can be felt in the early Meccan chapters, at the outset of the Prophet's missions.

The inimitability or *iʿjāz* of the Qurʾān is stated: "Do not make up any parables about God;" (16:74); one should never compare God with anything. "No falsehood shall approach it from either in front of it or behind it" (41:40).

Layout and Editing

It need hardly be said that writing materials were scarce in the ancient world, let alone in seventh-century Arabia, and Muḥammad could not have everything copied down verbatim as he received it through divine revelation. Men's breasts were important depositories for a limited time; their memories were more developed than our children's are today.

The initial collection of our sacred Text was possibly attempted by his close companion and protege Zayd ibn-Thabit; the Prophet's wife Hafsa is also mentioned as preserving much material, as is 'A'isha. The way in which the Prophet's wives were entrusted with the text is exemplary.

A committee was then set up to establish the canonical text of the Qurʾān by the third "rightly guided" caliph or Successor to the Prophet, 'Uthmąn ibn-ʿAffān. The commissioners worked at compiling the scattered Qurʾānic document during the years 650-655. Once this task was finished and the canon established, ʿUthmān then gave one copy each to Mecca and Madīna, and sent others to the new administrative centres of Basra and Kūfa in Iraq. Kūfa is said to have possessed a variant much later. ʿUthmān kept the original papers in Madīna for himself and the authorities there; this copy disappeared into the imperial German archives towards the end of the First World War when both Germany and Turkey suffered defeat, but may be in the Topkapı Museum in Istanbul today. Mention of old codices like the *Kitāb al-Maṣāḥif* of Ibn-Abī-Dāwūd, together with a collection of the variant readings can be found in Professor Arthur Jeffery's *Materials for the History of the Text of the Qurʾān* (Leiden 1938, and Watt-Bell, p. 40).

The layout of my translation has been reached through a gradual process of trial and error which came chiefly so that I could locate significant material for myself, which I needed to refer to. Layout and editing are important just as ancient *sajʿ* resembles the wild pigeon's broken cooing. Rhymed prose meets the ear, but since the invention of the printing press, it is punctuation and paragraphs that meet the reader's eye. Verse form and punctuation are both matters of literary structure; when the rhyme shifts in the Qurʾān, it is shown roughly in this version by using different lines and paragraphs in English, so that the reader can achieve a similar rhythmic effect, especially for public reading or recitation.

Layout on the page may seem more important than rhyming today, for the eye rather than the ear is our contemporary instrument: "the blind and the sighted are not equal / nor are darkness and light" (35:19-20). In the seventh century, and during the West European middle ages until the invention of the printing press and the growth of a general reading public, learning largely meant such oral training.

Further problems were those of paragraphing and capitalization so as to follow English usage. Straight adjectives which refer to the Deity are capitalized, as well as unique qualities or symbols like the Path, the Way, Truth and so on. All pronouns: We, He, You etc. representing the Deity are capitalized here, including their possessive form (His, Your, Our etc.) as occurs with other mention of the Deity. This use of capitals is employed to ensure a mood of reverence for the name and mention *(dhikr)* of God, especially with younger or non-Muslim readers. Thus the names of God, including the pronouns You and Your, He, Him and His etc., are kept distinct in this work.

Capital Roman numerals refer to one of the 30 more-or-less equal PARTS into which the Qurʾān has been traditionally divided for the purpose of continuous recitation. Lower-case Roman numerals refer to the SECTIONS into which each longer chapter is divided. I use the asterisk * to mark the beginning of a verse; two of these ** indicate the 5th, 10th etc. verses; triple asterisks *** show 100's.

Capital Roman numerals, placed in the upper inside corner of the page indicate the Part of the Qurʾān; following this are numbers (Arabic and lower-case Roman) indicating the Section and Verse. This system has been devised so that the Concordance, which *in Shā> Allāh* will follow with some 2000 pages, will provide easy reference for each page, without referring to future page numbers.

Marginal headings appear in the outside margin. The verse number for each 10th verse also appears. The Arabic names for chapter titles are to be found in the Table of Contents. Some titles are alternates even in the original Arabic, such as **Quraysh** OR **Winter** for Chapter 106, with no parentheses; others are further possibilities or alternates in English translation like **Eventide** (OR **Nightfall**) 103 because the Arabic word *Al-<Asr* has been difficult to render convincingly. Parentheses here indicate the alternative.

Long and short vowels need to be distinguished in Arabic, as well as emphatic consonants. The use of digraphs like *th, gh* and *dh* may be deplored, but English already has them in ch, sh, th, ng etc. These emphatic consonants are ḍ, ḍh (or ẓ), ṣ, ṭ and the occasional ḷ. Parentheses ( ) or so-called "round brackets" are used for implied statements, while "square" brackets [ ] are for elliptical insertions. Single quotation marks indicate direct translation from the Arabic: *ṣāliḥ* for 'honorable'; *al-Raḥīm* 'the Merciful'.

Also the system of underlining or the use of fonts should be explained. Italics have been saved for special emphasis, and especially with the Invocation: *In the Name of God, the Mercy-giving, the Merciful!*; and **black-face**, or **bold type** is for Chapter titles (**The Cow 2**), (**The House of <Imran 3**), etc., so these will be recognized as chapters and not as book titles. **Black-face** is also used for phrases with special importance. The use of hyphens must be more careful: Ibn-Rushd, Abū-Bakr, Ibn-Khaldūn, *<alay-kum* show pronouns and prefixes clearly for beginners and the amateur whom we have attracted to read this book. I am tired of reading student papers which talk of "Khaldūn" and "Rushd" quite baldly, not realizing that this person, if he ever existed, is an ancestor or a symbolic concept, and that *ibn-* and *banū-* mean 'sons of' (like Mac, Mc in Celtic), and *abū-* means 'father (of)'. We need a style here that will make Qur>ānic study valid and easier for our children and students.

SAY and SEE in small capitals denote God's own upcoming words and signs to the Prophet and to mankind. We also use NOTE and OR in the same small capitals for similar notations which are parallel.

An Index or Concordance will come later because it will consist of perhaps 2000 pages. I wish eventually to achieve a useful whole with notes and an index for North American and English-speaking Muslims the world over. It should be a document one can read with pleasure and for spiritual profit.

Translation as an Art

Finally we need some reflections on the art of translation: how does one use language, especially when it is the elevated expression of the Qur>ān? Is it possible to render such lofty style into a foreign tongue?

This new version of *The Noble Reading* which I am presenting has a serious purpose, which is to make its clear message available for the English-speaking world at the end of the twentieth Christian, or the beginning of the Islamic fifteenth century, which started in the last weeks of 1980 A.D. This task is comparable to translating any great classic like Homer, Virgil, *Quijote* or *Faust*, since it involves a transfer of true literature into the medium of a parallel culture. It is a problem more for the quality which must be matched in English than for any inherent difficulty or obscurity in the text itself.

This present version is not addressed so much to scholars as to godly minds and especially to those who are growing up speaking English, and thus need a simple, clear text of the historic writ to guide them. The Qurʾān itself says: "We have not sent any messenger unless he was to explain to them in his folk's own tongue" (14:1). For this reason, any attempt at translation has validity if each nation is to receive its message in its own language. It should be a document one can read, and it also, if possible, must offer a basis for ongoing research. We should respect the sacred text, yet interpret it accurately and reverently. This is not an intellectual game but has a serious purpose.

The Qurʾān could be considered untranslatable, because each time one returns to the Arabic text, he finds new meanings and fresh ways of interpreting it. It is a living document. I have at all times tried to find the simplest word so the Muslim child can understand it easily, and thereby feel strengthened by it. Any translation which is to have a use in divine worship must be simple yet noble, and not overladen with higher criticism. No translation should confuse, but teach and make things holy; we do not need criticism so much as constructive explanation. I myself must remember to act as a Westerner before this document in order to keep its meaning from being blurred. It must be translated respectfully for our own worship, and so that we and others can understand its message. The forms of piety are important, as well as the thought and mood which they engender. In our faith this leads to direct contact with God, with no need of any intercession, a condition achieved through literal and moral purification, and through prayer.

The Islamic world is growing again, its centre is widening, and Muslims everywhere, especially throughout the English-speaking part of it, need a version of their Scripture they can confidently give to their children as well as to friends who have not yet captured the full message of Islam. Our aim is to give pride to young English-speaking Muslims in North America especially, and also in Britain, the West Indies like Trinidad and Guyana, and the English-speaking parts of Africa. It can also be used by college students and interested non-Muslims who want a contemporary translation of this great world classic.

I have tried to be as objective as possible, but yet to provide the basis for evaluation by English-speaking readers who know no Arabic. This should make it usable so the intelligent person engaged in research can quote the Qurʾān in today's English. There is a necessity for an American version in contemporary English, to help in the revival of the Qurʾānic sciences during the coming fifteenth century of the Hijra, and this must occur in the English-speaking world. If my translation has any merit, it will simply be that it is intended for North Americans, so young American and Canadian Muslims can understand, when they are still teenagers or younger, what God told Muḥammad fourteen hundred years ago in Arabia, with no artifice or bombast, but in clear, simple and I hope beautiful English. Otherwise our message will be lost here in America. The next generation will speak English, and few of them will take the time or the trouble to learn Arabic properly, so someone has to put it into the language of the next two or three hundred years.

It would be a waste of time at present to do any work on Sunday school materials until we have a good copy of the Qurʾān we can trust. For this reason, several years ago I decided to dedicate time at the beginning of each morning to accomplishing this, so it would be done properly. This is the basic need for any propaganda in Islam on this continent, and until we have a version in good English, we will continue to read translations which evoke no reverence or beauty in the minds of the listeners.

We also need a good chapbook on prayers. Young American Muslims simply do not know their prayers, and that is the need in any "programmed learning" for Islam. But it must be done in Arabic, with the original text, in Romanized Arabic so those who cannot read the script can approximate the sound (and especially, avoid the dialectal variants one gets from Egyptian, Lebanese or Pakistani material), and again, a decent translation of the same into good English. This should be done with photos of the positions of prayer, and a tape recording of each of the individual prayers, not done in a hurry, but by a trained teacher with proper voicing of the material in Arabic, by a native speaker who reads the Qurʾān and recites prayers well, at slow speed, then at normal speed, and chanted if that is necessary; but all done so that Sunday school students can learn from them, and even an untrained Sunday school teacher would be able to handle the tapes. The chapbook should be published in a dignified way.

Some direct problems of translation might bear discussion at this point. Through the original Arabic we learn what Muḥammad was striving to express to his followers, but our problem is to catch *how* he might want this expressed for the people of today who speak English, and to translate it so that an intelligent and reverent American, especially in the teen-age group, can grasp the message which the Prophet received fourteen centuries ago in Arabia. Most versions give one the sensation of being thrust upon the reader through the translator's own mentality and purpose, a failing I cannot avoid completely. However, anything translated must lie close to the heart of future generations of English-speaking Muslims. I do not want to render a traditional paraphrase, nor to make a display of erudition with so many notes that they will confuse the younger student; notes must be such that they will help even the random reader. One's language should be meaningful above all, and its beauty come forth from the meaning, using the English of today in all of its richness, with both our Germanic and Latin roots. Our texts have been vitiated, and higher criticism has not led many to the faith. However if the

Arabic is clear (16:XIV, 26:XI), then why does it need to be worried over so intensely?

Most renditions have been so antiquated that they make the Qurʾān and Islam appear to have little connection with living circumstances. Thus I have tried to avoid strictly Christian terms like "infidel," "piety," "sin," etc., except where such are unavoidable. The Qurʾān possesses a definite language and style which becomes clearer as one works along with it. One English word if possible should be chosen in all of its range of meaning for each Arabic concept, using roots that can be turned into adjectives, verbs, nouns or other grammatical forms based on it. This in fact is not a translation but a version, a modest *tafsīr* for the English-speaking Muslim who has not been able to rely on Arabic for his meanings, and for sincere enquirers, those modern *Ḥanīfs* who are tired of the trinity, or of chaos and confusion in matters religious. The carper should look elsewhere.

Let us hope therefore that this enterprise will lead us on into the triumphant fifteenth century of Islam, which is now upon us. Our religion is once more resurgent, and its message can be stated with full clarity. Muslims everywhere hold their fate in their own hands now, and it is their will that in the end will prevail. Once we have trained our children.

I would like to thank Professor Thomas A. Lathrop of the University of Delaware for his work in typesetting the book. And lastly, I wish to thank my wife, Dr. Evelyn Uhrhan Irving, for her support in this project over more than twenty-three years, including typing of the final manuscript, and proof reading at many stages of the document.

T.B. Irving
October, 1985   *Cedar Rapids, Iowa*

Footnotes to Introduction

[1] For the order of the chapters, one should consult Dr. S. Abid Ahmad Ali's excellent pamphlet on "The Qurʾān, an Exposition of its Position" from *The Dawn* (Sargodha, Dec. 1961, pp. 23-55), where he discusses Arberry's original attempt at an anthology.

[2] This Noble Reading OR *al-Qurʾān al-Karīm* as it is called in 56:III; in 50:I and 85:I. It is called the *Majīd* or 'Glorious', 'Majestic', in 15:VI; it is also the 'Mighty', ʿAḍhīm. SEE R. A. Nicholson, *A Literary History of the Arabs*, p. 141, n. 1 and p. 159 on the word Qurʾān itself.

[3] A detailed discussion on Bible translation can be found in Barry Huberman's recent article, "Translating the Bible: an Endless Task" (*The Atlantic*, February 1985, pp. 43-58).

Further Observations 1993

T. B. Irving

1) Our 'Noble Reading' (*al-Qur'ān al-Karīm*) was revealed to the Prophet Muḥammad fourteen centuries ago in the cities of Mecca and Madīna, in the country that today is known as Saudi Arabia. It forms the revelation of God's word to mankind over a period of twenty-three years. The original text was preserved traditionally on a guarded tablet or *lawḥ* [1] and delivered during a Night of Power.[2] Its instrument of transmission was the archangel Gabriel, the Spirit or *Rūḥ al-Quds*.[3]

The revelation consists of 114 chapters of varying length. The Book is all encompassing, and requires expert explanation or commentary; this has been provided over the centuries by many learned commentators or *mufassirūn*. The earliest Muslims memorized this sacred text, while many wrote it down on whatever materials were available. The chapters which were revealed later, largely legislative and narrative Madinese ones, constitute the main body of the work, while the mostly Meccan earlier ones occur at the end, as a poetic postscript which is generally known as Part XXX. This XXXth Part with its shorter lyric verses is often published separately as a chapbook for general distribution or memorization by children.[4] The traditional arrangement, as given here, is orderly and canonical although several non-Muslim translators have tried to reorder the chapters, a rearrangement that adds little to their understanding.

How this document was collected by the early Muslims in the first decades of Islam and preserved zealously over fourteen centuries with no changes, is a true literary miracle. These thrilling events laid the foundation of the Islamic religion fourteen hundred years ago. The Qur'ān serves not only as a spiritual and moral guide but also as the constitution or political expression of the vast Commonwealth that emerged on the world scene within the years following the Prophet's death in the year 632 AD. It forms the fundamental document for understanding the religious and ethical system of one-fifth of present-day humanity, who are scattered across one of the most strategic zones of the world. Muslims live in the vast "Middle Belt" or *Ummat^{an} Wasaṭ^{an}*[5] where Islam stretches from Morocco and Nigeria on the Atlantic in a vast double prong that ends in Indonesia on the Pacific in the Far East on the one hand, and penetrates Central Asia to the northeast within the former Soviet Union on the other, in one of the most strategic zones of the world.

The Qur'ān forms the basic Scripture that should be studied in order to grasp the Islamic vision of man, and understand the society on which the individual Muslim builds in order to achieve the supreme art of life and living on this earth: "my living and my dying belong to God".[6] The need for this present contemporary translation arises because the Qur'ān is the fundamental Book for studying not only Middle Eastern morality, but also for much more. North Americans must know what the ethical system is that Muslims live by, as well as the basis for Muslim reactions to events. To date no adequate translation of the Qur'ān into North American English has been undertaken, although it is a Book that is as important to the Western world as Marx' *Das Capital*, which likewise remains largely unread by the general public, and even by "experts" in that field.

Since my target for this work is largely the American thinking public, such a translation must be made into contemporary American English, a version that states its message in clear English so that North Americans living in this and future generations can understand Islam. The Qur'ān itself states: *wa-mā arsalnā min rasūl[in] illā bi-lisān qawmi-hi, li-yubayyan la-hum* ('We have not sent any messenger unless he was to explain things to them in his folk's own tongue').[7]

This present edition initiates the reader into the Qur'ānic world view and its values, and aims at bringing the imagination into vivid contact with the Qur'ānic vision of man, society and life as Muslims have lived it for fourteen centuries. It is also meant for those who feel the need for a side-by-side edition of the Arabic and English texts, for easy reference.

In this translation I have tried to exchange many clichés for terms that I hope will capture the meaning of the Arabic text more appropriately. First of all, for the Arabic word *Islām* itself, instead of the meaning of "submission" which involves an abject and unmanly attitude, I prefer to use a 'Commitment (to live at *peace*)'. Rather than "prostration" for the act of worship in *sajada* (the alternate title to Chapter 41, pp. 268 ff.) with its nervous overtone in popular speech today, I prefer to describe this solemn religious act simply as to 'bow DOWN on one's knees (in worship before God Alone)'; and 'bowing from the waist' in the case of *rukū'*. "Ablution" is a clumsy word that has been used for 'washing UP before prayers') in order to attain the proper state of purity or cleanliness in which to meet the Divinity. The concept of 'washing up' provides both a noun and verb form required in the sacred text. "Circumnambulation" is another word that the Orientalists have invented for walking the seven times around the Ka'ba in Mecca; the term makes this sacred rite appear ridiculous, which it never is for any of us who have performed it.

Instead of "alms" which are voluntary and medieval in their concept (and a meaning which in Islam is covered more correctly by *ṣadaqa,* the impulsive urge to place a small coin in a beggar's hand), I use 'welfare tax', since this religious duty is obligatory and must reach much further: "Charity is [meant] only for the poor, the needy, those working at [collecting and distributing] it, those [possible converts] whose hearts are being reconciled [to yours], for freeing captives and debtors, and in [striving along] God's way, and for the wayfarer, as a duty imposed by God . . . "[8] "Infidel" is another term that dates from the Crusades and the European middle ages; I use 'disbelievers' which moreover has its useful verb 'to disbelieve' to accompany it. I prefer a 'plea' or 'appeal' for *du'ā'*, the spontaneous prayer of many a troubled worshipper, instead of "supplication" which somehow has even crept into some Muslims' vocabulary. "Cantillation" is best conceived of as 'chanting', which in Islam resembles the Gregorian chant, since neither is accompanied by any musical instrument.

Many of the terms I have replaced have crept into even Muslims' speech, especially if they received their education in British or missionary schools, or if they read current books on Islam written by non-Muslims. Such previous terminology makes Islam look ridiculous or quaint, and thus un-modern in spirit and unfit for men — or women — of today to consider living by. My desire is to present the Qur'ān in modern readable English so that Islam can be intelligently understood. True knowledge brings us certainty; other contemporary value judgments have left us with doubt, so that many learners have rejected the message.

* * *

2) Let us now consider the PROPHET MUḤAMMAD'S role in this historic process.

The Arabian Prophet (may God accept his prayers and grant him peace!), was born in the city of Mecca around the year 569 or 570 AD, and lived until 632. His father 'Abdullāh had died before his birth, and the boy became a full orphan at the age of six, when his mother Amīna passed away. She had been from Yathrib, later *al-Madīna al-Munawwara* or 'the Enlightened City', as it came to be called after the Prophet settled there; the city lies on a volcanic plain 240 miles or 400 kilometres to the north and slightly west of Mecca.

As a boy, Muḥammad knew what it was like to feel insecure; nevertheless he was protected by his extended family, and especially by his loving and respected grandfather 'Abd-al-Muṭṭalib, and later by his uncle Abū-Ṭālib when the former passed away. Mecca at that time was a trading town set in the Ḥijāz mountains on the caravan route leading from Yaman or 'Happy Arabia' (*'Arabia Felix* to the Romans) that lies to the south, and the markets of Syria and Egypt to the north and west.

At times Muḥammad is called the "Unlettered Prophet".[9] This does not mean that he was ignorant or illiterate, but rather that he had not received a formal education or, as we would say today, had gone to college. Few persons were able to do so in the ancient world; yet despite this apparent handicap, Muḥammad was intelligent and discerning, and above all, he was known as *al-Amīn* or 'the Trustworthy', and a man who could reason things out for himself.

Khadīja, his first wife, was a businesswoman who handled caravans that traded largely with Syria. She engaged the future Prophet to help her in this long-distance transport business. She was 40 years old, while Muḥammad was 25 when they married. Khadīja was an ideal and supportive wife such as a man needs who has a serious mission in life. They had several children before she died, but only their daughter Fāṭima lived to adulthood; she married 'Ali ibn-Abī-Tālib and was the mother of Muḥammad's grandsons Ḥasan and Ḥusayn.

Traditionally the older prophet and patriarch Abraham had come to Mecca with his elder son Ishmael to establish the pure worship of God Alone there after Sara, Abraham's first wife and cousin (as happens in the Semitic world, where they tend to marry closely within the family), expelled this other woman's child who formed a threat to her own son Isaac's full inheritance of the family property. In Mecca, Abraham and Ishmael together built the Kaᶜba, the son gladly helping the father; this legend of Abraham's presence in Mecca is still strong there. Ishmael's mother Hagar was an Egyptian, thus ushering in the racial equality that exists in Islam to this day.

In the Biblical book of Genesis (16:15) it is clearly stated that Ishmael had been born before his brother Isaac. It then dismisses Ishmael, although it has just described his birth, and speaks blandly of "thine only son Isaac".[10] This confused story supports Muslim claims that the present text of the Old Testament or Torah has been tampered with. This narrative is folk history that has been kept alive over the generations and centuries, through the Arabs' bounteous memory.

The Kaᶜba thus cherishes its memories of Abraham or *Ibrāhīm*, who came there to establish the true religion, *ad-Dīn al-Ḥanīf* with his elder son Ishmael, who remained there to serve it. Anyone who has visited Mecca with its surrounding mountains and valleys, drunk water from the well of Zamzan, and run between the hillocks of Ṣafà and Marwa[11] where Hagar, the Egyptian mother, ran looking desperately for water for her little boy Ishmael, participates in some of this 'experience' which is called the *'Umra* in Arabic.

In the year 610 AD at the age of 40, Muḥammad received his Message or *Risāla,* in full middle life. It might be called an Eastern reformation, but this reform aimed at replacing the paganism and idol worship that had crept into the worship at the Kaᶜba since the time of his ancestors Abraham and Ishmael, and restoring the worship of God Alone at that shrine.

The Prophet encountered many difficulties and rejection while he lived in Mecca. The Quraysh clan to which his family belonged was afraid that the pilgrimage business related to the idols that were by that time housed in the Kaᶜba, would be destroyed if they accepted the pure worhsip of God Alone, and were forced to cast out the images and idols contained therein. The goddess *Al-lāt,* an apparent feminine of *Allāh,* and thus supposedly and blasphemously His consort, along with *Al-Uzzà* ('the Almighty' in the feminine, and therefore also blasphemous), and *Manāt,* all formed a pagan trinity of false deities which are mentioned in Chapter 53, **The Star.**[12]

If few Meccans accepted the Message at first, many Arabs did, as well as Bilāl the Ethiopian, and Salmān the Persian; they became the Prophet's faithful henchmen, adding an international dimension to Islam even at this early stage. The Prophet's life was threatened, and his followers defended him. Some fled to Abyssinia, across the Red Sea, in an early *Hijra* or 'withdrawal' where the Christian monarch sheltered them after listening to a recital of the Chapter on **Mary.**[13]

Eventually Muḥammad undertook the historic *Hijra* or 'Transfer' to Yathrib, his mother's native city. This occurred in the year 622 AD, the date that forms the Zero year for the Islamic calendar (AH) that was established to avoid pagan fertility cults and festivals (and not through bad astronomy, as some carpers allege). In Madīna things went better although there were still intrigues and upsets fomented by the pagan Arabs and Jews who lived around that city, especially during the Prophet's fourth year there (626-7 AD). The warring tribes of Arabia eventually made peace however as they heard and accepted the Message; the Year of Delegations, which occurred just before the Prophet's death, might thus be said to have formally established the 'Commonwealth' or *Umma* of Islam in Arabia.(14

Thus a city state gradually evolved where the Prophet acted as judge and head of government, settling disputes and accepting the homage of various tribes and countless individuals. Three chapters, **The [Inner] Apartments, The Pleading Woman** and **Examining Her,**(15 all furnish examples of this growing judicial, political and diplomatic activity, to use contemporary terms. Actual power was slowly being forged during the ten years (622-632 AD) that the Prophet of Islam spent in Madīna, until the Arabian peninsula was transformed into a confederation out of what had been tribes in a more-or-less constant state of war: its new capital was the Prophet's 'City' or *Madīnat an-Nabi*. The principle of *Shūrà* or **Consultation**(16 guided them. Consensus or *ijmā'* among the faithful followed, and set general social policy during the coming years. This constitutional process was gradual and fruitful in nature, lasting twenty-three years in all, beginning with the Prophet's initial call in Mecca. No one could have conceived its success beforehand, and its appearance caught the great powers of that day, Byzantium or the Eastern Roman empire, Persia, and Abyssinia, by surprise.

When Muḥammad lived, the empires of Persia and Byzantium to the northeast and northwest of Arabia respectively, were destroying each other in savage wars. "The Byzantines have been defeated on the nearest front! Following their defeat, they shall conquer a few years later."(17 The full expansion of the new Islamic 'Commonwealth' or *Umma* occurred immediately following the Prophet's death and the War of Apostasy when some mainly central and eastern Arabian tribes revolted and attempted to revert to paganism. The new state however emerged with a ready-made army of recruits and trained leaders (or potential officers) who were no longer engaged in narrow tribal raids, but provided the new confederation with a standing army such as all empires require. The young bucks or camel jockeys of the formerly raiding tribes had now become the standing army of a confederation, the new 'Commonwealth' or *Umma* of Arabia and Islam.

These armies would soon sweep on to victory after victory over the jaundiced imperial forces of two empires, adding first the Fertile Crescent of Syria and Iraq with which the Arab caravans were already familiar; then Egypt and Persia to the west and east, the latter extending clear up into Central Asia where the Soviets hold sway today; and westward moving along the southern shore of the Mediterranean to North Africa and Spain on the Atlantic. These sweeps came at generational intervals of approximately thirty years, resting first in Iraq, Syria and Egypt where the conquerors bred a fresh generation of recruits by marrying local women. When the children of these Arab soldiers grew up, another wave of conquest followed into Libya, Tunisia and Algeria to the west (which countries are still firmly Arab and Islamic, based as their speech was on their Phoenician or Carthaginian antecedents, to the chagrin of the French and Italians, who failed to hold them in this century), and also further into Persia, taking Islam ever eastward. Finally Spain and India were reached in another set of forward leaps, although these last countries were never fully Islamized.

Such was the political and geographic achievement of the Arabian Prophet in its posthumous phase, soon after he had passed away. Muḥammad's lifework filled a strategic gap on the map of the world, and arrested the creeping medievalism that was leaving the Roman empire, especially its Western portion, in ruins. The new faith replaced this dying order with one of the world's great civilizations, the Islamic 'Commonwealth' which kept the Middle ages at bay for centuries from the southern Mediterranean, southwest Asia and much of the Indian ocean area.

This new political reality was soon based on an eclectic culture that was characterized by the oasis and the merchant city where the dome, courtyards, fountains and cool corridors made the new mosques, colleges and other public buildings liveable and attractive. It was an urban order based on irrigation in hot climates where the date palm and the olive grove were its symbols, and the camel and sailing ship plied the long distance trade routes that carried commerce over the deserts and the Mediterranean world and out into the Indian Ocean area. Islam could thus choose its materials and motifs from scores of countries on three continents, selecting its models wherever the early Muslims saw fit to borrow them.

The Iranian and Roman bureaucracies gave this new empire its essential administrative forms, while the useful Hindu numerals (which we in the West call the "Arabic" ones) made bookkeeping easier (have you ever tried to add or multiply with Roman numerals?). Words and phrases were coined from native Arabic speech to express concepts that the Beduin of the desert had never considered during his nomadic life. Philosophy and mathematics from Greece, new agricultural products like sugar and bananas from the Indian subcontinent all furnished this civilization with fresh features that promoted the spread of the religion and its outlook on society, rather than hindering it. Islam was quickly established as one of the great world civilizations, and certainly the greatest during its first period of glory. Its cities of Damascus, Baghdad, Cairo, Fez, Cordoba, Delhi, Lahore and Istanbul still shine like stars on the map of this middle belt in the world today.

* * *

3) How could ISLAM accomplish this new world order in such a short period of time, scarcely a few decades?

First of all, the word *Islām* in Arabic means living at 'peace' or in 'harmony' with God, with our fellow men, and within society. Thus this involves a solemn 'Commitment' to live at *peace* (rather than the abject sense of "submission", a term invented in Orientalist and Christian missionary manuals which has unfortunately slipped into many Muslims' speech as well). 'Commitment' is a more manly word and involves a responsible attitude, whereas "submission" is servile, and colonialist when it comes to the political sphere.

Muslim is the past participle of this verbal noun, meaning a man or woman who has accepted this 'peace' as his or her way of life. However there is no "other cheek" in Islam, a miscalculation by the British and the Zionists who planned the occupation of Palestine; Muslims are those "who protect themselves whenever any outrage happens to them".[18] "God will support anyone who retaliates insofar as he has suffered."[19] Moreover a Muslim is not a "Moslem" with its voiced "s" or "z" that is derived almost maliciously (and at times ignorantly) from the root of *ẓulm* or *dhulm* meaning 'harm' or 'injustice'; "Moslem" thus means a 'cruel' person, a concept that is diametrically opposed to the Islamic ideal of 'peaceful' coexistence.

The Qur'ān is the document that expresses these aims and values. Islam represents a pure and strict monotheism, *Tawḥīd* as it is called in Arabic. This concept tolerates no frivolous "death of God" since He is *al-Ḥayy al-Qayyūm* — 'the Living, the Eternal!'[20] God moreover is Creator of the Universe, *al-ᶜAlamīn* as this is known in Arabic, whose complex laws we, as Muslims, should try to fathom and understand. The will of God embraces the laws of nature as we know them; these rules are determined, not the result of some casual design or caprice.

Some passages from the Qur'ān express this pure Islamic idea of God lyrically: "Sure hearts feel tranquil whenever God is mentioned."[21] In Islam, God is Unique, Who must be contemplated in all of His majesty:

> *SAY:* "God is Unique!
> God is the Source [for everything];
> He has not fathered anyone
> nor was He fathered, and there
> is nothing comparable to Him.[22]

He is found everywhere:

> The East and West are God's:
> wherever you may turn,
> there will be God's countenance.[23]

God knows everything; He is Omniscient:

> God has knowledge about the Hour.
> He sends down showers and knows
> whatever wombs contain. Yet no person knows
> what he will earn tomorrow,
> nor does any person know

in what land he will die.
Still God is Aware, Informed! [24]

For this reason, we Muslims reverence God and pray to Him in gratitude for placing us here on earth. Because God sustains the Universe, Muslims can say "Yes" to life, and enjoy its benefits and prerogatives. Our intellectual love of God means simply that we accept the laws of nature as we find them and abide by the just rules of society gladly, finding our fulfilment within these limitations.

Proceeding further in this description of Islamic principles, the **Five Pillars** on which the faith is based, are as follows:

a) The *Profession of Faith* proclaims that "There is no deity except God," [25] and "Muḥammad is the messenger of God". [26] This formula is pronounced when one becomes a Muslim and accepts Islam as his faith. It is the inscription that is found on the green-and-white Saudi flag.

b) *Prayer* is the second Pillar of Islam. It is said five times a day while one is in a state of formal purity, during which we acknowledge God Alone as our sovereign Lord. Prayer is also performed on festival or special occasions like births, marriages and funerals.

We Muslims thus approach God directly five times a day to thank Him for the favor of creating us and granting us the privilege of living in this world and its society. We do not need any intercessor in order to approach Him, if our hearts and minds are pure and our bodies cleansed.

c) *Fasting* is practised during the daytime in the month of Ramaḍān, to discipline ourselves, and to learn how hungry people feel. This month changes each year, moving ahead ten days, so that it will not be influenced by pagan fertility cults, as happens in the celebration of Easter, Hallowe'en and Christmas. Thus if it began in mid-May this past year, then it will come ten days earlier next year, and gradually slip into the month of April, to come around eventually thirty years from now to the same Western month;

d) the *Welfare Tax* is levied to maintain essential public services, and prevent poverty and hardship among the faithful. *Zakāt* as it is called in Arabic, is designed to maintain state and essential welfare functions; in this translation it is called a 'welfare tax'. This is intended primarily to help orphans, relatives in one's own family, the poor and needy, the wayfarer, and those who administer the collection and distribution of this poor-due. Tithing is a similar duty among Christians, but this 'tax' is broader in concept (although today, lamentably, it is collected irregularly and by few proper authorities). Voluntary 'alms' is *ṣadaqa* in Arabic, for which SEE **Repentance** 9:58-60 [27] in this volume.

e) *Pilgrimage* to the Ka^cba in Mecca, the square black basalt box that Abraham and his elder son Ishmael raised together in that city is prescribed for those of us who can afford to make this journey, yet not leave our families in want. [28] Every faithful Muslim ought to see Mecca and share in the solemn, once a year Experience of that broader world of Islam where the representatives of that one-fifth of mankind who are our fellow Muslims come together and mingle in the sacred city.

These Five Pillars form the basis for the Islamic code of ethics and conduct. By contrast, the **Three Deadly Sins** of Islam are based on intellectual failings, and consist of:

a) *Disbelief* or 'Atheism', to state this in a contemporary manner.[29] God is not dead for Muslims, as we have said, but "the Living, the Eternal".[30] The word *kufr* in Arabic means 'ingratitude' (for divine favors, here), while its present participle, *kāfir*, means a 'disbeliever' or 'infidel' to use Orientalist or crusading terminology, or 'atheist' to be more modern, rather than a poor South African black as it is used derogatively.[31] The *Jahiliyya* that existed in Arabia before Islam was the time of pagan 'Ignorance' (or present-day 'agnosticism'); a *jāhil*, the Arabic present participle to this word, means an 'agnostic' or contemporary 'heathen'.

b) *Association,* the Unforgiveable Sin,[32] means giving "associates" or "partners" to God, or letting other gods or saints share in what should be His pure worship. *Allāh* in Arabic represents God Alone, the universal Deity Who has no associates, nor any saints to interfere in His adoration. A *mushrik,* another participial form on the pattern of "Muslim", is the sinful 'associator' whose blind error of polytheism or idolatry is never forgiven since he has thereby abdicated his sacred gift of human reason, by asking other gods or saints for favors: "The worst animals before God are the deaf and dumb, those who do not use their reason."[33]

c) The third sin of *Arrogation* or *ṭughyān* means acting as if we do not need to report to God for our actions.[34] Each one of us is responsible individually for his or her behavior, and will appear on Judgment Day to answer before God Alone for our good and evil deeds.

> Whoever has done an atom's weight
> of good will see it; while whoever
> has done an atom's weight of evil
> will see it.[35]

> Anyone whose scales are weighted down
> [will land] in easy living;
> while whoever's scales are light
> will have a Pit to mother him.
> What will make you realize
> what this will be like?
> Scorching fire![36]

The late Shah of Iran was a *ṭāghi* or 'tyrant', 'dictator' who fell from power because he despised Islam and relied instead on his non-Muslim allies for support. In private life this sin means acting like a 'bully' who does not consider the rights of other people, nor of God Himself.

Other sins such as murder, theft, adultery are considered more like civil crimes, that have their own punishments, just as good deeds reap their own rewards.

Much has been said by outsiders about the role of women in Islam, and how they should dress and behave. Naturally they should be modest and dress respectfully.[37] However men have a dress code as well, for the Qur'ān says clearly: "*Yā Banū-Adam, khudhū zīnata-kum fī kull masjid* — "Children of Adam, wear your best clothes to every place of worship!"[38] Sons (*banī-Adam,* not daughters — *banāt*) are exhorted here, so we see that men also have their own dress code for public worship. Traditionally men should be covered from their waist to their knees. Each and every one of us, whether a man or woman, has his or her obligations and duties before God Alone and society.

*   *   *

4) We now need to discuss how the Qur'ān should be read. In what manner should this pious duty be performed?

First of all, our sacred Book is one "which none but the purified may touch."[39] For this reason one must wash up before reading it, precisely as one prepares for prayers. Then we are told that "whenever you read the Qur'ān, seek refuge with God from Satan the Outcast."[40] Such reading is preferably done in the early hours of the morning because we are told that "reading [the Qur'ān] at daybreak will be witnessed."[41]

The preceding stipulates preparation for reading or reciting the sacred text. We are also told "whenever the Qur'ān is being recited, listen to it [attentively] and hush, so that you may receive mercy."[42] It can be read in short sittings or straight ahead.[43] During the fast of Ramaḍān, each night one of the thirty formal Parts of the Qur'ān is traditionally recited in the mosque; thus the total reading is completed during the course of that holy month.

Once we have read the Qur'ān in a devoted spirit, we begin to realize the essential *i*ᶜ*jāz* or inimitability which is expressed in the phrase: "Produce a chapter like it;[44] and also in the passage: "Even if men and sprites organized to produce something like this Reading, they would never bring anything like it no matter how much assistance they lent one another."[45]

In this present edition, most passages suitable for memorizing have been placed in blank verse if their mood is lyric, so that their spiritual beauty can be recognized and appreciated; while words and phrases that explain our religion and its outlook on life and society are set in **black face** or **bold** type.

The Introduction to each chapter can be found at the back of the volume in this edition, rather than introducing each individual chapter as in the original version. Each chapter is divided into its traditional Sections, which are indicated by the use of small Roman numerals (i, ii, iv &c.). This has been done because they are approximately the same length as a normal printed page, but never vary; this is for use with the Concordance which, God willing, I hope to publish eventually, to accompany this translation. Paragraphs have been used to help the flow and understanding of the sacred text, while verses set off important lyric passages. Square brackets [ ] embrace explanatory and implied material.

The Library of Congress method of transliteration is followed in my own transcription; this system began with the admirable cartography accomplished by the Board of Geographic Names during the Second

World War, and is now used on the *National Geographic* maps of North Africa and the Middle East. The ^c*ayn* and ' (*hamza* or the glottal stop) give some trouble in these transcriptions; yet they should be treated individually and not ignored as is sometimes done in newspapers whose type fonts are not equipped to distinguish these sounds.

Double quotation marks (" ") are for direct quotations; while single ones (' ') generally mean straight translation of an accompanying foreign word or term. **Bold-face** type, as mentioned previously, indicates the title of chapters or *sūras,* and other important passages. Hyphens join names and concepts that should be united semantically such as *ibn-* meaning 'son of-' and *abū* for 'father of-', and other particles that need to accompany the words they modify; these prefixes are inherent parts of proper names. I became tired of having students talk blandly of "Khaldūn", forgetting that if this Khaldūn ever existed, he was the eponymous ancestor of Ibn-Khaldūn, the great Tunisian (and Sevillian) philosopher of history and society. Similarly today reporters talk about the "terrorist" Nidal, forgetting that he, if he exists, is merely the figurative son of his father Abū-Niḍāl (meaning 'strife' or 'battle'), the Palestinian guerrillero. Such are the confusions that lack of linguistic training leaves the American public in, especially those of us who must read the press.

May God Alone bless this work as He sees fit, and make it comprehensible to those who wish to consider its message.

Cedar Rapids, December 1992

*　*　*

Footnotes to *Further Observations 1993*

1) SEE Chapter **Constellations** 85:22 in this edition, p. 590.

2) Chapter on **Power** (or **Fate,** 97, p. 598.

3) **The Cow,** ch. 2:87, p. 13; **The Night Journey** 17:85, p. 290; & **Power** 97:2, p. 598.

4) SEE the one prepared from this present edition by Professor M.A.J. Beg in Kuala Lumpur, 1986.

5) **The Cow** 2:143, p. 22.

6) **Livestock** 6:162, p. 150.

7) **Abraham** 14:4, p. 255.

8) **Repentance** 9:60, p. 196.

9) *an-Nabi al-Ummi,* **The Heights** 7:157, p. 170.

10) **Genesis** 22:2.

11) **The Cow** 2:158, p. 24.

12) Chapter 53:19-20, p. 526.

13) Chapter 19, pp. 305ff.

14) **The Coalition** Chapter 33, pp. 417-427.

15) Chapter 49, pp. 515-517; chapter 58, pp. 542-545; and chapter 60, pp. 549-551, respectively.

16) Chapter 42; SEE especially verse 38, p. 487.

17) **The [East] Romans,** Chapter 30:2-3, p. 404.

18) **Consultation** 42:39, p. 487.

19) **Pilgrimage** 22:60, p. 339.

20) **The Cow** 2:255, p. 42.

21) **Thunder** 13:28, p. 252.

22) **Sincerity,** Chapter 112:1-4 (complete), p. 604.

23) **The Cow** 2:115, p. 18.

24) **Luqmān** 31:24, p. 414.

25) **The Cow** 2:163, p. 24.

26) **Victory** 48:29, p. 515.

27) P. 196.

28) **The House of ᶜImrān** 3:97, p. 62.

29) **Abraham** 14:18, p. 257.

30) **The Cow** 2:255, p. 42.

31) **Disbelievers,** Chapter 109, p. 603.

32) **Women** 4:116, p. 97: "God does not forgive one's associating [others] with Him."

33) **Booty** 8:22, p. 179.

34) **The House of ᶜImrān** 3:77-80, pp. 59-60.

35) **The Earthquake** 99:7-8, p. 599.

36) **The Stunning [Blow]** 101:6-11, p. 600.

37) **The Coalition** 33:59, p. 426.

38) **The Heights** 7:31, p. 154.

39) **The Inevitable** 56:79, p. 537.

40) **Bees** 16:98, p. 278.

41) **The Night Journey** 17:78, p. 290.

42) **The Heights** 7:204, p. 176.

43) **The Night Journey** 17:106, p. 293.

44) **Jonah** 10:38, p. 213.

45) **The Night Journey** 17:88, p. 291.

I

The Opening

THIS INITIAL or prefatory chapter is made up of seven verses from the period which the Prophet passed in Mecca. It was revealed after **The Man Wearing a Cloak** 74 and before **The Flame** 111. The chapter has classical expression, and is "simple in wording but full of meaning," which eventually works into our consciousness as we repeat it daily.

This is the customary invocation used in Islamic ceremonies of all kinds, and it forms a true prayer, occupying somewhat the same place in Islam as the Lord's prayer does with Christians. The chapter is often said to contain the "essence" of the Qurɔān, and in 15:VI it is called the "Seven Oft-Repeated Verses."

This chapter should be read attentively since many Islamic terms are introduced here and are repeated daily by every Muslim. It also bears witness to God's presence everywhere.

In the name of God, the Mercy-giving, the Merciful!

* Praise be to God, * Lord of the Universe,
* the Mercy-giving, the Merciful!
* Ruler on the Day for Repayment!
** You do we worship and You do we call on for help.
* Guide us along the Straight Road,
* the road of those whom You have favored,
with whom You are not angry,
nor who are lost!

PART ONE

[Amen.]

2
The Cow

Tʜɪs ᴄʜᴀᴘᴛᴇʀ of 286 verses is arranged in forty sections. It, as well as Chapter 3 and Chapters 29-32 inclusive, begin with the mystic initials ᴀ.ʟ.ᴍ. It dates from the first year after the *Hijra* or Transfer from Mecca to Madīna, or around the year 623 ᴀ.ᴅ. It was revealed before Chapter 8 **Booty**, except for verse 281 (xxxvɪɪ) which was revealed at Mina, a suburb just east of Mecca, during the Farewell Pilgrimage shortly before the Prophet passed away. The title is taken from the Cow, ᴏʀ the Golden Calf, the story of which appears in section vɪɪɪ below, and which Moses wanted the Children of Israel to sacrifice to God Alone.

Because the chapter is quite long, it continues through two and a half of the thirty Parts into which the Qurʾān is traditionally divided, and comprises more than one-tenth of the whole text of the holy Book. The chapter mostly concerns legislation promulgated during the Madinese period. It begins with the majestic invocation to the Book which announces the first section, and then proceeds to describe disbelievers and those arrogant persons who take it upon themselves to dictate to others concerning religion. There is a parable on "The Gnat" in section ɪɪɪ, and we proceed to the story of Adam's creation in ɪv.

Prayer is discussed in v, and we are told in vɪ that intercession is not acceptable because God's face is to be found everywhere. The Direction of Prayer, or our *qibla*, is dealt with in xvɪɪ-xvɪɪɪ, and prayer itself once more in xxxɪ. Section xɪx instructs us that we should simply strive to meet God Alone. Abraham is introduced to us at Mecca (xv) while his signs appear in xxxv.

Fasting, the month of Ramaḍān and God's care are other themes discussed here (xxɪɪɪ). Food is mentioned in xxɪ; virtue and retaliation in xxɪɪ; the Pilgrimage appears in xxv. Charity is prescribed in xxxvɪ-xxxvɪɪ, and we are told to favor the genteel poor who do not go around begging in public. Death and wills are treated in xxɪɪ; waste and bribery in xxɪɪɪ. There is legislation against liquor and gambling in xxv, the loan business in xxxvɪɪɪ, while the matter of debts and loans is handled in xxxɪx. Then follow such matters as orphans, the sin of associating others with our worship of God Alone, menstruation (xxvɪɪɪ), marriage, oaths, divorce, nursing mothers and widows (xxx).

In Part III of the Qurʾān, towards the end of this chapter, we are offered the great vision of God's Seat or Throne, which embraces Heaven and Earth, and are admonished to observe tolerance (xxxɪv). The chapter ends with a statement of the Islamic creed, given as this is generally recited by Muslims (XL).

In the name of God, the Mercy-giving, the Merciful!

(I)* A.L.M.

   * This is the Book which contains no doubt; it means guidance for those who do their duty

     * who believe in the Unseen, keep up prayer, and spend something from whatever We have provided them with;

     * who believe in what has been sent down to you as well as what was sent down before you,

     While they are convinced about the Hereafter; ** such people hold on to guidance from their Lord; those will be successful.

Invocation to the Book

The Heedful Or Pious

* It is all the same whether you warn those who disbelieve or do not warn them; they still will not believe: * God has sealed off their hearts and their hearing, while over their sight there hangs a covering; they will have severe torment.

(II)* Some people say: "We believe in God and the Last Day," while they are not believers. * They would like to deceive God and those who believe, while they merely outwit themselves and do not even notice it! ** Their hearts contain malice so God has increased their [share of] malice. They will have painful torment because they have been lying.

   * Whenever someone tells them: "Dont act so depraved on earth," they say: "We are only improving matters!" * They are indeed mischief makers, but they are not aware of it. * When someone tells them: "Believe just as other people believe," they say: "Are we to believe just as simpletons believe?" Surely they are the fools even though they do not realize it!

   * Whenever they meet those who believe, they say: "We believe;" while once they go off alone with their ringleaders, they say: "We are with you; we were only joking!" ** God will joke with them and let them go on acting arrogantly in their blind fashion! * Those are the ones who have purchased error at the price of guidance, while their bargain does not profit them nor have they been guided.

8
Disbelievers (Arrogation Explained)

10

   * They may be compared to someone who kindles a fire, and once it lights up whatever lies around him, God takes away their light and leaves them in darkness. They do not see: * deaf, dumb and blind, they will never respond!

   * Or to a raincloud from the sky containing darkness, thunder and lightning; they stick their fingers in their ears to ward off death because of the thunderclaps, for God will soon be rounding up disbelievers. ** Lightning almost snatches their sight away: each time it lights things up for them, they walk along in it, while when darkness settles down on them, they stand stockstill. If God wanted, He would take away their hearing and eyesight; God is Capable of everything!

The Arrogant

20

21

(III) * Mankind, worship your Lord Who created you as well as those before you, so that you may do your duty! * [He is] the One Who has made the earth a carpet for you and had the sky built above you, and sent water to pour down from the sky and brought forth fruit by means of it as sustenance for you. Do not set up rivals for God while you know [better].

     * If you (all) are in any doubt about what We have sent down to Our servant, then **bring a chapter like it** and call in your witnesses besides God if you are so truthful. * If you do not—and you will never do so—then heed the Fire which has been prepared for disbelievers whose fuel is mankind and stones! ** Proclaim to those who believe and perform honorable deeds that they will have gardens through which rivers flow. Each time they are provided with fruits from it for their sustenance, they will say: "This is what we were provided with before!" They will be given similar things and have clean-living spouses there. They will live in it for ever!

Parables
(The Gnat)

     * God does not hesitate to compare things to a mosquito nor to anything bigger than it. Those who believe realize that it is the Truth from their Lord, while those who disbelieve say: "What does God want in such a comparison?" He lets so many go astray through it, and guides many by means of it. Yet only immoral persons are led astray by it! * Those who break God's covenant after they have pledged to keep it, and sever whatever God has ordered to be joined, and act depraved on earth, will be the losers. * How can you disbelieve in God when you once were dead and He furnished you with life? Soon He will let you die once more, then bring you back to life again; then unto Him will you return! * He is the One Who has created everything that is on earth for you; then He turned towards Heaven and perfected it as seven heavens. He is Aware of everything!

30
The Story
of Adam

(IV)** So when your Lord told the angels: "I am placing an overlord on earth", they said: "Will You place someone there who will corrupt it and shed blood, while we hymn Your praise and sanctify You?" He said: "I know something you do not know."

     * He taught Adam all the names of everything; then presented them to the angels, and said: "Tell me the names of these if you are so truthful." * They said: "Glory be to You; we have no knowledge except whatever You have taught us. You are the Aware, the Wise!" * He said: "Adam, tell them their names."

     Once he had told them their names, He said: "Did I not tell you that I know the Unseen in Heaven and Earth? I know whatever you disclose and whatever you have been hiding."

     * So We told the angels: "Bow down on your knees before Adam." They [all] knelt down except for Diabolis. He refused and acted proudly, and became a disbeliever.

     ** We said: "Adam, settle down in the Garden, both you and your wife, and eat freely from it anywhere either of you may wish. Yet do not approach this tree lest you become wrongdoers."

     * Satan made them stumble over it and had them both expelled from where they had been [living]. We said: "Clear out! Some of you will

[become] enemies of others. You will have a resting place on earth and enjoyment for a while."

* Adam received words [of inspiration] from his Lord and He turned towards him. He is the Relenting, the Merciful!

* We said: "Clear out from it together! If you should be handed guidance from Me, then anyone who follows My guidance will have no fear nor will they be saddened; * while those who disbelieve and reject Our signs will become inmates of the Fire; they shall remain in it!"

(v)** Children of Israel, remember My favor which I have shown you, and fulfil My agreement! I shall fulfil your covenant. I am the One you should revere! * Believe in what I have sent down to confirm what you already have, and do not be the first to disbelieve in it. Do not sell My signs for a paltry price. I am the One you should heed! * Do not cloak Truth with falsehood nor hide the Truth while you realize it.

* Keep up prayer, pay the welfare tax, and worship along with those who bow their heads. * Are you ordering people to be virtuous while forgetting it yourselves, even as you recite the Book? Will you not use your reason?

** Seek help through patience and prayer, since it is exacting except for the submissive * who assume they will meet their Lord, and that they will return to Him.

(vi)* Children of Israel, remember My favor which I have bestowed on you. I have preferred you over [the rest of] the Universe! * Heed a day when no soul will compensate for any other soul in any way. Intercession will not be accepted from him, nor will any alternative be taken for it. They will not be supported. * When We rescued you from Pharaoh's household, they had been subjecting you to the worst torment, slaying your sons and sparing your women. That meant such awful testing by your Lord! ** So We divided the sea for you and saved you, while We drowned Pharaoh's household as you were looking on. * When We appointed forty nights for Moses, you took the **Calf** after he [had left], and you became wrongdoers. * Then later on We still overlooked this for you, so that you might act grateful * when We gave Moses the Book and the Standard so that you might be guided. * When Moses told his folk: "My people, you have wronged yourselves in accepting the **Calf**, so turn towards your Maker in repentance and kill your own [guilty] selves; that will be better for you with your Maker. He will (then) relent towards you, since He is the Relenting, the Merciful."

** So you said: "Moses, we will never believe in you until we see God openly," the Thunderbolt caught you while you were (all) looking on. * Then We raised you up after you had died so that you might act grateful; * We spread the clouds out to shade you, and sent down manna and quail for you: "Eat some of the good things which We have provided you with!" They did not harm Us, but it was themselves whom they harmed.

40

Prayer

47

*Intercession
is not
Accepted*

50

* So We said: "Enter this town and eat wherever you may wish in it at your leisure. Enter the gate [walking] on your knees and say: 'Relieve us!' We will forgive you your mistakes and give even more to those who act kindly. * Yet those who do wrong altered the Statement to something else than what had been told them, so We sent a blight down from Heaven on those who did wrong since they had acted so immorally.

60   (VII)** Thus Moses looked for something for his people to drink, and We said: "Strike the rock with your staff!"; so twelve springs gushed forth from it. Each group of people knew its drinking spot: "Eat and drink from God's provisions, and do not cause any havoc on earth, as if you were mischief-makers."

* When you said: "Moses, we'll never stand one [kind of] food! Appeal to your Lord to produce whatever the earth will grow for us, such as its vegetables and cucumbers, and its garlic, lentils and onions;" He said: "Do you want to exchange something commonplace for something that is better?" Settle in some city to get what you have asked for!" Humiliation and poverty beat them down and they incurred anger from God. That was because they had disbelieved in God's signs and killed the prophets without having any right to. That happened because they disobeyed and had acted so defiant.

62   (VIII) * Those who believe and those who are Jews, Christians and Sabeans, [in fact] *anyone who believes in God and the Last Day, and acts honorably will receive their earnings from their Lord*: no fear will lie upon them nor need they feel saddened. * Thus we have made an agreement with you and raised the Mountain over you: "Hold firmly to what We have brought you and remember what it contains, so that you may do your duty;" * while later on you turned away, and if God's bounty and His mercy had not [rested] upon you, you would have turned out to be losers! ** Yet you knew which of you had been defiant on the Sabbath, so We told them: "Become apes, rejected!" * We set them up as an illustration of what had come before them and what would come after them, and as a lesson for the heedful.

The Cow   * When Moses told his folk: "God commands you to sacrifice a **cow**," they said: "Do you take us for a laughingstock?" He said: "I seek refuge with God lest I become so ignorant!" * They said: "Appeal to your Lord for us, to explain to us what she is."

He said: "He says she is neither a wornout **cow**, nor a heifer, but of an age in between. Do as you are ordered!" * They said: "Appeal to your Lord for us, to explain to us what color she is." He said: "He says that she is a bright yellow **cow**. Her color gladdens those who look at her."

70   ** They said: "Appeal to your Lord for us, to explain to us what she is like. Cows seem all alike to us and we should be guided properly, if God so wishes." * He said: "He says that she is a **cow** which has not yet been broken in to plow the earth nor to irrigate any crops; she is sound and has no blemish on her." They said: "Now you are telling the Truth!", and they slaughtered her though they almost had not done so.

(IX)* When you killed a soul and quarrelled over it, God was bound to bring forth whatever you had hidden. * We said: "Strike him with some part of it." Thus God revives the dead and shows you His signs so you may use your reason. * Even after that your hearts were hardened and became stony, and even harder yet, for there are some stones which rivers gush out of and there are others which water comes forth from when they split open, and there are still others which collapse out of awe for God. God is not oblivious of what you are doing!

** Are you so keen for them to believe for your own sake while a group of them have already heard God's word? Then they tamper with it once they have studied it, and they realize it. * Whenever they meet with those who believe, they say: "We believe!", while when some of them go off privately with one another, they say: "Will you report something to them which God has disclosed to you, so they may dispute with you about it in the presence of your Lord? Dont you use your reason?" * Do they not realize that God knows anything they hide and anything they display? * Some of them are illiterate and do not know the Book except to say "Amen" [to it]. They are merely guessing. * It will be too bad for those who write the Book down in their own hand[writing], then say: "This is from God!", so they may sell it for a paltry price. It will be too bad for them because of what their hands have written. Too bad for whatever they earn! ** They say: "The Fire will only touch us for several days."

SAY: "Have you taken it on oath from God? God never breaks His word. Or are you saying something about God which you really do not know?" * Rather anyone who commits evil will find his mistake will hem him in; those will become inmates of the Fire; they will remain in it for ever. * Those who believe and perform honorable deeds will be inhabitants of the Garden; they will live in it for ever.

(x)* Thus We made an agreement with the Children of Israel: "You shall serve God Alone, and treat your parents kindly, and [also] near relatives, orphans and the needy, and say kind things to [other] people, and keep up prayer and pay the welfare tax"; then you turned away and except for a few of you, you avoided doing anything. * So We made an agreement with you: "You must not shed your own blood, nor drive one another out of your homes;" then you ratified this and were witnesses [for it]. ** Then there you go killing one another and driving a group of you from their homes, backing one another up against them out of sin and enmity. If they are brought to you as prisoners, you ransom them, while it has been forbidden for you even to expel them!

Do you believe in part of the Book and disbelieve in another part of it? What reward has anyone of you who does so, except disgrace during worldly life, while on Resurrection Day they will be driven off to the harshest torment? God does not overlook anything you do! * Those are the ones who purchase worldly life instead of the Hereafter; punishment will not be lightened for them nor will they be supported.

72

Making a Living from Misinterpreting the Qurʾān

80

83

The Children of Israel

87   (XI)* We gave Moses the Book and followed him up with messengers later
            on. We gave Jesus the son of Mary evidence and assisted him with the
            Holy Spirit. Yet every time some messenger comes to you with what you
            yourselves do not fancy, why do you act so overbearing? One group you
            have rejected while another group you would [like to] kill.
                 * They said: "Our hearts are covered over." Rather God has cursed
Disbelief   them because of their disbelief; little do they believe. * Whenever a Book
            has come to them from God to confirm what they already have—whereas
            previously they had been seeking victory over those who disbelieve—so
            whenever something they can recognize is brought to them, they disbelieve
90   in it. God's curse lies on disbelievers! ** How wretchedly have they sold
            their own souls by disbelieving in what God has sent down to them,
            begrudging that God should send down some of His bounty on any of His
            servants He may wish. They have brought an exchange of anger for anger
            on themselves; disbelievers will have shameful torment. * Whenever some-
            one tells them: "Believe in what God has sent down;" they say: "We believe
            [only] in what has been sent down **to us**," while they disbelieve in what has
            come after that, even though it is the Truth confirming what they already
            have.
                 SAY: "Why did you kill God's prophets previously if you were believers?
            * Moses came to you with evidence; then later on you adopted the Calf
            and became wrongdoers." * When We made an agreement with you and
            raised the Mountain up over you [as a symbol]: "Take whatever We have
            brought you seriously, and listen;" they said: "We listen and [yet] we
            disobey!" They sucked the [spirit of the] Calf into their hearts because of
            their disbelief. SAY: "How wretchedly your faith commands you, if you ever
            have been believers!"
                 * SAY: "If a home in the Hereafter with God is exclusively yours instead
            of [other] people's, then long for death if you are so truthful!" ** They
            will never long for it because of what their hands have already prepared.
            God is Aware of wrongdoers! * You will find them the people most eager
            to live, even compared with those who associate [others with God]. Each
            one of them would like to live on for a thousand years! Yet it would never
            save anyone from torment, even should he live that long. God is Observant
            of whatever they do.

97   (XII)* SAY: "Who is Gabriel's enemy? He has brought it down for your
            heart with God's permission, to confirm what came before it and as
            guidance and good news for believers. * Who is an enemy of God and His
            angels and His messengers, as well as of Gabriel and Michael?'' Anyhow,
            God is an enemy of disbelievers! * We have sent you down clear signs;
100   only immoral people disbelieve in them. *** Each time they swear an
            oath, does a group of them shrug it off? Rather most of them do not even
            believe.
                 * Whenever a messenger from God has come to them to confirm what
            they already had, a group of those who were given the Book have tossed
            God's book behind their backs as if they did not know [any better]. *

They followed whatever the devils recited concerning Solomon's control. Solomon did not disbelieve but the devils disbelieved, teaching people magic and what was sent down to Hārūt and Mārūt, two angels at Babylon. Neither of these would teach anyone unless they [first] said: "We are only a temptation, so do not disbelieve!" They learned from them both what will separate a man from his wife. Yet they do not harm anyone through it except with God's permission. They learn what will harm them and does not benefit them. They know that anyone who deals in it will have no share in the Hereafter; how wretched is what they have sold themselves for, if they only knew! * If they had only believed and done their duty, a recompense from God would have been better, if they had realized it!

Learning Things Wrong

(XIII) * You who believe, do not say: "Herd us,"; and say [instead]: "Watch over us," and [then] "Listen!" Disbelievers will have painful torment. ** Neither those People of the Book who disbelieve, nor associators [of others with God] would like any good from your Lord to be sent down to you. God will single out anyone He wishes for His mercy; God possesses splendid bounty. * We do not cancel any verse nor let it be forgotten; instead We bring something better than it or else something similar. Do you not know that God is Capable of everything? * Do you not know that God [Alone] holds control over Heaven and Earth? You have no patron nor any supporter besides God. * Or do you (all) want to question your Messenger just as Moses was questioned previously? Anyone who exchanges faith for disbelief has strayed right down the line!

104

* Many People of the Book would like to turn you back into disbelievers following your [profession of] faith, out of envy for themselves, even though the Truth has been explained to them. Pardon [them] and disregard it till God brings His command; God is Capable of everything!

** Keep up prayer and pay the welfare tax; you will find any good you have sent on ahead for your own souls' sake is already [stored up] with God. God is Observant of whatever you do. * They say: "No one will enter the Garden unless he is a Jew or a Christian. Those individuals are merely saying "Amen" [to their leaders]. SAY: "Bring on your proof if you are so truthful." * Rather anyone who commits his person peacefully to God and is acting kindly will receive his earnings from his Lord. No fear shall come upon them nor will they be saddened.

110

Jews and Christians

(XIV) * Jews say: "Christians have no point to make;" while Christians say: "The Jews have no point to make." Yet they (all) quote from the [same] Book. Likewise those who do not know anything make a statement similar to theirs. God will judge between them on Resurrection Day concerning how they have been differing.

113

* Who is more in the wrong than someone who prevents God's name from being mentioned in His places of worship and attempts to ruin them? Such persons should not even enter them except in fear; they will suffer disgrace in this world as well as serious torment in the Hereafter.

God's Face

     ** The East and West are God's:
wherever you may turn,
there will be God's countenance,
for God is Boundless, Aware!

* They say: "God has adopted a son!" Glory be to Him! Rather He owns whatever is in Heaven and Earth. All things are devoted to Him. * Deviser of Heaven and Earth, whenever He decrees some affair, He merely tells it: "Be!" and it is.

* Those who do not know (anything) say: "If God would only speak to us, or a sign were brought us!" Likewise those before them said the same as they are saying; their hearts are all alike. We have explained signs for folk who are certain. * We have sent you with the Truth as a herald and a warner: you will not be questioned about the inmates of Hades.

120   ** Neither the Jews nor the Christians will ever be satisfied with you until you follow their sect. SAY:

"God's guidance means [real] guidance!"

If you followed their whims after the knowledge which has come to you, you would not have any patron nor supporter against God. * Those whom We have brought the Book, recite it in the way it should be recited; such men believe in it. Those who disbelieve in it will be the losers.

122   (xv)* O Children of Israel, remember My favor which I bestowed on you, and how I preferred you over [everyone in] the Universe. * Heed a day when no soul will make amends in any way for any other soul and no adjustment will be accepted from it nor any intercession benefit it. They will not be supported.

Abraham
at Mecca

     * When his Lord tested Abraham by means of [certain] words, and he fulfilled them, He said: "I am going to make you into a leader for mankind." He said: "What about my offspring?"; He said: "My pledge does not apply to evildoers."

     ** Thus We set up the House as a resort for mankind and a sanctuary, and [said]: "Adopt Abraham's station as a place for prayer." We entrusted Abraham and Ishmael with cleaning out My house for those who circle around it and are secluded [praying] there, and who bow down on their knees in worship.

     * So Abraham said: "My Lord, make this countryside safe and provide any of its people who believe in God and the Last Day with fruit from it." He said: "Even anyone who disbelieves, I'll let enjoy things for a while, then drive him along towards the torment of Fire. How awful is such a goal!"

     * Thus Abraham along with Ishmael laid the foundations for the House: "Our Lord, accept this from us! Indeed You are the Alert, the Aware! * Our Lord, leave us peacefully committed to You, and make our offspring into a nation which is at peace with You. Show us our cere-

monies and turn towards us. You are so Relenting, the Merciful! * Our
Lord, send a messenger in among them from among themselves who will
recite Your verses to them and teach them the Book and wisdom! He will
purify them, for You are the Powerful, the Wise!"

(XVI)** Who would shrink from [joining] Abraham's sect except someone
who fools himself? We selected him during worldly life, while in the
Hereafter he will be among the honorable ones. * So when his Lord told
him: "Commit yourself to [live in] peace"; he said: "I have already
committed myself peacefully to the Lord of the Universe!"

    * Abraham commissioned his sons with it [as a legacy], and [so did]
Jacob: "My sons, God has selected your religion for you. Do not die unless
you are Muslims." * Or were you present as death appeared for Jacob,
when he said to his sons: "What will you serve after I am gone?" They said:
"We shall worship your God and the God of your forefathers Abraham,
Ishmael and Isaac: God Alone! We are committed peacefully to Him."

    * That is a nation which has already passed away: there awaits it
whatever it has earned, while you will have what you have earned. You will
not be questioned about what they have been doing.

    ** They say: "Become Jews or Christians; you will [then] be guided."
SAY: "Rather Abraham's sect, [for he was] a seeker [afterTruth]; he was no
associator [of others with God Alone]." * SAY: "We believe in God and
what has been sent down to us, and what was sent down to Abraham,
Ishmael, Isaac, Jacob and their descendants, and what was given Moses
and Jesus, and what was given the [other] prophets by their Lord. We do
not discriminate against any one of them and are committed [to live] in
peace to Him."

    * If they believe the same as you believe, then they are guided, while if
they turn elsewhere, they will only fall into dissension. God will suffice for
you [in dealing with] them: He is the Alert, Aware. * [Such is] God's
design! Who is better than God for a design? We are serving Him. * SAY:
"Do you argue with us about God while He is our Lord and your Lord as
well? We have our actions while you have your actions, and we are loyal to
Him. ** Or do you say that Abraham, Ishmael, Isaac, Jacob and their
descendants were Jews or Christians?" SAY: "Are you more knowledgeable
than God?" Who is more unjust than someone who hides some evidence
from God which he holds? God is not heedless of what you are doing.
* That is a nation which has already passed away. There awaits it whatever
it has earned, while you will have what you have earned. You will not be
questioned about what they are doing.

marginalia: 130

*marginalia: Collective
Responsibility*

marginalia: 140

*marginalia: PART
TWO*

(XVII)* Some foolish folk will say: "Whatever turned them away from the
Direction [of Prayer] toward which they used to face?" SAY: "God holds the

*marginalia: 142
The
Direction
of Prayer*

East and West; He guides whomever He wishes towards a Straight Road."
* Thus We have set you up as a moderate nation so you may act as
witnesses for mankind, even as the Messenger is a witness for you. We have
only set up the Direction towards which you used to face so We might
know the one who is following the Messenger from someone who turns on
his heels. It is such a serious matter except for those whom God has
guided! God will never let your faith be forfeited; God is Gentle, Merciful
with mankind.

> * We see you shifting your face all over the sky, so We shall appoint a
> Direction for you which you will feel satisfied with; so turn your face
> towards the Hallowed Mosque. Wherever you (all) may be, turn your
> faces towards it!

Those who were given the Book know that it brings the Truth from their
Lord; while God is not unaware of what they do. ** Even though you
brought every sign for those who were given the Book they still would not
follow your Direction. You are not following their direction, nor will any
of them follow one another's direction. If you were to follow their whims
once knowledge has come to you, you would then be an evildoer. * Those
to whom We have given the Book recognize it just as they recognize their
own children. Nevertheless a group of them hide the Truth even though
they know it. * Truth comes from your Lord, so do not be a doubter!

148
*Direction
of Prayer
(cont'd)*

150

(XVIII) * Everyone has some course he steers by, so compete in [doing]
good deeds. Wherever you may be, God will bring you all together; God is
Capable of everything. * No matter where you may set out from, turn
your face towards the Hallowed Mosque. It means the Truth from your
Lord; nor will God overlook whatever you are doing. ** No matter where
you set out from, turn your face towards the Hallowed Mosque; wherever
you may be, turn your faces towards it, so that people will not have any
argument against you, except for those among them who do wrong. Do
not dread them but dread Me, so I may complete My favor towards you
and so that you may be guided; * just as We have sent a messenger to you
from among yourselves to recite My signs to you, and to cleanse you and
teach you the Book and wisdom, and to teach you what you did not
know. * Remember Me; I shall remember you. Thank Me, and do not act
ungrateful with Me!

153
*Striving
for God*

(XIX) *   You who believe, seek help through patience and prayer; God
stands alongside the patient!
     * Do not say: "They are dead!" about anyone who is
killed for God's sake. Rather they are living, even though you
do not notice it.
     ** We shall test you with a bit of fear and hunger, plus a
shortage of wealth and souls and produce. Announce such to
patient people * who say, whenever some misfortune strikes
them: "We belong to God, and are returning to Him!"

* Such will have their prayers [accepted] by their Lord, and [granted] mercy. Those have consented to be guided!

* Ṣafā and Marwa are some of God's waymarks. Anyone who goes on Pilgrimage to the House or visits [it] will not be blamed if he runs along between them. With anyone who volunteers some good, God is Appreciative, Aware. * God curses those who hide whatever We send down as explanations and guidance, once We have explained it to mankind in the Book, and cursers will curse them, ** except for those who repent, reform and explain; those I accept repentance from, for I am the Receiver of Repentance, the Merciful!

160

* Those who disbelieve and die while they are disbelievers will have God's curse upon them, as well as the angels' and all mankind's * to live with for ever. Torment will not be lightened for them nor will they be allowed to wait.

> * **Your God is God Alone;**
> there is no deity except Him,
> the Mercy-giving, the Merciful!

(xx)* In the creation of Heaven and Earth, the alternation between night and day, the ships which plow the sea with something to benefit mankind, and any water God sends down from the sky with which to revive the earth following its death, and to scatter every kind of animal throughout it, and directing the winds and clouds which are driven along between the sky and earth, are (all) signs for folk who use their reason. ** Yet there are some people who adopt rivals instead of God, whom they love just as they should love God. Those who believe are firmer in their love of God; if only those who commit evil might see, when they face torment, how strength is wholly God's, and God is Severe with torment. * When those who have been following them free themselves from those they have been following, and they see the torment, their bonds will be cut off from them! * Those they have been following will say: "If we only had another chance, then we would free ourselves from them just as they have freed themselves from us!" Thus God will show them their actions as regrets on their part. They will never leave the Fire!

164

(xxi)* Mankind, eat anything lawful, wholesome that exists on earth, and do not follow in Satan's footsteps; he is an open enemy of yours. * He merely orders you to commit evil and shocking deeds, and to say what you do not know about God. ** Whenever someone tells them: "Follow what God has sent down;" they say: "Rather we will follow what we discovered our forefathers were doing," even though their forefathers did not use their reason in any way nor were they guided. * Those who disbelieve may be compared to those who bleat away at something that only listens to calls and cries: deaf, dumb and blind, they do not use their reason. * You who believe, eat any wholesome things We have provided you with, and thank God if it is He Whom you worship.

168

170

Food

  * He has only forbidden you what has died by itself, blood and pork, and anything that has been consecrated to something besides God. Yet anyone who may be forced to do so, without craving or going too far, will have no offence held against him; for God is Forgiving, Merciful.

  * Those who hide what God has sent down in the Book and (then) barter it off for a paltry price only suck fire into their bellies. God will not speak to them on Resurrection Day nor will He purify them; they will have painful torment! ** Those are the ones who have purchased error instead of guidance, and torment instead of forgiveness. Why do they insist on facing the Fire? * That is because God has sent the Book down with the Truth, while those who disagree about the Book go much too far in dissension.

177

Virtue

(xxii) *   **Virtue** does not mean for you to turn your faces towards the East and West, but virtue means one should believe in God [Alone], the Last Day, angels, the Book and prophets; and no matter how he loves it, to give his wealth away to near relatives, orphans, the needy, the wayfarer and beggars, and towards freeing captives; and to keep up prayer and pay the welfare tax; and those who keep their word whenever they promise anything; and are patient under suffering and hardship and in time of violence. Those are the ones who act loyal, and they perform their duty.

Retaliation

  * You who believe, compensation for the murder(ed victim) has been prescribed for you: the freeman for the free, the slave for the slave, and the female for the female. Anyone who is pardoned in any way for it by his brother should follow this up appropriately, and handsomely make amends with him; that means a lightening as well as mercy from your Lord. Anyone who exceeds the limit after that shall have painful torment. * You will find [security for] life in [such] compensation, O prudent persons, so that you may do your duty!

180

Death and Wills

  ** It has been prescribed for you that whenever death faces one of you, he should draw up a will in a proper manner for both his parents and near relatives if he leaves any property behind, as a duty for the heedful. * Anyone who alters it once he has heard it [read] will have his sin fall upon only such as those who alter it; God is Alert, Aware. * However there is no sin to be charged anyone who fears some alteration or any sin on the part of an executor, and so patches things up among them. God is Forgiving, Merciful.

183

Fasting

(xxiii)* You who believe, fasting has been prescribed for you just as it was prescribed for those before you, so that you may do your duty, * on days which have been planned ahead. Any of you who is ill or on a journey [should choose] a number of other days. For those who can [scarcely] afford it, making up for it means feeding a poor man. It is even better for anyone who can volunteer some wealth; although it is better yet for you to fast, if you only knew.

** The month of Ramadan is when the Qurʾān was sent down as guidance for mankind, and with explanations for guidance, and as a Standard. Let any of you who is at home during the month, fast in it; while anyone who is ill or on a journey should [set an equal] number of other days.

The Month of Ramadan

God wants things to be easy for you and does not want any hardship for you, so complete the number and magnify God because He has guided you, so that you may act grateful.

* Whenever My servants ask you about Me,
[it means] **I am Near**.
I answer the appeal of the prayerful one
whenever he appeals to Me.
Let them respond to Me,
and believe in Me
so they may be directed!

God's Care

* It is lawful for you to have intercourse with **your wives** on the night of the Fast: they **are garments for you while you are garments for them**. God knows how you have been deceiving yourselves, so He has relented towards you and pardoned you. Now [feel free to] frequent them and seek what God has prescribed for you.

Eat and drink until the white streak [of dawn] can be distinguished by you from the black thread [of night] at daybreak. Then complete the Fast until nightfall and have no dealings with women while you are secluded at your devotions in the mosques. Such are God's limits, so do not attempt to cross them! Thus God explains His signs to mankind so they may do their duty.

* Do not eat up one another's wealth to no good purpose, nor try to bribe authorities with it so you may consume a share of [other] people's wealth viciously while you realize [what you are doing].

Waste and Bribery

(xxiv)* They will ask you about the phases of the moon. SAY: "They serve as datelines for mankind as well as the Pilgrimage. It is no virtue for you to go into houses through their backdoors, but **virtue lies in doing one's duty**; approach houses through their [front] doors and heed God, so that you may prosper.

189

** Fight those who fight against you along God's way, yet do not initiate hostilities; God does not love aggressors. * Kill them wherever you may catch them, and expel them from anywhere they may have expelled you. **Sedition is more serious than killing!** Yet do not fight them at the Hallowed Mosque unless they fight you there. If they should fight you, then fight them back; such is the reward for disbelievers. * However if they stop, God will be Forgiving, Merciful. * Fight them until there is no more subversion and [all] religion belongs to God. If they stop, let there be no [more] hostility except towards wrongdoers.

190
Aggression

* One hallowed month matches [another] hallowed month, while sacred matters have [their] means of compensation. Attack anyone who attacks you to the same extent as he has attacked you. Heed God, and know that God stands by the heedful. ** Spend for God's sake, yet do not expose yourselves to ruin through your own hands. Do good: God loves those who act kindly.

Pilgrimage

* Accomplish the Pilgrimage and the Experience for God's sake. If you are prevented from doing so, then make some offering available. Do not shave your heads until after the offering has reached its destination. For anyone of you who is ill or has some rash on his head, redemption means fasting, or some other act of charity or devotion. Once you feel safe, anyone who is enjoying the Experience along with the Pilgrimage should [send along] whatever he may make available in the form of an offering. Whoever does not find any should fast three days during the Pilgrimage and seven [more] when you return [home]; those make ten exactly. That is for anyone whose family is not present at the Hallowed Mosque. Heed God and know that God is Firm in retribution.

197   (XXV) *   Pilgrimage falls during specific months. Anyone who undertakes the Pilgrimage during them should not indulge in amorous intercourse, nor any immorality nor wrangling during the Pilgrimage. God knows about any good you may do. Make provision; yet **the best provision is doing your duty.** Heed Me, those who are prudent!

* It will not be held against you if you seek bounty from your Lord. When you stream forth from ‹Arafāt, remember God at the Hallowed Monument. Remember Him just as He has guided you, even if previously you acted like those who are lost. * Then stream forth from wherever the people stream forth, and seek forgiveness from God. God is Forgiving,

200   Merciful! *** Once you have performed your ceremonies, remember God just as you remember your forefathers, or even more fervently. There is the occasional man who says: "Our Lord, give us [such and such] during this world!" while he will have no share in the Hereafter. * There is another kind who says:

A Short Prayer

"Our Lord, give us something fine in this world,
as well as something fine in the Hereafter,
and shield us from the torment of Fire!"

* Those will have a portion of anything they have earned: God is Swift in reckoning!

* Remember God during the calculated days. Anyone who is anxious to leave within two days commits no offence, while anyone who stays on, commits no offence either, provided he does his duty. Heed God, and know that you will be summoned to Him.

Frivolity and Anarchy Condemned

* There is a certain man whose talk about worldly life intrigues you. He calls God to witness whatever is in his heart. He is extremely violent in quarreling. ** Whenever he holds the upper hand, he rushes around the earth ruining it. He destroys [people's] crops and breeding stock even though God does not like ruination. * When someone tells him: "Heed God," a [false] sense of importance leads him off to sin. He can count on Hell; what an awful couch!

* Another type sells his own soul while craving God's approval, even though God is Gentle with [His] servants. * You who believe, enter absolutely into peace! Do not follow Satan's footsteps; he is an open enemy of yours. * If you should lapse after explanations have come to you, then know that God is Powerful, Wise. ** Are they only waiting for God as well as angels to come along to them under canopies of clouds, so the matter will be settled? Unto God do matters return!

(xxvi)* Ask the Children of Israel how many clear signs We have given them. Anyone who changes God's favor once it has come to him will find God is Stern in punishment. * Worldly life has attracted those who disbelieve. They ridicule those who believe! Yet those who do their duty will stand ahead of them on Resurrection Day; God provides for anyone He wishes without any reckoning!

* Mankind was [once] one nation, so God despatched prophets as heralds and warners. He sent the Book down along with them to bring the Truth, so as to decide among mankind concerning whatever they had been disagreeing about. However only those to whom it was given disagreed about it out of envy towards one another, after explanations had been brought them. By His permission God has guided those who believe to any Truth they may have disagreed about. God guides anyone He wishes to a Straight Road.

* Or did you reckon you will enter the Garden when the same thing never happened to you such as [happened] to those who have passed away before you? Suffering and hardship assailed them, and they were battered about until the Messenger and those who believed along with him said: "When is God's support [due]? Is not God's support near?"

** They will ask you about what they should spend [in taxes]. SAY: "Any money you contribute should be [first] spent on both your parents, close relatives, orphans, the needy and the wayfarer. God is Aware of any good you do. * Fighting is also prescribed for you even though it may seem detestable to you. It may be that you detest something which is good for you; while perhaps you love something even though it is bad for you. God knows, while you do not know."

(xxvii)* They will ask you about fighting during the hallowed month. SAY: "Fighting in it is serious, while obstructing God's way, disbelief in Him and the Hallowed Mosque, and turning His people out of it are even more serious with God. Even dissension is more serious than killing."

They will never stop fighting you until they make you abandon your religion if they can manage to do so. Anyone of you who abandons his religion and dies while he is a disbeliever will find their actions will

210

211

Taxes

217

miscarry in this world and the Hereafter. Those [will become] inmates of the Fire; they will remain there. * Those who have believed and who have migrated and striven for God's sake may expect to receive God's mercy, for God is Forgiving, Merciful.

Liquor and Gambling

* They will ask you about liquor and gambling. SAY: In each of them there lies serious vice as well as some benefits for mankind. Yet their vice is greater than their usefulness."

220

They may ask you what to spend. SAY: "As much as you can spare!" Thus God explains His signs to you so that you may meditate ** concerning this world and the Hereafter.

Orphans

They will ask you about orphans. SAY: "To improve their lot is best; if you have any dealings with them, [remember] they are your brethren. God distinguishes the plunderer from the improver. If God so wished, He might crush you. God is Powerful, Wise.

Marriage with Associators

* Do not marry women who associate [others with God] until they believe. A believing maid is better than an associating woman, no matter how attractive she may seem to you. Do not let [your daughters] marry men who associate [others with God] until the latter believe; a believing slave is better than an associator, no matter how attractive he may seem to you. Those people invite (one) to the Fire while God invites (us) to the Garden and to forgiveness through His permission. He explains His signs to mankind in order that they may bear them in mind.

222
Menstruation

(XXVIII)* They will ask you about menstruation. SAY: "It is a nuisance, so keep away from women during menstruation. Do not approach them until they are cleansed. Once they cleanse themselves, then go to them just as God has commanded you to do. God loves the penitent and He loves those who try to keep clean.

Marriage

* Your wives are [meant] for you to cultivate: so go to your cultivation as you wish. Prepare yourselves while heeding God; know that you will be meeting Him. Proclaim such to believers!

Oaths

* Do not use God as an excuse in your oaths, to keep yourselves from being virtuous, doing your duty, and improving matters among mankind. God is Alert, Aware. ** God does not take you to task for any idle talk in your oaths, but He does take you to task for whatever your hearts have earned. God is Forgiving, Lenient.

Divorce

* Those who abstain from [having intercourse with] their wives, should lie low for four months longer. If they should then change their minds, well God is Forgiving, Merciful. * However if they insist on a divorce, God is Alert, Aware.

* Divorced women should wait [alone] by themselves for three menstrual periods; it is not lawful for them to hide what God has created in their wombs if they believe in God and the Last Day. Their husbands ought to take them back meanwhile in case they want a reconciliation. Women have the same [rights in relation to their husbands] as are expected in all decency from them; while men stand a step above them. God is Powerful, Wise.

(XXIX) * Divorce may be [pronounced] twice; then [it means] either to retain [your mate] in all decency, or else part from [the other partner] with (all) kindness. It is not lawful for you to take anything you have given any women unless both parties fear they will not keep within God's limits. If you fear they will not keep within God's limits, then there is no blame on either of them if she buys him off. Such are God's limits, so do not exceed them; those who exceed God's limits are wrongdoers. ** If he [finally] divorces her, she is not allowed [to remarry] him afterward, until she marries some husband other than him [in between]. If [the latter later] divorces her, there is no blame on either of them if they return to one another, provided they both think they can keep within God's limits.

Such are God's limits; He explains them to folk who know. * Once you divorce women, and they have reached the end of their waiting period, then either retain them in all decency or part from them decently. Do not retain them just to act mean with them; anyone who does that merely hurts himself. Do not take God's signs as a joke! Remember God's favor towards you, and anything He has sent down to you out of the Book and wisdom for your instruction. Heed God and know that God is Aware of everything.

(XXX) * Whenever you divorce women and they have reached the end of their waiting period, do not hinder them from marrying their [former] husbands if they have agreed to do so with proper formalities among themselves. Whoever among you believes in God and the Last Day is instructed to act thus; that is purer for you as well as more orderly. God knows while you do not know [what is fitting].

* Mothers should breastfeed their children two full years, provided they want to complete the nursing. The family head must support women and clothe them properly. Yet no person is charged with more than he can cope with. No mother should be made to suffer because of her child, nor any family head because of his child. An heir has the same [duties] in that respect. If they both prefer to wean [the child] when they have agreed on terms and consulted together, it should not be held against them; so if you want to find a wetnurse for your children, it should not be held against you, provided you hand over whatever you may have given in all decency. Heed God and know that God is Observant of anything you do.

* Those of you who pass away and leave spouses behind, let [the latter] hold themselves back for four months and ten [days more]. Once they reach the end of their term, you are not responsible for however they may dispose of themselves with due formality. God is Informed of anything you do. ** It should not be held against you concerning whatever you may propose in the way of becoming engaged to such women, or may keep to yourselves; God knows that you will bear them in mind. However do not propose anything to them secretly unless you utter a formal statement. Do not tie the marriage knot until the decree has become final; know that God knows whatever is on your minds, so be careful with Him! Know that God is Forgiving, Lenient.

(XXXI) * It will not be held against you if you divorce women when you have never had any contact with them, nor assigned them any living. Provide for

229
*Divorce
(cont'd)*

230

232

*Nursing
Mothers*

Widows

*Proposals
of
Marriage*

236
Alimony

them, the well-to-do according to his means and the straitened according to his means; an assignment is due in all decency from those who act kindly. * If you divorce women before you have had contact with them and have already assigned them a living, then [give them] half of what you have assigned [them] unless they forego it, or the man in whose hand lies the marriage knot foregoes it. That you forego it is nearer heedfulness. Do not forget to be generous with one another; God is Observant of whatever you do.

Prayer

* Watch over prayers and [especially] the Middle Prayer; and stand up devoutly to [worship] God. * If you feel afraid while on foot or out riding, then [perform it] once you feel safe. Remember God just as He has taught you what you did not know.

240
Wills and Inheritance

** For those of you who pass away leaving [widowed] spouses, a will means making provision for a year without having them leave [home]. If any women should leave, then you are not to blame for however they may dispose of themselves in all decency. God is Powerful, Wise. * Divorced women should have some provision [made] for them as a duty binding on the heedful. * Thus God explains His signs to you, so you may use your reason.

243
Refugees

(xxxii)* Have you not seen those who have left their homes? There were thousands of them risking death! God told them: "Die!"; then He revived them. God possesses bounty for mankind, even though most men do not act grateful.

Fighting for God's Sake

* Fight in God's way and know that God is Alert, Aware. ** Who is there to offer God a handsome loan, so He may compound it many times over for him? God both withholds and bestows; to Him will you return.

* Have you not seen how the councillors for the Children of Israel told a prophet of theirs [who came] after Moses: "Send us a king; we will fight for God's sake." He said: "Perhaps you will not fight even though fighting has been prescribed for you." They said: "What do we have to keep us from fighting for God's sake? We and our children have been turned out of our homes!"

Yet whenever fighting was prescribed for them, all but a few of them turned away. God is Aware as to who are evildoers. * Their prophet told

King Saul

them: "God has sent Saul as a king for you." They said: "How could he hold control over us, since we are fitter to exercise control than he is? He has not been given ample wealth."

He said: "God has singled him out for you and added plenty to his knowledge and physique. God gives his control to anyone He wishes; God is Boundless, Aware." * Their prophet told them: "A sign of his control will be that the Ark shall come to you containing Serenity from your Lord, as well as some relics which Moses' house and Aaron's house have left behind. The angels will bring it; in that there will be a sign for you if you are believers.

249

(xxxiii)* When Saul set out with the troops, he said: "God will test you at a river: anyone who drinks from it will not be on my side; while anyone who does not taste it is with me, except for someone who scoops up only a palmful in his hand." Yet all but a few of them drank some of it!

When he and those who were along with him and believed had crossed over, they said: "We have no way today to prevail over Goliath and his troops!" Those who thought they were going to meet God said: "How often has a small detachment defeated a larger detachment with God's permission! God stands alongside the patient!"

** When they marched forth to face Goliath and his troops, they said 250 [in prayer]: "Our Lord, fill us full of patience and brace our feet. Support us against such disbelieving folk!"

* They routed them with God's permission. David killed Goliath, and God gave him control and wisdom, and taught him whatever He wished. If God did not defend some men by means of others, the earth would be ruined; but God possesses bounty for [everybody in] the Universe. * These are God's verses which We recite to you for the Truth, since you are one of the messengers.

PART
THREE

(XXXIII cont'd)* We have preferred some of these messengers over others. 253 Some of them God spoke to, while others He raised in rank. We gave Jesus the son of Mary explanations, and endorsed him by means of the Holy Spirit. If God had wished, the ones who came after them would not have fallen out with one another once explanations had come to them; however they disagreed. Some of them believed while others disbelieved. If God had wished, they would not have fallen out with one another, but God does whatever He wants.

(XXXIV)* You who believe, spend some of what We have provided you 254 with before a day comes along in which there will be no bartering, friendship, nor any intercession! Disbelievers are such evildoers.

** God! There is no deity except Him,
the Living, the Eternal!
Slumber does not overtake Him, nor does sleep. *God's*
What the Heavens hold and what Earth holds *Seat*
[belongs] to Him. Who is there
to intercede with Him except by His permission?
He knows what lies before them and what's behind them,
while they embrace nothing of His knowledge
except whatever He may wish.
His **Seat** extends far over Heaven and Earth;
preserving them both does not overburden Him.
He is the Sublime, the Almighty!

Tolerance

* There should be no compulsion in religion. Normal behavior stands out clearly from error; so anyone who rejects the Arrogant ones and believes in God has grasped the Firmest Handle which will never break. God is Alert, Aware.

> * God is the Patron of those who believe.
> He brings them out of darkness into Light,
> while those who disbelieve have the Arrogant ones
> for their patrons; they will lead them
> out of Light into darkness. Those are
> inmates of the Fire; they shall remain there!

258

Abraham's Proof With The Sun

(XXXV)* Have you not considered the person who argued with Abraham about his Lord, concerning whether God would grant him any control? When Abraham said: "My Lord is the One Who gives life and brings death;" [the former] said: "I (too) give life and bring death!" Abraham said: "God brings the sun from the East, so you bring it from the West." The man who disbelieved was dumbfounded. God does not guide such wrong-doing folk.

The Stranger at the Ghost Town

* Or like the man who passed by a town whose roofs had caved in. He said: "How will God revive this following its death?" God let him die for a hundred years; then raised him up again.

He said: "How long have you been waiting here?" He said: "I've been waiting a day or part of a day." He said: "Rather you have stayed here a hundred years. Yet look at your food and drink: they have not yet even become stale! And look at your donkey. We will grant you it as a sign for mankind. Look how We set its bones together, then clothe them with flesh."

When it was explained to him, he said: "I know that God is Capable of everything!"

260

** When Abraham said: "My Lord, show me how You revive the dead;" He said: "Why, do you not believe?" He said: "Of course [I do], but just to set my heart at ease." He said: "Take four [kinds] of birds and train them to [follow] you; then place a part of them on every mountain. Then call them; they will come to you at once. Know that God is Powerful, Wise."

261

Charity is Like Sprouting Grain

Grudging Forbidden

The Bare Boulder

(XXXVI)* Those who spend their wealth for God's sake may be compared to a grain which sprouts into seven ears with a hundred grains in each ear. God multiplies things for anyone He wishes; God is Boundless, Aware. * Those who spend their wealth for God's sake, then do not follow up what they have spent with any reproach or scolding, shall receive their earnings from their Lord. No fear will lie upon them nor should they feel saddened. * Polite conversation and forgiveness are better than any act of charity followed by a scolding. God is Transcendent, Lenient.

* You who believe, do not cancel your acts of charity by [making] any reproach or scolding like someone who spends his money simply for people to see it while he does not believe in God and the Last Day. He may be compared to a boulder covered with some soil which a rainstorm strikes and leaves bare. They cannot do anything with whatever they have earned. God does not guide such disbelieving folk.

** Those who spend their wealth seeking God's approval and to strengthen their souls may be compared to a garden on a hilltop; should a rainstorm strike it, its produce is doubled, while if a rainstorm does not strike it, then drizzle does. God is Observant of anything you do. * Would any of you like to have a garden full of palms and grapes through which rivers flow? He would have all [sorts of] fruit in it. Yet old age will afflict him while he still has some helpless offspring, and a windstorm containing fire will strike it, so it is burned off. Thus God explains signs to you so that you (all) may think things over.

The Hilltop Garden

(XXXVII)* You who believe, spend some of the wholesome things you may have acquired as well as anything We produce from the earth for you. Do not choose the poorest parts of it for anything you spend [in taxes or on charity] which you yourselves would only accept disdainfully. Know that God is Transcendent, Praiseworthy. * Satan threatens you with poverty and orders you to misbehave sexually, while God promises you forgiveness from Himself as well as bounty. God is Boundless, Aware. * He gives wisdom to anyone He wishes, and anyone He gives wisdom to, receives an abundant boon. Yet only prudent persons will reflect on it.

267
Charity and Taxes

** God knows any expenses you may have incurred, or any promise you may have sworn. Wrongdoers will have no supporters. * If you publicize any acts of charity, it is quite worthwhile; while if you conceal them and give [directly] to the poor, it will be even better for you, and will cancel out some of your evil deeds for you. God is Informed about anything you do. * Guiding them is not your duty, but God guides anyone He wishes to. Any [tax] money you may spend is for your own good and whatever you spend is only through a craving to see God's face. Any money you spend will be repaid you, and you will not be harmed.

270

* Take care of the poor who, being totally absorbed in working for God's cause, cannot manage to travel [freely] around the earth seeking their livelihood. An ignorant person might assume they are rich because of their modesty; yet you will recognize them from their features: they do not make insistent demands on people. Yet God is Aware of any money you may so spend.

The Genteel Poor

(XXXVIII)* Those who spend their wealth night and day, both privately and publicly, will receive their earnings from their Lord. No fear will lie upon them nor need they ever feel saddened.

274

** Those who live off the interest on loans will never stand up, except in the way those whom Satan knocks down with a fit rise up again. That is because they say: "Trading is just like taking interest." **Yet God has permitted trading and forbidden taking interest.** Anyone who receives such an instruction from his Lord and stops doing so, may keep whatever

The Loan Business

[capital] is a thing of the past, while his case rests with God; yet those who do so over and over again will become inmates of the Fire, to remain there for ever. * God wipes out usury and nourishes acts of charity; God does not love every vicious disbeliever.

* Those who believe and perform honorable actions, keep up prayer and pay the welfare tax, will receive their wages from their Lord; no fear shall lie upon them nor should they feel saddened. * You who believe, heed God and write off anything that remains outstanding from lending at interest if you are [true] believers. * If you do not do so, then be prepared to face war declared by God and His messenger! If you repent, you may retain your principal. Do not wrong [others] and you will not be wronged.
** If any debtor suffers hardship, then postpone [repaying] it until conditions become easier [for him]; while if you treat it as an act of charity, it would be better for you, if you only knew! * Heed a day when you will be brought back to God; then every soul will be paid in full according to whatever he has earned, and they will not be treated unjustly.

280

(XXXIX)* You who believe, whenever you contract a debt for a stated period, write it down. Let some literate person write [what goes on] between you properly; no literate person should refuse to write it down. Just as God has taught him, so let him write it down, and let the borrower dictate. May he heed God and not omit any part of it.

If the borrower is feeble-minded or incapacitated or cannot manage to dictate himself, then let his guardian dictate it in all fairness, and seek out two witnesses from among your men-folk to act as witnesses. If there are not two men [available], then one man and two women [may serve] as witnesses from anyone you may approve of, so that if either of them should slip up, then the other woman may remind the other. Witnesses must not refuse [to serve] when they are called upon, nor try to get out of writing anything down whether it is small or large, along with its due date.

Such [procedure] is more equitable so far as God is concerned and it makes for more valid testimony, as well as reducing the chances for doubt; unless it is some transaction handled on the spot that you pass around among yourselves, in which case it will not be held against you for not writing it down. Call in witnesses whenever you engage in trade, and let no literate man nor any witness feel obligated if you do so; that would be immoral on your part. Heed God, for God teaches you! God is Aware of everything.

* If you are on a journey and do not find any literate person, then a deposit may be withheld as a lien. If one of you entrusts [something to] another, the one who has been entrusted with it should hand over his security and he should heed God his Lord and not hide any testimony. Anyone who hides it has a vicious heart. God is Aware of anything you do!

282

Debts and Loans; Buying on Credit

284

(XL)* God holds whatever is in Heaven and whatever is on Earth; whether you disclose what is on your minds, or hide it, God will bring you to account for it. He forgives anyone He wishes to and punishes anyone He wishes; God is Capable of everything!

** The Messenger believes in what has been sent down to him from his Lord, and [so do] believers; everyone believes in God and His angels, His books and His messengers. We do not differentiate between any of His messengers. They say: "We have heard and obey; [we beg] Your pardon, our Lord! Toward You lies the Goal!"

An Islamic Profession of Faith

* God only assigns a soul something it can cope with: it is credited with whatever it has earned, while it is debited with whatever it has brought upon itself.

> Our Lord, do not take us to task
> if we have forgotten or slipped up!
> Our Lord, do not lay any obligation upon us
> such as You placed on those before us.
> Our Lord, do not overburden us
> with more than we can bear!
> Pardon us, forgive us, and show us mercy!
> You are our Protector,
> so support us against disbelieving folk!

3
The House of ʿImrān

THIS CHAPTER consists of 200 verses arranged in twenty sections; like the previous one and Chapters 29 through 32, it begins with the initials A.L.M. It was revealed during the third or fourth year which the Prophet spent in Madīna (approximately 625 A.D.), after the chapter on **Booty** 7 and before **The Coalition** 33.

ʿImrān was a common ancestor of Moses and Jesus. The first section teaches us how to read the Qurʾān; the second explains the principle of God's Oneness. Persecution and the concept of God as the Sovereign are discussed in section III. The stories of Zachariah (IV) and Jesus (V-VI) follow. Abraham appears in VII. Exploitation and arrogation are explained in VIII, and how to treat turncoats in IX. The parable of "The Bitter Wind" comes in XII while the pious or heedful are described in XIV. We learn about the Prophet's trials with the battle of Uḥud in the year 3 / 625 (XIII & XVI). The Town Crier gives us another figure; with him the chapter ends (XX).

In the name of God, the Mercy-giving, the Merciful!

(I)* A.L.M.

> * God, there is no deity except Him,
> the Living, the Eternal!

* He has sent down the Book to you with Truth to confirm whatever existed before it. He sent down the Torah and the Gospel * in the past as guidance for mankind; He has (also) sent down the Standard. Those who disbelieve in God's signs will have severe torment; God is Powerful, the Master of Retribution!

> ** Nothing is hidden from God, on Earth nor in Heaven. * He it is Who shapes you just as He wishes in [your mothers'] wombs. There is no deity except Him, the Powerful, the Wise! * He is the One Who sent you down the Book which contains decisive verses. They [form] the basis of the Book; while others are allegorical.

Those whose hearts are prone to falter follow whatever is allegorical in it, seeking to create dissension by giving [their own] interpretation of it. Yet only God knows its interpretation; those who are versed in knowledge say: "We believe in it; it all comes from our Lord!" However only prudent persons bear it in mind.

* Our Lord, do not let our hearts falter once You have guided us; grant us mercy from Your presence, for You are the Bountiful! * Our Lord, You will be gathering mankind together on a day there is no doubt about; God will never go back on the Promise!

(II)** Neither their wealth nor their children will ever save those who disbelieve in any way from God; those will be fuel for the Fire. * In the case of Pharaoh's house as well as those before them, they denied Our signs, so God seized them because of their offences; God is Stern in punishment.

    * TELL those who disbelieve: "You will be defeated and summoned to Hell! How awful is such a resting place!" * You have already had a sign in the two detachments which met, one detachment fighting for God's sake and the other disbelieving; they saw them with their own eyes as twice the same [number] as themselves. God assists anyone He wishes through His support; in that there lies a lesson for persons with insight. * The love of passions [that come] from women and children has attracted mankind, as well as accumulated gold and silver treasures, pedigreed horses, livestock and crops. That means enjoyment during worldly life, while God holds the finest retreat.

    ** SAY: "Should I give you news of something even better than that? Those who do their duty will have gardens through which rivers flow to live in for ever with their Lord, plus purified spouses and approval from God. God is Observant of [His] worshippers * who say: "Our Lord, we believe, so forgive us our offences and shield us from the torment of Fire!" * [They are] the patient ones, loyal and steadfast, who spend [in charity] and seek forgiveness before dawn each morning.

    * God testifies there is no deity except Himself, and so do the angels and persons possessing knowledge. Maintaining fairplay, there is no deity except Him, the Powerful, the Wise.

    *** Religion with God means [Islam:]
a commitment to [live in] peace.**

Those who have already been given the Book did not disagree until after knowledge had come to them, out of envy for one another. Anyone who disbelieves in God's signs [will find] God is Prompt in reckoning!

    ** If they should argue with you, then say: "I have committed my person peacefully to God, and [so has] anyone who follows me. Tell both those who have been given the Book as well as the unlettered: "Have you become Muslims?" If they commit themselves to [live in] peace, then they are guided; while if they turn away, you need merely to state things plainly. God is Observant of [His] worshippers.

(III)* Announce painful torment for those who disbelieve in God's signs and kill prophets without any right to, and kill those people who order fairplay. * Those are the ones whose actions will miscarry in this world as well as the Hereafter; they will have no supporters.

    * Have you not considered those who were given a portion [of knowledge] from the Book? They were invited to [accept] God's book

10

20

21

so it might judge between them; then a group of them turned away and disregarded [it].

* That is because they say: "The Fire will never touch us except for several days." Whatever they have invented about their religion has led them astray.

** How will it be when We gather them in on a day there is no doubt about, and each soul will be paid off according to whatever it has earned? They will not be wronged!

God the Sovereign

* SAY: "O God, Holder of control!
You give control to anyone You wish
and snatch control from anyone You wish.
You exalt anyone You wish
and humble anyone You wish.
Good lies within Your hand;
You are Capable of everything!

    * ''You wrap night up in daylight,
and wrap daytime up in night.
You draw the living from the dead,
and draw the dead from the living.
You provide for anyone You wish
without any reckoning!''

* Believers should not enlist disbelievers as patrons in preference to [other] believers. Anyone who does so will have nothing to do with God, so you should take precautions against them. God warns you about Himself; for towards God lies the Goal!

* SAY: "Whether you hide what is on your minds or disclose it, God knows it [anyhow]; He knows whatever is in Heaven and whatever is on
30   Earth. God is Capable of everything!" ** Some day when every person will find whatever good he has done is presented [as evidence] as well as whatever bad he has done, he would like a long stretch [to lie] between them and himself. God cautions you about Himself; though God is Gentle with [His] worshippers.

31   (IV)* SAY: "If you have been loving God, then follow me; God will then love you and forgive you your offences. God is Forgiving, Merciful!" * SAY: "Obey God and the Messenger." Yet if they should turn away, [remember that] God does not love disbelievers. * God selected Adam and Noah, Abraham's House and **‹Imrān's House** over [everyone in] the Universe. * Some of their offspring are descended from others. God is Alert, Aware. ** Thus a woman [from **the House] of ‹Imrān** said: "My Lord, I have freely consecrated whatever is in my womb to You. Accept it from me; You are Alert, Aware!

* When she gave birth, she said: "My Lord, I have given birth to a daughter."—(God was quite Aware of what she had given birth to, for a male is not like a female)—"I have named her Mary, and ask You to protect her and her offspring from Satan the Outcast."

* Her Lord accepted her in a handsome manner and caused her to grow like a lovely plant, and told Zachariah to take care of her. Every time Zachariah entered the shrine to [see] her, he found she had already been supplied with food. He said: "Mary, how can this be meant for you?" She said: "It comes from God, for God provides for anyone He wishes without any reckoning." * With that Zachariah appealed to his Lord; he said: "My Lord, grant me goodly offspring from Your presence, for You are the Hearer of Appeals."

Zachariah

* The angels called him while he was standing praying in the shrine: "God gives you news of John, who will confirm word from God, masterful yet circumspect, and a prophet [chosen] from among honorable people." ** He said: "My Lord, how can I have a boy? Old age has overtaken me, while my wife is barren."

40

He said: "Even so does God do anything He wishes!" * He said: "My Lord, grant me a sign." He said: "Your sign is that you will not speak to people for three days except through gestures. Mention your Lord often and glorify [Him] in the evening and early morning hours."

(v)* So the angels said: "Mary, God has selected you and purified you. He has selected you over [all] the women in the Universe. * Mary, devote yourself to your Lord; fall down on your knees and bow alongside those who so bow down."

42
*The Story
of Jesus*

* Such is some information about the Unseen We have revealed to you. You were not in their presence as they cast [lots with] their pens [to see] which of them would be entrusted with Mary. You were not in their presence while they were so disputing.

** Thus the angels said: "Mary, God announces word to you about someone whose name will be Christ Jesus, the son of Mary, [who is] well regarded in this world and the Hereafter, and one of those drawn near [to God]. * He will speak to people while still an infant and as an adult, and will be an honorable person." * She said: "My Lord, how can I have a child while no human being has ever touched me?"

He said: "That is how God creates anything He wishes. Whenever He decides upon some matter, He merely tells it: 'Be!', and it is. * He will teach him the Book and wisdom, plus the Torah and the Gospel * as a messenger to the Children of Israel: 'I have brought you a sign from your Lord. I shall create something in the shape of a bird for you out of clay, and blow into it so it will become a [real] bird with God's permission. I shall cure those who are blind from birth and lepers, and revive the dead with God's permission. I shall announce to you what you may eat and what you should store up in your houses. That will serve as a sign for you if you are believers, ** confirming what I have already [learned] from the Torah. I shall permit you some things which have been forbidden you. I have brought you a sign from your Lord, so heed God and obey me! * God is both my Lord and your Lord, so serve Him. This is a Straight Road!'"

50

* When Jesus sensed disbelief among them, he said: "Who will be my supporters in the cause of God?" The disciples said: "We are God's

*His
Disciples*

supporters! We believe in God; take note that we are Muslims. * Our Lord, we believe in what You have sent down and [thus] have followed the Messenger, so enroll us among the witnesses." * They plotted, while God plotted; however God is the best Plotter!

55

Jesus (cont'd)

(VI)** So God said: "Jesus, I shall gather you up and lift you towards Me, and purify you from those who disbelieve, and place those who follow you ahead of those who disbelieve until Resurrection Day. Then to Me will be your return, and I shall decide among you (all) concerning anything you have been disagreeing about. * As for those who disbelieve, I will punish them severely in this world and the Hereafter. They will have no supporters." * As for those who believe and perform honorable deeds, He will repay them their earnings. God does not love wrongdoers!

* That which We recite to you comes from the signs and the wise Reminder. * Jesus' case with God was the same as Adam's: He created

60

him from dust; then told him: "Be!" and he was. ** Truth comes from your Lord, so do not be a waverer. * Tell anyone who argues with you concerning it, once knowledge has come to you: "Come, let us call our children and your children, our women and your women, ourselves and yourselves together; then let us plead, and place God's curse upon the liars."

* These are true stories. There is no deity except God; while God is Powerful, Wise. * However if they should turn away, God is Aware as to who are mischief makers.

64

(VII)* SAY: "People of the Book, [let us] rally to a common formula to be binding on both us and you, that we shall worship only God [Alone] and associate nothing else with Him, nor shall any of us take on others as lords instead of God." If they should turn away, then say: "Bear witness that we are Muslims."

** People of the Book, why do you argue about Abraham when the Torah and the Gospel were not sent down until after him? Do you not use

Abraham

your reason? * There you go, arguing on about someone you (actually) have some knowledge about! Yet why do you (then) argue about something you have no knowledge about? God knows while you do not know.

> * Abraham was neither a Jew nor a Christian,
> but he was a Seeker [after Truth], a Muslim;
> he was no associator [of others with God].

* The closest people to Abraham are those who follow him, as well as this Prophet and those who believe. God is the believers' Patron. * A faction from the People of the Book would like to lead you (all) astray; yet they

70

only lead themselves astray, even though they do not notice it. ** People of the Book, why do you disbelieve in God's signs while you watch them happen? * People of the Book, why do you dress Truth up with falsehood and knowingly conceal the Truth?

72

(VIII)* A faction from among the People of the Book say: "Believe in what has been sent down to those who believe," at the outset of the day; while towards the end of it, [they say]: "Disbelieve". That may be so they will

keep coming back [to argue with you]. * Believe only in someone who
follows your own religion. SAY: **"Guidance [means] guidance from God,** lest
one person should be given the same as what you (all) have been given, or
they should argue with you concerning your Lord." SAY: **"Bounty [rests] in
God's hand.** He gives it to anyone He wishes; God is Boundless, Aware.
* He claims anyone He wishes for His mercy; God possesses tremendous
Bounty!"

** If you entrusted some People of the Book with a large sum, he
would hand it back to you; while if you entrusted another with a gold coin,
he would never hand it back to you unless you dunned him for it *Exploitation*
constantly. That is because they say: "There is no way for such illiterates
[to complain] against us." They tell a lie about God while they realize
it! * Instead, anyone who keeps his word and performs his duty [will find]
God loves the heedful.

* Those who barter God's pledge plus their [own] faith for a paltry
price will have no share in the Hereafter, nor will God ever speak to them *Arrogation*
nor even notice them on Resurrection Day. He will not purify them while *Explained*
they will have painful torment. * A group of them twist their tongues
around concerning the Book so you will reckon [something] comes from
the Book while it is not from the Book. They say: "It comes from God!",
while it is not from God. They knowingly tell a lie about God!

* It is not proper for God to give the Book plus discretion and
prophethood to any human being, then that [the latter] should tell
people: "Be worshippers of mine instead of God's," but rather: "Be the
Lord's [Alone] since you have been teaching the Book and because you
have been studying it." ** He does not order you to adopt angels and 80
prophets as lords; would He order you to disbelieve once you have
become Muslims?"

(IX)* So God accepted an agreement from the prophets: "Have I not given 81
you some of a Book plus wisdom?" Then a messenger came to you to
confirm what you already had, so you might believe in him and support
him. He said: "Have you acknowledged and accepted that obligation of
mine?" They said: "We so acknowledge it." He said: "Then act as witnesses;
I am one of those testifying along with you."

* Those who turn away later on act immorally. * Do they crave
something besides God's religion? Whoever is in Heaven and Earth is *Who Are*
committed to [make] peace with Him, whether willingly or reluctantly; to *Muslims*
Him will they be returned.

* SAY: "We believe in God and what has been sent down to us, and
what was sent down to Abraham, Ishmael, Isaac, Jacob and their
descendants, and what was given Moses, Jesus and the prophets by
their Lord. We do not differentiate between any one of them, and we
are committed to [live at] peace with Him."

** Anyone who desires something other than Islām as a religion will never
have it accepted from him, while in the Hereafter he will be among the *What is*
losers. * How should God guide a folk who disbelieve following their *Islām*

Renegades or Turncoats

[profession of] faith, and have testified that the Messenger was right and evidence had come to them? God does not guide wrongdoing folk. * Those will have their reward since God's curse will lie upon them, as well as the angels' and all mankind's, * to live with for ever; punishment will not be lightened for them nor will they be granted any respite * except for those who repent later on and reform. God is Forgiving, Merciful! ** Those who disbelieve following their [profession of] faith, then increase in disbelief, will never have their repentance accepted; those are lost [souls]! * Those who disbelieve and die while they are disbelievers will never have even all the earth filled with gold accepted from any one of them, even though they tried to use it as a ransom. Those will have painful torment while they will have no supporters.

90

PART
FOUR

92

Food

(x)* You will never attain virtue until you spend something you are fond of; while God is Aware of anything you may spend. * Every [kind of] food was permitted the Children of Israel except what Israel had banned herself before the Torah came down. SAY: "Bring the Torah and recite it if you have been truthful." * Those who invent a lie concerning God after that will be wrongdoers. ** SAY: "God has spoken truly, so follow the sect of Abraham the Seeker; he was no one to associate [others with God]."

* The first House [of worship] set up for mankind was the one at Becca (sic); it was blessed and a guidance for [everyone in] the Universe. * In it are clear signs [such as] Abraham's station. Anyone who enters it will be secure.

Pilgrimage

Pilgrimage to the House is a duty imposed on mankind by God, for anyone who can afford a way to do so. Anyone who disbelieves [will find] that God is Transcendent, beyond [any need of] the Universe.

* SAY: "People of the Book, why do you disbelieve in God's signs while God is a Witness for anything you do?" * SAY: "People of the Book, why do you obstruct God's way for anyone who believes, seeking to make it crooked, while [moreover], you (are) watching it happen? God is not oblivious of what you are doing.***You who believe, if you were to obey a group of those who have been given the Book, they would turn you back into disbelievers following your [profession of] faith. * How can you disbelieve while God's verses are being recited to you and His messenger is among you? Anyone who clings to God will be guided to a Straight Road.

100

102
*Who are
True
Muslims*

(xi)* You who believe, heed God the way He should be heeded, and do not die unless you are Muslims.

* Cling firmly together by means of God's rope, and do not separate. Remember God's favor towards you when you were enemies; He united your hearts so you became brothers because of His favor.

You were on the brink of a fiery pit, and He saved you from it! Thus God explains His signs to you, so that you may be guided.

* Let there be a community among you who will invite [others] to [do] good, command what is proper and prevent dishonor; those will be prosperous. ** Do not be like those who split up and disagreed after explanations had come to them; those will have awful torment!

* One day some faces will turn white while other faces will turn black. Those whose faces are blackened [will be asked]: "Did you disbelieve after your [profession of] faith? Taste torment because you have disbelieved!" * while those whose faces are whitened will live for ever in God's mercy.

* Those are God's verses which We recite to you for the Truth. God does not want any harm [to happen] to the Universe. * God holds whatever is in Heaven and whatever is on Earth, while [all] matters will be returned to God.

(XII) ** You are the best community which has been produced for mankind. You command decency and forbid dishonor, and you believe in God [Alone]. If the People of the Book would only believe, it would be better for them; some of them are believers while most of them are perverse. * They will never harm you except by annoying [you]. Yet if they should fight you, they will [soon] turn their backs; then they will not be supported. * Disgrace will be branded on them wherever they are overtaken unless they have a bond [leading] to God and a bond with other men. They have incurred anger from God while misery has been branded on them. That is because they have disbelieved in God's signs and killed the prophets without any right to; that is because they disobey and act so aggressive.

* Yet they are not [all] alike: some People of the Book form an upright community; they recite God's verses through the small hours of the night as they bow down on their knees. * They believe in God and the Last Day; they command decency and forbid dishonor, and compete in doing good deeds. Those are honorable men; ** any good they do will never be denied them. God is Aware of the heedful. * Neither their wealth nor their children will ever help out those who disbelieve against God in any way; those will become inmates of the Fire, they will remain there for ever.

110

* What they spend during this worldly life can be compared to a wind containing bitter frost which strikes the crop of people who have injured themselves, and so destroys it. God has not injured them, but rather they injure themselves.

The Bitter Wind

* You who believe, do not take up with any other persons than your own fellows as intimates. They will continually cause you turmoil, and they like anything that will distress you. Loathing shows through their mouths while what their minds conceal is even greater. We have explained the signs to you provided you will use your reason. * Here you are, loving such people while they do not love you! You believe in the whole Book. Yet whenever they meet you, they say: "We believe;" while when they go off by themselves, they gnaw away at their fingertips in rage over you.

120

SAY: "Die in your rage!" God is Aware of what is on your minds. ** Whenever something good happens to you, it annoys them, while if any evil happens to you, they delight in it. If you are patient and do your duty, their plotting will not harm you in any way; God embraces anything they do.

121
The Battle of Uḥud

(XIII) * When you rose earlier than your people did in order to station believers at their battle positions, God was Alert, Aware. * As two factions of you worried as to whether they should both fall back, God acted as a Patron for both of them. Believers should rely on God! * God already supported you (all) at Badr where you were underdogs, so heed God in order that you may be grateful.

* So you told believers: "Will it never be enough for you if your Lord furnishes you with three thousand angels who have been sent down?" ** Of course if you act disciplined and obey orders, and they should come at you all of a sudden just like this, your Lord will supply you with five thousand angels sent on purpose. * God has merely turned it into good news for you, so your hearts may feel tranquil over it. Support comes only from God, the Powerful, the Wise, * so He may cut off a flank from those who disbelieve and restrain them, and they will be sent home disappointed. * It is no concern at all of yours whether He relents towards them or punishes them, since they are wrongdoers.

* God possesses whatever is in Heaven and whatever is on Earth. He pardons anyone He wishes and punishes anyone He wishes; God is Forgiving, Merciful.

130
The Loan Business

(XIV) ** You who believe, do not live off usury which is compounded over and over again. Heed God so that you may prosper: * heed the Fire which has been prepared for disbelievers; * obey God and the Messenger so you may find mercy!

The Pious
OR *Heedful*

140

* Hasten towards forgiveness from your Lord and a garden broader than Heaven and Earth which has been prepared for those who do their duty, * who spend [for others] throughout happiness and hardship, and suppress their anger and overlook what other people do. God loves the kindly, ** and those who remember God and seek forgiveness for their offences when they commit some shocking deed or harm themselves—for who forgives offences besides God?—and do not knowingly persist in whatever they have been doing. * Those will have forgiveness from their Lord, as their reward, plus gardens through which rivers flow to live in for ever. How blissful will [such] workers' wages be!

140

* Institutions have passed away before you: travel around the earth and observe what the outcome was for those who deny [it all]. * This is an explanation for mankind, as well as guidance and instruction for the heedful: * do not falter nor feel saddened since you are superior, if you are believers. ** If some sore should afflict you, well sores just like them have afflicted [other] folk. We deal out such days to mankind, so God may recognize those who believe and accept witnesses from among you—God does not love wrongdoers— * and so God may purge those who believe

and wipe out disbelievers. * Or did you reckon that you would enter the Garden while God still does not recognize those among you who strive nor does He know the patient ones. * You used to long for death even before you met it, so now you have seen it while you were facing it!

(XV) * Muḥammad is only a messenger. Messengers have passed away   144
before him. If he should die or be killed, will you (all) revert to your old ways? Anyone who turns on his heels will never injure God in any way, while God will reward the grateful.

** No soul shall die except with God's permission according to specific writ. As for anyone who wants this world's prize, We shall give him part of it; while We shall give anyone who wants the prize of the Hereafter, some of it. We will repay the grateful! * How many a prophet has fought with many devout men alongside him! They never faltered despite what had afflicted them for God's sake; they did not weaken nor yield. God loves the patient! * Their statement was merely to say: "Our Lord, pardon us our offences and our excesses in business. Brace our footsteps and support us against disbelieving folk!" * So God gave them this world's prize, although the prize in the Hereafter will be even finer. God loves the kindly.

(XVI) * You who believe, if you should obey those who disbelieve, they will   149
turn you around on your heels and send you home as losers. ** Rather   150
God is your Protector; He is the best Supporter! * We will cast panic into
the hearts of those who disbelieve, because they have associated others with   *The Battle*
God for which He has sent down no authority. Their refuge will be the   *of Uḥud*
Fire, and how wretched will such wrongdoers' lodging be!   *Again*
    * God confirmed His promise to you as you grappled with them by His permission, until you faltered and argued about the matter; you disobeyed after He had shown you what you would love (to have). Some of you want this world, while others of you want the Hereafter.
    Then he diverted you from them so He might test you. Yet He has overlooked it in you; God possesses bounty for believers. * When you were climbing up [the hillside] and did not follow anyone, and the Messenger was calling to you from your rear, He rewarded you with one worry after another so you would not feel so sad because of what had eluded your grasp nor for what had afflicted you. God is Informed about anything you do!
    * Then following [your] worry, He sent down confidence upon you; a drowsiness overcame one squadron of yours, while another squadron fretted themselves thinking something besides the Truth about God, guesswork from [the times of] Ignorance. They said: "Is this a concern of ours in any way?" SAY: "The whole concern is up to God." They hide something they do not show in their souls; they say: "If we had had anything to do with the matter, we would not have had to fight here."
    SAY: "Even though you were in your own homes, those for whom killing has been prescribed would have shown up on their deathbeds, so that God might test what is on your minds and purge whatever is in your hearts. God is Aware of whatever is on your minds! ** Those of you who turned away on the day when both troops met, were only tripped up by

Satan because of something they had earned. However God has pardoned them, for God is Forgiving, Lenient."

156

(XVII) * You who believe, do not be like those who disbelieve and tell their brethren when they travel around the earth or are out on some campaign: "If they had been with us, they would not have died nor been killed," so that God places that [sort of] despair in their hearts. God gives life and brings death; God is Observant of anything you do. * If you should be killed for God's sake or die, forgiveness and mercy from God are better than what they are gathering; * yet if you should die or be killed, you will still be summoned [to appear] before God.

* However since mercy from God does exist, you have been easy on them. If you had been harsh and cruel-hearted, they would have dispersed from around you. Pardon them, seek forgiveness for them, and consult with them on the matter.

Reliance on God

> **Yet once you have reached a decision,
> then rely on God;
> God loves those who are reliant**.

160

** If God supports you (all), there is no one who will overcome you; while if He should forsake you, who is there [left] to support you later on? On God should believers rely!

* No prophet should hold back anything; and anyone who defrauds [someone else] will bring along whatever he has been withholding on Resurrection Day. Then every soul will be repaid for whatever it has earned, and they will not be harmed. * Is someone who follows after God's approval like someone else who incurs wrath from God? His refuge will be Hell, and how awful is such a goal!

* There are ranks with God, and God is Observant of whatever they are doing. * God has benefited believers whenever He sent them **a messenger from among themselves**, to recite His verses to them and purify them, and teach them the Book and wisdom, whereas previously they had been in plain error. ** Yet whenever some disaster strikes you, such as has struck you twice as heavy already, you have said: "What's this for?" SAY: "It is your own doing; God is Capable of everything."

* Whatever happened to you on the day when both troops clashed, occurred with God's permission, so He might recognize believers * and recognize those who act hypocritically. They were told: "Come fight in God's way or [at least] defend yourselves." They said: "If we knew how to fight, we would follow you." They were nearer disbelief than faith that day. They say with their mouths what is not in their hearts; although God is quite Aware of what they are concealing. * Those who tell their brethren while they remain behind: "If they had obeyed us, they would not have been killed," should be told: "Avert death from yourselves if you are so truthful!"

Martyrs

170

* Do not reckon those who are killed for God's sake are dead, but rather [they are] living; they will be provided for by their Lord, ** so happy will they be with whatever God has given them out of His bounty, and rejoicing for those they left behind who have not yet overtaken them.

No fear will fall on them nor will they be saddened; * they will rejoice because of favor and bounty from God, since God does not deprive believers of their wages.

(XVIII)* Any persons who respond to God and the Messenger after some   172
sore has afflicted them, those who act kindly and do their duty, will have a splendid fee. * Those whom people have told: "Some people have gathered to [oppose] you, so be on your guard against them!"; yet it increased them in faith and they said: "God is our Reckoning, and how splendid is such an Administrator!" * They returned home with favor and bounty from God; no evil ever touched them because they followed God's pleasure. God possesses such splendid bounty! ** That was only Satan who intimidated his adherents. Do not fear them and [instead] fear Me, if you are believers! * Let not those who hasten on to disbelief sadden you; they will never injure God in any way. God wants to grant them no fortune in the Hereafter, where they will have terrible torment. * Those who purchase disbelief at the price of faith will never injure God in any way, while they will have painful torment.

* Let not those who disbelieve consider how Our acting indulgent with them is good so far as their own persons are concerned: We are merely postponing things for them so they may increase in vice; they will have disgraceful torment. * God is no One to leave believers where you are now, until He sorts out bad from good. It is not God's role to acquaint you with the Unseen, but God chooses anyone He wishes from among His messengers. So believe in God and His messenger; if you believe and do your duty, you will have a splendid fee. ** Let not those who act   180
niggardly with any of His bounty God has given them consider it is better for them; rather it will be worse for them: they will be charged on Resurrection Day with anything they were so niggardly about. God holds the inheritance of Heaven and Earth; God is Informed about anything you do.

(XIX)* God has heard the statement of those who say: "God is poor while   181
we are rich!" We will write down whatever they say and how they killed the prophets without any right to [do so]. We will say: "Taste the torment of burning." * That [has happened] because of what your hands sent on ahead. God is no One to harm [His] worshippers, * such as those who say: "God has charged us not to believe in any messenger until He brings us some offering which fire will consume." SAY: "Messengers before me have already brought you explanations and just what you have said; why did you kill them if you are so truthful? * If they reject you, messengers before you have already been rejected when they came even with explanations, the Psalms and the Enlightening Book."

** **Every soul will be tasting death**: you will merely be repaid your earnings on Resurrection Day. Anyone who is snatched from the Fire and shown into the Garden will have triumphed. What does worldly life mean except the enjoyment of illusion? * You will be tested by means of your wealth and through your own selves, and you will hear much abuse from those who were given the Book before you, as well as those who associate [others with God]. If you are patient and do your duty, that is what will determine matters.

* When God made an agreement with those who were given the Book [saying]: "You shall explain it to mankind and not conceal it," they tossed it away behind their backs and sold it for a paltry price. How wretched was what they bought [instead]! * Do not consider those who feel delighted about what they have been given and love to be praised for something they have not done, do not reckon they [have found] any means to triumph over torment. They will have painful torment! * God holds control over Heaven and Earth; God is Capable of everything!

190
Creation

(xx)** In the creation of Heaven and Earth, and the alternation between night and daylight, there are signs for prudent persons * who **remember God while standing, sitting and [lying] on their sides**, and meditate on the creation of Heaven and Earth [by saying]:

"Our Lord, You have not created this in vain! Glory be to You! Shield us from the torment of Fire!

* "Our Lord, anyone You sentence to the Fire, You will humiliate. Wrongdoers will have no supporters.

The Town Crier

* "Our Lord, we heard a crier appealing for belief, [calling out]: 'Believe in your Lord;' and so we have believed.

"Our Lord, forgive us our offences, remove our evil deeds from us, and gather us up [at death] with the virtuous.

* "Our Lord, give us what you have promised us through Your messengers, and do not humiliate us on Resurrection Day. You never go back on any promise!"

** So their Lord responded to them: "I shall never waste the work of any worker among you, whether it is a man or a woman. Some of you [have sprung] from others. I shall remove their evil deeds for those who have

Refugees

migrated and were driven out of their homes and mistreated for My sake, and have fought and were killed; and I shall admit them to a Garden through which rivers flow, as a prize from God Himself. God holds the finest prize!

* Do not let it deceive you how those who disbelieve bustle about the land: * [it means such] brief enjoyment; then their refuge will be Hell, and how awful will be such a couch! * However those who heed their Lord will have gardens through which rivers flow, to live in for ever as a welcome from God. What God possesses is best for the virtuous.

* Some People of the Book do believe in God and what has been sent down to you and what has been sent down to them, acting reverently towards God. They do not sell God's signs for a paltry price: those will

200

receive their wages from their Lord; God is Prompt in reckoning! *** You who believe, act patient, discipline yourselves, and hold yourselves ready! Heed God so that you may succeed.

4
Women

THIS LONG chapter contains 176 verses arranged in twenty-four sections which date from the fourth year that the Prophet spent in Madīna, or 625-6 A.D. It was revealed after **Examining Her** 60 and before **The Earthquake** 99, and it deals with women's rights and conditions after the battle of Uḥud 3 / 625. These concern marriage laws (I & IV), and how to treat women, as the title itself suggests; in fact, the word **"women"** echoes constantly throughout this chapter.

It also takes up the subject of orphans (I & XIX), especially those girls left after the battle of Uḥud, men's duty in maintaining their own households (VI), and matrimonial rifts (VI & XIX). Inheritance is also dealt with (I-II, XXIV). Sexual offences form a further theme (III), as does etiquette and politeness (XI). The sin of Association is mentioned several times (VI, VII & XVIII). Conditions for prayer are stated (VII) and the problem of performing prayers during warfare when they are probably most needed, is worked out (XV). Manslaughter and murder come up in XIII. We are told to obey constituted authority (VIII), and to strive to please God (X). Lackeys or "yesmen" are described in XX, while the Jews are mentioned in XXII.

In the name of God, the Mercy-giving, the Merciful!

(I)* Mankind, heed your Lord Who has created you from a single soul, and created its mate from it, and propagated so many men and **women** from them both. Heed God through Whom you hold one another responsible, as well as any ties of kinship. God is Watching over you.

* Give orphans their property and do not substitute something bad for something good nor swallow up their wealth along with your own wealth. It would be a great outrage. * If you are afraid you will not deal fairly with orphans, then marry off such **women** as may seem good to you, in pairs, or three or four [at a time]. If you [still] fear you will not act justly, then [marry] one woman [only] or someone your right hand controls. That is more likely to keep you from committing an injustice. * Give **women** their marriage portions with no strings attached. If they themselves waive some of it for you, then consume it at leisure and with good cheer.

Orphans and Marriage

** Do not give the feebleminded your property which God has granted you for [their] support; provide for them out of it, and clothe them and address them decently. * Test orphans as soon as they reach a marriageable age. If you are sure of their maturity, then turn their property over to them; do not use it up extravagantly, overanxious lest they should grow

Inheritance

up. Anyone who is rich should restrain himself; while anyone who is poor may live off it in decency. Whenever you hand their property over to them, have it witnessed for them. God suffices as a Reckoner!

* Men shall have a portion of whatever parents and near relatives leave, while **women** should have a portion of whatever parents and near relatives leave; no matter how small nor how large it is, a portion is stipulated. * When near relatives, orphans and paupers are present at the probate, provide for them out of it and speak politely to them. * Let anyone act cautiously just as they themselves would fear to leave helpless offspring behind; let them heed God and speak in a proper manner.

10

** Those who live off orphans' property without having any right to do so will only suck up fire into their bellies, and they will (eventually) roast in a blaze!

11

Inheritance (cont'd)

(II)* God instructs you concerning your children: a son should have a share equivalent to that of two daughters. If the **women** [left behind] are more than two, then two-thirds of whatever he leaves belongs to them; yet if there is only one, then she has half. Both his parents shall each receive a sixth of whatever he may leave, if he had a son. If he had no son, and both his parents inherit from him, then his mother receives a third. If he has siblings, then his mother will have a sixth, once the will or any [outstanding] debt has been settled. You do not know whether your parents or your children are closer to you in usefulness, as an obligation [laid down] by God, for God is Aware, Wise.

* You will have half of anything your wives leave, provided they have no child. If they should leave a child, then you will have a fourth of whatever they may leave, once the will has been settled or any [outstanding] debt; while they [your widows] will have a fourth of anything you leave provided you have left no child. Should you have a child, then they will have an eighth of anything you leave, after settling any legacy or debt. If either a man or a woman bequeaths anything to more distant kin while he still has a brother or sister, then each one of them will have a sixth. If there are more than that, then they should be partners in a third after settling any legacy or debt, yet without causing any hardship. It is an instruction from God; God is Aware, Lenient.

God's Limits

* These are God's limits. Anyone who obeys God and His messenger will be admitted to gardens through which rivers flow, to live there for ever. That will be the supreme Achievement! * Anyone who disobeys God and His messenger and oversteps His limits, will be shown into a Fire to live there for ever; he will have humiliating torment.

15

(III)** Should any of your **women** commit some sexual offence, collect evidence about them from four [persons] among yourselves. If they so testify, then confine the **women** to their houses until death claims them or God grants them some other way out. * If two of you should indulge in it, trounce them both. If they repent and reform, then ostracize them both. God is Relenting, Merciful.

Repentance

* Repentance holds with God only for those who do evil out of ignorance, then repent shortly after; those God turns to. God is Aware,

Wise. * Repentance is not for those who perform evil deeds until one
of them says: "I have just now repented!", just as death faces him. Nor
is it for those who die while they are disbelievers; for those We have
reserved painful torment.

* You who believe, it is not lawful for you to inherit anything from **women**
against their will; do not hinder them from remarrying so that you may
make off with part of what you have given them, unless they indulge in
flagrant sexual misconduct. Treat them politely; even if you dislike them,
perhaps you dislike something in which God has placed much good.
*Marriage
and
Divorce*

20

  ** If you want to exchange one wife for another, and have given one of
them a large sum of money, do not hold back any of it. Would you
withhold it through slander and open sin? * How can you hold it back when
you have had intercourse with each other, and they have made a solemn
agreement with you? * Do not marry any **women** whom your fathers have
already married, unless this is a thing of the past; it is a shocking act and
disgusting, and the worst possible way.

(IV)* Forbidden to you [in marriage] are your mothers, your [own]
daughters, your sisters, your aunts on your father's side as well as your
aunts on your mother's side, and your brother's and your sister's daughters,
your foster mothers and your foster sisters, your mothers-in-law and step-
daughters who are under your guardianship [since their mothers are] wives
of yours with whom you have consummated marriage (however if you have
not consummated it with them, it will not be held against you), and the
wives of your sons who are your own flesh-and-blood; nor may you bring
two sisters together [under one roof] unless this is a thing of the past. God
is Forgiving, Merciful.
23

PART
FIVE

24
*Marriage
(cont'd)*

(IV cont'd) * Nor [should you marry] any [already] married **women**, except
the ones under your control. [Such is] God's legislation as it applies to you.
Anything beyond that is lawful for you, provided you court them by means
of your wealth, marrying them properly, rather than taking them on as
mistresses. Since you have thereby sought enjoyment with them, give them
their marriage portions as is stipulated. Yet it will not be held against you
should you come to other terms about it even after what has been
stipulated. God is Aware, Wise.

  ** Any of you who cannot afford to marry respectable believing
matrons, should then [seek] one of your believing maids under your
control. God is quite Aware as to what your faith consists of. Each one of
you has ties to others, so marry them off with their family's consent and
give them their marriage portions decently as matrons rather than taking
them on as mistresses, nor having [any secret affairs with] them as
girlfriends. Once they are so married off and should they then commit
some sexual offence, they should have half the punishment that [ordinary]
matrons would receive. That goes for any of you who worries lest he may

not control his [sexual] impulses; however it is better for you to discipline yourselves. God is Forgiving, Merciful.

26   (v)* God wants to explain things to you (all) and to guide you in the customs of those who have preceded you. He turns to you; God is Aware, Wise.

Controlling Passion

             * God wants to turn to you,
             while those who follow their own passions
             want you to give in utterly.
             * God wants to lighten things for you,
             since man was created weak!

* You who believe, do not use up your wealth idly, [squandering it] on one another, unless it is for some business based on mutual consent among
30   you. Do not kill one another; God has been Merciful towards you! ** We shall roast anyone in a Fire who does so out of enmity and wrongfully. That will be easy for God [to do]!

       * If you will avoid the great [sins] you are forbidden [to commit], We will cancel out your [other] evil deeds for you, and send you into [Paradise] through a noble entrance.

* Do not envy the way that God has made some of you excel over others: men should have a portion of whatever they have earned, while **women** should have a portion of whatever they have earned. Ask God for some of His bounty; God is Aware of everything. * For everyone We have placed executors for whatever either parents and close relatives may leave. Give their share to those whom you have sworn to trust; God is a Witness for everything!

34   (vi)* Men are the ones who should support **women** since God has given some persons advantages over others, and because they should
A Man's Responsibility   spend their wealth [on them]. Honorable women are steadfast, guarding the Unseen just as God has it guarded.

Admonish those women whose surliness you fear, and leave them alone in their beds, and [even] beat them [if necessary]. If they obey you, do not
Matrimonial Rifts   seek any way [to proceed] against them. God is Sublime, Great. ** If you fear a split between a man and his wife, send for an arbiter from his family and an arbiter from her family. If both want to be reconciled, God will arrange things between them. God is Aware, Informed. * Worship God
Association   [Alone] and do not associate anything with Him.

       Show kindness to both [your] parents and with near relatives, orphans, the needy, the neighbor who is related [to you] as well as the neighbor who is a stranger, and your companion by your side and the wayfarer, and
Kindness and Charity   anyone else under your control. God does not love someone who is conceited, boastful, * nor those who are tight-fisted and order [other] people to be stingy, and hide anything that God has given them out of His bounty. We have reserved humiliating torment for disbelievers * who spend their wealth to be seen by other people and yet neither believe in

God nor the Last Day. Anyone who has Satan for an intimate has such an evil soulmate! * What does it matter for them whether they believe in God and the Last Day and spend something from what God has supplied them with? God is Aware of them!

** God does not harm anything so much as an atom's weight: if a fine deed exists, he multiplies it and adds a splendid fee from Himself besides. * How would it be if We were to bring a witness from every nation, and bring you as a witness against such people? * On that day those who have disbelieved and defied the Messenger would like to have the earth levelled off while they are still [standing] on it! They will not hide anything that happens from God!

40

(VII)* You who believe, do not attempt to pray while you are drunk, **until you know what you are saying**; nor after a seminal emission—except when travelling along some road—until you take a full bath. If you are ill or on a journey, or one of you has come from the toilet, or has had contact with any **women**, and you do not find any water, then pick up some wholesome soil and wipe your faces and your hands with it. God is Pardoning, Forgiving.

43
Conditions for Prayer

* Have you not watched those who were given a portion of the Book? They buy up error and want you to lose your Way. ** God is quite Aware as to who your enemies are; God suffices as a Patron, and God suffices as a Supporter.

* Some persons who are Jews lift words out of their context and say: "We have heard and disobeyed;" and "Hear without listening" or "Lead us on!", twisting their tongues around and stabbing at religion as if they had [really] said: "We have heard and obeyed," and "Hear!" and "Watch over us!", which would be better for them and more straightforward; however God has cursed them for their disbelief, since only a few believe. * You who have received the Book, believe in what We have sent down to you as a confirmation of what you already have, lest We dazzle your faces and set them on backwards, or curse them just as We cursed the masters of the Sabbath. God's command must be fulfilled!

Jews and Christians

* God does not forgive anyone for associating something with Him, while He does forgive whomever He wishes to for anything besides that. Anyone who gives God associates has invented such an awful offence!

Association Again

* Have you not seen those who purify themselves? Indeed God will purify anyone He wishes to, and they will not be harmed one bit. ** Look how they invent a lie about God! That is enough in itself as a clear offence.

50

(VIII)* Have you not watched those who were given a portion of the Book? They believe in witchcraft and arrogant leaders and tell those who disbelieve: "Those are better guided to a way than are the ones who believe." * Those are the ones whom God has cursed; anyone God has cursed will never find a supporter for himself. * Or have they any share in control? Why, they will not give a speck to anybody!

51

* Or do they envy people because of what God has given them out of His bounty? We already gave Abraham's family the Book and wisdom, and

We gave them splendid control. ** Some of them believed in it while
others of them blocked it out. Hell will suffice as a blaze! * Those who
disbelieve in Our signs We will roast in a Fire: each time their hides are
toasted, We shall exchange them for some other skins so they may taste the
torment [again]. God is Powerful, Wise. * We will show those who believe
and perform honorable actions into gardens through which rivers flow, to
live there for ever; they will have clean-living spouses there, and We will
show them into shady nooks.

Trusts and
Ownership

* God orders you to restore deposits entrusted [to you] to their
[rightful] owners. Whenever you judge between people, you should judge
with [a sense of] justice. How superbly God instructs you to do so; God is
Alert, Observant!

Obeying
Authority

* You who believe, obey God and obey the Messenger and those from
among you who hold command.

If you should quarrel over anything, refer it to God and the
Messenger if you believe in God and the Last Day; that will be better,
and finer in the long run.

60

(IX)** Have you not considered those who claim they believe in what has
been sent down to you and what was sent down before you? They want to
seek judgment from arrogant leaders and so they are ordered to disbelieve
in it. Satan wants to lead them far astray. * Whenever someone tells
them: "Come to what God has sent down, and to the Messenger," you will
see hypocrites barring the way for you. * How will it be when some disaster
strikes them because of what their hands have already prepared? Then they
will come to you swearing by God: "We only wanted to have kindness and
success!" * Those are the ones whom God knows what their hearts
contain, so shun them and reprove them. Give them a convincing statement
about themselves.

* We have not sent any messenger unless he was to be obeyed in
accordance with God's permission. If they had come to you and sought
forgiveness from God whenever they harmed themselves, and the Messenger had prayed for forgiveness for them, they would have found that God
is Ever-Turning, Merciful.

** Yet by your Lord, they will never believe until they name you to
judge concerning what they are quarreling over among themselves; then
they will find no inconvenience for themselves concerning whatever you
have decided, and will accept it wholeheartedly. * If We had prescribed for
them: "Let yourselves be killed or expelled from your homes," only a few
of them would have done so. If they had done what they were instructed to
do, it would have been better for them, as well as more stabilizing: * then
We would have given them splendid earnings from Our very presence
* and guided them to a Straight Road. * Anyone who obeys God and the
Messenger stands by those whom God has favored, such as prophets, loyal
persons, martyrs and honorable men. How fine are such companions!

70

** That means bounty from God; it is enough for God to be Aware.

71

(X)* You who believe, take your precautions and march off in detachments, or march off all together. * Among you there are some who

procrastinate. If any disaster strikes you, they say: "God has favored me, for I was not a witness along with them." * Yet if some bounty from God strikes you, he will say, as if no affection had existed between you and him: "If only I had been with them, I should have achieved something splendid!"

* Let those who barter worldly life for the Hereafter fight for God's sake; We shall pay a splendid fee to anyone who fights in God's way, and is either killed or is victorious. ** Why should you not fight for God's sake when men, **women** and children who are considered helpless say: "Our Lord, lead us out of this town whose people are so oppressive, and grant us a patron from Your presence and grant us a supporter from Your presence!" * Those who believe, fight in God's way, while those who disbelieve fight in the way of the arrogant ones; therefore fight Satan's patrons. Satan's plot is weak.

Striving for God's Sake

(XI)* Have you not watched those who have been told: "Restrain your hands, keep up prayer and pay the welfare tax"? Yet whenever any fighting is prescribed for them, then a group of them feel afraid of people just as they should be afraid of God, or they are even more afraid. They say: "Our Lord, why have You prescribed fighting for us? If You would only postpone it for a little while longer!"

77

SAY: "Worldly enjoyment means little while the Hereafter is better for anyone who does his duty. You will not be wronged a bit. * Wherever you may be, death shall still overtake you even though you are in well-built towers." Yet if something fine happens to them, they say: "This is from God;" while if something bad happens to them, they say: "This is because of you!" SAY: "Everything comes from God." What is wrong with such folk that they scarcely understand why anything happens?

Good and Evil

* Any good that happens to you comes from God, while anything bad that happens to you is through yourself.

We have sent you as a Messenger to [instruct] mankind; and God suffices as a Witness. ** Anyone who obeys the Messenger has obeyed God [Himself], while We have not sent you to be a taskmaster set up over anyone who turns away.

80

* They will say: "At your orders!", yet when they show up somewhere else than with you, a faction of them will spend the night at something quite different from what you tell [them to do]. God writes down whatever they do at night, so avoid them and rely on God. God suffices as a Trustee.

* Have they not meditated on the Reading? If it had come from some other source than God, they would have found a great deal of contradiction in it.

The Qurʾān

* Whenever some order concerning [public] safety or fear comes to them, they broadcast it. If they would only refer it to the Messenger and those among them who hold command, those of them who investigate matters would have known about it. If it had not been for God's bounty and mercy towards you, all but a few would have followed Satan; * so fight for God's sake, since you are only held responsible for yourself. Encourage believers; perhaps God will fend off the violence of those who disbelieve. God is Strongest when things come to violence and Sternest in punishment.

Handling Rumors

Etiquette
OR
Politeness

** Anyone who intercedes in a fine manner shall have a share in it, while someone who intercedes in an evil way will be held liable for it. God is a Developer for everything. * Whenever you are welcomed with some greeting, then answer back with something finer than it, or [at least] return it. God is a Reckoner for everything.

* God, there is no deity except Him. He will bring you all together on Resurrection Day; there is no doubt about it. Who is more Reliable than God as a Narrator?

88

(XII)* Why should you take both sides concerning hypocrites? God has discarded them because of what they have earned. Do you want to guide someone whom God has let go astray? Anyone whom God lets go astray will never find a way back to Him. * They would love for you to disbelieve just as they disbelieve, so you will be exactly like them.

Do not adopt sponsors from among them until they migrate along God's way. If they should ever turn against you, then seize them and kill them wherever you may find them. Do not adopt any sponsor nor supporter from among them, ** except those who join a folk with whom you have a treaty or who come to you because their breasts shrink from fighting you or fighting with their own people. If God so wished, He would have given them authority over you so that they would have fought you. Yet if they keep aloof from you and do not fight you, and they propose peace to you, God does not grant you any way against them.

90

Agitators

* You will find others who want to feel safe from you as well as safe from their own people, yet every time they come upon another chance for dissension, they plunge into it. If they neither keep aloof from you nor yet propose peace to you and hold back their hands, then take them and slay them wherever you may run across them. Over such persons We have given you clear authority.

92
Manslaughter

(XIII)* No believer should kill any other believer unless it happens by mistake. Anyone who kills a believer by mistake should free a believing captive and deliver blood-money to his family unless they forego it as an act of charity. If he was from a nation which is at war with you and yet he was a believer, then free a believing captive; while if he were from a people with whom you have a treaty, then it means blood-money should be delivered to his family and freeing a believing captive. Anyone who does not find the wherewithal for it should fast for two consecutive months as penance from God. God is Aware, Wise!

Murder

* Anyone who kills a believer deliberately will receive as his reward [a sentence] to live in Hell for ever. God will be Angry with him and curse him, and prepare dreadful torment for him.

* You who believe, whenever you campaign for God's sake, discriminate carefully and do not tell someone who proffers you a greeting: "You are no believer!" You crave the display of worldly life, while God holds many more prizes. That is what you were like previously, though God has showered His

benefits on you; so discriminate. God is Informed about anything you do.

** Those believers who sit around and yet have no physical disability are not equal to those who strive for God's sake with their property and persons. God shows preference to those who strive with their property and persons through [higher] rank, than with those who just sit around; for each, God has promised handsome things, yet God shows preference to strivers with a better wage over those who stay at home, * such as [higher] ranks from Him, as well as forgiveness and mercy. God is Forgiving, Merciful.

Public Service

(XIV)* Those whom the angels will gather up [and] tell, as they are harming themselves: "What were you [busy] with?", will say: "We were acting as weaklings on earth." They will say: "Is not God's earth so vast you might settle down elsewhere on it?" Those will have their refuge in Hell, and how evil is such a goal * except for those men, **women** and children who are [really] helpless and cannot find any other means nor are they guided in any way; * those God may eventually pardon. God is Pardoning, Forgiving.

97

*** Anyone who migrates for God's sake will find many places for asylum and accommodation on earth. Whoever leaves his home as a refugee for God's and His messenger's sake, then has death overtake him, will receive his earnings as God's responsibility. God is Forgiving, Merciful.

100
Refugees

(XV)* It will not be held against you when you travel out into the world should you shorten prayer, if you fear those who disbelieve may harass you. Disbelievers are open enemies of yours.

101
Prayers During Warfare

* When you are among them, [Muhammad], and have stood up to pray in front of them, then let a squad of them stand up along with you and hold on to their weapons. Once they have bowed down on their knees, then let them fall back to your rear, and another squad who have not yet prayed come up to pray along with you. Let them hold on to [both] their precautions and their weapons. Those who disbelieve would like to catch you napping with your weapons and your baggage, so they may overpower you (all) at one stroke.

Nor will it be held against you if you are bothered by rain or are ill, should you lay down your weapons and take [similar] precautions for yourselves. God has prepared humiliating torment for disbelievers.

* Once you have finished praying, remember God while standing, sitting and [lying] on your sides. Even when you are at leisure, still keep up prayer:

Prayer in General

Prayer is a timely prescription for believers!

* Yet do not flag in pursuit of people: if you have been suffering, then they are suffering just as keenly as you are suffering; while you expect something from God that they do not expect. God is Aware, Wise.

(XVI)** We have sent the Book down to you with the Truth so that you may judge among mankind by means of what God has shown you. Do not act as an advocate for traitors; * seek forgiveness from God: God is

105

Forgiving, Merciful. * Do not plead for those who betray themselves; God does not love anyone who has been a vicious traitor.

* They may try to hide from people while they can never hide from God: He stands alongside them when they spend the night talking about something He does not approve of; God surrounds anything they do. * There you are, those who have pleaded in favor of them during worldly life! Who will plead with God about them on Resurrection Day, or who will act as an agent for them?

110 ** Anyone who commits evil or harms himself, then seeks forgiveness from God, will find God is Forgiving, Merciful; * while anyone who acquires a vice, only acquires it personally. God is Aware, Wise. * Anyone who commits a blunder or vice, then casts [the blame] against some innocent person, will burden himself with slander and flagrant vice.

113 (XVII)* If God's bounty and mercy had not lain upon you, a faction of them would have worried about how to lead you astray. They only lead themselves astray and do not injure you in any way. God has sent the Book and wisdom down to you and taught you what you did not know; God's bounty towards you has been splendid!

* There is no good in much of their intrigue except with someone who calls for charity, decency or reconciliation among people; We shall give a splendid wage to anyone who does that in pursuit of God's approval. ** Anyone who splits off from the Messenger once guidance has been explained to him, and follows some path other than the believers', We shall turn over to whatever he has turned to, and lead him off to Hell. How evil is such a goal!

116

Association the Worst Sin

(XVIII)* God does not forgive one's associating [others] with Him; He forgives anyone He wishes to for anything beyond that. Anyone who associates [others] with God has strayed far afield. * They only appeal to females instead of to Him; they only call upon some upstart Satan!

Satan and Pagan Practices

* God cursed him, and he said: "I shall take some of Your servants as a stipulated portion; * I will lead them astray and urge them on. I will order them to slit the ears on livestock and order them to alter what God has created. Anyone who adopts Satan as a patron instead of God has obviously lost out. ** He promises them [things] and urges them on; yet Satan promises them nothing except delusion. * Those will have Hell as their refuge and find no escape from it.

120

* We will show the ones who believe and perform honorable deeds into gardens through which rivers flow, to live there for ever. God's promise is true; who is more reliable in the way he speaks than God? * There is nothing in your saying "Amens" nor in the way the People of the Book say "Amen". Anyone who commits evil will be rewarded accordingly and not find any patron nor protector for himself besides God. * Anyone who performs honorable deeds, whether it is a man or a woman, provided he is a believer, those will enter the Garden and not be harmed a speck. ** Who is finer in religion than someone who peacefully commends his person to God while he acts kindly and follows the sect of Abraham the Enquirer? God adopted Abraham as a bosom friend. * God

Those Who Go to Paradise

holds whatever is in Heaven and whatever is on Earth; God embraces everything!

(XIX)* They will consult you concerning **women**. SAY: "God advises you about them, and what is recited to you from the Book concerning orphan **women** whom you have not given what was assigned to them while you are disinclined to marry them; and minor children, and supporting orphans with [all] fairness. God is Aware of any good you do.

   * If some woman fears abuse or desertion by her husband, it should not be held against either of them if they should try to come to terms: coming to terms is best, while greed is ever present in [our] souls. If you act kindly and do your duty, God will be Informed about anything you do.
 * You will never manage to deal equitably with **women** no matter how eager you may be [to do so]; yet do not turn completely aside [from one] so you leave another in suspense. If you (all) come to terms and do your duty, God will be Forgiving, Merciful. ** Yet if they should separate, God will enrich each out of His abundance; God is Boundless, Wise.
* God holds whatever is in Heaven and whatever is on Earth.

   We have instructed those who were given the Book before you, and you (all) as well, to heed God. If you should disbelieve, God still owns whatever is in Heaven and whatever is on Earth. God is Transcendent, Praiseworthy!
* God holds whatever is in Heaven and whatever is on Earth; God suffices as a Trustee: * if He wished, He might take you people away and bring in others. God is Capable of that! * Anyone who wants a worldly prize [should know] God holds the worldly prize plus another in the Hereafter. God is Alert, Observant.

(XX)** You who believe, act steadfast before God as witnesses for fairplay even though it is against yourselves, your own parents and near relatives; whether it concerns a rich or a poor man, God [stands] closer to them both. Do not follow any passion so that you may deal justly. If you swerve about or turn aside, God is still Informed about whatever you do.

   * You who believe, believe in God and His messenger, and the Book which He has sent down to His messenger as well as the Book which He had sent down previously. Anyone who disbelieves in God and His angels, His books, His messengers and the Last Day will stray far afield. * Those who believe, then disbelieve, then believe, then [again] disbelieve, then increase in their disbelief, will have no means for God to forgive them nor to guide them in any way.

   * Spread word to hypocrites that they shall have painful torment.
* Do those who enlist disbelievers as sponsors instead of believers, seek [to gain] prestige through them? Prestige rests entirely with God.

** In the Book, He has revealed to you that whenever you hear God's signs disbelieved in and ridiculed, you should not sit with them until they change to some other topic. You would be just like them then! God will gather all the hypocrites and disbelievers into Hell; * such as those who try to catch you off guard, so if you receive some victory from God, they

127
Orphans

Marriage Difficulties

130

135
Oaths and Evidence; Courtroom Procedure

Belief

Wavering

Lackeys OR *Yesmen*

140

say: "Were we not with you?" Yet if disbelievers have any share [in it], they say: "Did we not help you win, and held off believers from you?" God will judge between you (all) on Resurrection Day; God will never grant disbelievers any way to [harm] believers.

142   (xxi)* Hypocrites try to outwit God while He is outwitting them! Whenever they stand up to pray, they stand up lazily to be seen by other people, and seldom mention God, * wavering in between, [leaning] neither towards these nor those. You will never find any way [to follow] someone whom God lets go astray.

* You who believe, do not enlist disbelievers as sponsors, instead of believers. Do you want to give God clear authority against you? ** Hypocrites will stand on the lowest level of the Fire; you will never find any supporter for them * except for those who repent and reform, cling to God and dedicate their religion solely to God. Those stand alongside believers, and God will give believers a splendid wage. * What does God accomplish through your torment, provided you act grateful and believe? God is Appreciative, Aware.

Part Six

148   (xxi cont'd)* God does not love evil talk in public unless it is by someone who has been injured thereby. God is Alert, Aware. * Whether you reveal any good or hide it, or pardon any evil, God is Pardoning, Capable.

150   ** Those who disbelieve in God and His messengers, and want to distinguish between God and His messengers, and say: "We believe in some and disbelieve in others;" wanting to adopt a course in between, * are really disbelievers. We have reserved humiliating torment for

Saints'
Worship
disbelievers. * Those who believe in God and His messengers, and do not single out any one of them [especially], will be given their earnings. God is Forgiving, Merciful.

153   (xxii)* The People of the Book ask you to have a book sent down from Heaven for them. They asked Moses for something even greater than that, and said: "Show us God directly." The Thunderbolt caught them in their wrongdoing.

Then they adopted the Calf even after explanations had come to them. We still pardoned that, and gave Moses clear authority. * We raised the Mountain up over them as their charter, and told them: "Enter the gate while on your knees." We told them [further]: "Do not go too far on the Sabbath," and made a solemn pledge with them.

** Because of their breaking the charter, their disbelief in God's signs, their killing the prophets without any right to do so, and their saying: "Our hearts are covered over," instead, God has stamped them with their disbelief. They only believe a little * because of their disbelief and their

Jesus
talking such terrible slander about Mary * and (also) for their saying: "We killed God's messenger Christ Jesus, the son of Mary!" They neither killed

nor crucified him, even though it seemed so to them. Those who disagree about it are in doubt concerning it; they have no [real] knowledge about it except by following conjecture. No one is certain they killed him! * Rather God lifted him up towards Himself. God is Powerful, Wise!

* There is nobody from the People of the Book but who will believe in him before his death, while on Resurrection Day he will act as a witness against them. ** Because of wrongdoing on the part of those who are Jews, We have forbidden them certain wholesome things which had been permitted them; and because they blocked off so many people from God's way * and took usury although they had been forbidden to, and idly consumed other people's wealth, We have reserved painful torment for those among them who are disbelievers. * Yet those of them who are versed in knowledge, as well as believers, believe in what is sent down to you and what has been sent down [to those] before you; and We shall give a splendid wage to those who keep up prayer and pay the welfare tax, and who believe in God and the Last Day.

160

(XXIII)* We have inspired you just as We inspired Noah and the prophets following him, and as We inspired Abraham, Ishmael, Isaac, Jacob and the patriarchs, and Jesus, Job, Jonah, Aaron and Solomon; and just as We gave David the Psalms.

163
Other Prophets

* We have told you about some messengers [sent] previously, while **other messengers We have not yet told you about**—God spoke directly to Moses— ** messengers bringing good news plus a warning so that mankind would have no argument against God once the messengers [had come]. God is Powerful, Wise.

* Nevertheless God bears witness through what He has sent down to you; He sent it down with His (own full) knowledge. And angels so testify, though God suffices as a Witness. * Those who disbelieve and obstruct God's way have strayed far afield. * Those who disbelieve and act wrongfully will not find that God will forgive them nor guide them along any road * except the road to Hell, to remain there for ever. That will be so easy for God [to do]! ** O mankind, the Messenger has brought you the Truth from your Lord, so believe, since it is best for you. If you should disbelieve, God still holds whatever is in Heaven and Earth; God is Aware, Wise.

170

* People of the Book, do not exaggerate in [practising] your religion and tell nothing except the Truth about God. Christ Jesus, the son of Mary, was merely God's messenger and His word which He cast into Mary, and a spirit [proceeding] from Him.

Jesus Again

Believe in God [Alone] and His messengers, and **do not say: "Three!" Stopping [it] will be better for you**. God is only One God; glory be to Him, beyond His having any son! He owns whatever is in Heaven and whatever is on Earth; God suffices as a Trustee.

The Trinity

(XXIV)* The Messiah would never disdain to be God's servant, nor would the angels who are closest. He will summon anyone to Him who disdains to worship Him and acts too proud [for it]. * As for those who believe

172

and perform honorable deeds, He will pay them their earnings and add even more for them out of His bounty. He will punish those who act scornful and proud with painful torment; they will not find any sponsor for themselves nor any supporter besides God. * Mankind, proof has come to you from your Lord; We have sent a clear Light down to you. ** He will show those who believe in God and cling to Him, into mercy and bounty from Himself, and guide them along a Straight Road towards Himself.

Inheritance   * They will ask you for your verdict. SAY: "God advises you (all) concerning indirect heirs. If some man should pass away and has no son while he leaves a sister, then she shall have half of anything he may leave; while he inherits from her if she has no child. If they are two women [who are sisters], they shall both have two thirds of whatever he may leave. If they are siblings, both men and **women**, then each brother shall have the same share as two sisters would have.

God explains things to you
lest you go astray.
God is (all) Aware of everything!

5

The Table

THIS CHAPTER of 120 verses arranged in sixteen sections was revealed at Madīna (except for v. 3, which was announced after the stay at ʿArafāt during the Farewell Pilgrimage in the 10th year of the Hijra, or March 632 A.D.). The chapter comes after **[Divine] Support** 110 and before **Dispensation** 9 in the sequence of revelation. It is called **The Table** from section XV towards the end, where Jesus' disciples asked for the rules governing food, and he was challenged to have a table sent down from Heaven.

The chapter starts out like **The House of ʿImrān** 3, with important statements on Islam as a religion, so as to consolidate the nascent Islamic community. This begins by considering behavior during Pilgrimage (I), a subject which is resumed in XIII. Food, marriage (I), and washing before prayer (II) come next; also oaths, liquor and gambling (XII). Good and evil (XIII) are moral issues which are likewise discussed. Judicial procedure is recorded (VI) while Mosaic law is mentioned in VII. Adam's sons Cain and Abel were participants in the first murder (V), although they are not named in the Qurʾān. Theft (VI) and wills (XIV) are other matters discussed.

Christians are addressed and we are told that Christ is not God (III). Jesus himself is discussed in VII; as well as Christians, the trinity and the figure of Christ again in X. The Jews are mentioned in XI, but we are advised that Christians are closer than they are to Islam. Jesus' miracles are described in XV, and we are informed how Jesus himself rejected Godhood at the end of section XVI, which closes the chapter.

In the name of God, the Mercy-giving, the Merciful!

(I)* You who believe, fulfil any contracts [you may make].

Any animals from livestock are permitted you except for what has already been listed for you. What is not permitted you is game while you are in pilgrim dress. God judges anything He wishes. * You who believe, do not profane God's monuments nor the hallowed month, nor the offerings and [beasts with] garlands, nor those intent on visiting the Hallowed House to seek bounty and approval from their Lord. Once you are permitted to [go on your way], then go hunting. Do not let ill will towards any folk incriminate you, just because they blocked your way to the Hallowed Mosque, so that you act aggressive; cooperate with one another for virtue and heedfulness, and do not cooperate with one another for the purpose of vice and aggression. Heed God [Alone]; God is Strict with punishment!

Conduct and Food During Pilgrimage

* Forbidden to you is anything that dies by itself, and blood and pork, as well as whatever has been consecrated to something besides God, and whatever has been strangled, beaten to death, trapped in a pit, gored, and what some beast of prey has begun to eat, unless you give it the final blow; and what has been slaughtered before some idol, or what you divide up in a raffle; (all) that is immoral!

Today those who disbelieve despair about your religion, so do not dread them, and (rather) dread Me.
(**Today I have perfected your religion for you, and completed My favor towards you, and have consented to grant you [Islām] as a religion: a commitment to live in peace.**)

Anyone who is obliged to do so while (he is) starving, yet without deliberately sinning, [will find] God is Forgiving, Merciful.

Food Again

* They will ask you what has been made allowable for them. SAY: "It is lawful for you [to eat] wholesome things, and what you have trained beasts and birds of prey to catch—you have trained them to do something just as God has taught you. So eat anything they may catch for you, and mention God's name over it. Heed God; God is Swift in reckoning. ** Today wholesome things are [made] lawful for you, and so is the food of those who were given the Book lawful for you, while your food is lawful for them.

Marriage

And believing matrons [are lawful to marry] as well as matrons from among those who were given the Book before you, once you have given them their marriage-portions and taken them in wedlock respectably, not seeking any thrills nor taking [them on as] mistresses. Anyone who rejects faith [will find] his action will miscarry, while he will be one who will lose out in the Hereafter.

6
Washing Before Prayer

(II)* You who believe, whenever you intend to pray, wash your faces and your hands up to the elbows, and wipe off your heads and [wash] your feet up to the ankles. If you are [ritually] soiled, then take a full bath. If you are ill or on a journey, or one of you has just come from the toilet or had contact with any women, and you do not find any water, then resort to wholesome soil and wipe your faces and hands off with some of it. God does not want to place any inconvenience on you, but He does want to purify you and to complete His favor towards you, in order that you (all) may act grateful.

* Remember God's favor towards you and His charter which He ratified for you when you said: "We hear and obey." Heed God; God is Aware of whatever is on your minds."

* You who believe, act steadfast towards God, as witnesses for fairplay, and do not let ill-will toward any folk incriminate you so that you swerve from dealing justly. **Be just: that is nearest to heedfulness**; and heed God [Alone]. God is Informed about anything you do. * God has promised those who believe and perform honorable deeds that they will have forgiveness plus a splendid wage. ** Those who disbelieve, and refute Our signs, will

10

become inmates of Hades. * You who believe, remember God's favor towards you when some folk intended to stretch their hands out towards you, and He fended their hands off from you. Heed God, and let believers rely on God.

(III)* God made a covenant with the Children of Israel, and We despatched twelve of them as captains. God said: "I shall be with you if you will keep up prayer and pay the welfare tax, and believe in My messengers and respect them, and advance God a handsome loan. I shall overlook your evil deeds for you and show you into gardens through which rivers flow. Anyone of you who disbelieves following that will have strayed from the Level Path."

12
The
Children
of Israel

* Since they broke their covenant, We have cursed them and planted a hard shell over their hearts. They lift words out of their context and have forgotten a portion of what they should have memorized. Except for a few of them, you will always catch some of them committing some act of treachery. Yet pardon them and overlook it; God loves those who act kindly.

* We accepted their agreement from those who say: "We are Christians;" then they forgot a portion of what they had been reminded of, so We have stirred up enmity and jealousy among them until Resurrection Day. God will notify them about whatever they have been accomplishing. ** People of the Book, Our messenger has come to you to explain much of what you have been concealing out of the Book, and to dispense with much of it. Light and a Clear Book have been brought to you from God. * God thereby guides anyone who seeks His approval along pathways of peace; He leads them out of darkness into Light by His permission, and guides them along a Straight Road.

Christians

* Those who say: "God is Christ, the son of Mary," **disbelieve**.

Christ is
not God

SAY: "Who would control anything from God if He ever wanted to do away with Christ, the son of Mary and his mother, plus everyone on earth? God holds control over Heaven and Earth, as well as anything in between them. He creates anything He wishes. God is Capable of everything!
* Jews and Christians say: "We are God's children and His favorites." SAY: "Then why does He punish you for your offences?" Rather you are human beings just like anyone else He has created. He forgives anyone He wishes and punishes anyone He wishes. God holds control over Heaven and Earth, and whatever lies between them. Towards Him lies the goal!"
* O People of the Book, Our messenger has come to explain [things] to you after an interval between the messengers, lest you say: "No herald nor any warner has ever come to us." A herald and a warner has indeed come to you! God is Capable of everything!

(IV)** So Moses told his people: "My people, remember God's favor towards you when He planted prophets among you and set you up as kings; and gave you what no one else in the Universe had ever been given. * My people, enter the Holy Land which God has assigned to you; do not turn your backs on it, lest you be sent away as losers.

20

* They said: "Moses, there is a heavy-handed folk in it. We will never enter it until they leave. If they should leave it, then we will enter." * Two men from among those who fear—God favored them both—said: "Walk right in through the gate on them. Once you have entered it, you will be victorious. You should rely on God if you are believers." * They said: "Moses, we will never enter it at all so long as they remain in it! You go off and fight, both you and your Lord; we will be sitting around here."

** He said: "My Lord, I control only myself and my brother. Distinguish between us and such perverse folk!" * He said: "It will be proscribed them for forty years. They will wander around the earth, so do not worry about such perverse people.

27

*Murder
(Cain and
Abel)*

(v)* Recite information to them about the Truth concerning Adam's two sons. When they both presented an offering, it was accepted from one of them and not accepted from the other. He said: "I'll kill you!" [The former] said: "God only accepts [things] from the heedful. * Even if you stretch forth your hand towards me in order to kill me, I'll never stretch out my hand towards you to kill you. I fear God, Lord of the Universe! * I want you to atone for my sin as well as for your own sin; you will become an inmate of the Fire. That is the wrongdoers' reward."

30

** His own self urged him on to kill his brother, so he killed him, and one morning he turned out to be a loser. * God sent a raven to scratch the earth in order to show him how to dispose of his brother's corpse. He said: "It's too bad for me! Have I failed to be like this raven and dispose of my brother's corpse?" So one morning he felt full of remorse.

*Handling
Sedition*

* On account of that, We prescribed with the Children of Israel that anyone who kills any person without another soul being involved or for causing mischief in the land, acts as if he had killed all mankind. Anyone who spares life acts as if he had granted life to all mankind. Our messengers have brought them explanations; then later on many of them committed excesses on earth.

* The penalty for those who wage war on God and His messenger, and spread havoc through the land, is to be slaughtered or crucified, or have their hands and feet cut off on opposite sides, or to be banished from the land. That will mean their disgrace in this world, while they will have serious torment in the Hereafter, * except for those who come to terms before you overpower them. Know that God is Forgiving, Merciful.

35

(VI)** You who believe, heed God and aspire for contact with him; strive for His sake so that you may prosper. * Even if those who disbelieve owned whatever is on earth plus its like besides, in order to redeem themselves from torment by means of it on Resurrection Day, it would not be accepted from them; they will have painful torment. * They may want to leave the Fire, yet they will not leave it; theirs will be constant torment.

Theft

* A thief, whether a man or a woman, shall have his or her hands cut off as a penalty for whatever he or she has earned, as an example set by God. God is Powerful, Wise. * God will relent towards anyone who repents following his wrongdoing, and reforms; God is Forgiving, Merciful.

40

** Do you not know that God holds control over Heaven and Earth? He punishes anyone He wants to and forgives anyone He wants. God is Capable of everything!

* O Messenger, do not let those who rush off into disbelief worry you, such as those who say: "We believe" with their mouths, while their hearts do not believe. Some of those are Jews who are listening for [the sake of] lying, listening for other folk who do not come to you. They lift words out of their context, saying: "If you are given this, then take it; while if you are not given it, then watch out!" God will never let you control someone whom God wants to test in any way; those are the ones whose hearts God does not want to purify. They will have disgrace in this world, while in the Hereafter they will have terrible punishment, * as listeners to lying, living off graft.

Consolation with Intrigue

If they should come to you, then judge between them or else put them ·off. If you put them off, they will never harm you in any way, while if you judge among them, then **judge fairly**. God loves those who deal fairly. * How can they choose you as a judge when they have the Torah, which contains God's judgment? Yet even then they will turn away, and such persons are not believers.

Judicial Procedure

(VII)* We have sent down the Torah containing guidance and Light. The prophets who were committed to [live in] peace judge those who were Jews by means of it, and [so do] the rabbis and scholars, because of what they sought to observe from God's book. They have even acted as witnesses for it.

44

So do not dread mankind, and dread Me; do not buy up My signs for a paltry price. *Those who do not judge by what God has sent down are disbelievers!*

** There We prescribed for them a life for a life, an eye for an eye, a nose for a nose, an ear for an ear, a tooth for a tooth, and wounds should have [similar] compensation. Yet anyone who treats it as charity, [will find] it serves as an atonement for him. *Those who do not judge by what God has sent down are wrongdoers!*

Mosaic Law

* We had Jesus, the son of Mary, follow in their footsteps in order to confirm what had come before him from the Torah and We gave him the Gospel which contains guidance and Light, to confirm what he already had in the Old Testament, and as guidance and a lesson for those who do their duty. * Let the people of the Gospel judge by what God has sent down in it; *Those who do not judge by what God has sent down are perverse!*

Jesus' Role

* We have sent you down the Book with the Truth, to confirm what was already there from the [previous] Book, and to safeguard it. Judge among them according to whatever God has sent down, and do not follow their whims concerning any Truth that has been given to you.

We have given each of you a code of law plus a program [for action]. If God had wished, He might have made you into one community, but compete rather in doing good deeds so He may test you by means of

The Diversity of Human Life

what He has given you. To God is your return entirely, and He will notify you concerning anything you have been disagreeing about.

* So judge among them according to what God has sent down, and do not follow their whims. Beware of them lest they seduce you away from what God has sent down to you. If they should turn away, then know that God only wants to afflict them with some of their own offences; many men are so immoral! ** Do they crave judgment [from the time] of Ignorance? Yet who is finer in judgment than God for any folk who are convinced?

50

51

(VIII)* You who believe, do not accept Jews or Christians as sponsors; some of them act as sponsors for one another. Any of you who makes friends with them becomes one of them. God does not guide such wrongdoing folk. * You will see those in whose hearts there lurks malice dashing in among them saying: "We dread lest a turn of fortune strike us!" Perhaps God will bring some victory or command from Himself, so some morning they will awaken regretful about what they have concealed within themselves.

    * Those who believe will say: "Are these the ones who swore by God with their most solemn oaths that they stood alongside you?" Their works have failed and they have turned out to be losers. * You who believe, any one of you who abandons his religion [will find] God will bring a people whom He will love just as they love Him, docile towards believers, stern against disbelievers; they will strive for God's sake and not fear reproach from any critic. Such is God's bounty which He gives to anyone He wishes. God is Boundless, Aware.

    ** **Your Patron is God [Alone]**, as well as His messenger and those who believe—who keep up prayer, pay the welfare tax and bow their heads [in worship]. * Anyone who enlists God as a patron, and His messenger and those who believe, [will find] God's side will be victorious!

57

(IX)* You who believe, do not accept as sponsors those from among the ones who were given the Book before you nor any disbelievers, if they treat your religion as a joke and a sport. Heed God if you are believers. * Whenever you call [people] to prayer, they take it as a joke and a sport. That is because they are folk who do not use their reason. * SAY: "People of the Book, do you persecute us just because we believe in God and what has been sent down to us, and what was sent down previously? Most of you are perverse!"

60

    ** SAY: "Shall I announce to you something worse than this as a recompense from God?" Those whom God has cursed and become angry at, and made them into monkeys and swine, and who serve the arrogant ones, are in a worse plight and even further astray from the Level Path. * When they come to you, they say: "We believe," while they have entered with disbelief and they leave with it. God is quite Aware as to what they have been hiding. * You will see many of them plunging into vice and hostility, and living off graft. What they have been doing is so wretched! * If their rabbis and scholars had only forbidden them from speaking sinfully and living off graft! How wretched is what they have been producing.

* The Jews say: "God's hand is shackled." May their own hands be shackled and themselves cursed because of what they have said! Rather both His hands are outstretched; He dispenses [things] just as He wishes. Anything sent down to you from your Lord increases many of them in arrogation and disbelief. We have tossed hostility and hatred between them until Resurrection Day. **Every time they kindle a fire for war, God snuffs it out.** They rush around the earth creating havoc. God does not love those who create havoc. ** If the People of the Book would only believe and do their duty, We would overlook their evil deeds for them and show them into gardens full of Bliss. * If they had only kept up the Torah and the Gospel, and whatever was sent down to them by their Lord, they would have eaten anything above them and from beneath their feet. Some of them form a moderate community, while many of them act badly in anything they do.

War

(x)* O Messenger, deliver whatever has been sent down to you by your Lord. If you do not do so, you will not have conveyed His message. God will defend you from mankind: God does not guide disbelieving folk. * SAY: "People of the Book, you will not make any point until you keep up the Torah and the Gospel, as well as anything that has been sent down to you by your Lord." What has been sent down to you by your Lord increases many of them in arrogation and disbelief, yet do not despair about disbelieving folk.

67

    * Those who believe and those who are Jews, Sabeans and Christians—anyone who believes in God and the Last Day, and acts honorably, should have no fear nor will they be saddened. ** We made an agreement with the Children of Israel and sent them messengers. Every time a messenger would come to them with what they themselves did not fancy, one group they accused of lying while another group they killed. * They reckoned there would be no testing, so they acted blind and deaf. Then God relented toward them; still many of them acted blind and deaf. Yet God is Observant of whatever they do.

Other Believers
70

    * Those who say that God is Christ the son of Mary have disbelieved. Christ [himself] said: "Children of Israel, worship God [Alone, Who is] my Lord as well as your Lord." God will ban the Garden for anyone who associates anything else with God; his lodging will be the Fire. Wrongdoers will have no supporters.

Christians

    * Those who say: "God is the third of three," have disbelieved! There is no deity except God Alone. If they do not stop saying what they say, painful torment will afflict those among them who disbelieve. * Why do they not turn towards God and seek His forgiveness? God is Forgiving, Merciful. ** Christ the son of Mary was only a messenger; messengers have passed away before him. His mother was sincere. They both ate food.

The Trinity

Christ

Look how We explain signs to them; then look [again] how they shrug them off! * SAY: "Do you worship something instead of God that does not control any harm nor any advantage for you while God is Alert, Aware?" * SAY: "People of the Book, do not exaggerate in your religion beyond the

Truth, nor follow the whims of a folk who have already gone astray and misled many as they stray from the Level Path.

78

*Jews
Again*

80

(xi)* Those Children of Israel who disbelieved were cursed by the tongue of David and Jesus, the son of Mary. That was because they disobeyed and had acted defiantly. * They did not refrain from the debauchery they were indulging in; how awful is what they had been doing! ** You will see many of them making friends with those who disbelieve. How wretched is what their souls have sent on ahead for them, since God is exasperated with them and they will live in torment for ever. * If they had believed in God and the Prophet, and what was sent down to him, they would not have adopted them as patrons; but so many of them are perverse.

*Christians
are Closer
To Islam*

* You will find the most violently hostile people towards those who believe are the Jews and those who associate [others with God]; while you will find the most affectionate of them towards those who believe, are those who say: "We are Christians." That is because some of them are priests and monks; they do not behave so proudly.

**PART
SEVEN**

83
*Christians
(cont'd)*

(xi cont'd.) * When they listen to what has been sent down to the Messenger, you will see their eyes well up with tears because of the Truth they recognize. They say: "Our Lord, we believe, so enroll us among the witnesses! * Why should we not believe in God and any Truth that has come to us? We yearn for our Lord to admit us along with honorable folk."

** God will compensate them with gardens through which rivers flow to live in for ever because of what they have said. Such will be the reward of those who act kindly, * while those who disbelieve and reject Our signs will become the inmates of· Hades!

87
Food

(xii)* You who believe, do not forbid any wholesome things which God has permitted you, nor exceed the limits. God does not love the defiant. * Eat any lawful, wholesome thing which God has provided you with. Heed God in Whom you are believers.

*Oaths
(Perjury)*

* God will not take you to task for what you may rattle off in your oaths, but He does take you to task for anything you have sworn to solemnly [and then ignored]. Exoneration for it means feeding ten paupers with the average of what you would feed your own families, or clothing them, or freeing a captive. Whoever does not find the wherewithal [to do so], should fast for three days. This is what penance involves in order to free yourselves from any oath you have sworn [loosely]. Keep your word; thus God explains His signs to you, so you may act grateful.

90
*Liquor
and
Gambling*

** You who believe, liquor and gambling, idols and raffles, are only the filthy work of Satan; turn aside from it so that you may prosper. * Satan only wants to stir up enmity and jealousy among you by means of liquor and gambling, and to hinder you from remembering God and from praying. So will you stop?

* Obey God and obey the Messenger, and be on your guard. If you should ever turn away, know that Our messenger need only state things clearly. * It will not be held against those who believe and perform honorable deeds for what they may have fed on while they did not do their duty, since they did believe and performed honorable deeds. So do your duty and believe—and then again, do your duty and act kindly: God loves those who act kindly!

(XIII)* You who believe, God will test you by means of some of the game which your hands and spears have caught, so that God may know who fears Him even though [He is] Unseen. Anyone who acts defiant later on, will have painful torment. ** You who believe, do not kill any game while you are forbidden [this while on Pilgrimage]. Anyone of you who kills some deliberately may make compensation through the same [type of animal] as he has killed, in livestock, with two fairminded men from among you judging it, which should be sent as an offering to reach the Ka⸲ba; or else exoneration may mean feeding paupers or the equivalent of that in fasting, so that he may taste the effect of his action. God pardons whatever is a thing of the past. God will avenge Himself on anyone who does so over again; God is Powerful, the Wielder of Retribution.

94

Pilgrimage

* Game from the sea is lawful for you; eating it means provision for you as well as for travellers. Game from land is forbidden you so long as you are under taboo [on Pilgrimage]. Heed God, before Whom you will be summoned.

Seafood

* God has placed the Ka⸲ba as the Hallowed House to be maintained for mankind, as well as the Hallowed Month and the offerings and garlands; that is so you may know that God knows whatever is in Heaven and whatever is on Earth, and that God is Aware of everything. * Know that God is Stern in punishment and (also) that God is Forgiving, Merciful. * The Messenger has only to proclaim matters; while God knows whatever you show and whatever you hide.

*** SAY: "**Evil and good are not equal**, even though the abundance of evil may fascinate you; so heed God, you prudent persons, so that you may prosper!"

100
Good and Evil

(XIV)* You who believe, do not ask about such things as would worry you if they were shown to you. Yet if you should ask about them while the Qur⸲ān is being sent down, they will be explained to you. God pardons it, for God is Forgiving, Lenient. * A folk before you asked about them; then became disbelievers because of it.

101
How to Believe

* God has not set up [specially] any slit-eared camel, nor is any [livestock] to be turned loose [to pasture freely], nor any twin-bearing goat or ewe, nor any pensioned stallion, but rather those who disbelieve make up a lie about God. Most of them do not use their reason. * Whenever they are told: "Come to what God has sent down, and to [hear] the Messenger," they say: "We are satisfied with what we found our forefathers doing;" even though their forefathers did not know anything and were not guided!

Pagan Practices

*Personal
Responsibility*

** You who believe, your souls are in your own care. No one who goes astray will harm you, provided you are guided. Toward God will you all return together, and He will notify you about whatever you have been doing.

Wills

* You who believe, testimony should be taken by you whenever death appears for one of you; at the time for drawing up any will, two of you who are fairminded, or two others besides yourselves if you are travelling around the earth and the calamity of death should strike you. Detain them both after prayer so they may swear by God if you (all) have any doubts: "We will not sell it for any price, not even to a near relative, nor will we hide God's testimony: otherwise we would be sinners!" * If it turns out that either of them has been accused of any sin, then let two others than the first two from among those who deserve to be [executors] stand up in their stead. Let them both swear by God: "Our testimony is more valid than the testimony by either of them; we have never defied [God] for then we would be wrongdoers!" * That is more appropriate for you in order to secure testimony at its face value, or for them to fear you may check back by means of [fresh] oaths following their own oaths [now]. Heed God and listen; God does not guide immoral folk.

109

110

*Jesus'
Miracles*

(xv) * Some day God will assemble [His] messengers and say: "What response have you received?" They will say: "We possess no knowledge; You are the Knower of Unseen things!" ** So God will say: "Jesus, son of Mary, remember My favor towards you and towards your mother when I assisted you with the Holy Spirit. You spoke to people from the cradle and as an adult when I taught you the Book and wisdom, the Torah and the Gospel. So you created something out of clay looking like a bird with My permission; you breathed into it, and by My permission it became a bird! You cured anyone born blind, and the leper with My permission. So you brought forth the dead by My permission, and I fended off the Children of Israel from you, when you brought them explanations, so those among them who disbelieved said: 'This is sheer magic!'

* "When I inspired the disciples to believe in Me and in My messenger, they said: 'We believe, so take witness that we are Muslims.' * When the disciples said: 'Jesus, son of Mary, can your Lord send a **Table** down from Heaven for us?', he said: 'Heed God if you are believers!' * They said: 'We want to eat from it, and for our hearts to feel at rest, and so we know that you have told us the Truth, and that we should be witnesses for it.' * Jesus the son of Mary said: 'O God our Lord, send us down a **Table** from Heaven so it may be a recurring feast for us, for both the first of us and the last of us, and as a sign from You! Provide for us, since you are the best Provider.' ** God said: 'I shall send it down to you. Any of you who disbelieves afterward, I shall punish with such torment as I have never punished anyone in the Universe!'"

116

*Jesus
Himself
Rejects
Godhood*

(xvi)* When God said: "Jesus, son of Mary, have you told people: 'Take me and my mother as two gods instead of God [Alone]?';" he said: "Glory be to You! It is not my place to say what I have no right to [say]. If I had said it, You would have known it already: You know what is on my mind, while I do not know anything that is on Yours. You are the Knower of Unseen things. * I have never told them anything except what You have ordered me to: 'Worship God as my Lord and your Lord.' I was a witness for them so long as I was among them. When You gathered me up, You became the Watcher over them; You are a Witness for everything. * If you should punish them, they are still Your servants; while if You should forgive them, surely You are Powerful, Wise."

* God said: "This is a day when their truthfulness will benefit the truthful: they shall have gardens through which rivers flow, to live in for ever and ever." God approves of them, while they are pleased with Him; that will be the supreme Achievement. ** God holds control over Heaven and Earth, as well as whatever lies within them. He is Capable of everything!

120

6
Livestock

THIS CHAPTER contains 165 late Meccan verses arranged in twenty sections. Verses 60, 63, 91, 114, 141 and 151-153 however all date from Madīna. The chapter was revealed after **Stoneland** 15 and before **(Drawn Up In) Ranks** 37. Livestock here comprises first of all camels, then bovine cattle, sheep and goats which are all mentioned in sections XVI & XVII as having been dedicated to other deities than God Alone; consequently their presence in sacrifice did not help advance the cause of true religion.

The beginning sections and XVI deal with the sin of associating other things in our worship of God Alone. The chapter contains several lyric descriptions of the Deity, such as "Keys to the Unseen" (VII). Two important statements are made on the subject of tolerance in VI and XIII. What might be called an Islamic decalogue or Ten Commandments, and God's Straight Road are found in XIX. The final section (XX) is pregnant with meaning.

In the name of God, the Mercy-giving, the Merciful!

(I)* Praise be to God, Who created Heaven and Earth and granted darkness and light! Yet those who disbelieve make other things equal to their Lord. * He is the One Who has created you (all) from clay; then fixed a term. A deadline has been set by Him, yet you go on doubting! * He is God in (both) Heaven and Earth. He knows your secret and anything you publish; He knows whatever you earn.

* Not one of their Lord's signs ever reaches them except they shun it. ** They have rejected Truth whenever it came to them, yet (more) news will reach them concerning what they have been making fun of. * Have they not seen how many generations We wiped out whom We had established on earth before them in a way We did not establish you? We sent [water down from] the sky upon them in torrents and let rivers flow beneath them; and yet We wiped them out because of their offences and raised up other generations to succeed them.

* Even though We sent you down something written on a papyrus scroll so they might touch it with their own hands, those who disbelieve would still say: "This is just sheer magic!" * They say: "If an angel were only sent down to him!" Yet if We were to send an angel down, the matter would be settled; then they would no longer be allowed to wait. * Even if We made him into an angel, We would have made him a man as well, to confuse them just as they confuse themselves. ** Messengers have been

scoffed at before you, till whatever they were ridiculing swept in around those who had been doing the scoffing.

(II)* SAY: "Travel around the earth and see what the outcome was for those who denied [it all]."

* SAY: "Who owns whatever is in Heaven and Earth?" SAY: "God does. He has prescribed mercy for Himself so He may gather you in on Resurrection Day, concerning which there is no doubt. Yet those who have lost their souls will never believe. * He has anything that rests at night and by daylight. He is the Alert, Aware." * SAY: "Shall I adopt someone as a patron besides God, the Deviser of the Heavens and Earth? He feeds [everybody], yet is not fed!" SAY: "I have been ordered to be the first who has committed himself to (live at) peace. Do not be an associator!"

** SAY: "I fear the torment of an awful day if I should disobey my Lord." * He will show mercy to anyone who is spared on that day: that will be the clear Triumph. * If God should let any harm touch you, no one would remove it except He Himself; while if He should let some good touch you, well He is Capable of everything. * He is the Irrresistible, [High] above His servants. He is the Wise, the Informed.

* SAY: "What thing is most important as evidence?" SAY: "God is a Witness for both me and you. This Reading has been revealed to me so that I may warn you (all) by means of it, as well as anyone it may reach. Do you testify that there are other gods along with God?" SAY: "I will not swear so!" SAY: "He is God Alone, while I am innocent of whatever you associate [with Him].'' ** Those whom We have given the Book know Him just as they recognize their own sons; [yet] those who have lost their souls will never believe.

(III)* Who is worse off than someone who invents a lie about God or has rejected His signs? Wrongdoers will never prosper. * Some day We will summon them all together, then tell those who have associated [others with Us]: "Where are your associates which you have been claiming [to have]?" * Then there will be no test for them unless they say: "By God our Lord, we have not been associators!" * See how they lie even about themselves! Whatever they have invented has misled them.

** Some of them listen to you even though We have placed wrappings over their hearts and dullness in their ears lest they should understand it. Even if they saw every sign, they still would not believe in them; so whenever they come to you, they argue with you. Those who disbelieve say: "These are only legends by primitive people." * They try to refute it and remain aloof from it; yet they only destroy their own souls while they do not even notice it! * If you could see when they are set before the Fire and say: "Alas, if we might only be sent back and had not rejected our Lord's signs, and we had been believers!"

* Rather what they had been hiding previously has appeared to them; even though they were sent back, they would still return to what they have been forbidden. They are such liars! * They say: "Only our worldly life exists; we will not be raised up again." ** If you could only see as they are made to stand before their Lord! He will say: "Isn't this real?" They will

I I

*God is
One*

20

2 I
*Association
is Wrong*

30

say: "Of course, by our Lord!" He will say: "Taste torment, since you have been disbelieving!"

31 (IV)* Those who deny [they will have] any meeting with God have already lost out, so that when the Hour comes suddenly upon them, they will say: "Have pity on us for how we neglected it!" They will carry their burdens on their own backs. Is not whatever they bear something evil?

* What does worldly life mean except some sport and amusement? The future Home is better for those who do their duty. Will you (all) not use your reason? * We well know how anything they say saddens you. Yet they are not rejecting merely you, but wrongdoers even repudiate God's signs. * Messengers before you have been rejected, yet they held firm on being rejected and abused, until Our support came to them. **There is no way to change God's words!** News from (other) emissaries has already come to you. ** If their reluctance bears so heavily upon you, then how would it be if you managed to bore a tunnel through the earth or to climb a ladder up to Heaven, and brought a sign to them? If God so wished, He would gather them together for guidance; so do not act so ignorant as well. * Only those who listen will respond, plus the dead whom God will raise; then unto Him will they return.

* They say: "If a sign were only sent down to him by his Lord!" SAY: "God is Able to send down a sign, even though most of them will not know it." * There is no animal [walking] on earth nor any bird flying on its wings unless they exist as communities like yourselves. * We have not neglected anything in the Book; then to their Lord will they be summoned.
* Those who reject Our signs are deaf and dumb, [groping along] in darkness. God lets anyone He wishes go astray, while He sets anyone He wishes upon a Straight Road.

40   ** SAY: "Have you considered whether, once God's torment comes to you (all) or the Hour comes to you, you will appeal to someone instead of God if you are so truthful?" * Rather it is to Him you will appeal and if He wishes, He will remove whatever you have appealed to Him about, and you will forget what you have associated [with Him].

42 (V)* We sent [word] to nations before you and seized them with suffering and hardship so that they might act submissively. * Why then did they not act submissive when Our violence came to them, but instead their hearts were hardened and Satan made whatever they were doing seem attractive to them? * So once they forgot what they had been reminded of, We opened up the doors to everything for them until just when they were happiest with what they had been given, We caught them suddenly and there they were confounded! ** The last remnant of the folk who had been doing wrong was cut off. Praise be to God, Lord of the Universe!

* SAY: "Have you (all) considered whether, if God should snatch away your hearing and your eyesight, and sealed off your hearts, who is the god besides God [Himself] who can give them back to you?" Watch how We deal out signs, yet they still keep aloof! * SAY: "Have you yourselves considered whether, if God's torment should come to you suddenly or openly, any except wrong-doing folk would be wiped out?" * We do not

send any emissaries except as newsbearers and warners. Anyone who believes and reforms should have no fear nor will they be saddened, * while punishment will alight on those who reject Our signs because of how immoral they have been.

** SAY: "I do not say God's treasures lie with me nor do I know the Unseen, nor do I even tell you I am an angel. I merely follow what has been inspired in me." SAY: "Are the blind and the sighted man equal? Will you not think such matters over?"

50

(VI)* Warn those who fear that they will be summoned to their Lord concerning it: they will have no patron nor any intercessor besides Him— so that they may do their duty.

51

* Do not drive away those who appeal to their Lord, wanting His presence in the early morning and the evening. You have nothing to do with their reckoning, while they have nothing to do with your reckoning. Should you drive them off, you would be a wrongdoer.

Tolerance

* Even so do We try some of them by means of others, so they may say: "Are those the ones among us towards whom God has been gracious? Is God not quite Aware as to who are grateful?"

* Whenever those who believe in Our signs come to you, SAY: "Peace be upon you!" Your Lord has prescribed mercy for Himself so He will be Forgiving, Merciful to any of you who commits evil out of ignorance, then repents later on and reforms. ** Thus We spell out signs so the criminals' way may be evident.

Good Manners

(VII)* SAY: "I am forbidden to serve those whom you appeal to instead of to God." SAY: "I do not follow your whims: in that case I would go astray and not be guided." * SAY: "I am [looking] for evidence from my Lord while you have rejected it. I do not have what you are trying to hurry up; discretion lies only with God. He relates the Truth and is the best Decider." * SAY: "If I had what you seek to hurry up, the matter would have been settled between me and you. God is quite Aware as to who are wrongdoers."

56

* He holds the keys to the Unseen;
only He knows them! He knows
whatever exists on land and at sea;
no leaf drops down unless He knows it,
nor any seed [lies] in the darkness of the earth,
nor any tender [shoot] nor any withered [stalk]
unless it is [written down] in a clear Book.

Keys to The Unseen

** He is the One Who gathers you (all) in at night.
He knows what you have accomplished by day;
then He revives you in it
so a stated period may be fulfilled.
Then your return will be unto Him,
when He will notify you
about whatever you have been doing.

60

61

More on
God

(VIII) * He is the Irresistible,
[reigns Supreme] Above His servants!
He sends guardians [to watch] over you
so that whenever death comes for one of you,
Our messengers will gather him in.
They will not neglect [their duty];
* then they will be sent back to God,
their true Patron.
Surely discretion belongs to Him!
He is the Swiftest Reckoner.

* SAY: "Who saves you from darkness on land and at sea?" You appeal to Him beseeching and in secret: "If He will rescue us from this, we'll be so grateful!"

     * SAY: "God will rescue you from it, and from all anxiety. Yet you still associate others with Him!"

     ** SAY: "He is Able to send torment down upon you or from underneath your feet, or to confuse you with factions and make some of you experience the violence of others."

     Watch how We handle signs so that they may understand. * Even so your folk reject it although it is the Truth.

SAY: "I am no administrator set up over you. * Every piece of news has some purpose, as you shall realize."

Handling
Discussions

     * Whenever you see those who speculate about Our signs, avoid them till they speculate about some other topic of conversation. Even if Satan should cause you to forget [to do so], still do not sit around with such wrongful folk once you remember. * Those who do their duty are not accountable for them in any way except to remind [them], so that they [in turn] may do their duty.

70

     ** Stay away from those who take their religion as a sport and amusement. Worldly life has lured them on. Remind [them] of it lest any soul become reckless because of what he has earned; he will have no patron nor any other intercessor besides God. Even if he were to proffer every alternative, such would not be accepted from him. Those who let themselves act recklessly concerning what they have earned must drink boiling water and suffer painful torment because of how they have disbelieved.

71

(IX)* SAY: "Should we appeal to something that can neither benefit nor harm us, instead of to God? Shall we turn on our heels now that God has guided us, bewildered like someone whom the devils have enticed away on earth, while his companions are calling him to guidance: 'Come to us!'?"

God's
Guidance

SAY: "God's guidance means [real] guidance. We have been ordered to commit ourselves peacefully to the Lord of the Universe. * 'Keep up prayer and heed Him!' He is the One before Whom you will (all) be summoned. * He is the One Who really created Heaven and Earth. Any day He says: 'Be!'; then it **is**!

     "His speech [means] the Truth and He will hold control on the day when the Trumpet is sounded. Knowing the Unseen and Visible, He is Wise, Informed."

* Thus Abraham said to his father Āzar: "Do you accept idols as gods? I see you and your folk are in obvious error." ** Therefore We showed Abraham sovereignty over Heaven and Earth so he might feel reassured.

   * When night descended on him, he saw a star. He said: "Will this be my lord?" So when it set, he said: "I do not like setting things."

   * So then as he saw the moon rising, he said: "Will this be my lord?"; and when it set, he said: "If my Lord did not guide me, I would be a member of the lost folk."

   * So when he saw the sun rising (again), he said: "Will this be my lord? This is [even] greater." As it set, he said: "My people, I am innocent of what you associate [with God]! * **I have turned my face enquiringly to Him Who originated Heaven and Earth.** I am no associator."

   ** His people argued with him. He said: "Are you arguing with me concerning God, while He has guided me? I do not fear what you associate with Him, unless my Lord should wish for something else. My Lord comprises everything in knowledge. Will you not be reminded? * How should I fear what you associate [with Him] while you do not fear having associated something with God for which He has not sent you down any authority? Which of either group deserves more security, if you know anything? * Those who believe and do not cloak their faith in wrongdoing will feel more secure and will be [better] guided."

   (x)* Such was Our argument which We furnished Abraham with against his folk: We raise anyone We wish to in rank. Your Lord is Wise, Aware. * We bestowed Isaac and Jacob on him; each We guided. Noah We had guided before, and from his offspring [came] David, Solomon, Job, Joseph, Moses and Aaron; thus We reward those who act kindly. ** Zachariah, John, Jesus and Elijah were all honorable men. * And Ishmael, Elisha, Jonah and Lot; each We preferred over [everybody else in] the Universe. * We picked out some of their forefathers, their offspring and their brethren, and guided them to a Straight Road.

   * Such is God's guidance: He thereby guides any of His servants He may wish. If they had associated [others with Him], whatever they were doing would have collapsed on them. * Those are the ones to whom We have given the Book, along with discretion and prophethood; if such men should disbelieve in it, then We will entrust it to a folk who will not disbelieve in it. ** Such are the ones whom God has guided, so copy their guidance. SAY: "I do not ask you any fee for it; it is only a Reminder to [everybody in] the Universe!"

   (xi)* They do not value God the way He should be valued when they say: "God has not sent down anything to a human being." SAY: "Who sent down the Book which Moses came with, as Light and guidance for mankind? You publish it on (separate) sheets to show it around, while you (also) hide a great deal [of it]. You have been taught what neither you yourselves nor your forefathers ever knew." SAY: "God [has sent it];" then leave them toying away with their speculation.

   * This is a blessed Book We have sent down to confirm whatever came before it, so you may warn the Mother of Towns and anyone around her. Those who believe in the Hereafter believe in it and attend to their

Abraham's Search for God

80

83

Other Prophets

90

91

prayer. * Yet who is more in the wrong than someone who invents a lie about God? Or says: "Something has been revealed to me...", while nothing has been revealed to him; and who says: "I shall send down the same as God has sent down"?

If you could only see when wrongdoers are in their death throes and the angels stretch forth their hands: "Away with your souls! Today you are awarded the torment of shame because you have been saying something that is not true about God. You have acted too proud for His signs." * You have (all) come to Us individually, now, just as We created you in the first place. You have left behind what We conferred on you, nor do We see your intercessors alongside you whom you claimed were associated with you. They have been cut off from you, and what you have been claiming has merely led you astray!"

95
*Proof
of God*

(XII)** God is the One Who splits the seed and kernel,
He brings the living from the dead, and is the One
Who brings the dead from the living.
Such is God; yet still you shrug Him off!

* Kindler of morn, He grants night for repose,
and the sun and moon for telling time.
Such is the measure of the Powerful, the Aware!

* He is the One Who has placed the stars
to guide you through darkness on land and at sea.
We have spelled out signs for people who know!

* It is He Who has reproduced you from a single soul,
and [granted you] a settlement [on earth]
and a resting place [after death].
We have spelled out signs for people who understand.

* It is He Who sends down water from the sky. Thus We bring forth plants of every type with it; We produce green vegetation from it. We produce grain from it piled tight packed on one another, and from the datepalm, clusters close at hand produced from its pollen, as well as orchards full of grapes, olives and pomegranates, which are so similar and yet dissimilar. Look at their fruit as He causes it to grow and ripen. **In that are signs for folk who believe.**

100

*** They have set up sprites as associates with God, even though He created them! They have even dared to impute sons and daughters to Him without having any knowledge. Glory be to Him; Exalted is He over whatever they describe!

101

(XIII)* Deviser of Heaven and Earth! How can He have a son while He has no consort? He created everything and is Aware of everything!

*God the
Creator of
Everything*

* Such is God, your Lord;
there is no deity except Him,
the Creator of everything,
so serve Him. He is
a Trustee for everything!

* No powers of vision can comprehend Him, while He comprehends [all] vision; He is the Subtle, the Informed. * Insights have come to you from your Lord; anyone who observes [them] does so for his own sake, while anyone who acts blindly has himself to blame. I am not [set up as] any guardian over you.

The Limits of Responsibility

** Thus we spell out signs so they will say: "You have been studying!"; and so We may explain it to folk who know. * Follow whatever has been revealed to you by your Lord; there is no deity except Him. Avoid anyone who associates [others with God]. * If God had so wished, they would not have associated [anything with Him]. We have not set you up as a guardian over them, nor are you an administrator for them.

* Do not insult those they appeal to instead of to God, lest they insult God as an enemy without even realizing it. Thus We have made their action seem attractive to every nation; then their return shall be to their Lord, so He may notify them about how they have been acting.

Tolerance

* They swear by God with their stiffest oaths that if a sign were given them, they would believe in it. SAY: "Signs belong only to God." What will make you perceive that even when they are given them, they will still not believe? ** We upset their vital organs and their eyesight since they did not believe it in the first place. We will leave them groping along in their arrogance.

110

PART
EIGHT

III

(XIV)* Even though We were to send angels down to them and the dead were to speak to them, and We mustered everything against them, they still would not believe unless God so wishes; yet most of them act so out of ignorance. * Thus We have granted each messenger an opponent, devils from humankind and sprites, some of whom have inspired others with seductive talk in order to deceive them. If your Lord had so wished, they would not have done so; so leave them alone as well as anything they may be inventing. * Let the vital organs of those who do not believe in the Hereafter incline towards it, and let them feel satisfied with it and acquire whatever they may be acquiring.

* Should I crave someone besides God to settle matters? He is the One Who has sent the Book down to you to set things forth in detail. Those whom We have given the Book recognize that it has been sent down from your Lord with the Truth, so do not be a doubter. ** Your Lord's word has been completed so far as [its] credibility and justice are concerned; there is no way to change His words. He is the Alert, the Aware. * If you obeyed most of those who are on earth, they would lead you astray from God's path; they only follow conjecture and are merely guessing. * Your Lord is quite Aware as to who is straying from His path, just as He is quite Aware as to who are guided.

* So eat whatever God's name has been mentioned over if you are believers in His signs. * What is wrong with you that you do not eat something God's name has been mentioned over? He has spelled out for you what has been forbidden you—unless you are obliged to [eat it]. Many [people] lead others astray through their own passions without having any knowledge; your Lord is quite Aware as to who are disobedient. ** Leave off obvious vice and its inner source; those who acquire a vice will be rewarded for whatever they may have committed. * Do not eat anything over which God's name has not been mentioned; it is so immoral! The devils inspire their adherents to argue with you; if you (all) obeyed them, you would become associators [of others in your worship of God Alone].

120

(xv) * Is someone who has been dead and whom We revived and granted light to so he may walk among people with it, to be compared to someone who is in such darkness he cannot leave it? Thus anything they have been doing seems attractive to disbelievers.

122

* Thus We have granted each town great men who are its criminals, to plot away in it. They merely plot against themselves and do not even notice it. * Whenever some sign comes to them, they say: "We will never believe until we are given the same as God's messengers were given." God is quite Aware as to where He should place His message; belittlement by God and stern torment will strike those who commit crimes because of what they have been plotting.

** God lays anyone's breast open to Islām whom He wants to guide, while He makes the breast of anyone He wants to be led astray seem cramped, tight, just as if he were climbing up to Heaven. Thus God places a blight on those who do not believe. * This is your Lord's Straight Road. We have spelled out signs for folk who remember: * they will have **a peaceful home** with their Lord; He will be their Patron because of what they have been doing.

* Some day He will summon them all together: "O company of sprites, you have required too much from humankind." Their adherents among humanity will say: "Our Lord, some of us have taken advantage of one another, and have [now] reached our deadline which You appointed for us." He will say: "The Fire will be your lodging to live in for ever, except for whatever God may wish. Your Lord is Wise, Aware." * Thus We let some wrongdoers manage others because of what they had been earning.

130

(xvi)** "O company of sprites and humankind, have not messengers from among yourselves come to relate My signs to you and warn you about a meeting on this day of yours?" They will say: "We bear witness even against ourselves." Worldly life has lured them on and they bear witness against themselves for having been disbelievers.

* That is because your Lord will not destroy any towns unjustly while their people are heedless: * everyone will have ranks according to what they have been doing. Your Lord is not oblivious of what they are doing. * Your Lord is Transcendent, the Master of Mercy; if He so wished, He would remove you and bring replacements for you in any way He wishes, just as He has produced you from the offspring of other people. * What you are promised is coming; you will never avert it.

** SAY: "My people, act according to your situation; I [too] am Acting! You will know who will have the Home as a result. The fact is that wrongdoers will not prosper. * They grant God a share in what He has produced such as crops and **livestock**, and they say: "This is God's," according to their claim, and: "This is our associates'." Anything that is meant for their associates never reaches God, while what is God's reaches their associates (too); how evil is whatever they decide! * Even so, their associates have made killing their children seem attractive to many associators, to lead them on to ruin and to confuse their religion for them. If God so wishes, they would not do so; so leave them alone and whatever they are inventing.

* They say: "This **livestock** and (these) crops are taboo; only someone we wish to may eat them!", according to their claim. There are some **livestock** whose backs one is forbidden to ride, as well as (other) **livestock** over which God's name has not been mentioned, as something invented despite Him. He will reward them according to what they have been inventing. * They say: "What is in this **livestock**'s bellies is reserved exclusively for our menfolk, and forbidden to our wives." Yet if it is stillborn, then they may be partners in it!

He will reward them for their description; He is Wise, Aware. ** Those who have stupidly killed their own children without having any knowledge and forbidden something God has provided them with, have lost out through inventing things about God; they have gone astray and not accepted guidance.

(XVII)* He it is Who has produced gardens, both trellised and untrellised, and datepalms and field crops whose food [tastes] different, as well as olives and pomegranates which are so alike and yet so unlike! Eat some of their fruit as they ripen, and give away whatever they ought to on their harvest day. Yet do not overdo things for He does not love extravagant people.

* Some **livestock** is for transport and some meant for use at home. Eat anything God has provided you with and do not follow in Satan's footsteps, for he is an open enemy of yours. * Eight exist in pairs: two [pairs] of sheep and two of goats. SAY: "Does He forbid both males or both females, or what the females' wombs contain? Inform me scientifically if you are so truthful!" * Camels also [come] in twos and cattle in twos. SAY: "Did He forbid both males or both females, or what both females' wombs contain? Were you witnesses when God instructed you concerning this?" Who does more harm than someone who invents a lie about God, so he may lead mankind astray without having any knowledge? God does not guide wrong-doing folk.

(XVIII)** SAY: "I do not find anything forbidden in what has been revealed to me for anyone needing to eat something, unless it is something that has died [by itself] or it is blood which has already been shed, or pork—that is so filthy!—or a sinful offering that has been consecrated to something besides God. Concerning anyone who is obliged to do so, without either meaning to disobey nor exceeding his [barest] needs, your Lord is Forgiving, Merciful.

* We have forbidden those who are Jews everything having a claw, and in the case of cattle, sheep and goats, We have forbidden them their tallow, unless it is located in their backs or intestines, or what is mingled with their bones. That is how We have rewarded them because of their insolence. We are Truthful; * so if they should reject you, then say: "Your Lord possesses boundless Mercy. His might will not be withheld from criminal folk."

Associators

* Those who associate [others in their worship of God] will say: "If God had so wished, neither we nor our forefathers would have associated [anything with Him] nor have forbidden anything." Even so did those before them reject [Us] until they tasted Our might. SAY: "Have you (all) any knowledge? Then bring it here for us! Why, you only follow conjecture; you are merely guessing!"

150

* SAY: "God holds the convincing argument; if He so wished, He would have guided every one of you." ** SAY: "Produce your witnesses who will testify that God has forbidden this!" If they so testify, still do not testify along with them nor follow the whims of those who reject Our signs and do not believe in the Hereafter. They make all things equal to their Lord!

151

(XIX)* SAY: "Come close, I will recite what your Lord has forbidden you:

I

Do not associate anything with Him;

II

And [show] kindness towards both [your] parents.

III

Do not kill your children because of poverty; We shall provide for you as well as for them.

IV

Do not indulge in shocking acts which you may practise either openly or keep secret.

V

Ten Commandments

Do not kill any person whom God has forbidden, except through [due process of] law. He has instructed you in this so that you may use your reason.

VI

* Do not approach an orphan's estate before he comes of age, except to improve it.

VII

Grant full measure and weight in all fairness. **We do not assign any person to do more than he can cope with**.

VIII

Whenever you speak, be just even though it concerns a close relative.

IX

Fulfil God's agreement. Thus has He instructed you so that you may bear it in mind.

X

The Straight Road

* This is My Straight Road, so follow it and do not follow [other] paths which will separate you from His path. Thus has He instructed you so that you may do your duty.

* Then We gave Moses the Book as a fulfilment for someone who acts kindly, and an analysis of everything, as well as for guidance and mercy so they may believe about meeting their Lord.

(xx)** This is a Blessed Book We have sent down, so follow it and do   155
your duty so that you may receive mercy, * lest you say: "The Book was
sent down to only two factions before us. We have been unaware of what
they study." * Or you may say: "If the Book had been sent down to us,
We would be better guided than they are."

Evidence has now come to you from your Lord, as well as guidance
and mercy. Who is more in the wrong than someone who rejects God's
signs and even evades them? We will reward those who evade Our signs
with the worst torment because they have acted so evasive. * Are they
only waiting for angels to come to them or for your Lord to arrive, or for
some of your Lord's signs to come? On the day when some of your Lord's
signs arrive, belief in them will not benefit any person who has not believed
in them already, nor earned some good through his [profession of] faith.
SAY: "Wait; we too are waiting!"

* Concerning those who permit divisions in their religion and form
sects, you should have nothing to do with them in any way. Their case   *Sectarian
rests entirely with God; soon He will notify them about whatever they   Divisions*
have been doing.

    ** Anyone who comes with a fine deed   160
    will have ten more like it,
    while anyone who comes with an evil deed
    will only be rewarded with its like;
    they will not be treated unjustly.

* SAY: "As for me, my Lord has guided me along a Straight Road,
[leading to] an established religion, the creed of Abraham the Enquirer.   *Abraham*
He was no associator."

    * SAY: "My prayer and my devotion,
    my living and my dying,
    (all) belong to God, Lord of the Universe;
    * no associate has He,
    with that am I commanded,
    and I am the first of the Muslims."

* SAY: "Should I seek some other lord than God, while He is Lord
of Everything? Each soul is responsible only for its own self, while no   *Individual
burdened [soul] shall bear another's burden. Soon your return will be   Responsibility*
unto your Lord, so He may advise you concerning whatever you have
been differing over.

** "He is the One Who has placed you as overlords on earth and raised
some of you higher than others in rank so He may test you by means of   *Collective
what He has given you. Your Lord is Swift in punishment; yet He is   Responsibility*
Forgiving, Merciful."

7
The Heights

THIS LONG chapter of 206 Meccan verses is arranged in twenty-four sections. Vv. 163-170 in section XXI date however from Madīna. The chapter was revealed after [**The Letter**] **Ṣād** 38 and before **Sprites** 72, and concerns our eventual reward for our conduct during this life. It contains a series of parallel yet not identical passages on the case histories or messages that have been conveyed through various prophets.

In section II the Devil tempts Adam before the tree of Good and Evil. **The Heights** which give the chapter its title are mentioned in sections V-VI, and they present a vivid picture of Heaven and Hell which furnishes some of the imagery for the Divine Comedy by the Italian poet Dante Alighieri. Some consider them to be a lofty bridge or the site of Purgatory that lies between Heaven and Hell.

Sections IX-X reflect on the future and on God's Oneness. Then there follows in detail Moses' wonderful story, especially on Mt. Sinai with the Golden Calf (XIII-XVIII), and then his troubles with the Children of Israel. The last section (XXIV, along with VII), offers the vast picture of man's creation along with the resultant process of animal and human reproduction.

In the name of God, the Mercy-giving, the Merciful!

(I)* A.L.M.S.

* A Book has been sent down to you, so do not let your breast feel it is under any constraint because of it, so you may warn by means of it; [it is] a Reminder for believers.
* Follow whatever has been sent down to you by your Lord and do not follow any sponsors besides Him; yet how seldom do you remember!
* How many towns have We wiped out? Our might has come upon them at dead of night or while they were napping. ** Once Our might came to them, their appeal was merely to say: "We have been such wrongdoers!"
* Let Us ask those to whom it was sent and let Us (also) ask the emissaries; * let Us relate what We know about them since We have not been absent.

* The weighing-in that day will be correct: those whose scales are heavy will be prosperous; * while those whose scales are light are the ones who have lost their souls because they have been damaging Our signs. ** We have established you on earth and granted you means by which to live on it. Yet seldom are you grateful!

10

(II)* We created you (all); then We shaped you. Then We told the angels: "Bow down before Adam". They bowed down on their knees except for Diabolis; he was no one to bow down on his knees!

* He said: "What prevents you from bowing down when I have commanded you to [do so]?" He said: "I am better than he is; You created me from fire, while You created him from clay." * He said: "Clear out of here; you have no reason to act so proud about it. Get out; you are such a petty person!"

* He said: "Let me wait until the day when they are raised up again." ** He said: "You are one who will be allowed to wait." * He said: "Since you have let me wander off, I'll waylay them along Your Straight Road; * then I'll come at them from in front of them and from behind them, on their right and on their left. You will not find that most of them are grateful." * He said: "Get out of here, despised, rejected! I'll fill Hell with all of those who follow you.

* "And Adam, settle down in the garden, you and your wife. Eat wherever you wish; yet do not approach this tree lest either of you should become wrongdoers."

** So Satan whispered to them to show them both their private parts which had gone unnoticed by either of them. He said: "Your Lord only forbids you this tree so that you will not become two angels, or lest you both become immortal." * He swore to them: "I am a sincere counsellor with both of you!" * He led them on by deceiving [them].

Once they had tasted the tree['s fruit], their private parts became apparent to both of them, and they started to patch together leaves from the Garden for themselves.

Their Lord called out to them: "Did I not forbid you that tree and tell you both that Satan is an open enemy of yours?" * They said: "Our Lord, we have harmed ourselves! If You do not forgive us and grant us mercy, we'll be losers." * He said: "Clear out! You will become one another's enemies. Yet you may have a residence on earth and enjoyment for a while." ** He [further] said: "You will live on it and you will die on it, and from it will you be brought forth [again]."

(III)* "Children of Adam, We have sent you down clothing with which to conceal your private parts and to dress up in. Yet **the clothing of heedfulness is best!**"

That is one of God's signs, so that they may bear it in mind.

* Children of Adam, do not let Satan tempt you just as he turned your two ancestors out of the Garden, stripping them of their clothing in order to show them their private parts. He and his tribe watch you from where you do not see them! We have placed devils as patrons for those who do not believe. * Whenever they perform any obscene act they say: "We found out our forefathers were performing it, and God has ordered us to do so." SAY: "God does not order any sexual misconduct. Do you say something you do not know about God?"

* SAY: "My Lord has ordered me to play fair. Keep your faces set towards every place of prayer and appeal to Him sincerely; religion belongs to Him. Even as He started you off, so will you return. ** One party has

11
*The Devil
with Adam*

*The Tree
of Good
and Evil*

20

26

*Sexual
Misconduct*

30

He guided while another party ought to be allowed to go astray: they have adopted the devils as patrons instead of God, and reckon they are guided!

Etiquette

* Children of Adam, **wear your best clothes to every place of worship!** Eat and drink, yet do not overdo things; He does not love the extravagant.

32

(IV)* SAY: "Who has forbidden God's amenities which He has produced for His servants, and the wholesome things from [His] provision?" SAY: "On Resurrection Day they will be [reserved] exclusively for those who have believed during worldly life." Thus do We set forth signs for folk who know.

*More
Do Not's*

* SAY: "My Lord has only forbidden shocking deeds whether they are flagrant or kept hidden; and vice and sedition without any right to do so; and that you should associate anything with God for which He has not sent down any authority; and that you should say something you do not know concerning God.

*Philosophy
of History*

> * Every nation has its term;
> so whenever their deadline comes,
> they will not postpone it for an hour,
> nor will they advance it.

** Children of Adam, whenever any messengers from among yourselves come to relate My signs to you, then anyone who does his duty and reforms will have no fear nor need they feel saddened; * while those who reject My signs and act too haughty towards them will become inmates of the Fire; they will remain there for ever.

* Who is more in the wrong than someone who invents a lie about God or rejects His signs? Those will have their portion from the Book presented to them so that when Our messengers come to carry them off, they will say: "Where are whatever you used to appeal to instead of to God?" They will say: "They have left us in the lurch," and so they shall testify against themselves as to how they have been disbelievers. * He will say: "Enter the Fire along with the nations of sprites and humankind who have passed away before you."

Every time some nation enters it, it will curse its sister[-nation] until, when they have all caught up with one another, the last of them will say to the first: "Our Lord, these [people] have misled us, so give them double torment from the Fire!" He will say: "Each shall have double, even though you do not realize it." * The first of them will tell the last: "What advantage have you over us? Taste torment because of what you have earned!"

40

*Heaven
and Hell*

(V)** Heaven's gates will not swing open for those who reject Our signs and feel too proud for them, nor will they enter the Garden until a camel can be led through the eye of a needle. Thus We reward criminals: * they will have a couch in Hell while over them there will hang awnings. Thus We reward wrongdoers!

* Those who believe and perform honorable deeds [will find] We never assign any soul more than it can cope with. Those will become inhabitants of the Garden; they will live in it for ever. * We will strip away any rancor

[that lingers] in their breasts. Rivers will flow beneath them and they will say: "Praise be to God Who led us to this! We would never have been guided if God had not led us on. Our Lord's messengers have brought the Truth." They will hear someone call out: "Here is the Garden you have inherited because of what you have done!"

* The inhabitants of the Garden will call out to the inmates of the Fire: "We have found out that what our Lord promised us is true. Have you found what your Lord promised you to be true?" They will say: "Yes!" So an announcer among them will call out: "God's curse rests on wrong-doers ** who obstruct God's path and try to make it crooked, and are disbelievers in the Hereafter."

* Between them both there will hang a curtain, while on the **Heights** above there will be men who recognize everyone by their features. They will call out to the inhabitants of the Garden: "Peace be upon you!" They have not yet entered it even though they long to. * When their sight is shifted towards the inmates of the Fire, they will say: "Our Lord, do not place us alongside such wrongdoing folk!"

(vi)* The Companions on the **Heights** will call out to some men whom they will recognize by their features; they will say: "How did all your storing things up and how proud you acted benefit you? * Are you those who swore that God would not confer any mercy on them? Enter the Garden; there is no [need] for you to fear nor should you feel saddened."   48

** The inmates of the Fire will call out to the inhabitants of the Garden: "Pour some water over us, or anything God has provided you with!" They will say: "God has forbidden either of them to disbelievers * who have taken their religion as a pastime and for amusement; worldly life has lured them on."   50

Today We shall forget them just as they forgot about meeting on this day of theirs. Did they not repudiate Our signs? * We have given them the Book; We have spelled it out knowingly as a guideline and mercy for folk who believe. * Are they only waiting for it to be interpreted? The day its interpretation comes along, those who have already forgotten it will say: "Our Lord's messengers did bring the Truth! Have we any intercessors to intercede for us? Or should we be sent back, then we would act so differently from the way we have been acting." They have lost their souls and what they have been inventing has left them in the lurch.

(vii)* Your Lord is God, Who created Heaven and Earth in six days; then He mounted on the Throne. He wraps night up with daytime, seeking it automatically. The sun, moon and stars are regulated by His command. Surely creation and authority belong to Him. Blessed be God, Lord of the Universe!   54

Creation

** Appeal to your Lord beseeching and in private; He does not love those who are aggressive. * Do not spoil things on earth once they have been improved. Appeal to Him out of fear and expectation; God's mercy lies close to those who act kindly. * He is the One Who sends winds to announce His mercy directly, so that whenever they lift up heavy clouds, We drive them along to a dead countryside and send down water from

The Winds

them; and thus We bring forth every kind of fruit. Thus We bring forth the dead too so you may bear this in mind. * A good land brings forth its plants with its Lord's permission, while whatever is sterile will produce only grudgingly. Thus We spell out signs for folk who act grateful.

59

60

Noah's Mission

(VIII)* We sent Noah to his people, and he said: "My folk, serve God [Alone]; you have no other deity than Him. I fear the torment of an awful day for you!" ** The elders of his people said: "We see you are in obvious error." * He said: "My folk, no trace of error lies in me, but I am a messenger from the Lord of the Universe. * I transmit my Lord's messages to you, and counsel you sincerely. I know something you do not know about God. * Are you surprised that a Reminder should come to you from your Lord through one of your own men, so He may warn you and you will do your duty, and in order that you may receive mercy?"

* Yet they said he was lying, so We saved him and those who were along with him in the Ark. We let those who rejected Our signs drown; they were such blind folk!

65

'Ād and Their Prophet Hūd

(IX)** To ‹Ād [there was sent] their brother Hūd: "O my people, serve God [Alone]. You have no other deity than Him. Will you not do your duty?" * The elders who disbelieved among his folk said: "We see you are [full] of nonsense, and think you are a liar!"

* He said: "My people, there is no nonsense in me, but I am a messenger from the Lord of the Universe! * I transmit my Lord's messages to you; I am a trustworthy counsellor for you. * Are you surprised that a Reminder from your Lord should come to you through one of your own men, so that He may warn you? Remember when He set you up as overlords following Noah's folk, and made you grow so very tall. Remember God's benefits so that you may prosper.''

70

** They said: "Have you come to us so we will worship God Alone and forsake whatever our forefathers have been serving? Bring us whatever you threaten us with if you are so truthful." * He said: "A blight plus wrath from your Lord have already fallen on you. Are you arguing with me about some names that you and your forefathers have made up? God has not sent down any authority for them. Just wait: I am waiting alongside you."

* So We saved him and those who stood with him through mercy from Ourself, and We cut off the last remnant of those who rejected Our signs and were not believers.

73

Thamūd and Their Prophet [Methu] Ṣāliḥ

(X)* To Thamūd [there was sent] their brother Ṣāliḥ. He said: "My folk, worship God! You have no other deity than Him. A proof has come to you from your Lord: this camel belonging to God is a sign for you, so leave her grazing on God's earth and do not let any harm touch her lest some painful torment should overtake you. * Remember when He set you up as overlords after ‹Ād, and settled you down on the earth. You occupy palaces on its plains and carve houses out of the mountains. Remember God's benefits and do not cause havoc on earth like mischief makers."

** The elders among his people who acted proudly told the ones they considered helpless, even though they still believed: "Do you know whether

Ṣāliḥ is an emissary from his Lord?" They said: "We are believers in whatever he has been sent with." * Those who acted proudly said: "We are disbelievers in what you believe in." * So they hamstrung the camel, objected to their Lord's command, and said: "Ṣāliḥ, bring us what you promise us with if you are an emissary!"

* A tremor caught them; so one morning they lay cowering in their home. * He turned away from them and said: "My people, I have delivered my Lord's message to you and counselled you sincerely, but you do not like sincere advisors."

** And there was Lot when he told his people: "Do you indulge in a sexual practice such as no one in the Universe has ever indulged in previously? * You approach men lustfully instead of women! Rather you are dissipated folk."

80

Lot

* His people's answer was merely to say: "Run them out of your town: they are persons who are trying to keep pure." * We saved him and his family except for his wife; she was one of those who lagged behind. * We sent a rain down on them: look how the outcome was for such criminals!

(xi)** To Midian [We sent] their brother Shuᶜayb. He said: "My people, worship God [Alone]! You have no other deity besides Him. A token has come to you from your Lord, so offer full measure and weight, and do not undersell people in their dealings nor spoil things on earth once it has been set right; that will be best for you if you are believers. * Do not lurk along every road, threatening and blocking anyone off from God's way who believes in Him, and seeking to make it crooked. Remember how few you were and He increased you. See what the outcome was for those who act depraved. * If there is a faction of you who believe in what I have been sent with, and another faction which does not so believe, still be patient until God judges between us. He is the best of Judges."

85

Midian and Their Messenger Shuᶜayb

PART
NINE

(xi cont'd) * The elders among his people who had acted proudly said: "We'll run you out of our town, Shuᶜayb, as well as those who believe along with you; or else you will return to our sect!" He said: "Even though we detest it? * We'd invent a lie about God if we returned to your sect now after God has saved us from it. There is no means for us to return to it unless God our Lord should wish us to; our Lord comprises everything in knowledge. On God have we relied. Our Lord, really deliver us from our own people; You are the best Deliverer."

88

** The elders among his people who disbelieved said: "If you follow Shuᶜayb, you will then be losers." * So the Tremor caught them, and one morning they lay cowering in their homes: * those who rejected Shuᶜayb [ended up] as if they had never been so wealthy in them; those who rejected Shuᶜayb were the losers! * So he turned away from them and said: "My people, I have delivered my Lord's messages to you and counselled you sincerely. Why should I grieve over a disbelieving folk?"

90

94
*Prosperity
and
Depression*

(XII)* We have never sent a prophet into any town unless We [first] seized its people with suffering and hardship, so that they might be humbled. ** Then We turned evil into good so that they were thriving, and said: "Both hardship and happiness befell our ancestors." So We seized them suddenly while they did not even notice it.

* If the townsfolk had (only) believed and done their duty, We would have showered blessings from Heaven and Earth on them, but they rejected [them], so We seized them because of what they had been acquiring. * Do townsfolk feel secure from Our might's striking them at dead of night while they are asleep? * Or do the people of the towns feel safe from Our might's striking them in broad daylight while they are playing around? * Do they feel safe from God's design? No one should feel safe from God's design except for folk who will lose out.

100

(XIII)*** Were those who will inherit the earth after its [present] people never shown how We would strike them down for their offences and seal off their hearts if We so wished, so they would not hear? * We have related news concerning those towns to you: their messengers came to them with explanations, yet they were not in any mood to believe in something they had already rejected. Thus God seals off disbelievers' hearts. * We did not find any agreement was ever kept by most of them, although We did find most of them were quite immoral!

Moses

* Then after them, we despatched Moses with Our signs to Pharaoh and his courtiers, and they mistreated them. See how the outcome was for mischiefmakers! * Moses said: "Pharaoh, I am a messenger from the Lord of the Universe. ** It is (only) right for me to say nothing except the Truth about God. I have brought you an explanation from your Lord, so send the Children of Israel away with me." * He said: "If you have brought some sign, well produce it then if you are so truthful!" * He tossed his staff down and imagine, it obviously became a snake! * He pulled out his hand [from his shirtfront], and imagine, it was white to the onlookers!

109
110

(XIV)* The notables among Pharaoh's people said: "This is some clever magician! ** He wants to drive you out of your land; so what do you command?" * They said: "Put him and his brother off, and send recruiters out through the cities * who will bring you in every clever magician."

* The magicians came to Pharaoh. They said: "Will we have some payment if we are the winners?" * He said: "Yes, and you will become courtiers."

** They said: "Moses, will you throw something down or shall we be the ones to throw [first]?" * He said: "You throw [first]!" So when they threw, they charmed the people's eyes and overawed them. They produced a splendid trick!

* We inspired Moses with: "Throw your staff," and imagine, it swallowed up whatever they had trumped up! * Truth prevailed and what they had been doing collapsed; * those men were defeated and were turned

120

back belittled. ** The magicians dropped down on their knees; * they said: "We believe in the Lord of the Universe, * the Lord of Moses and Aaron."

* Pharaoh said: "You have believed in Him before I permit you to! This is some scheme which you have hatched in the city in order to drive its people out. You will soon find out! * I'll cut off your hands and feet on opposite sides; then I'll crucify you all." ** They said: "We will be sent home to our Lord. * You are persecuting us only because we have believed in our Lord's signs once they were brought us. Our Lord, pour patience over us, and gather us up [at death] as Muslims!"

(xv)* The notables among Pharaoh's people said: "Are you letting Moses and his people ruin the earth, and forsake you and your gods?" He said: "We shall slaughter their sons and let their women live; we stand irresistible over them."

* Moses told his people: "Seek help from God and act patient; the earth belongs to God. Anyone He wishes from among His servants will inherit it, and the outcome belongs to the heedful." * They said: "We were oppressed before you came to us, and [will be again] after you have come to us." He said: "Perhaps your Lord will wipe out your enemy and leave you as overlords on earth, so He may observe how you act."

(xvi)** We gripped Pharaoh's household with years [of trial] and a   130
shortage of fruit so they might bear it in mind. * Whenever something fine came to them, they said: "This is ours;" while if something evil afflicted them, they took it as an omen connected with Moses and whoever was with him. Did not their omen only lie with God? Yet most of them do not realize it. * They said: "No matter what sign you may bring us to charm us with, we will never believe in you."

* We sent the flood and grasshoppers, lice, frogs and blood on them as distinguishing signs, yet they (still) acted proudly and were criminal folk. * Whenever some plague fell upon them, they said: "Moses, appeal to your Lord for us, because of what He has pledged for you; if you will lift the plague from us, we will believe in you and send the Children of Israel away with you."

** Yet whenever We lifted the plague from them for a period which they were to observe, why, they failed to keep it! * We avenged Ourselves on them and drowned them in the deep, because they had rejected Our signs and been so heedless of them. * We let a folk whom they considered to be inferior inherit the Eastern and Western parts of the land which We had blessed. Your Lord's finest word was accomplished for the Children of Israel because they had been so patient. We destroyed everything Pharaoh and his people had been producing and whatever they had been building.

* We led the Children of Israel across the sea. They came upon a people who were dedicated to some idols they had. They said: "Moses, make a god for us like the gods they have." He said: "You are a folk who act ignorantly. * Anything those people are busy at is doomed and whatever they have been doing is absurd." ** He said: "Should I seek   140
something instead of God as a deity for you, while He has preferred you ahead of [everyone in] the Universe? * When We saved you from Pharaoh's household, they were imposing the worst torment on you: they slaughtered your sons and spared your women. That meant a serious trial from your Lord."

142

*Moses on
Mt. Sinai*

(XVII)* We appointed thirty nights for Moses and completed them with ten; the appointment with his Lord was complete in forty nights. Moses told his brother Aaron: "Rule my people in my stead and set a good example; do not pursue the mischiefmakers' course."

* When Moses came for Our appointment and his Lord spoke to him, he said: "My Lord, show [yourself] to me so I may look at You." He said: "You will never see Me, but look at the mountain [instead]. If it remains in its place, then you shall see Me." When his Lord displayed his glory to the mountain, He left it flattened off, and Moses fell down stunned.

When he came back to his senses, he said: "Glory be to You! I have turned to You and am the first believer!" * He said: "Moses, I have selected you ahead of [all] mankind for My messages and My word; so accept whatever I may give you and act grateful [for it]." ** We wrote down a bit of everything for him on Tablets for instruction and as an analysis of everything: "Hold to it firmly and command your folk to hold on to whatever is best in it. I shall show you (all) the home for immoral people. * I shall divert those from My signs who have strutted around the earth so proudly without having any right to do so."

Even if they saw every sign, they still would not believe in them. If they saw the way to normal behavior they would not accept it as any way [to behave], while if they saw any way to err, they would accept it as a course [of action]. That is because they have rejected Our signs and been heedless of them.

* Those who reject Our signs and [the idea of] a meeting in the Hereafter will [see] their works collapse. Will they not be rewarded for just what they have been doing?

*Modesty and
Good Conduct*

148

*The Golden
Calf*

(XVIII)* After he had gone, Moses' folk designed a calf [made] out of their jewelry, a (mere) body that mooed. Did they not see that it neither spoke to them nor guided them along any way? They adopted it and (thereby) became wrongdoers.

* When the matter was dropped in their hands and they saw that they were lost, they said: "If our Lord does not show us mercy and forgive us, we will be losers."

150

** When Moses returned angry, sorrowful to his folk, he said: "What an awful thing you have committed behind my back! Have you tried to hurry up your Lord's command?" He dropped the Tablets and seized his brother by the head, pulling him towards himself. He said: "Son of my mother, the people felt I was weak and they almost killed me! Dont let any enemies gloat over me nor place me with such wrongdoing folk!" * He said: "My Lord, forgive me and my brother, and let us enter Your mercy! You are the most Merciful of those who show mercy!"

152

(XIX)* Anger and disgrace from their Lord will be awarded those who accepted the Calf during worldly life. Thus We reward those who invent [such things]; * as for those who perform evil deeds, then repent later on and believe, your Lord will later on be Forgiving, Merciful.

* When his anger had subsided, Moses picked up the Tablets whose text contained guidance and mercy for those who revere their Lord.

** Moses chose his people, seventy men, for an appointment with Us. When the Tremor seized them, he said: "My Lord, even though You may have wished to wipe them out and myself (as well) earlier, are You wiping us out just because of what some fools among us have done? It is only Your manner of testing: You let anyone You wish to, go astray by means of it, and let anyone You wish, to be guided. You are our Patron, so pardon us and show us mercy; You are the best Pardoner. * Prescribe a fine thing for us in this world and in the Hereafter; let us be guided towards You!"

He said: "I afflict anyone I wish with My torment while My mercy embraces everything; I shall prescribe it for those who do their duty, pay the welfare tax, and who believe in Our signs, * those who follow the Messenger, the Unlettered Prophet whom they will find written down for them in the Torah and the Gospel. He commands them to be decent and forbids them dishonor. He permits them wholesome things and prohibits them evil things, and relieves them of their obligation and the shackles which have lain upon them. Those who believe in him, revere him and support him, and follow the Light which was sent down with him; those will be successful."

The Unlettered Prophet

(xx)* SAY: "Mankind, for all of you I am but a messenger from God [Alone], Who holds control over Heaven and Earth. There is no deity except Him; He gives life and brings death. Believe in God and His messenger, the Unlettered Prophet who himself believes in God [Alone] and His words: follow him so you may be guided."

158

* Out of Moses' folk [there grew] a nation who guided by means of the Truth and dealt justly by means of it. ** We split them up into twelve tribes, communities, and inspired Moses when his people asked for water: "Strike the rock with your staff." Twelve springs gushed forth from it. Each set of people knew its own drinking-place.

160

We shaded them with clouds and sent down manna and quail for them: "Eat some of the wholesome things which We have supplied you with." Yet they did not harm Us, but they themselves were the persons whom they harmed. * When they were told: "Settle down in this town and eat wherever you wish in it, and say: 'Relieve [us]!' Enter the gate [walking] on your knees. We will forgive you your mistakes; We will give even more to those who act kindly," * those among them who did wrong changed the statement into something else than what had been told them; so We sent a plague from Heaven upon them because of how wrong they had been acting.

(xxi)* Ask them about the town which lay facing the sea, when they broke the Sabbath. Their fish came to them swimming on the surface on their Sabbath Day, while any day they did not cease work, it did not come to them. Thus We tested them since they had been acting so immorally.

163

The Sabbath Breakers

* Whenever a community among them said: "Why do you lecture a folk whom God will destroy anyhow, or [at least] punish them severely?" they said: "To gain absolution from your Lord, and so they may do their duty." ** When they forgot what they had been reminded of, We rescued

those who had forbidden evil while We seized those who were doing wrong with dreadful torment because they had been acting so immorally. * When they became insolent about what had been forbidden them, We told them: "Become apes who will be chased away." * So your Lord announced that He would send someone against them who would impose the worst torment on them until Resurrection Day. Your Lord is Prompt with punishment, while He is (also) Forgiving, Merciful.

Imperfect Messages

* We split them up into nations (that exist) on earth. Some of them are honorable while some of them are otherwise. We have tested them with fine things and evil things so they might repent. * Successors replaced them afterward who inherited the Book, taking on the show of this lowly place and saying: "It will be forgiven us." If a show like it were given them (again), they would accept it. Was not an agreement concerning the Book accepted by them: that they would tell nothing but the Truth about God? They studied what was in it.

170

A home in the Hereafter is better for those who do their duty—do they not use their reason? ** As for those who hold onto the Book and keep up prayer—We shall never forfeit reformers' wages. * Thus We suspended the Mountain over them as if it were an awning, and they thought it was going to fall down on them: "Hold on firmly to anything We have given you and remember what is in it, so that you may do your duty!"

172

The Islamic Covenant

(XXII)* When your Lord took their offspring from the Children of Adam's loins, and made them bear witness about themselves: "Am I not your Lord?"; they said: "Of course, we testify to it!" lest you (all) might say on Resurrection Day: "We were unaware of this;" * or lest you say: "It was only our forefathers who associated [others with God] previously; we are offspring following them. Will You wipe us out because of what futile men have done?" * Thus We spell out signs so that they may repent.

The Dog

** Recite news to them about someone to whom We gave Our signs. He slipped away from them, so Satan followed him and he became misguided. * If We had so wished, We might have raised him up by means of them, but he clung to the earth and followed his own whim. He might be compared to a dog: no matter how you drive him off, he just pants away. Or if you leave him alone, he still pants on. That is what folk who reject Our signs are like; tell such stories so they may think things over. * How evil is the comparison of folk who reject Our signs; it is their own souls they hurt!

The Losers

* Anyone whom God guides
has been (really) guided;
while those He lets go astray
will be the losers. * We have bred
many sprites and humans for Hell:
they have hearts they do not understand with,
and eyes they do not see with,
and ears they do not hear with.
Those persons are like livestock;
in fact, they are even further off the track,
they are so heedless!

** God has the Finest Names, so appeal to Him by name and leave   180
those who blaspheme against His names alone; they will be rewarded
for whatever they have been doing.
   * Some of those whom We have created form a nation which
guides [men] by means of the Truth, and because of it they act justly.

(XXIII)* We shall gradually bring those who reject Our signs from a place   182
they do not recognize. * I shall let them go on, for My scheme is
sure. * Have they not thought things over? There is no madness in their
companion; he is merely a plain warner. ** Have they not observed in the
sovereignty over Heaven and Earth and whatever God has created of any
sort, that perhaps their deadline may be approaching? In what report will
they believe later on? * Anyone whom God lets go astray will have no
guide; He leaves them groping along in their arrogance.
   * They may ask you about the Hour: "When will it arrive?" SAY:
"Knowledge about it rests only with my Lord; He Alone will disclose its
time. Things will seem heavy in Heaven and Earth; it will simply come
upon you all of a sudden!"
   They will even ask you as if you yourself were anxious about it. SAY:
"Knowledge about it rests only with God, though most people do not
realize it." * SAY: "I control no advantage nor any disadvantage by myself
except whatever God may wish. If I had known the Unseen, I would have
tried to increase [my share] of good, while no evil would ever touch me. I
am merely a warner and newsbearer for people who believe."

(XXIV)* He is the One Who has created you (all) from a single soul, and   189
made its mate from it, so he may settle down with her. Once he has
covered her, she conceives a light burden and walks around [unnoticed]   *Man's*
with it; then when she begins to feel heavy, they both appeal to God, their   *Reproduction*
Lord: "If You will grant us a healthy [child], we will be grateful."
   ** Once He gives them a healthy child, they both set up associates for   190
Him despite what He has given them. Exalted is God over anything they
may associate [with Him]! * Do they associate something [with God] that   *Association*
has never created anything, while they themselves have been created?
   * They cannot offer them any support nor can they even assist themselves!
   * If you summon them to guidance, they will not follow you; it is the same
for you whether you appeal to them or keep silent: * "Those you appeal
to instead of to God are servants just like yourselves. Appeal to them so   *Idol*
they may respond to you if you are so truthful! ** Have they feet to walk   *Worship*
with, or hands to grasp things with, or eyes to see with, or ears to listen
with?"
   SAY: "Appeal to your associates [instead of to God]; then plot away
against me, and do not wait for me [to act]! * My Patron is God [Alone],
who has sent down the Book. He befriends the honorable * while those
you appeal to instead of Him cannot lend you any support nor do they
even support themselves. * If you summon them to guidance, they will not
hear, and you will see them looking towards you while they are [really] not
seeing [anything]."
   * Practise forgiveness, command decency; and avoid ignorant people.

200

*** If some urge from Satan should prompt you, seek refuge with God; He is Alert, Aware. * The ones who perform their duty bear it in mind whenever some impulse from Satan bothers them, and so they are granted insight. * Their brethren will trail off into aimlessness; therefore do not interfere with them.

     * If you had not brought them any sign, they would (still) say: "Why didnt you pick one out?" SAY: "I follow only what has been inspired in me by my Lord. These are insights from Your Lord, as well as guidance and mercy for folk who believe."

How to Listen to the Qurᶜan

     * Whenever the Qurɔān is being recited, listen to it [attentively] and hush, so that you may receive mercy. ** Keep your Lord in mind within your own soul, beseeching and fearfully, without raising your voice, both in the early morning and in the evening; do not act so heedless!

BOW DOWN HERE

         * Those who are with your Lord
do not feel too proud to worship Him;
they glorify Him and drop down
on their knees before Him.

8
Booty
(also called *The Struggle*)

T HIS CHAPTER contains 75 verses from Madīna arranged in ten sections; however vv. 30-36 in Section IV date from Mecca. The chapter was revealed after **The Cow** 2 and before **The House of ‹Imrān** 3.

It refers to events surrounding the battle of Badr in the year 2 / 624; this occurred in hilly country about three days' camel journey from Madīna on the road southwest to Mecca in an action directed against a Meccan caravan financed by Abū-Sufyān which was returning from Syria. This crisis occurred when 319 Muslims faced nearly one thousand Meccans, and it was decisive in the formation of the new Islamic state. It is also known as the chapter of the "fighting men."

The usual title comes from the problems discussed at the beginning of the chapter concerning the disposal of the windfalls or spoils acquired in such battles. God's support is promised in I, III and VIII. The Prophet is finally assured that quality will overcome quantity during his trials (IX). The **Struggle** is described in the final section (X). Forced migration has been a serious problem from the beginning of Islam.

In the name of God, the Mercy-giving, the Merciful!

(I)* They will ask you about **Booty**. SAY: "**Booty** belongs to God and the Messenger, so heed God and patch up any [differences] that may stand between you. Obey God and His messenger if you are believers."

True Believers

* Believers are merely those whose hearts feel wary whenever God is mentioned and whose faith increases when His verses are recited to them. On their Lord do they rely. * Those who keep up prayer and spend some of whatever We have provided them with * are truly believers. They hold rank before their Lord, as well as forgiveness and generous provision, ** just as your Lord sent you forth from your home with the Truth, even though a group of believers disliked it. * They will argue with you about the Truth even after it has been explained, just as if they were only being driven along towards death and were expecting it.

* When God promised you that one of the two bands would be yours, you preferred the one that had no weapons [to fall] to you, while God wanted the Truth to be verified through His words and to cut off the last remnant of the disbelievers * so He might verify the Truth and disprove falsehood no matter how criminals might dislike it. * Thus you (all) implored your Lord, so He responded to you: "I will reinforce you with a

10   thousand angels riding up one after another." ** God granted it merely as good tidings to calm your hearts. Support comes only from God; God is Powerful, Wise.

11   (II) * Thus He caused drowsiness to overcome you as an assurance from Him, and sent down water from the sky on you to cleanse you with and to remove Satan's blight from you, and to bind up your hearts and brace your feet with it. * So your Lord inspired the angels: "I am with you, so brace those who believe. I shall cast panic into the hearts of those who disbelieve; so strike at the nape of their necks and beat every [last] fingertip of theirs!"

     * That is because they have split off from God and His messenger. Anyone who splits off from God and His messenger [will find out] that God is Stern in punishment. * That is [how it is], so taste it; disbelievers

Battle Tactics   will have fiery torment! ** You who believe, whenever you meet those who disbelieve, do not turn your backs on them as they go marching along. * Anyone who turns his back on them on such a day, except while manoeuvring for battle or wheeling towards some detachment, will incur wrath from God; his lodging will be Hell and how awful is such a goal! * You (all) do not kill them but God kills them. You did not shoot [anything] when you shot [arrows or spears] but God threw [them] so He may test believers, as a handsome test from Himself. God is Alert, Wise. * That is [how it is]; since God is the One Who will frustrate the disbelievers' plot.

     * If you sought to conquer, then victory has already come to you. Yet if you would only stop, it would be better for you; while if you do it over again, We too shall do so again. Your detachment will not give you any advantage no matter how numerous it is. God stands alongside believers.

20   (III) ** You who believe, **obey God and His messenger**; do not turn away from Him while you are within earshot. * Do not be like those who say: "We have heard," while they were not even listening.

> * The worst animals before God
> are the deaf and dumb, those
> who do not use their reason.

* If God had known about any good in them, He would have made them hear; yet even though He were to make them hear, they would still turn away and shun [Him]. * You who believe, respond to God and the Messenger whenever He invites you to something that will make you live.

> Know that **God slips in between a man and his heart**,
> and to Him you will (all) be summoned.

** Do your duty lest dissension strike those of you especially who do wrong. Know that God is Severe in punishment. * Remember when you were so few, disdained as helpless souls on earth, fearing lest men would kidnap you, and how He sheltered you and aided you with His support, and provided you with wholesome things so that you might act grateful.

* You who believe, do not betray God and the Messenger, nor knowingly betray your own trusts. * Know that your possessions and children are merely a trial, while God holds a splendid wage.

(IV) * You who believe, if you heed God, He will grant you a Standard, absolve your evil deeds for you, and forgive you. God possesses such splendid bounty! 29

** Whenever those who disbelieve plot against you, to pin you down or kill you or exile you, they plot away while God is plotting too, and God is the best Plotter! * Whenever Our verses are recited to them, they say: "We have heard (it) already; if we wished to, we'd say the same as this. These are only legends by primitive people!" * When they say: "O God, if this is the Truth from You, then rain down stones from Heaven on us, or give us painful torment!" * God is not apt to punish them while you are among them, nor will God be their tormenter so long as they seek forgiveness. 30

* What do they have, that God should not punish them for blocking off the Hallowed Mosque while they are not its protectors? Its protectors are only the heedful, even though most of them do not realize it. ** Their prayer at the House consists only of whistling and clapping: "Taste torment since you have disbelieved!" * Those who disbelieve spend their money to block off God's way. They will go on spending it; then regret will be their lot. Next they will be defeated and those who disbelieve will be summoned unto Hell * so God may sort out the bad from the good and pile some of the bad on top of the rest, so He may heap them all up together and drop them into Hell. Those will be the losers!

(V) * Tell those who disbelieve that anything they have done in the past will be forgiven once they stop [doing so], while if they should ever do it over again, the precedent with the earliest men has already been set. * Fight them off until there is no more persecution, and **Religion belongs wholly to God**: yet if they do stop, then God is Observant of anything they do. ** If they should turn away, then know that God is your Protector; how splendid such a Protector is, and how favored is such a Supporter! 38

40

PART TEN

(V cont'd) * Know that with anything you may acquire as spoils, a Fifth of it belongs to God and the Messenger, close relatives and orphans, paupers and the wayfarer, if you believe in God and what We have sent down to Our servant on the Day of Distinction, the day when both forces met. God is Capable of everything. 41

* When you (all) were on the nearer bank and they were on the further bank, and the baggage train was lower than you were, even if you had made [previous] arrangements with one another, you would have failed to keep the appointment; but [it happened] so God might settle a matter which had already been determined, so that anyone who perished might

The Battle Scene at Badr

perish in order to set an example, and anyone who survived might (also) survive as an example. God is so Alert, Aware! * When God pointed them out to you as a few in your dream, you (all) would have felt discouraged and debated the matter even if He had shown you that they were many; but God kept things safely in hand. He is Aware of whatever is on your minds. * When He showed you them as a few in your eyes as you met, He made you seem few in their eyes too, so God might settle a matter which had already been determined. To God do matters return.

45

*Facing
Aggression*

(VI) ** You who believe, whenever you meet with any armed force, hold firm and remember God often, so that you may succeed. * Obey God and His messenger and do not argue with one another, so that you will falter and lose your courage. Show patience; God stands beside the patient. * Do not be like those who left their homes recklessly and in order to be seen by everybody, and they obstructed God's way. God is Embracing whatever they are doing.

* So Satan made their actions seem attractive to them, and said: "There will be no man who will overcome you today: I'll stand close by you." Yet as both detachments sighted one another, he wheeled around on his heels and said: "I am innocent of you; I see something you do not see! I fear God, and God is Severe in punishment."

49

50

(VII) * Whenever hypocrites and those in whose hearts [there lurks] malice say: "Their religion has lured these people on," anyone who relies on God [will find] that God is Powerful, Wise. ** If you could only see when the angels gather up [the souls of] those who disbelieve, striking their faces and backs: "Taste the torment of the Blaze! * That is because of what your hands have sent on ahead. Yet God is no One to harm any worshippers."

*Philosophy
of History*

* In the case of Pharaoh's house as well as those who lived before them, they disbelieved in God's signs, so God seized them for their offences. God is Strong, Severe with punishment! * That is because **God is no One to alter any favor He has granted a folk unless they alter what they themselves have**. God is Alert, Aware. * In the case of Pharaoh's house and those who lived before them, they had rejected their Lord's signs, so We let them perish because of their offences and let Pharaoh's household drown. They were all such wrongdoers! ** The worst animals for God are those who disbelieve and do not even want to believe; * those with whom you have pledged some undertaking, then they break their word in every case and do not heed. * Should you encounter them in war, then use them to frighten off anyone who comes in their rear, so that they may (all) learn a lesson. * Should you fear treachery from any folk, confront them with it in exactly the same manner. God does not love traitors.

*Handing
Treachery*

59

60

(VIII) * Let not those who disbelieve reckon they will thus forge ahead; they will not forestall a thing. ** Prepare any [military] strength you can muster against them, and any cavalry posts with which you can overawe God's enemy and your own enemy as well, plus others besides them whom you do not know. God however knows them!

Anything you spend for God's sake will be repaid you, and you will not be harmed. * If they should incline to peace, then incline to it too and rely on God. He is Alert, Aware. * If they want to outwit you, then let God serve as your [final] reckoning; He is the One Who aids you through his own support and by means of believers. * He has united their hearts: even though you spent everything on earth, you could never unite their hearts; but God has united them. He is Powerful, Wise. * O Prophet, let God be your Reckoning, and that of any believers who may follow you.

(IX) ** O Prophet, urge believers on to fight! If there are twenty disciplined   65
men among you, they will overcome two hundred, while if there are a hundred of you, they will defeat a thousand of those who disbelieve, since those are folk who do not understand. * Now God has lightened things for you; He knows how much weakness exists among you. If there are a hundred patient men among you, they will overcome two hundred, while if there are a thousand of you, they will overcome two thousand with God's permission. God stands alongside the disciplined.

* It is not proper for a Prophet to have any prisoners [of war] until he has subdued [everyone] on earth. You (all) want worldly show while God wants the Hereafter [for you]. God is Powerful, Wise. * Had it not been for a writ from God that had come previously, awful torment might have afflicted you because of what you have taken; * so (now) consume any lawful and wholesome thing out of what you have captured, and heed God. God is Forgiving, Merciful.

(x) ** O Prophet, tell any captives who are in your hands: "If God knows   70
of any good in your hearts, He will give you something even better than what has been taken away from you, as well as forgive you. God is Forgiving, Merciful." * If they should want to betray you, they have already betrayed God previously, so He has made them available. God is Aware, Wise.

* Those who believe, and have migrated and **struggled** for God's sake   *Refugees*
with their property and persons, as well as those who have given them asylum and support, [will find] some of those are friends of one another. You do not owe any protection to those who believe and have not migrated, until they become refugees. If they should plead for support however from you concerning religious matters, you must support them except against any folk with whom you have made a treaty. God is Observant of anything you do. * Some of those who disbelieve are allies of one another. Unless you [Muslims] do not do likewise, dissension will exist on earth, and [cause] great havoc. * Those who believe and become refugees, and **struggle** for God's sake, as well as those who grant them asylum and support, are truly believers; they will have forgiveness and generous provision. ** Those who believe later on, and migrate and **struggle** alongside you are (also) part of you. [Nevertheless] some blood relationships are closer to others according to God's writ. God is Aware of everything!

9
Repentance
(OR *Dispensation*)

THIS CHAPTER contains 129 verses arranged in sixteen sections. They are all from Madīna except for the two final verses which date from the Farewell Pilgrimage to Mecca (as does Chapter 110 on **[Divine] Support**). This chapter was revealed after **The Table** 5 and the expedition to Tabūk on the road to Damascus which occurred in A.H. 9 / 630 A.D., or two years before the Prophet's death (VI, XIII). The alternate title of **Dispensation** (OR **Release**) comes from v.1, while the main one of **Repentance** (which is preferred by the great commentator Ibn-Kathīr) is to be found in vv. 5, 11 and 103. The battle of Ḥunayn which occurred in the year 8 / 630 is discussed in sections XIII & XIV.

There is no invocation to this chapter since it is really a continuation of the previous one on **Booty** 8, and the first verse invokes God's name. It strongly advises us against associating other deities in our pure worship of God Alone or the sin of idolatry, as it is called, and against trusting treacherous neighbors. Associators should not visit mosques (III), while priests and clergy are called unnecessary since God can be approached directly; likewise God has no son (V). Charity is another theme which is discussed (VII-VIII), especially its use in missionary effort (VIII).

We also read biographical details about the Prophet's suffering during his Transfer or the Hijra from Mecca to Yathrib, which was then to be called Madīna (the Enlightened 'City'—*al-Madīna al-Munawwara*—or the Prophet's 'City'). We likewise learn about his troubles in imposing a draft or military service, especially on the rich (VII) and the nomads (XI-XII) which are described in an especially vivid manner. Dissension had been stirred up by hypocritical agitators and draft dodgers who went out among the fickle desert folk, The Migrants or refugees similarly had their troubles in settling down in his new capital of Madīna. The ending is one of the last sections in the whole Qurʾān to be revealed.

(I) * **Dispensation** [comes] from God and His messenger for those associators with whom you have made a treaty: * travel around the earth for four months, and realize that you (all) cannot escape from God. God will shame disbelievers.

Treaty
Rights

* [This is] a proclamation by God and His messenger for mankind [assembled] on the day of the greater Pilgrimage, to wit: God may dissolve

treaty obligations with associators and [so may] His messenger. If you **repent**, then it will be better for you; while if you turn aside, know that you cannot escape from God. Announce painful torment to those who disbelieve, * except for those associators with whom you have already made a treaty; provided they have not failed you in any respect nor backed up anyone against you. Fulfil any treaty [you have] with them until their period is up. God loves those who do their duty!

** When the hallowed months have slipped away, then fight associators wherever you may find them; take them and besiege them, and waylay them at every outpost. If they should **repent**, keep up prayer and pay the welfare tax, then let them go their way. God is Forgiving, Merciful. * If one of the associators should ask you for protection, then grant him asylum until he has heard God's word. Later on escort him to where he can find safety. That is because they are folk who do not know anything.

(II) * How can there be any treaty with associators on the part of God and His messenger, except for those with whom you have ratified one at the Hallowed Mosque? So long as they act straightforwardly with you, be straightforward with them. God loves those who do their duty! * How, if they should overcome you, will they honor any pact or obligation with you? They seek to please you in whatever they say while their hearts refuse to. Most of them are immoral: * they have bought up God's signs for a paltry price, and obstructed His way. How evil is what they have been doing! ** They honor no pact nor any obligation with a believer; those are aggressors! * Yet if they should **repent**, keep up prayer and pay the welfare tax, then [they may be] your brethren in religion. We spell out signs for folk who know.

* If they should violate their trust once they have sworn it, and insult your religion, then fight the leaders of disbelief; they have no faith to make them stop. * Will you not fight folk who have violated their trust and intended to exile the Messenger? They attacked you first! Are you afraid of them? You ought to be even more afraid of God if you are believers. * Fight them, so God may punish them at your hands and disgrace them, and support you against them, and heal the breasts of believing folk, ** and remove the fury from their hearts. God turns to anyone He wishes; God is Aware, Wise. * Or do you reckon you will be abandoned once God knows which of you have struggled, and did not adopt anyone as an ally besides God, His messenger and believers? God is Informed about anything you do.

(III) * Associators must not frequent God's mosques since they act as witnesses for their own disbelief. Those [people will find] their actions will miscarry and they will remain for ever in the Fire. * Only someone who believes in God and the Last Day, keeps up prayer, pays the welfare tax, and dreads only God [Alone], shall frequent God's mosques. Perhaps those may be the ones who submit to guidance.

* Have you made those giving pilgrims something to drink and taking care of the Hallowed Mosque just like someone who believes in God and the Last Day, and struggles on for God's sake? They are not equal before

Marginal notes:

7

10

*Self
Defence*

17

*Associators
Should Not
Visit Mosques*

20

God; God does not guide such wrongdoing folk! ** Those who believe and migrate, and struggle for God's sake with their property and persons, stand much higher in rank with God. Those will be triumphant! * Their Lord proclaims mercy and approval from Himself for them, and gardens where they will have lasting bliss * to live in for ever and ever; with God there lies a splendid wage.

* You who believe, do not take your fathers and your brothers on as sponsors if they prefer disbelief rather than faith. Anyone of you who enlists them as sponsors are wrongdoers. * SAY: "If your fathers, your sons, your brothers, your spouses and your family ties, as well as the wealth you have acquired and the business you dread will fall off, plus the dwellings you are so fond of, are all dearer to you than God and His messenger, or striving for His sake, then wait around till God brings His command to pass. God does not guide such immoral folk!

The Proper Use of Property and Wealth

25

(IV) ** God has supported you on many battlefields and the day of Ḥunayn when your own numbers amazed you; yet it did not spare you in any way and the earth seemed cramped for you, spacious as it is. Then you fell back in retreat. * Next God sent His serenity down upon His messenger and on believers; He sent down armies you did not even see and punished those who disbelieved. Such is the reward for disbelievers.

* Then later on God will turn towards anyone He wishes. God is Forgiving, Merciful. * You who believe, associators are nothing but filthy, so they should not approach the Hallowed Mosque after this year that they still have. If you should fear destitution, God will enrich you out of His bounty if He so wishes. God is Aware, Wise. * Fight the ones among those who were given the Book who do not believe in God nor the Last Day, nor forbid whatever God and His messenger have forbidden, nor profess the True Religion, until they pay the polltax of their own accord and act submissive.

Fighting

30

(v) ** Jews say: "Ezra was God's son," while Christians say: "Christ was God's son." That is what they say with their mouths, imitating what those have said who disbelieved before them. May God fight them off for what they have trumped up! * They have adopted their scholars and monks as lords instead of God, plus Christ, the son of Mary. Yet they have been ordered to serve only God Alone; there is no deity except Him. Glory be to Him ahead of whatever they may associate [with Him]! * They want to blow out God's light with their mouths while God refuses [everything] except that His light must be perfected, no matter how disbelievers may hate it. * He is the One Who has sent His messenger with guidance and the True Religion so He may cause it to prevail over all [other] religion, no matter how associators may hate it.

God Has No Son

* You who believe, many [Jewish] scholars and [Christian] monks do consume people's wealth to no good purpose and they obstruct God's way. Announce painful torment to those who hoard gold and silver and do not spend them for God's sake. ** Some day [these metals] will be heated up in Hell fire, so their foreheads, sides and backs may be branded with it: "This is what you have hoarded up for yourselves, so taste what you have been hoarding!"

Clergy are Branded

* The number of months with God is twelve: [they were] in God's book on the day He created Heaven and Earth. Out of them, four are sacred; such is the established religion. Do not harm yourselves during them, yet fight associators to a finish, just as they fight you to a finish. Know that God stands by the heedful. * Postponing it will only [lead to] an increase in [their] disbelief: those who disbelieve are led astray by it; they permit it one year and ban it another year so they make up for any number that God has forbidden and (even) permit something God has forbidden. Their evil actions seem attractive to them, although God does not guide disbelieving folk.

The Hijra OR *Sacred Year*

(VI) * You who believe, what is wrong with you when you are told: "March off in God's cause!"? Do you feel weighted down to the ground? Are you more satisfied with worldly life than with the [prospect of the] Hereafter? The comfort of worldly life will mean so little in the Hereafter. * Unless you march away, He will punish you with painful torment and substitute you with some other folk. You will not harm Him in any way, for God is Capable of everything!

38

Draft Dodging

** If you do not support him, well God did support him when those who disbelieved expelled him as the second of two, when they were both in the Cave, as he told his companion: "Do not worry; for God is with us." So God sent His serenity down on him and aided him with troops you did not see, and placed the word of those who disbelieved lowest, while God's word remained supreme. God is Powerful, Wise.

40

* March forth light or heavy[-armed], and strive in God's cause with your property and persons. That will be best for you if you only realize it. * If there had been some goods to be acquired closer by and on a shorter journey, they would have followed you; but the expedition seemed much too far for them. They will swear by God; "If we could have managed to, we would have left along with you (all)." They destroy their own souls while God knows what liars they are!

(VII) * May God pardon you! Why did you permit them to do so before it was explained to you which ones were truthful so you might recognize the liars? * Those who believe in God and the Last Day do not ask you to excuse them from striving with their property and persons. God is Aware as to who are heedful. ** Only those who do not believe in God and the Last Day ask you to excuse them. Their hearts are in such doubt that they even waver in their doubt!

43

* If they had wanted to sally forth, they would have made some preparation for it; but God disliked their being delegated to do so, so He let them lag behind. They were told: "Sit around among the shirkers!" * Even if they had left with you, they would only have meant more turmoil for you; they would have galloped in among you and stirred up dissension for you. Among you there were some who would listen to them. God is Aware of those who do wrong. * They have already sown such dissension previously and upset matters for you until Truth came along and God's command prevailed no matter how they hated it.

Agitators

* Among them someone may say: "Leave me alone and do not stir me up." Have they not already fallen into dissension? Hell will engulf dis-

50

Charity

believers! ** If some fine thing happens to you, it bothers them, while if a misfortune happens to you, they say: "We already took our matter in hand previously." They stalk away rejoicing. * SAY: "Nothing will ever happen to us unless God has prescribed it." He is our Protector, and on God [Alone] should believers rely." * SAY: "Are you expecting only one out of two fine things for us, while we are expecting you to have God afflict you with torment from His very presence or at our hands? So wait around: we are waiting along with you."

* SAY: "Spend either willingly or unwillingly, it will never be accepted from you, since you have been such immoral folk.'' * The reason that prevents them from having their expenditures accepted from them is merely that they have disbelieved in God and His messenger and do not come to pray except when they are lazy, nor do they spend anything [on charity or taxes] unless they are reluctant. ** Do not let their wealth nor children astonish you; God only wants to punish them by means of them during worldly life and for their souls to perish while they are disbelievers. * They swear by God that they are with you while they do not stand with you, but are a folk who are easily scared off. * If they should find some refuge or some caverns, or an entrance they could creep into, they would bolt away!

* Some of them criticize you concerning the [distribution of] charity. If they are given some of it, they are pleased, while if they are not given any, why they act resentful. * If they had only been pleased with what God and His messenger have given them, and said: "God is our Reckoning. God and His messenger will give us something out of His bounty. We are beseeching [it] from God."

60

Charity (cont'd)

(VIII) ** Charity is [meant] only for the poor, the needy, those working at [collecting and distributing] it, those [possible converts] whose hearts are being reconciled [to yours], for freeing captives and debtors, and in [striving along] God's way, and for the wayfarer, as a duty imposed by God. God is Aware, Wise.

* There are some [people] who annoy the Prophet by saying: "He's (all) ears!" SAY: "[He's] an ear for good for you! He believes in God and believes for the believers' sake, and is a mercy for any of you who do believe." Those who annoy God's messenger will have painful torment. * They swear by God for you just to please you (all). It is more correct to please God and His messenger if they are [really] believers. * Do they not know that anyone who places any limits on God and His messenger will have Hell fire to remain in for ever? That will be an awful disgrace!

Hypocrites

Turncoats

* Hypocrites act anxious lest a chapter be sent down for them to notify them as to what is in their hearts. SAY: "Joke away: God will produce what you are so anxious about." ** If you question them, they say: "We have only been toying (with words) and playing around." SAY: "Have you been joking about God, and His signs and His messenger?" * Make no excuses! You have disbelieved following your profession of faith. If We should pardon one faction of you, We will still punish another faction since they have been such criminals.

(IX) * Hypocrites, whether men or women, resemble one another: they command wickedness, forbid decency, and clench their fists. They have forgotten God, so He has forgotten them. Hypocrites are so immoral! * God has promised hypocrites, whether they are men or women, as well as [outright] disbelievers, Hell fire to live in for ever: it will be their reckoning. God has cursed them, and they will have constant torment.

* Just as those before them were firmer than you are in strength, and possessed more wealth and children, and they exploited their advantage, even so have you sought to enjoy your opportunity, just as those who came before you enjoyed their advantage. You have talked a lot just as they have talked on and on. Yet those [will find] their actions will miscarry in this world and the Hereafter; those will be the losers! ** Has not the story come to them about those who preceded them, Noah's folk, and ʿĀd's and Thamūd's, and Abraham's folk and the inhabitants of Midian and the Overthrown [Towns]? Their messengers brought them clear explanations; it was not God Who injured them, but they themselves who inflicted the injury.

* Believers, whether men or women, must [act as] friends to one another; they should command decency and forbid wickedness, keep up prayer, and pay the welfare tax as well as obey God and His messenger. Those God will grant mercy to; God is Powerful, Wise! * God has promised believers, whether they are men or women, gardens through which rivers flow to live in for ever, and goodly dwellings in the gardens of Eden. Yet approval by God is greatest; that will be the supreme Achievement!

(X) * O Prophet, struggle with disbelievers and hypocrites; deal harshly with them: their lodging will be Hell, and how awful is such a destination! * They swear by God they have said nothing while they did pronounce the word of disbelief; they disbelieve after their commitment to [live in] peace; and worry over what they do not accomplish. How spitefully they act merely because God and His messenger have enriched them out of His bounty. If they should **repent**, it would be better for them; while if they turn back again, God will punish them with painful torment in this world and the Hereafter. They will have no sponsor nor any supporter on earth.

** Some of them have pledged to God: "If He gives us some of His bounty, we will act charitably and be loyal." * Yet whenever He has given them some of His bounty, they have acted miserably with it: they turn away and become evasive; * so He planted hypocrisy in their hearts till the day when they will meet Him because they broke their word to God which they had promised Him and for how they had been lying.

* Do they not realize that God knows their secrets and their intrigue, and that God is the Knower of Unseen things? * May God scoff at those who criticize such believers as dedicate themselves to charitable works and those who do not find anything [to offer] except their own effort, so they scoff at them too. They will have painful torment. ** Seek forgiveness for them or else do not seek forgiveness for them; even if you sought forgiveness for them seventy times over, God would never pardon them. That is because they disbelieve in God and His messenger. God does not guide immoral folk.

67

70

73

80

81

*Shirkers
Again*

(XI) * Those who were left behind are delighted to sit around inactive behind God's messenger, and they hate to struggle in God's way with their property and persons. They say: "Don't march off in such heat!" SAY: "Hell fire will be even hotter," if they could only understand.

* Let them laugh a little and weep a lot as a reward for what they have been earning. * If God should send you back to a faction of them, and they should ask you for permission to sally forth, SAY: "You will never march forth with me, nor fight any enemy alongside me! You were satisfied to sit around inactive in the first instance, so sit around [now] with the stay-behinds."

* Never pray over any of them who dies nor stand at his graveside; they have disbelieved in God and His messenger, and died while they were rebellious. ** Do not let their wealth and children astonish you; God only wants to punish them by means of them during this world, and let their souls perish while they are disbelievers.

* Whenever a chapter is sent down saying: "Believe in God and struggle alongside His messenger," influential persons among them ask you to exempt them and say [instead]: "Let us stay with those who are just sitting around." * They are so pleased to be among the stay-behinds. It is stamped on their hearts so they do not understand; * but the Messenger and those who believe along with him, do struggle with their property and persons. Those will have even better things; such will be successful! * God has prepared gardens through which rivers will flow for them to live in for ever; that will be the supreme Achievement!

90

Nomads

(XII) ** Excuse-makers have come from the desert Arabs to beg off for them. Those who tell lies before God and His messenger have merely sat around (at home). Painful torment will afflict those of them who disbelieve.
* Yet it will not be held against the helpless nor the sick, nor those who cannot find anything to spend [on God's cause], provided they act sincerely towards God and His messenger; there is no way [open] against those who act kindly since God is Forgiving, Merciful. * Nor [will it be held] against those whom you told, when they came for you to transport them: "I do not find any means of transporting you." They turned away, and their eyes were welling up with tears from sadness since they could not find any way to provide for their expenses. * A way is [open] only against those who beg you to exempt them while they are rich; they are satisfied to be [numbered] among those who stay behind. God has placed a stamp on their hearts while they do not realize it.

**PART
ELEVEN**

94

(XII cont'd) * They will apologize to you when you (all) return to them. SAY: "Don't apologize; we will never believe you! God has already notified us concerning everything about you. God and His messenger will see how you act; then you will be sent back to the Knower of the Unseen and the Visible, and He will notify you about whatever you have been doing."

** They will swear [anything] to you by God when you go back home to them, provided you will overlook them. Overlook them anyhow: they are a blight and their lodging will be Hell as a compensation for what they have been earning. * They swear to you so you will (all) feel satisfied with them. Even if you should approve of them, God is still not pleased with such immoral folk. * Desert Arabs are quite stubborn when it comes to disbelief and hypocrisy, and the least inclined to acknowledge the limits that God has revealed to His messenger; yet God is Aware, Wise. * Some desert tribesmen assume that anything they spend [in taxes] is a fine, and they try to catch you in some reverses. On them will fall the worst reverse! God is Alert, Aware.

* Still other desert Arabs believe in God and the Last Day, and consider anything that is spent as a means of access to God and the Messenger's prayers. Yet are they indeed not such an access for them? God will admit them into His mercy; God is Forgiving, Merciful!

(xiii) *** Pioneers comprise the first Migrants and Supporters, as well as those who have adhered to them by showing any kindness. God is pleased with them, while they are pleased with Him; He has prepared gardens through which rivers flow for them to remain in for ever. That will mean the supreme Achievement!

* Some desert Arabs around you are hypocrites as well as some of the people from Madīna; they even persist in hypocrisy. You do not know them; however We know them. We shall punish them twice; then they will be handed over to terrible torment.

* Others have acknowledged their offences. They have mixed up an honorable action with another evil one. Perhaps God will relent towards them; for God is Forgiving, Merciful. * Accept charity out of their wealth; you will cleanse and purify them by means of it. Pray for them; your prayers will mean relief for them. God is Alert, Aware. * Do they not know that it is God Who receives **Repentance** from His servants and accepts such acts of charity, and that God is the Ever-Turning, the Merciful?

** SAY: "Work away; God will see your labor, and so will His messenger and believers. You will be brought back to the Knower of the Unseen and the Visible, and He will notify you about how well you have been working." * Others are still expecting [to receive] God's command, [and to see] whether He will punish them or relent towards them. God is Aware, Wise.

* Those who adopt a mosque for [working] mischief and disbelief, as well as disunion among believers and as an outpost for anyone who has already warred on God and His messenger, will swear: "We only wanted to be kind!" God witnesses what sort of liars they are. * Never stand in it! It is more fitting for you to stand in a mosque which has been founded on performing one's duty from the very first day in which there are men who love to be purified. God loves those who cleanse themselves.

* Is someone who founds his building on heeding and pleasing God better, or someone who founds his building along the edge of a

100

*Always
Build
Firmly*

110

crumbling bluff, so it crumbles along with him into Hell fire? God does not guide such wrongful folk: ** the building which they have built is continually in doubt within their hearts, till their hearts are torn to pieces. God is Aware, Wise!

111

The Believers' Reward

(XIV) * God has bought up their persons and their property from believers, so they may have the Garden [instead]. **They fight for God's sake; they kill and are killed as a rightful promise from Him** [to be found] in the Old Testament, the Gospel and the Qurɔān. Who is more Trustworthy with His word than God? So rejoice in your bargain which you have reached with Him. That will be the supreme Achievement * [for] those who **repent**, worship, praise [God], observe fasting, bow their heads and knees [in prayer], those who command decency, forbid wickedness, and keep within God's limits; spread such news to believers. * It is not proper for the Prophet and those who believe to seek forgiveness for associators, even though they are close relatives, once it has been explained to them how they will become the inmates of Hades.

* Abraham pleaded for forgiveness on behalf of his father only because of a promise he had made to him. When it became clear to him that he was God's enemy, he declared his innocence of him. Abraham was concerned, lenient. ** God is not apt to let any folk go astray once He has guided them to the point where He explains to them how they should do their duty. God is Aware of everything. * God holds control over Heaven and Earth. He both grants life and brings death, while you (all) have no patron nor any supporter besides Him.

* God has relented towards the Prophet, and the Refugees and Supporters who followed him in the hour of hardship, after the hearts of a group of them had almost faltered; then He turned towards them, for He is Compassionate, Merciful, with them. * As for the three who were left behind, until the earth seemed too cramped for them, spacious though it is, and even their souls seemed to strangle them and they thought there would be no refuge from God except through Himself; then He **relented** towards them so they might **repent**. God is **Ever-Turning**, Merciful.

119
120

(XV) * You who believe, heed God and stand by those who are truthful. ** It is not for the people of Madīna nor any desert Arabs who (live) around them, to lag behind God's messenger nor to prefer themselves ahead of himself. That is so no thirst would afflict them, nor any stress nor starvation along God's way, nor would they adopt any stand which would irritate disbelievers, nor gain any acquisition from an enemy, unless some honorable action were recorded for them because of it.

God does not waste the wages of those who act kindly. * They could not provide for any outlay small or great, nor cut across a valley unless it were prescribed for them, so that God may reward them for the finest things they have been doing. * Believers should not march forth in a body; if a squadron from each division of them should march forth, they should still instruct [others] in religion and warn their folk when they return to them so that they may take precautions.

(XVI) * You who believe, fight any disbelievers who hem you in so they may find out how tough you are. Know that God stands by the heedful. * Whenever a chapter is sent down, some of them say: "Which of you has this increased in faith?" Well, it increases those who believe in faith and so they rejoice. ** As for those whose hearts contain malice, well it adds squalor to their own squalor. They will die while they are (still) disbelievers.

* Do they not see how they are being tested once or twice each year? Yet they neither **repent** nor do they remember. * Whenever a chapter is sent down, some of them look at one another [as if to say]: "Is anyone watching you?" Then they slip away. God has slipped their hearts away since they are a folk who do not comprehend.

* A Messenger has come to you from among yourselves; he takes it seriously how you have come to grief, is anxious about you, compassionate, merciful towards believers.

* If they should turn away, then SAY:

"God is enough for me!
There is no deity except Him;
on Him do I rely.
He is Lord of the mighty Throne!"

IO
Jonah

THIS CHAPTER was revealed after **Eventide** 103 and before **Hūd [the Messenger]** 11 which immediately follows it. It is the first of a group of five chapters which all begin with the initials "A. L. R." (10, 11, 12, 14, 15), just as the second and third chapters and the 29th to the 32nd begin with "A. L. M." Chapter 13 has the combination "A. L. M. R."

This consists of 109 late Meccan verses arranged in eleven sections; except for vv. 40, 49, 59 and 96 which date from Madīna. It begins with a description of how the world was created. The prophet Jonah is mentioned only in section X; a fuller story of the prophet Jonah is actually given in 37:V, and he is mentioned again in 21:VI and 68:II. There is a close connection with the previous chapter, 9, because this one rounds off its contents and shows how God's mercy predominates.

The sin of Association is taken up in Sections II, III and XI; rain from Heaven in III; the Qurɔān in IV; personal responsibility, and the different nations in V; and freewill and tolerance in X. The chapter also is concerned with Truth (III, IV, VIII, XI). At the end of Section VII we are told emphatically that God has no son. Noah and Moses are other prophets who are discussed in VIII.

In the name of God, the Mercy-giving, the Merciful!

(I) * A. L. R.

These are verses from the Wise Book. * Does it seem astonishing to mankind that We should inspire a man from among themselves: "Warn mankind, and spread news to those who believe that they are on a sound footing with their Lord"? Disbelievers say: "This is an obvious magician."

Creation OR *Cosmogony*

* Your Lord is God [Alone], Who created Heaven and Earth in six days. Then He ascended the Throne to regulate the matter. There is no intercessor until He gives permission [for it]. Such is God, your Lord, so worship Him. Will you not reflect? * To Him will you all return. God's promise is true; He begins with creation then performs it all over again so He may reward those who believe and perform honorable deeds in (all) fairness. Those who disbelieve will have scalding water to drink and painful torment because they have been disbelieving.

** He it is Who has placed the sun for radiance and the moon for (reflected) light, and measured it out in phases so you may know how to count out the years and [to make other such] reckoning. God did not create that except for the Truth. He spells out signs for folk who know.

* In the alternation between night and daytime, and whatever God has created in Heaven and Earth, there are signs for folk who heed.

* Those who do not expect to meet Us and are pleased with worldly life, and feel at ease about it, as well as those who are heedless of Our signs * will find their lodging in the Fire because of what they have been earning. * Their Lord guides those who believe and perform honorable deeds according to their faith: rivers will flow beneath them in gardens of delight; ** their cry in it will be:

"Glory be to You, O God!",
while their greeting in it will be:
"Peace!",
and the close of their appeal:
"Praise be to God, Lord of the Universe!"

10

(II) * If God were to hasten up evil for mankind just as they seek to hasten good, then their deadline would have been decreed for them. We leave those who do not hope to meet Us groping along in their arrogance. * Whenever any trouble touches man, he appeals to Us while [lying] on his side, seated, or standing; yet when We remove his trouble from him, he walks away as if he had never appealed to Us (at all) because of the trouble which had afflicted him. Thus anything they have been doing seems attractive to the dissipated. * We have destroyed generations before you when they did wrong and their messengers had brought them explanations, and they would still not believe. Thus We reward criminal folk. * Then We placed you as overlords on earth after them, so We might see how you would act.

** When Our clear signs are recited to those who do not expect to meet Us, they say: "Bring some other Reading than this, or else change it!" SAY: "It is not up to me to change it of my own accord, because of whatever I may encounter in it on my own. I merely follow what is inspired in me. I fear torment on an awful day if I should disobey my Lord!" * SAY: "If God had so wished, I would not have recited it to you nor advised you about it. I lived for a lifetime among you before [receiving] it. So will you not use your reason?" * Who is more in the wrong than someone who invents a lie about God or rejects His signs? It is a fact that criminals will not succeed!

* Instead of God they serve what neither harms nor benefits them, and they say: "These are our intercessors with God." SAY: "Do you [presume to] notify God about something in Heaven and on Earth that He already does not know? Glory be to Him; Exalted is He over whatever they associate [with Him]!"

* Mankind was once just one nation; then they disagreed. If word had not come on ahead from your Lord, what they had been disagreeing over would have been settled for them. ** They say: "If a sign were only sent down by his Lord for him!"; so SAY: "The Unseen belongs only to God, so wait: I am waiting alongside you."

11

The Arrogant

*Facing
Trouble*

Skeptics

*Association
as a Sin*

20

21

(III) * Whenever We let mankind taste mercy after some adversity has afflicted them, why they cook up some scheme about Our signs! SAY: "God is much Swifter in scheming." Our messengers write down whatever they are plotting.

* He is the One Who sends you travelling along on land and at sea until when you are on board a ship, and sailing along under a fair wind and they feel happy about it, a stormy wind comes upon them and waves reach at them from all sides and they think they are being surrounded by them. They appeal to God sincerely, [offering their] religion to Him: "If You will save us from this, we will be grateful!"

* Yet once He has saved them, why they act wilfully on earth without any right to [do so]. Mankind, your wilfulness falls only on yourselves to be enjoyed during worldly life; then to Us will be your return, and We will notify you (all) about whatever you have been doing!

Rain from Heaven

* **Worldly life** may be compared to water We send down from the sky. It mingles with the plants of the earth on which mankind and livestock feed until, when the earth takes on its trimmings and looks attractive, and its people think that they will be able to use them as they like, Our command comes along to it by night or daytime, and We mow it down ahead of time just as though it had not been so lush the day before. Thus We spell out signs for folk who will think things over.

The Final Judgment

** God invites [us] to the Home of Peace, and guides anyone He wishes to, to a Straight Road. * Those who act kindly will have kindness and even more besides, while neither soot nor any disgrace will line their faces. Those will be inhabitants of the Garden; they will live in it for ever. * Those who have acquired evil deeds will have an evil reward similar to them. Disgrace will overshadow them; they will have no defender from God, just as if their faces had been covered with a strip of darkest night. Those will become inmates of the Fire; they will live there for ever.

Associates Will Renounce Their Own Worship

30

* Some day We will summon them all together; then We shall tell those who have associated [others in Our worship]; "[Keep to] your place, you and your associates!" We will sort them out, and their associates will say: "You did not worship us! * God suffices as a Witness between us and you. We were unaware that you were even worshipping us." ** There each soul will be tested for whatever it has sent on ahead in the past, and they will be handed over to God, their rightful Patron. Anything they have invented will leave them in the lurch.

31

God Alone

(IV) * SAY: "Who provides for you out of Heaven and Earth? Who controls hearing and eyesight? Who brings the living forth from the dead, and brings the dead forth from the living? Who regulates the affair?"

They will say: "God [Alone]" so SAY: "Will you not then do your duty?"
* Such is God, your rightful Lord!

What exists except error after Truth, so why do you disregard it? * Thus your Lord's word proves itself to be true with those who act

Truth

immorally. They do not believe. * SAY: "Has any of your associates ever attempted to create anything, then repeated it?" SAY: "God begins with creation; then performs it (all over again). How is it that you shrug it off?'' ** SAY: "Does any of your partners guide one to Truth?" SAY: "God guides to Truth. So is someone who guides to Truth worthier to be followed than someone who does not guide unless he himself is guided? What is the matter with you? How do you decide things?"

    * Most of them merely follow conjecture.
    However **guessing is no substitute for Truth**.
    God is Aware of whatever they are doing.

* This Reading was not invented by anyone except God; but [it exists] as a confirmation from the Lord of the Universe for what He already has and [serves] as an analysis of the Book which contains no doubt. * Or do they say: "He has made it up!"? SAY: **"Produce a chapter like it,** and appeal to anyone you can manage to besides God if you are so truthful."

The Qur'ān

    * Instead they reject what they cannot grasp any knowledge about, [especially] when its interpretation has never come to them. Likewise those before them rejected [it]; so watch how the outcome will be for wrong-doers! ** Some of them believe in it while others do not believe in it. Your Lord is quite Aware as to who are corrupt.

40

    (v) * If they should reject you, then SAY: "My behavior is my own concern, while your behavior is your concern. You are innocent of anything I do, while I am innocent of what you are doing."

41

*Personal
Responsibility*

* Some of them however do listen to you. Yet can you make the deaf hear, even though they do not use their reason? * Others of them will look towards you. Yet will you guide the blind, no matter how they do not see? * God does not harm mankind in any way, but men do harm themselves. ** Some day He will summon them; it will be as if they had merely been hanging around for an hour during daylight. They will recognize one another. Those who have denied they will meet God will lose out and never be guided. * Whether We show you some of what We have promised them or let you pass away [instead], to Us is their return; moreover God will be a Witness for whatever they have been doing.

    * Every nation has a messenger. Once their messenger has come, judgment will be passed upon them in all fairness and they will not be wronged. * They will say: "When will this promise be, if you have been so truthful?" * SAY: "I control no harm nor any advantage by myself, except concerning whatever God may wish.

Nations

    Each nation has a deadline: whenever their deadline comes, they will not postpone it for an hour nor will they advance it.

** SAY: "Have you considered whether His torment will come to you (all) at dead of night or by daylight? What part of it will criminals try to hurry up? * Yet now when it is happening, will you believe in it? Still you were just trying to hurry it on!"

50

    * Then those who have done wrong will be told: "Taste the torment of eternity. Have you not been rewarded merely with something you have earned?" * They will enquire from you: "Is it true?" SAY: "Indeed, by my Lord, it is true! You cannot avert it."

54

(VI) * Even though each person who has done something wrong had everything on earth, he would still try to ransom himself with it. They will conceal regret once they see the torment. Judgment will be passed upon them in all fairness, and they will not be wronged. ** Does God not possess whatever is in Heaven and Earth? Is not God's promise true? Yet most of them do not realize it. * He gives life and brings about death, and to Him will you (all) return.

* O mankind, instruction has been given you by your Lord, and healing for whatever is in your breasts, plus guidance and mercy for believers. * SAY: "In God's bounty and mercy, therein let them rejoice. It is better than what they are collecting." * SAY: "Have you considered what sort of sustenance God has sent down to you, and what you have been forbidden and permitted?" SAY: "Has God allowed you it or are you inventing something about God?" ** What will be the thought of those who invent a lie about God, on Resurrection Day? God possesses bounty for mankind, yet most of them are not grateful.

60

61

(VII) * No matter what business you may be engaged in as well as whatever you may quote from any reading, you (all) do not perform any action unless We act as Witness for you when you are occupied with it. No atom's weight escapes your Lord on Earth nor in Heaven, nor anything smaller than that nor larger, unless it is [recorded] in a plain Book. * God's adherents should have no fear nor need they worry. * Those who believe and have done their duty * will have good news concerning worldly life as well as about the Hereafter. There is no way to alter God's words; that will be the supreme Achievement.

** Do not let their talk sadden you; prestige rests entirely with God. He is the Alert, Aware. * Does not anyone in Heaven and anyone on Earth belong to God? What do those follow, who appeal to associates instead of to God? They merely follow conjecture and they are only guessing. * He is the One Who has granted you night to settle down in, and daylight to see your way around. In that are signs for folk who listen.

*God Needs
No Son*

* They say: "God has adopted a son." Glory be to Him! He is Transcendent. He holds whatever is in Heaven and whatever is on Earth!

Do you have any authority for this? Are you saying something you do not know about God? * SAY: "Those who invent such a lie about God will not prosper." ** Enjoyment is [meant] for this world; then to Us will be their return. Then We will let them taste severe torment because of how they have disbelieved.

70

71

Noah

(VIII) * Quote Noah's story to them when he told his people: "My people, if my staying around here bothers you and my reminding you about God's signs, well I rely on God, so make your designs on me and those you have associated [with God]; then do not let your business seem so gloomy. Next decide about me, and do not put me off. * So should you turn away, I have not asked you for any payment; my payment comes only from God, and I have been ordered to become a Muslim."

* Yet they still rejected him, so We saved him and whoever was in the Ark along with him. We set them up as survivors and drowned those who

had rejected Our signs. Watch how the outcome will be for those who were warned!

* Then We despatched messengers to their people later on, and they brought explanations with them. Still they were not going to believe in something they had already rejected; thus We seal off the hearts of the defiant.

** Next We sent Moses and Aaron after them with Our signs for Pharaoh and his councillors. Yet they acted proudly and were criminal folk. * When Truth came to them from Our very presence, they said: "This is sheer magic!" * Moses said: "Do you say about Truth when it has come to you: 'Is this magic?' Magicians never prosper." * They said: "Have you come to us to turn us away from what we found our forefathers doing? And so greatness on earth may belong to both of you? We do not believe in either of you." * Pharaoh said: "Bring me every cunning magician!"

Moses and Aaron

** When the magicians came, Moses told them: "Cast whatever you are going to cast." * When they cast [it], Moses said: "What you have produced is magic. God will cancel it out; God does not promote the work of mischief-makers. * God verifies the Truth through His own words no matter how criminals may hate it."

80

The Tournament of Magic

(IX) * Only some offspring among his own folk believed in Moses because of fear for Pharaoh and his councillors, lest he might put them to some test. Pharaoh was so haughty on earth and besides he was a dissipated man. * Moses said: "My people, if you believe in God, then rely on Him if you are Muslims." ** They said: "On God do we rely. Our Lord, do not turn us into a trial for wrongdoing folk! * Save us through Your mercy from such disbelieving folk!"

83

* So We inspired Moses and his brother [as follows]: "Settle your people down in houses in Egypt and turn your houses into shrines; keep up prayer and announce good news to believers." * Moses said: "Our Lord, You have given Pharaoh and his councillors splendor and wealth during worldly life. Our Lord, is it so they may lead [us] off from Your way? Our Lord, wipe out their wealth and firm up their hearts so they may not believe until they see painful torment." * He said: "Your appeal has been answered, so act straightforward and do not follow along the way of those who do not know."

** So We brought the Children of Israel across the sea. Pharaoh and his armies had them followed in hot pursuit and fought [them] off until, as drowning overtook him, he said: "I believe that there is no deity except the One Whom the Children of Israel believe in. I am [now] a Muslim."

90

* Now, you had disobeyed before and been a mischief-maker! * However today We will preserve you in your body so you may be a sign to anyone who comes after you. Yet many people are quite heedless of Our signs.

(X) * We settled the Children of Israel in a respectable dwelling and provided them with wholesome things. They did not disagree until knowledge came to them. Your Lord will decide among them on Resurrection Day concerning whatever they have been disagreeing about.

93

Freewill

* If you are in any doubt concerning what We have sent down to you, then question those who have read the Book before you: Truth has come to you from your Lord, so do not be a waverer; ** do not be someone who rejects God's signs, so you [turn out to] be a loser. * Those against whom your Lord's word has been confirmed will never believe * until they see painful torment, even though every sign should be brought them. * If only there had been a town which believed and whose faith had benefited it besides **Jonah's** people. Once they believed, We lifted the torment of shame from them during worldly life and let them enjoy things for a while. * If your Lord had so wished, everyone on earth would have believed, all of them together!

100

Tolerance

So will you force mankind to become believers? *** It is not up to any soul to believe unless it [happens] with God's permission; He places a blight on those who do not use their reason. * SAY: Look at whatever [exists] in Heaven and Earth.'' Signs and warning do not benefit any people who do not believe.

* Do they expect anything except days like the ones which happened to those who passed away before them? SAY: "So wait; I am one of those waiting alongside you." * Then We will save Our messengers and those who believe; it is thus right for Us to save believers!

104

God's Role Explained

(XI) * SAY: "Mankind, if you are in any doubt concerning my religion, well, I do not serve those whom you serve instead of God but rather I worship God [Alone], Who will gather you (all) in. I am commanded to be a believer: ** 'Keep your face set towards religion, seeking [God] righteously and do not be an associator * nor appeal to something that will neither benefit nor harm you, instead of to God [Alone]. If you should do so, you would then be a wrongdoer.' * If God should afflict you with any trouble, there is no one to remove it except Him, while if He wants some good for you, there is no one who can spurn His bounty; He strikes any of His servants He wants to with it. He is the Forgiving, the Merciful!"

* SAY: "Mankind, Truth has come to you from your Lord! Anyone who accepts guidance is guided only for his own sake; while anyone who strays away, will only become lost at his own risk. I am no custodian set up over you."

* Follow whatever has been inspired in you and be patient until God judges, for He is the best Judge.

11
Hūd
[*the Messenger*]

THIS CHAPTER contains 123 late Meccan verses, except for vv. 12, 17 and 114, which date from Madīna. They are arranged in ten sections. The chapter was revealed after the previous one on **Jonah** 10 and is thus the second in the A.L.R. series; it likewise precedes the next one on **Joseph** 12.

Hūd was an ancient prophet who was sent to the nation of ʿĀd which lived in southern Arabia along the Indian Ocean. His story begins at v. 50 in section v, following that of Noah (III-IV). The chapter also mentions two other Arabian prophets at length, Shuʿayb (VIII) and Ṣāliḥ (OR Methusaleh in Genesis 5:25-27 in the Old Testament) (VI); and then Abraham (VII), Lot (VII) and Moses (IX).

A quality of 'Mercy,' God's essential *raḥma*, flows through this chapter as each prophet's message to his own people comes up in turn (II, III, V, VI, VIII). These parallel stories which contrast the Arabian prophets with the strictly Biblical or Hebrew ones show us they are meant to be analogies. A picture of the Day of Judgment comes at the end of section IX.

In the name of God, the Mercy-giving, the Merciful!

(I) * A.L.R.

[This is] a Book whose verses are decisive, and have been set forth in detail in the presence of Someone [Who is] Wise, Informed * so that you will serve only God [Alone]: "I am a warner, a herald from Him to you;" * and so you will seek forgiveness from your Lord; then turn towards Him [in repentance]. He will let you enjoy a handsome allotment for a specific period, and grant His bounty to everyone possessing bounty. If you should turn away, then I fear the torment of a great day for you. * Unto God is your return; He is Capable of everything!

** Indeed they wrap their breasts up to try to hide things from Him. Whenever they attempt to cover themselves up with their clothing, does He not know whatever they conceal and what they disclose? He is Aware of whatever [their] breasts contain.

PART
TWELVE

6

(I, cont'd) * No animal exists on earth unless God provides for it. He knows its lair and its burrow; everything is [to be found] in a clear Book. * He is the One Who created Heaven and Earth in six days. His Throne rises over the water, so He may test which of you is finest in action. If you should say: "You will (all) be raised up after death," those who disbelieve would say: "This is just sheer magic!" * If We postponed torment for them till a period to be counted out, they would say: "What is delaying it?" On the day when it comes to them, there will be no means for them to dodge it, while whatever they had been sneering at will sweep in around them.

9
10

*Building
Character*

(II) * If We ever let man taste any mercy from Us, then snatched it away from him, he would become despondent, ungrateful. ** Yet if We let him taste favor after some hardship has afflicted him, he says: "Evil things have departed from me!" He is so cheerful, boastful, * except for the ones who act patiently and perform honorable deeds; those will have forgiveness and a big wage. * Perhaps you are abandoning something that has been inspired in you, and your breast is feeling cramped because of it, since they say: "Why has not a treasure been sent down to him, or some angel come along with him?": You are only a warner, while God is a Trustee for everything.

* Or do they say: "He has made it all up!" SAY: "Well then bring chapters made up like it! Appeal to anyone you can manage to instead of to God if you are so truthful. * If they do not respond to you, then know it has only been sent down with God's knowledge. There is no deity except Him. Will you not become Muslims?"

15

** We shall repay anyone who has been wanting worldly life and its attraction according to their actions in it; they will not be caught short there. * Yet those will have only the Fire during the Hereafter while anything they have been producing in it will collapse and whatever they have been doing will [prove to] be useless.

* What about someone who has [received] an explanation from his Lord and to whom a witness from Him is reciting while Moses' book lies before him as a token and a mercy? Such persons believe in it. Anyone from the factions who disbelieve in it will have the Fire for his appointment, so do not be in any quandary about it; it is the Truth from your Lord, even though most men do not believe so.

* Who is more in the wrong than someone who invents a lie about God? Those will be turned over to their Lord and witnesses will say: "These are the ones who have lied about their Lord!" Does not God's curse rest on wrongdoers, * those who obstruct God's way and attempt to make it crooked, and are disbelievers in the Hereafter? ** Those will not prevent anything from happening on earth nor will they have any patrons besides God. Torment will be doubled for them. They have not been enabled to hear nor have they been observing [anything]. * Such are the ones who

20

have lost their own souls, while whatever they were inventing has led them astray. * It is positive they will lose most in the Hereafter!

* Those who believe, perform honorable deeds, and yield unto their Lord, will become inhabitants of the Garden; they will live in it for ever. * Both groups can be compared to a blind and dumb man, alongside a sighted and hearing one. Are they alike for the purpose of comparison? Will you not bear this in mind?

(III) ** We sent Noah to his folk: "I am a plain warner for you, * so that you may worship nobody except God [Alone]. I fear the torment of a painful day for you!"

25

Noah

* The notables from among his own people who disbelieved said: "We regard you only as a human being like ourselves. We do not see that anyone follows you except those who are the meanest among us, who are just beginning to form opinions. We do not consider that you (all) have any advantage over us; rather we think you are lying.

* He said: "My people, have you considered whether I have [brought] any explanation from my Lord? He has sent me mercy from His presence, although it has been disguised so far as you are concerned. Shall we compel you to [accept] it while you dislike it? * And my folk, I do not ask you for any money for it; my wages come only from God. Nor am I driving away those who believe: they will be meeting their Lord [anyhow]. Yet I do see you are a folk who act out of ignorance. ** My people, who will support me against God if I should drive them off? Will you not bear this in mind?

30

* "I do not tell you that I hold God's treasures, nor do I know the Unseen nor say I am an angel, nor do I tell those whom you eye with contempt that God will not give them anything good. God is quite Aware of what lies in their souls. I should then be a wrongdoer."

* They said: "Noah, you have pleaded with us, and kept on pleading with us. Bring us whatever you threaten us with if you are so truthful!" * He said: "Only God will bring you it, if He so wishes. You will not prevent it. * My advice will not benefit you no matter how sincerely I want to advise you, should God be wanting to let you wander off. He is your Lord and to Him will you (all) return."

** Or do they say: "He has invented it!"? SAY: "If I have invented it, then my crime rests on myself; while I am innocent of any crimes you may be committing."

(IV) * It was revealed to Noah that: "None of your folk will ever believe except for someone who has already believed. Do not despair about what they have been doing. * Build the Ark under Our eyes and Our inspiration. Do not preach to me about those who have done wrong; they will be drowned."

36

* As he was building the Ark, each time any gentlemen from his own people passed by him, they would sneer at him. He said: "If you ridicule us, then we'll ridicule you just the way you are sneering. You will come to know who will be given torment which will shame him, and have lasting torment settle down upon him."

40

** So when Our command came and the bowels (of the earth) welled up, We said: "Load her up with two apiece from every species, and your own family—except for anyone against whom the Sentence has already been pronounced—as well as anyone who believes." Yet only a few believed along with him.

Noah's Embarkation Prayer

He said: "Board her:

**"In the name of God
is her sailing and her mooring;
my Lord is so Forgiving, Merciful!"**

* She sailed on with them through waves that were like mountains. Noah called out to his son who stood aloof by himself: "My dear son, sail away with us, and do not stay with the disbelievers." * He said: "I'll take refuge on a mountain which will protect me from the water." He said: "Nothing is safe today from God's command except for someone who has been shown mercy." A wave swept in between them so he was one of those who were drowned.

* It was said: "Earth, swallow your water!", and: "Sky, clear up!" So the water receded, the Command was accomplished, and she settled down on [Mt.] Jūdi.

* It was (also) said: "Away with such wrongdoing folk!" ** Noah called upon his Lord and said: "My Lord, my son belonged to my own family, while Your promise is true, and You are the wisest Judge!" * He said: "Noah, he no longer belongs to your family: his behavior was dishonorable. Do not ask Me about something you have no knowledge about; I so caution you lest you become ignorant." * He said: "My Lord, I take refuge with You from asking You something I have no knowledge about. If You do not forgive me and show me mercy, I may become a loser."

* It was said: "Noah, land in peace from Us; blessings will [rest] on you and on some of the nations who [will spring] from you. We shall let some [other] communities enjoy themselves; then painful torment from Us will afflict them."

The Unseen

* This is some of the news about the Unseen which We reveal to you. Neither you nor your people knew them before this, so be patient. The outcome belongs to those who do their duty.

50

Hūd Himself

(v) ** To ʿĀd [we sent] their brother **Hūd**. He said: "My people, worship God [Alone]! You have no other deity except Him. Otherwise you are only making things up. * My folk, I ask you for no payment for it: my wage comes only from the One Who fashioned me. Will you not reason [things out]? * My folk, seek forgiveness from your Lord, then turn to Him [repentant]. He will send the heavens down upon you in torrents and add strength to you even beyond your own strength. Do not turn away like criminals.

* They said: "**Hūd**, you have not brought us any explanation, nor are we apt to leave our gods merely on your say-so. We are no believers in you; * we only say: 'Some of our gods have stricken you with evil.'" He said: "I take God as a witness, and bear witness yourselves that I am inno-

cent of what you associate with ** instead of Him. Plot away all together against me; then do not keep me waiting! * I have relied on God, [Who is both] my Lord and your Lord. There is no animal which He does not grasp by its forelock. My Lord is on a Straight Road. * Even if you should turn away, I have still delivered to you what I have been sent to you with. My Lord will replace you with some other people than yourselves, while you will not harm Him in any way. My Lord acts as a Keeper over everything.

* Once Our command came, We rescued **Hūd** as well as those who believed along with him through mercy from Ourself; We saved them from stern torment. * Such [people] were ‹Ād: they repudiated their Lord's signs, defied their messengers, and followed the command of every stubborn oppressor. ** They were followed by a curse in this world as well as on Resurrection Day. Did not ‹Ād disown their Lord? Well, it meant: "Away with ‹Ād, **Hūd**'s folk!"

60

(vi) * To Thamūd [We sent] their brother Ṣāliḥ. He said: "My people, worship God; you have no deity besides Him. He has produced you from the earth and let you settle down on it, so seek forgiveness from Him. Then turn to Him; my Lord is Near, Responsive." * They said: "Ṣāliḥ, you have been a source of expectation among us until now. Do you prohibit us from serving what our fathers worshipped? We feel suspicious doubt about what you are appealing for us to do."

61

Ṣāliḥ

* He said: "My folk, have you considered whether I bring any explanation from my Lord? He has given me mercy from Himself. Who will support me against God if I were to disobey Him? You would only make me lose even more.

* "My people, this she-camel belonging to God is a sign for you. Let her pasture on God's earth and do not hurt her in any way lest some torment should overtake you from near at hand." ** Still they mistreated her, so he said: "Enjoy yourselves in your homes for three days [more]! That is a promise which will never be repudiated."

* Once Our command came along, We saved Ṣāliḥ and those who believed along with him from the disgrace of that day through mercy from Ourself. Your Lord is the Strong, the Powerful. * The Blast caught those who had been doing wrong, so one morning they lay cowering in their homes. * It was just as if they had never prospered there. Had not Thamūd disbelieved in their Lord? Was it not: "Away with Thamūd!"?

(vii) * Our messengers came to Abraham with good news. They said: "Peace!"; he said: "Peace!", and immediately set about bringing in a roast calf. ** When he saw their hands did not reach out towards it, he felt uneasy with them and started to be afraid of them. They said: "Do not act afraid; we have been sent to Lot's folk."

69

Abraham

70

* His wife was standing by and she laughed, so We informed her about Isaac, and following Isaac, Jacob. * She said: "It's too bad for me! Shall I bear a child while I am an old woman and this husband of mine is elderly? That would be an amazing thing!" * They said: "Do you marvel at God's command? God's mercy and blessings are on all you people in [this] house. He is Praiseworthy, Glorious!"

* So when his dismay left Abraham and the news came (home) to him, he pleaded with Us about Lot's folk; ** Abraham was so lenient, worried, concerned. * "Abraham, avoid this! It is merely that your Lord's command has come, and torment which cannot be averted has been brought them."

* When Our messengers came to Lot, he was uneasy concerning them and felt helpless about warding off anything they might do, He said: "This is a critical day!" * His people came hurrying up to him; while just before they had been performing such evil deeds! He said: "My people, these are my daughters; they are purer for you. Heed God and do not shame me through my guests. Is there not a normal man among you?" * They said: "You know we have no right to your daughters. You know what we

want!" ** He said: "If only I had some power over you or could seek safety at some firm support!"

* They said: "Lot, we are your Lord's messengers. They will not overtake you, so travel with your family during part of the night and do not let anyone of you turn around except for your wife. Her fate is what will strike them [too]. Their appointment will be in the morning. Is not morning near?"

* When Our command came along, We turned them upside down and rained stones on them from tablets which had been sorted out, * stamped by your Lord. They never lie far from wrongdoers!

(VIII) * To Midian [God sent] their brother Shuᶜayb. He said: "My people, worship God [Alone]! You have no other deity except Him. Do not give short measure and weight. I see you enjoy well-being while I fear the torment of an overpowering day for you. ** My people, give full measure and weight with all fairness, and do not cheat men of their belongings nor cause havoc on earth as mischief makers do. * Anything God leaves over is best for you provided you believe. I am no guardian set up over you."

* They said: "Shuᶜayb, does your prayer command you that we must abandon what our forefathers worshipped, or that we should [not] do what we wish to with our property? Yet you are such a lenient, normal person!"

* He said: "My people, have you considered whether I bear any explanation from my Lord? He has provided me with handsome sustenance from Himself. I do not want to oppose you in what I am forbidding you; I only want to improve matters so far as I can manage to. My success lies only with God; on Him have I relied and to Him do I refer. * My people, let not disagreement with me involve you in any crime, so the same fate as struck Noah's folk, or **Hūd**'s folk or Ṣāliḥ's folk, will strike you.

Lot's folk even lived not far away from you. ** Seek forgiveness from your Lord; then turn towards him; my Lord is Merciful, Affectionate.''

* They said; "Shuᶜayb, we do not understand most of what you say. We do see you are weak compared to us, and were it not for your immediate family, we'd expel you. You are not so dear to us."

* He said: "My folk, are my family ties dearer to you than God is? You thrust Him behind you, turning your backs on Him! Yet my Lord embraces anything you do. * My people, do anything that lies within your

power; I am (likewise) acting. You will soon know who will be brought torment which will disgrace him, and who is lying. Watch out! I am watching along with you."

* When Our command came, We saved Shuᶜayb and those who believed with him through mercy from Ourself, while the Blast overtook those who had been doing wrong, so they lay cowering in their homes one morning ** just as if they had never prospered there. Was it not away with Midian, just as Thamūd was also sent away?

(IX) * We sent Moses with Our signs and clear authority * to Pharaoh and his notables; so they followed Pharaoh's command, even though what Pharaoh commanded was not sensible. * He will appear before his folk on Resurrection Day and lead them on to the Fire. How awful will be (their) arrival wherever they are led! * They will be followed by a curse in this [world] and on Resurrection Day; how awful is the gift which will be presented [them]!

*** That is some of the news from towns We are telling you about; some of them are still standing there while [others have been] mown down. * We did no wrong to them but they had (already) wronged themselves; their (false) gods which they had been appealing to instead of to God [Alone] did not benefit them in any way once your Lord's command came along, and they increased them in nothing except destruction. * Even so will your Lord seize things when He takes over any towns while they are doing wrong; His seizing will be painful, severe.

* In that lies **a sign** for anyone who fears torment in the Hereafter; that will be a day on which mankind will be gathered, and such is a day when (every)one should be present. * We will not postpone it except till a deadline which shall be counted out. ** The day it comes, no soul will speak up except with His permission. Some of them will feel miserable while [others] will be happy. * Those who are miserable will be in the Fire; they shall (hear) moaning and groaning in it, * remaining there so long as Heaven and Earth will last, except for whatever your Lord may wish. Your Lord is a Doer of whatever He wants!

* Those who have found happiness will be in the Garden, living there so long as Heaven and Earth may endure, except for whatever your Lord may wish, as a gift that will never crumble away. * Do not be in any quandary about what those [people] serve; they only worship as their forefathers worshipped previously. We will repay them their share without omitting anything.

(X) ** We gave Moses the Book, yet disagreement arose concerning it. Had it not been for a statement which had previously gone forth from your Lord, it would have been decided among them. They are in such suspicious doubt about it! * Your Lord will repay everyone for their actions, for He is Informed about whatever they are doing. * Carry on just as you have been ordered to, as well as anyone who repents along with you. Do not act arrogantly: He is Observant of anything you do! * Do not lean on those who do wrong lest the Fire should touch you. You have no patrons besides God; otherwise you will not be supported.

96

Moses

100

110

Prayer

> * Keep up prayer at both ends of the day;
> and at the approach of night.
> **Good deeds remove evil deeds**:
> that is a Reminder for such persons
> as will be reminded.

** Act patiently; God does not let the wages of those who act kindly be wasted. * If there had only been a few persons with a little [sense] left to forbid corruption on earth out of those We saved among the generations before you! They followed those who did wrong in whatever they had been luxuriating in, and were criminals. * Your Lord would never destroy any towns for doing wrong while their people were trying to reform.

* If your Lord had wished, He would have made mankind into one community, but they will not stop disagreeing, * except for those to whom your Lord has shown mercy.

120

For that reason did He create them, and your Lord's word was completed: "I shall fill Hell with sprites and mankind all together!" ** Everything We relate to you concerning the history of messengers is what We brace your vitals with; through this, Truth comes to you, as well as a lesson and Reminder for believers. * Tell those who do not believe: "Do whatever lies within your capacity; we are [likewise] acting. * Wait! We are waiting (too)."

> * God holds the Unseen in Heaven and Earth,
> and unto Him does every matter return;
> so **serve Him, and rely on Him**.
> Your Lord is not unmindful
> of what you (all) are doing.

12
Joseph

THIS CHAPTER has 111 Meccan verses, except for vv. 1, 2, 3 and 7 which date from Madīna. It comprises twelve sections, and was revealed after the previous one which is entitled **Hūd [the Messenger]** 11 and before **Stoneland** 15. It might almost be considered a short story, for it forms one of the enduring tales in world literature, and a great theme that has been known for millenia throughout the Middle East. It has even inspired modern writers like Thomas Mann.

Joseph at the beginning is clearly a boy, a younger brother who will relax and play while the rest of the family are out working (II). Thus he provokes sibling jealousy. He matures through trial and misfortune until he ends as an advanced civil servant or statesman.

If this chapter carries any message, it is the need for trusting God entirely through any period of trial. Moses' mystic journey (18:IX-X) serves as another example of this advice. Watch for the unkind cut when Joseph was falsely accused of stealing (IX), and especially for the noble figure of the here nameless elder brother who also appears at II and X; the family was not all bad. It is interesting too that the ruler of Egypt is here called a king rather than Pharaoh (VI-VII).

In the name of God, the Mercy-giving, the Merciful!

(I) * A.L.R.

These are verses from the Clear Book. * We have sent it down as an Arabic reading so that you may reason.

* We relate the best stories to you, since We have revealed this Reading to you. You were someone quite unaware previously.

* So Joseph told his father: "My father, I saw eleven stars, and the sun and moon; I saw them bowing down before me!" ** He said: "My dear son, do not relate your vision to your brothers lest they may lay some trap for you; Satan is an open enemy to man. * Thus your Lord is choosing you and teaching you how to interpret events, and completing His favor towards you and Jacob's house, just as He has already completed it towards both your forefathers Abraham and Isaac. Your Lord is Aware, Wise!"

(II) * There were signs for inquirers in Joseph and his brothers * when they said; "Joseph and his brother are dearer to our father than we are,

7

even though we are a closed group. Our father is clearly mistaken. * [Let's] kill Joseph or throw him into exile in some land so your father's attention will be absorbed in (all of) you, and later on you will be honorable folk." ** One among them spoke up and said: "Don't kill Joseph; toss him into the bottom of the cistern so some travellers may pick him up, if you must do something."

* They said: "Our father, what's wrong with you that you do not trust us with Joseph? We are quite sincere about him. * Send him along with us tomorrow to relax and play. We'll look after him." * He said: "It would worry me for you to go off with him. I fear a wolf will eat him up while you are careless about him." * They said: "How could a wolf eat him when we are a closed group? Then we would be losers!"

** As they went away with him, they agreed on how to place him in the bottom of a cistern. We inspired him as follows: "You will inform them about this business of theirs while they will not catch on about it."

* They came back weeping to their father in the evening. * They said: "Our father, we went off racing and left Joseph with our belongings, and the wolf ate him up! You will not believe us even though we are telling the truth." * They even came with false blood on his shirt. He said: "Rather you yourselves have been fooled in the matter. **Patience is beautiful!** God is the One to seek help from against what you describe."

* Some travellers came along who sent their waterboy and he let down his bucket. He said: "What a godsend! This is a boy!" So they hid him as a piece of merchandise; yet God was Aware of what they were doing. ** They sold him for a trifling price, just a few coins which were counted out. They were quite indifferent about him.

(III) * The person from Egypt who [eventually] bought him told his wife: "Let his stay here be dignified; perhaps he will benefit us or we'll adopt him as a son." Thus We established Joseph in the land and taught him how to interpret events. God was Dominant in his affair, even though most men do not realize it.

* When he became of age, We gave him discretion and knowledge; thus We reward those who act kindly. * However the woman in whose house he lived, wanted to seduce him. She bolted the doors and said: "Come here, you!" He said: "God protect me! He is my Lord, the best shelter to hold on by. He does not let wrongdoers prosper."

* She kept him on her mind, while he would have had her on his, had it not been that he saw a proof from his Lord. Thus We warded off evil and sexual misconduct from him; he was one of Our sincere servants. ** They both raced for the door, and she ripped his shirt from behind; and they met her husband at the door! She said: "What is the penalty for someone who wants [to commit] evil with your wife except for him to be jailed or [suffer] painful torment?" * He said: "She tried to seduce me."

A witness from her side of the family testified: "If his shirt has been ripped from in front, then she has told the truth and he is a liar; * while if his shirt has been ripped from behind, then she has lied and he is truthful." * When he saw his shirt was ripped from behind, he said: "It is one of your women's tricks. Your wiles are serious! * Joseph, avoid this.

10

20

21

Potiphar's Wife

[My wife], ask forgiveness for your sin. You're someone who has slipped up."

(IV) ** Some women in the city said: "The official's wife wants to seduce her houseboy. He's set her madly in love! We see she has gone clear astray."

   * When she heard about their remarks, she sent for them and prepared a party for them. To each of them she gave a knife. She told [him]: "Come out to [see] them!"

   When they saw him, they praised him and cut their hands. They said: "God forbid! This is no human being; this is simply a noble angel!" * She said: "Well this is the person whom you blamed me for. Yes, I wanted to seduce him, and he held himself back! If he doesn't do what I order him to, he'll be jailed, and taken down a notch or two."

   * He said: "My Lord, jail is more precious to me than what they are inviting me to do. Unless You ward off their tricks from me, I'll fall for them and act as if I do not know a thing." * His Lord responded to his plea and warded off their tricks from him. He is the Alert, Aware. ** Then it occurred to them to jail him for a while even after they had seen the signs.

(V) * Two young men entered the prison along with him. One of them said: "I dreamed I was pressing wine." The other said: "I dreamed I was carrying bread on my head from which the birds were eating. Tell us about their interpretation; we see you are someone who acts kindly."

   * He said: "Food will not be brought either of you to sustain you, unless I will tell you their interpretation even before it reaches you. That is something my Lord has taught me. I have left the sect of folk who do not believe in God and are disbelievers in the Hereafter: * I follow the sect of my forefathers Abraham, Isaac and Jacob. We may not associate anything in [our worship of] God [Alone]. That is part of God's bounty towards us and towards mankind; even though most men are not grateful.

   * "Both my jailmates, are separate lords better than God Alone, the Irresistible? ** Instead of Him you do not serve anything except some names which you and your forefathers have given them. God has not sent down any authority for them. Discretion belongs only to God. He has ordered you to serve Him Alone; such is the established religion, even though most men do not realize it.

   * "My two jailmates, one of you will pour wine for his lord, while the other will be crucified so birds will eat from his head. The case has been decided which you have been seeking my opinion about."

   * He told the one whom he thought would be released: "Mention me to your lord." However Satan made him forget to mention it to his lord, so he languished in jail for several years.

(VI) * The king said; "I [dreamed I] saw seven fat cows which seven lean ones were eating, and seven green ears plus some others all dried up. Councilmen, explain my dream to me if you know how to explain any vision." * They said: "Jumbles of dreams; we do not know how to interpret dreams." ** The one from the pair who had been released said

30

*Joseph
in Prison*

36

*Polytheism
Condemned*

40

43

*Pharaoh's
Dream*

(for he recalled things after a lapse of time): "I'll inform you about its interpretation. Send me [after it]!"

* "Joseph, you truthful man, explain to us about seven fat cows which seven lean ones were eating, and seven green ears and others all dried up, so that I may return to the people so they may know." * He said: "You will farm for seven years as usual, and with anything you harvest, leave it in its ear except for a little which you may eat. * Then later on, seven severe ones will come which will eat up anything you have planned ahead for them, except for a little which you will store up. * Then a year will come after that when people will receive showers, and in which they will press [grapes]."

50   (VII) ** The king said: "Bring him to me." When the messenger came to him, he said: "Return to your lord and ask him what [was on] the mind of the women who cut their hands. My Lord is Aware of their tricks."

* He said: "What were you after when you tried to seduce Joseph?" The women said: "God forbid! We have not known about any evil concerning him." The official's wife said: "Now the Truth has prevailed! I tried to seduce him; he is someone who is telling the truth. * That was so he may know that I have not betrayed him during his absence, and that God does not guide the plotting of traitors.

PART
THIRTEEN

53   (VII, cont'd) * "I do not claim to be innocent myself: **one's soul is prone to [commit] evil**, except for anything my Lord shows mercy for. My Lord is Forgiving, Merciful." * The king said: "Bring him to me; I'll select him for my special service."

When he spoke to him, he said: "Today you stand before us secure, trusted." ** He said: "Place me over the storehouses in the land. I will be a careful overseer."

* Thus We established Joseph in the land, to budget for it in any way he wished. We confer Our mercy on anyone We wish to and never let the earnings of those who act kindly get lost. * Earnings in the Hereafter will be even better for those who believe and have done their duty.

58   (VIII) * Joseph's brothers came, and they entered his office. He recognized them, while they remained ignorant as to who he was. * When he had equipped them with their supplies, he said: "Bring me a brother of yours [who is] with your father. Dont you see that I give full measure and have
60   been the best of hosts? ** If you do not bring me him, I'll have no [further] measure for you nor need you ever approach me [again]."

* They said: "We'll try to coax his father to let him go, We [promise] to do so." * He told his houseboys: "Place their trading goods back in their saddlebags, so they will recognize it when they return home to their family; thus they may come back."

* When they returned to their father, they said: "Our father, any [further] measure has been denied us, so send our brother [Benjamin] along

with us so we may be treated as customers. We'll look after him." * He said: "How dare I trust you with him except as I entrusted you with his brother long ago? God is the best Guardian and the most Merciful of Mercy-granters."

** When they opened their baggage, they found their trading goods had been returned to them. They said: "Our father, what more do we desire than this? This merchandise of ours has been returned to us! We shall supply our family, look after our brother, and add a camel's load [to it] besides: that should be such an easy load!" * He said: "I will never send him with you until you give me some assurance before God that you will bring him back to me, unless you have been ambushed."

When they had given him their pledge, he said: "God is a Trustee for what we say." * He said: "My sons, do not enter by a single gate; enter rather by separate gates. I cannot help you in any way against God; discretion rests only with God. On Him have I relied, and on Him should reliant persons rely."

* When they had entered [the city] just as their father ordered them to, it did not help them in any way against God except as a need which He fulfilled in Jacob's soul. He possessed knowledge since We had taught him, although most men do not realize it.

(IX) * As they entered Joseph's quarters, he took his brother [Benjamin] aside. He said: "I am your brother, so do not feel distressed about whatever they have been doing."   69

** When he furnished them with their supplies, he placed a mug in his brother's saddlebag. Then a crier called out: "Caravaners, you are thieves!"   70
* They said as they approached them: "What have you lost?" * They said: "We are missing the king's goblet. Whoever brings it back will have a camel's load; I can vouch for it." * They said: "By God, you [ought to] know we have not come here to cause any trouble in the land. We are not thieves!" * They said: "What will the penalty be for it if you are liars?" ** They said: "Its penalty? Whoever's saddlebag it is found in will [act as] his own penalty. Thus we penalize wrongdoers."

* He began with their baggage before his brother's bag. Then he pulled it out of his brother [Benjamin]'s bag. Thus We contrived [things] for Joseph; he would never have taken his brother according to the king's code unless God had so wished it. We raise anyone We wish to in rank, while Someone Aware [stands] over everyone possessing knowledge.

* They said: "If he has been [caught] stealing, then a brother of his stole something previously." Joseph kept his secret to himself and did not reveal it to them. He said: "You are in a worse plight! God is quite Aware of what you describe."

* They said: "Sir, he has a father who is an elderly gentleman. Take one of us in his place; we see you are someone who acts kindly." * He said: "God prevent us from taking anyone except the one whom we found our property with! We'd then be wrongdoers."

(X) ** When they despaired of influencing him, they held counsel by themselves. The eldest of them said: "Dont you realize that your father   80 took a pledge from you before God? You have already been remiss concerning Joseph so I shall never leave the land until my father permits me to, or God decides [things] for me. He is the best Judge! * Return to your father and say: 'Our father, your son has stolen something! Yet we testify only about what we know and are not guardians of the Unseen. * Ask the town[sfolk] where we have been and the caravan which we came back in; we are telling the truth!'"

Jacob's Grief

* He said: "Rather you have fooled yourselves in the matter. **Patience is a virtue**! Perhaps God will bring them all back to me; He is the Aware, the Wise." * He turned away from them and said: "How upset I feel over Joseph!" Both his eyes clouded over from sadness, so he choked back his grief. ** They said: "By God, you keep on remembering Joseph until you will be exhausted or will be ready to die!" * He said: "I complain only to God about my sorrow and my sadness. Through God I know something you do not know. * My sons, go and search for Joseph and his brother; do not despair of [finding] God's comfort; only disbelieving folk despair of God's comfort."

* When they entered his office, they said: "Sir, trouble has afflicted us and our family, and we have come with meagre merchandise. Fill up the load for us and act charitably towards us. God rewards the charitable." * He said: "Do you know what you did to Joseph and his brother while

90

you were acting out of ignorance?" ** They said: "Why, are you Joseph?" He said: "I am Joseph, and this is my brother. God has compensated us; with anyone who does his duty and perseveres, God does not lose track of the wages for those who act kindly." * They said: "By God, God has preferred you ahead of us, while we have been mistaken." * He said: "There is no [way for me to] find fault with you today. God will forgive you; He is the most Merciful of the Mercy-granting. * Take this shirt of mine and throw it over my father's face; he will become sighted [again]. Bring me all your family."

94

(xi) * As the caravan set out, their father said: "I smell a breath from Joseph, even though you may think I am doting." ** They said: "By God, you are still in your old error!"

* When an advance rider came, he threw it over his face, and his sight was restored. He said: "Did I not tell you that through God I know something that you do not know?" * They said: "Our father, seek us forgiveness for our offences! We have been mistaken." * He said: "I shall seek forgiveness for you from my Lord; He is the Forgiving, the Merciful."

100

* When they entered Joseph's office, he took both his parents aside and said: ''Enter Egypt safely, if God wishes.'' *** He helped his parents up on to the platform, and they fell down on their knees before him. He said: "My father, this is the interpretation of my earlier vision. My Lord has made it come true! He was Kind to me when He let me out of jail, and brought you in from wandering on the desert after Satan had stirred up trouble between me and my brothers. My Lord is Gracious in whatever way He wishes; He is the Aware, the Wise.

Joseph's Prayer

* "My lord, you have given me control and taught me how to interpret events. Originator of Heaven and Earth, You are my Patron in this

world and the Hereafter. Gather me in as a Muslim and unite me with honorable men!"

* Such are some of the news from the Unseen We inspire you with. You were not in their presence when they agreed on their affair and were plotting. * Yet most men will not become believers, no matter how eager you may be. * You need not ask them for any payment for it; it [serves] only as a Reminder to [everybody in] the Universe.

The Universal Message

(XII) ** How many a sign do they pass by in Heaven and Earth, and pay no attention to them? * Most of them do not believe in God unless they associate [others with Him]. * Do they feel confident that a sample of God's torment may not come to them, or the [final] Hour will come upon them suddenly, while they do not suspect it? * SAY: "This is my way. I and anyone who follows me, appeal to God through insight. Glory be to God! I am no associator."

105

* We have not sent anyone before you except men from among the townspeople whom We have inspired. Have they not travelled around the earth and seen what the outcome was for those who preceded them? A home in the Hereafter will be better for those who do their duty. Will they not use their reason— ** so that once messengers despair and think that they have been lied to, Our support will come to them and anyone We wish to will be saved? Our might is never averted from criminal folk.

110

* There is a lesson in their stories for prudent persons. It is not some report which has been invented but confirmation of what has existed previously and an analysis of everything, as well as guidance and mercy for folk who believe.

13
Thunder

HESE 43 VERSES arranged in six sections are mostly late Meccan, although some date from Madīna. The chapter was revealed after **Muhammad** 47 and before **The Mercy-giving** 55. It has A.L.M.R. for its initials, almost like the second, third and twenty-ninth to thirty-second chapters.

The law of consequences is stated here, and in section III we are told who will go to Heaven and who to Hell. We are warned against other failings that may lead us astray.

In the name of God, the Mercy-giving, the Merciful!

(I) * A.L.M.R.

These are verses from the Book; what has been sent down to you by your Lord is the Truth, even though most men do not believe so. * God is the One Who has raised up the Heavens without any support you can see. Then He mounted on the Throne and regulated the sun and moon; each runs along on a specific course. He directs the matter; He manifests signs so that you may be convinced about meeting your Lord.

God as Creator

* He is the One Who has spread the earth out and placed headlands and rivers on it, and has placed two pairs for every kind of fruit on it. He wraps daylight up in night. In that are signs for folk who meditate. * On the earth are neighboring tracts, and vineyards, cultivated fields and datepalms, [growing] in clumps and all alone, watered from a single source. We make some of them excel others in food value. In that are signs for folk who use their reason.

** If you should feel astonished, then how much more astonishing is their statement: "When we have become dust, shall we [end up] in some fresh creation?" Those are the ones who disbelieve in their Lord; such (persons) will have fetters [placed] around their necks and those will become inmates of the Fire, to live there for ever. * They want to hasten you on to commit evil rather than [to perform] a fine deed.

Examples have already been set before them.
> **Your Lord possesses forgiveness for mankind,**
> **no matter how wrong they are**; though
> your Lord still is Stern with punishment.

* Those who disbelieve say: "If only a sign were sent down from his Lord!" Yet you are only a warner; each folk has a guide.

(II) * God knows what every female bears, and how some wombs may miscarry or else may wait too long. Everything has its measure with Him; * Knowing the Unseen and the Visible, [He is] the Great, the Exalted! ** It is all the same for you whether one of you is secretive about what he says or speaks out about it, and whether one keeps to himself at night and struts around by day: * he has [angels] checking from both before him and behind him; they guard him at God's command.

**God does not change what any people may have
until they change whatever they themselves have.**

Whenever God wants something bad [to happen] to any people, there is no way to avert it nor have they any patron except for Him. * He is the One Who shows you lightning to inspire both fear and expectation. He whips up the heavy clouds. * **Thunder** hymns His praise while angels stand in awe of Him. He sends down thunderbolts and strikes anyone He wishes with them. Yet they argue on and on about God while He is Stern in strategy.

* To Him should go the appeal for Truth; those they appeal to instead of Him will never respond to them in any way, except as someone does who stretches out his palms for water, so it may reach his mouth since he himself can never reach it. An appeal by disbelievers merely goes astray.

** Whoever is in Heaven and Earth **bows down on their knees** before God obediently or grudgingly, just as their shadows do so in the morning and the evening. * SAY: "Who is Lord of Heaven and Earth?" SAY: "God [Alone]." SAY: "Yet have you adopted patrons besides Him who control no benefit nor any harm by themselves?" SAY: "Are the blind and the sighted person equal? Or is darkness equal to light? Or have they given God associates whom they have created just as He creates, so that all creation seems just the same to them?"

SAY: "God is the Creator of everything;
He exists Alone, the Irresistible.

* He sends down water from the sky so that river valleys flow according to how much there is. The torrent carries along swelling foam, foam just like what comes out of fire they have kindled to smelt jewelry or some equipment with.
    Even so God knocks Truth and falsehood together [to compare them]. As for the foam, the scum will go away; while whatever benefits mankind lingers on in the earth. Thus God compares things with one another.

* Those who respond to their Lord will have the finest [reward] while those who do not respond to Him, even if they had everything on earth and the like of it besides, would never redeem themselves with it. Those will have the worst reckoning; their refuge will be Hell and how awful a resting place it is!

Margin notes:

8
*God the
All-Knowing*
10

*The Object
of Prayer;
Association
is Futile*

*BOW DOWN
HERE*

God Alone

*Foam in
Floods*

19

20

*Who Will
Go to
Heaven*

*Who Will
Go to
Hell*

27

30

32

(III) * Is someone who knows how whatever has been sent down to you from your Lord is the Truth, like someone who is blind?

Only prudent persons bear it in mind, ** those who fulfil God's agreement and do not break the covenant, * who transmit anything God has ordered to be transmitted, and dread their Lord and fear the worst reckoning, * who persevere in seeking their Lord's countenance and keep up prayer and spend whatever We have provided them with both secretly and publicly, and **ward off evil with good**; those will have the compensation of the [final] Home, * gardens of Eden which they will enter, as well as anyone who has acted honorably among their forefathers, their spouses and their offspring. Angels will come in on them by every gate: * "Peace be upon you because you have acted so patiently!" How blissful will the compensation of the Home be!

** Those who have broken God's agreement after having pledged it, and intercepted what God has commanded to be transmitted, and acted depraved on earth will have the Curse and theirs will be the worst home! * God extends and measures out sustenance for anyone He wishes, while they are happy with worldly life. Yet what is worldly life compared with the Hereafter except as something to be enjoyed [as it passes]?

(IV) * Those who disbelieve say: "If only a sign were sent down to him from his Lord!" SAY: "God lets anyone He wishes go astray, and guides to Himself anyone who feels concerned— * the ones who believe and whose hearts feel tranquil through remembering God—

"Surely hearts feel tranquil
whenever God is mentioned!"

— * Those who believe and perform honorable deeds will find gladness and the finest journey's end.

** Thus We have sent you to a nation—nations have passed away long before it—so you may recite to them what We have inspired you with even though they disbelieve in the Mercy-giving! SAY: "He is my Lord: there is no god except Him. On Him do I rely and towards Him [goes] my repentance."

* If there were only some Qurɔān by which the mountains would travel away or the earth would crack open, or the dead would speak out! Rather command is wholly God's. Do not those who believe despair, because God might have guided all mankind had He so wished? Disaster will continually afflict those who disbelieve because of what they produce, or it will settle down close to their home until God's promise comes true. God does not break any appointment.

(V) * Messengers have been ridiculed before you (came), and I have been indulgent with those who disbelieve; then I seized them. What was My punishment like? * Who is there standing over every soul [checking up] on whatever it has earned, while they give God associates? SAY: "Name them! Or will you inform Him about something on earth He does not know, or is it just a display of words?" Rather those who disbelieve feel their scheme is attractive while they are diverted from the Path. Anyone whom God lets go astray will have no guide. * Theirs will be torment during worldly life, while torment in the Hereafter will be even more heartrending. They will have no one to shield them from God.

** [Here] is what the Garden which the heedful are promised will be like: rivers will flow through it; its food and its shade shall be perpetual. Such is the compensation for those who have done their duty, while the outcome for disbelievers will be the Fire.

The Garden

* Those whom We have given the Book to are happy with what has been sent down to you; yet among the factions there are some who disregard part of it. SAY: "I am only ordered to serve God [Alone] and not associate anything with Him. To Him do I appeal and towards Him will be my retreat." * Thus We have sent it down for Arab discretion. If you followed their whims after the sort of knowledge which has come to you, you would have no protector nor any shield against God.

People of the Book

(VI) * We have sent messengers before you [came], and granted them spouses and offspring. No messenger would have brought any sign except with God's permission. For each period there is something written (down).

38

* God erases and consolidates whatever He wishes; He retains the Mother of the Book. ** Whether We merely show you part of what We have promised them or cause you to pass away, you merely have to proclaim it, while We must reckon. * Have they not seen how We come to clip the land off at its borders? God decides; there is no way to reverse His decision. He is Swift in reckoning!

40

* Those before them have plotted, even though God [controls] all plotting; He knows what every soul is earning. Disbelievers shall know who has compensation in the Home. * Those who disbelieve say: "You are no emissary." SAY: "God suffices as a Witness between me and you (all), as well as anyone who has knowledge about the Book."

14
Abraham

THIS CHAPTER consists of 52 verses arranged in seven sections which are all late Meccan, except for vv. 28 & 29 which date from Madīna. It was revealed after **Noah** 71 and before **Prophets** 21.

The chapter contains two parables, "Ashes in the Wind" (III) and "The Good and the Bad Tree" (IV). Abraham's famous prayer is found in section VI (vv. 35-41); this is followed by a graphic picture of the Day of Reckoning with which the chapter ends.

In the name of God, the Mercy-giving, the Merciful!

(I) * A.L.R.

We have sent down a Book to you in order to bring men out of darkness into Light by their Lord's permission, towards the road of the Powerful, the Praiseworthy, * God, Who holds whatever is in Heaven and whatever is on Earth. Alas, because disbelievers will have harsh torment, * those who would rather have worldly life in preference to the Hereafter and obstruct God's way, seeking to make it crooked; those stray far afield.

* We have not sent any messenger unless he was to explain to them in his folk's own tongue. God lets anyone He wishes go astray, and guides anyone He wishes; He is the Powerful, the Wise. ** We sent Moses with Our signs: "Lead your people out of darkness into Light, and remind them of God's days. In that are signs for every patient, grateful person."

Moses' Mission

* So Moses told his folk: "Remember God's favor towards you when He saved you from Pharaoh's court, who had imposed the worst torment on you, and slaughtered your sons while letting your women live. That was a serious trial from your Lord."

7

(II) * So your Lord announced: **"If you act grateful, I shall give you even more**, while if you are thankless, then My torment will be severe." * Moses said: "Even if you and whoever is on earth should disregard it, God will still be Transcendent, Praiseworthy."

* Has not news come to you concerning those who preceded you such as Noah's folk, and ʿĀd's and Thamūd's, as well as those who came after them? Only God knows who they were. Messengers brought them explanations yet they merely stuffed their hands into their mouths and said: "We disbelieve in what you have been sent with. We are in suspicious doubt

10

about what you are inviting us to do." ** Their messengers said: "Is there any doubt about God, the Originator of Heaven and Earth? He invites you in order to forgive you some of your offences and to postpone things for you during a specific period." They said: "You are only human beings like ourselves! You want to divert us from what our forefathers have been worshipping, so bring us some clear authority."

* Their messengers told them: "We are only human like yourselves, but God showers blessings on any of His servants whom He wishes. It is not for us to bring you any authority except with God's permission. On God should believers rely." * Why should we not rely on God when He has guided us along our [several] ways? And so we may patiently endure how you persecute us? On God [Alone] should the reliant rely!

(III) * Those who disbelieved told their messengers: "We'll run you out of our land unless you return to our sect!" Their Lord [however] inspired them [as follows]: "We shall wipe out wrongdoers * and settle you on the land to succeed them." That is [in store] for anyone who fears My position and fears My threat.

13

** They sought to conquer, and every stubborn oppressor blundered. * Beyond him there lies Hell where he will be given stagnant water to drink. * He will gag on it and not quite swallow it. Death will come at him from everywhere, while he will not quite die. Beyond him lies harsh torment.

Hell

* The works of those who disbelieve in their Lord may be compared to ashes which the wind whips around on a stormy day. They cannot do a thing with anything they have earned. That is going far afield!

Ashes in the Wind

* Have you not seen how God has really created Heaven and Earth? If He so wished, He would remove you and bring on a fresh creation. ** That is not unfeasible for God [to do]. * They will all march forth to [meet] God, and the weaklings will tell those who acted so proudly: "We formed a following for you; can you help us out now in any way against God's torment?" They will say: "If God had guided us, then we'd have guided you. It's all the same for us whether we panic or act patient; we'll have no escape."

20

(IV) * Satan will say, once the matter has been settled: "God has given you a true promise, while I have both promised you and then broken my word with you. I have no authority over you except that I appealed to you, and you responded to me. Do not blame me but blame yourselves! I have no claim on you nor have you any claim on me. I disown how you have associated me [with God] up till now. Wrongdoers will have painful torment."

22
Blame is not Shifted

* Those who believe and perform honorable deeds will be shown into gardens through which rivers flow, to live there with their Lord's permission. Their greeting in it will be: "Peace!"

* Do you not consider how God makes up a parable? A good word may be compared to a good tree whose root is firm and whose branches soar up into the sky. ** It yields its food each season with its Lord's permission.

The Good and the Bad Tree

God composes parables for mankind so that they may be reminded.
* A bad word may be compared to a bad tree: it will be uprooted from
the face of the earth; it has no foothold.

* God braces those who believe with firm speech during worldly life and in
the Hereafter; while God lets wrongdoers stray away. God does whatever
He wishes!

28

30

(v)* Have you not seen those who pay back God's favor with disbelief and
settle their folk in the home of Perdition— * Hell! They will roast there,
and how awful is such a plight! ** They place rivals alongside God to lead
others astray from His path.

SAY: "Enjoy yourselves even though your goal will be the Fire!" * Tell
My servants who believe to keep up prayer and spend what We have
provided them with both secretly and openly before a day comes along
when there will be no bartering nor any intimacy.

God's Role

* God is the One Who has created Heaven and Earth, and sends down
water from the sky. He brings forth produce by means of it as
sustenance for you. He has subjected ships to you so they may sail at
sea by His command; and subjected rivers to you. * He regulates the
sun and moon for you, both journeying on and on, and regulates night
and day for you.

* He gives you everything you ever ask Him for. If you counted up
God's favor(s), you would never [be able to] number them; yet man is
so unfair, ungrateful.

35

** So **Abraham** said:

*Abraham's
Prayer*

"My Lord, make this countryside safe and keep me and my sons away
from worshipping idols. * My Lord, they have led so many men
astray! Anyone who follows me belongs to me, just as anyone who
disobeys me [will still find] You are Forgiving, Merciful.

* "Our Lord, I have had some of my offspring reside in a valley
without any crops alongside Your Hallowed House, our Lord, so that
they may keep up prayer. Make men's vitals feel fond of them, and
provide them with fruit so they may act grateful.

* "Our Lord, You know whatever we hide and whatever We
display; nothing on earth nor in the sky is hidden from God. * Praise
be to God Who has bestowed Ishmael and Isaac on me in my old age.
My Lord is so Alert to anyone's appeal!

40

** "My Lord, make me keep up prayer,
and have my offspring [do so too].
* "Our Lord, accept my appeal!
Our Lord, forgive me, both my parents,
and believers on the Day
when the Reckoning will be set up!"

42
Doomsday

(VII) * Do not reckon God is oblivious of what wrongdoers are doing; He
is merely putting them off till a day when their eyesight will be glazed * as

they dash along with their heads tilted forward, their glances not checking back for them, and their vital organs gaping open. * Warn mankind against a day when torment will come upon them. Those who have done wrong will say: "Our Lord, put us off for a short while; we will answer Your appeal and follow the messengers!"

(Did you not use to swear previously that you would never [face] extinction? ** You have inhabited the dwellings of those who wronged themselves; it was explained to you how We had dealt with them, and We made up parables for you.)

* They hatched their plot while God held up their plot, even though their plan had been to transport the mountains by means of it! * Do not reckon God will break His promise to His messengers; God is Powerful, the Wielder of Retribution.

* Some day the earth will be changed into a different earth, and [so will] Heaven; they will emerge for God Alone, the Irresistible! * You will see criminals linked together by means of fetters on that day; ** their garments will be [smeared] with tar while fire will cover their faces, * so God may reward each soul according to whatever it has earned. God is Prompt at reckoning!

50

> * This is a proclamation for mankind;
> let them feel they are warned through it
> and know that He is God Alone.
> May prudent persons bear it in mind!

15
Stoneland
(OR *Rock* [*City*])

HERE WE have 99 quite early Meccan verses arranged in six sections (except for v. 87 which dates from Madīna). The title refers to a community north of Madīna to whom Thamūd came, which lived in a stone or rock city like that at Petra. It lay on the route from Madīna to Syria, as we see in the last section of the chapter, and may have been near Taymāʾ in Midian.

This reference is preceded by mention of the early prophets, Abraham (IV) who gave his name to the previous chapter, and Lot (V). This chapter is important for its cosmogony or the description of how the world was formed. Diabolis is present at man's creation too (III).

This chapter was revealed after **Joseph** 12 and before **Livestock** 6, and is the last of the older group from Mecca, as can be seen by the initials at the beginning of the first verse. This mood can be sensed in the style and differing rhythm of the first verses. The chapter becomes quite personal towards the end, and sounds almost like a cry of distress uttered by someone seeking solace; it ends with a short hymn in this vein.

In the name of God, the Mercy-giving, the Merciful!

(I) * A.L.R.
These are verses from the Book, and a clear Reading.

PART
FOURTEEN

2

(I cont'd) * Perhaps those who disbelieve would like to become Muslims. * Leave them eating and enjoying themselves; let hope distract them, for they soon will know (anyhow). * We have never wiped out any town unless it had [received] a known term; ** no nation can forestall its deadline, nor will they ever postpone it. * Yet they say: "You to whom the Reminder has been sent down, why you're crazy! * Why don't you bring us angels if you are so truthful?"

Past and Present

10

* We do not send down any angels except with the Truth, and even then they would not be allowed to wait. * We Ourself have sent down the Reminder just as We are safeguarding it. ** Even before you, We sent [some] down among the sects of early people; * yet no messenger ever came to them whom they did not sneer at.

* Thus We slip it into criminals' hearts; * they will not believe in it, even though the custom of early people has already preceded it. * Even though We opened up a gate to Heaven for them so they might keep on climbing into it, ** they still would say: "Our eyesight has been dazzled—in fact, we are enchanted folk!"

(II) * We have placed constellations in the sky and embellished it for onlookers. * We have safeguarded them against every outcast Satan * except for such as may try to eavesdrop, so a blazing meteor follows him.

    * Earth have We spread out and cast headlands upon it, and planted a bit of everything to grow there (so it is) well balanced. ** We have placed various means of livelihood on it for (all of) you as well as anyone you do not have to provide for. * There is nothing whose stores are not [controlled] by Us, and We send it down only according to a fixed quantity.

    * We send forth fertilizing winds and send down water from the sky and offer you something to drink from it. You are not the ones who store it up. * We give life and bring death, and We are the Heirs [to everything]! * We know which of you try to get ahead and We know those who hold back. ** Your Lord will summon them; He is Wise, Aware.

(III) * We created man from ringing clay, from moulded slime; * while the sprites We had created earlier from smokeless fire.

    * So your Lord told the angels: "I am about to create a human being from ringing clay, from moulded slime. * When I have finished with him and breathed some of My spirit into him, then drop down on your knees before him." ** The angels all bowed down together * except for Diabolis; he refused to be one of those bowing down on their knees.

    * He said: "Diabolis, what is wrong with you that you are not among those who bow down on their knees?" * He said: "I am no one to kneel before a human being You have created from ringing clay, from moulded slime."

    * He said: "Then get out of here, for you are an outcast! ** On you lies the Curse until the Day for Repayment!"

    * He said: "My Lord, let me wait till the day when they are raised up again." * He said: "You will be allowed to wait * until a day in known time."

    * He said: "My Lord, since You have let me go astray, I shall make things on earth seem attractive to them; I'll mislead them all ** except for any of Your sincere servants who may be among them."

    * He said: "Here will be a Straight Road [leading] up to Me! * You will not hold any authority over My servants except for someone who may follow you from among those who are misguided. * Hell will [serve as] an appointment for all of them together. * It has seven gates; each gate will have a portion assigned from them."

(IV) ** The heedful will be in gardens and by springs:

16

Heaven and Earth

20

26

Diabolis at Man's Creation

30

40

45
Paradise

* "Enter them safely, at peace!"
* We will strip away any rancor
that [lingers] in their breasts;
like brethren they will face
one another on couches.

* Toil will not touch them there,
nor will they ever be expelled
from it. * Advise My servants
that I am the Forgiving, Merciful One,
50   ** although My torment will be painful torment.

Abraham   * Advise them about Abraham's guests * how, when they entered his presence and said: "Peace!", he said: "We feel wary of you." * They said: "Don't feel so wary; We bring you word about a clever boy."

* He said: "Have you brought me word like this once old age has set in on me? What sort of word do you want to spread?" ** They said: "We have brought you word of the Truth, so do not act so discouraged." * He said: "Who despairs of his Lord's mercy except those who are lost?"

Lot   * He said: "Yet what is your errand, you emissaries?" * They said: "We have been sent for some criminal folk, * except for Lot's house; we
60   will rescue them all ** except his wife. We have decreed that she will be one of those who will be left behind."

61   (v) * When the emissaries came to Lot's household, * he said: "You are
Lot (cont'd)   folk who should be ignored." * They said: "Rather we have come to you about something they have been puzzling over. * We have brought you the Truth, for we are reliable. ** Travel with your family at dead of night; you should follow in their rear, and let none of you glance around! Keep on going wherever you are ordered to. * We have passed judgment on that case for him so that those people's last remnant shall be cut off once morning dawns for them."

Sodom   * The people of the city came up gay with the news. * He said: "These are my guests so do not disgrace me. * Heed God, and do not shame
70   me." ** They said: "Didnt we forbid you to have contact with [anyone in] the Universe [outside]?" * He said: "These are my daughters if you are going to do (something)."

* Upon your life, they were groping along in their drunkenness * so the Blast caught them at sunrise: * We turned things upside down and rained down stones which had been stamped with their names on them. ** In that are signs for investigators; * and it lies along a permanent highway.

Midian   * In that is a sign for believers. * The Companions in the Forest had been wrongdoers, * so We avenged Ourself on them. Both are a clear indication.

80   (VI) ** The inhabitants of **Stoneland** rejected the emissaries. * We gave them Our signs even though they had shunned them. * They had confidently hewn houses out of the mountains. * So the Blast caught them

early one morning * and what they had been earning did not help them out.

** We have only created Heaven and Earth and whatever lies between them for the sake of Truth. The Hour is coming on, so examine [matters] with fine discrimination. * Your Lord is the Clever Creator!

* We have brought you seven Oft-Repeated [verses] plus the Mighty Qurʾān. * Do not strain your eyes towards what We let some types of them enjoy; do not feel saddened by them, and lower your [sheltering] wing over believers.

* SAY: "I am the plain Warner," ** (such as We have sent down for the quibblers * who have torn the Qur'ān apart. * By your Lord, We shall question them all * about whatever they have been doing!) * So proclaim whatever you are ordered to and shun associators; * We will suffice for you against such scoffers ** who place another deity alongside God [Alone]. They soon will know!

90
Handling Critics

* We already know how cramped your breast feels because of what they say: * so hymn your Lord's praise and be one of those who bow down on their knees (in worship).

Prayer is Consoling

* Serve your Lord until conviction comes to you!

16
Bees

128

THIS SIXTEEN-SECTION chapter consists of 128 late Meccan verses, except for the last three which date from Madina. It was revealed after **The Cave** 18 and before **Noah** 71, and belongs to a new group of chapters dating from the late Meccan period. The chapter is slightly longer than the others in this part and quite beautiful, containing many elevated thoughts.

The theme includes exhortations which give a clue to good behavior and commendable conduct. Pagan practices and beliefs are condemned in sections V-VIII. **The Bee** appears in v. 68 (IX). Agriculture has been mentioned first in II, and the food which God provides us with in IX and XV. Parables like "The Slave, the Master and the Dumb Man" (X) and "The Disbelieving Town" (XV) also form part of this chapter. The advantage of keeping one's word or oaths and avoiding mutual deceit appears in section XIII, where we are instructed on how to recite the Qurʾān.

In the name of God, the Mercy-giving, the Merciful!

Association is Foolish

(I) * God's command is coming, so do not seek to hasten its appearance.

Glory be to Him!
Exalted is He over anything
they may associate [with Him]!

* He sends down angels with the Breath of His command on any of His servants He may wish: "Warn [mankind] that there is no deity except Me; so heed Me!" * He has created Heaven and Earth in all Truth; Exalted is He over anything they associate [with Him]!

God's Favors; Livestock

* He creates man from a drop of semen, yet he is an open opponent; ** and livestock has He created for you in which are warmth and [other] advantages and some of which you use for food. * You have beauty in them when you drive them home to rest, and whenever you lead them out to pasture. * They transport your loads to lands you would not reach except through travail for yourselves—your Lord is so Gentle, Merciful— * as well as horses, mules and donkeys for you to ride on and to show them off. He even creates something you do not know. * On God rests the search for the Way, though sideroads may branch off from it. If He so wished, He would even guide you all.

10

Agriculture

(II) ** He is the One Who sends down water from the sky. You have something to drink from it, and from it shrubs you use for forage. * He grows you crops by means of it: olives, datepalms, grapevines and every sort of fruit. In that is a sign for folk who will think things over. * He has regulated night and daylight for you, while the sun, moon and stars are subjected to His command. In that are signs for folk who use their minds; * as well as in anything He has scattered over the earth for you with different colors. In that is a sign for folk who remember.

* He is the One Who regulates the sea so you may eat fresh meat from it and extract jewelry you may wear from it. You see ships sailing along through it so you (all) may seek some of His bounty, in order that you may feel grateful. ** He has set up headlands on the earth lest it sway with you, and rivers and paths so that you may be guided, * as well as landmarks, and by stars are they guided [too].

* Is Someone Who creates like someone who does not create anything? Will you not bear this in mind? * If you counted up God's favor, you would never calculate it; God is Forgiving, Merciful. * God knows anything you hide and anything you display. ** Those whom they invoke instead of God do not create a thing, while they themselves have been created; * dead, lifeless, they do not even perceive the times when they will be raised up again.

20

*False
Gods*

(III)   * Your God is God Alone!

22

Those who do not believe in the Hereafter have hearts which refuse to learn while they are overproud. * God knows absolutely anything they hide and anything they disclose; yet He does not love the prideful.

* Whenever someone tells them: "What has your Lord sent down?", they say: "Legends by primitive people!" ** Let them carry all their own burdens on Resurrection Day as well as some burdens for those whom they have misled without having any knowledge! Surely what they bear is evil!

(IV) * Those before them schemed, and God reached for their building through its foundations, so the roof caved in on them and torment came at them from where they did not even suspect it. * Then He will shame them on Resurrection Day and say: "Where are My associates through whom you have fallen into disagreement?" Those who have been given knowledge will say: "Shame and evil [will fall] today on disbelievers, * whom the angels will carry away while they are harming themselves."

26

*Scheming
Goes Awry*

They will offer to surrender: "We were not doing anything evil!" Nevertheless God is Aware of what you have been doing, * so enter Hell's gates to remain there. How awful will the lodging of the prideful be!

** Those who have done their duty will be told: "What has your Lord sent down?" They will say: "(The very) Best!" Those who have acted kindly in this world will have a fine thing, while their Home in the Hereafter will be even better. How splendid will the Home for the heedful be: * gardens of Eden will they enter where rivers will flow beneath them. They will have whatever they wish in it; thus God rewards those who do their duty, * whom the angels carry off while they are good persons, saying: "Peace be upon you! Enter the Garden because of what you have been doing."

30

*Future
Bliss*

* Are they merely waiting for the angels to come to them, or your Lord's command to come along? That is what those before them did, and God did not harm them but rather they harmed themselves. * The evil

deeds which they had been doing assailed them, and what they had been sneering at swept in around them!

35 (v) ** Those who associate [others with God] say: "If God so wished, neither we nor our forefathers would have served anything besides Him, nor would we have forbidden anything besides Him." Thus have those before them done!

Need messengers do anything except to proclaim things clearly? * We have despatched a messenger to every nation [who said]: "Serve God [Alone] and turn aside from the Arrogant ones." Some of them God has guided, while others there are for whom error has been confirmed. Travel around the earth and see how the outcome was for those who deny [everything].

* Even if you are eager to guide them, God still does not guide someone who misleads another and they will have no supporters. * They have sworn by God with their most solemn oaths, God will not raise up anyone who dies. Nonetheless it is a promise truly binding on Him, even though most men do not realize it, * so He may explain to them what they have been differing over, and so those who disbelieve may know that

40 they have been lying. ** Our statement for anything We have willed, is only for Us to tell it: "Be!", and it exists.

41 (vi) * We shall settle those who have migrated for God's sake after they were wronged, in something fine during this world, while the wages in the Hereafter will be even greater, * did those who act patient and rely on their Lord only know. * Before you We have only sent men whom We have inspired so ask people about the Reminder: "If you have not known * about explanations and the Psalms, We still sent you down the Reminder so you may explain to mankind what was sent down to them, so that they may meditate."

** Do those who plot evil deeds feel safe that God will not have the earth swallow them up, or torment come upon them from where they do not notice it? * Or lest He should overtake them as they bustle around and they cannot prevent it, * or catch them so they waste away? Yet your Lord is Gentle, Merciful!

* Have they not considered how everything God has created has its
BOW DOWN shadows move from right to left, **bowing down to God** so they themselves
HERE feel of lessened importance? * Whatever is in Heaven and whatever is on Earth **bows down** before God, whether they are animals or angels, and they
50 do not act proudly; ** they fear their Lord Above them, and do whatever they are ordered to.

51 (vii) * God says: "Do not adopt two gods:
Dualism there exists only God Alone,
Condemned and I am the One you should revere.

* He owns whatever is in Heaven and Earth, while religion is His for ever and ever. Will you heed something besides God? * You will receive no favor unless it comes from God. Yet whenever some harm touches you, you plead with Him; * then when He removes the harm from you, why a

group of you will associate (others) with your Lord, ** renouncing whatever We have given them! "So enjoy yourselves, for you soon shall know!"

* They assign a portion of what We have provided them with, to
something they do not know (by God, you shall be questioned about
whatever you have been inventing)! * They (even) assign daughters to
God. Glory be to Him! They themselves have what they desire. * Yet
whenever one of them receives word he has had a daughter, his face
becomes black with gloom and he feels like choking. * He hides from folk
because of the bad news that he has just received. Will he hold on to her
and feel disgraced, or bury her in the dust?

Paganism as well

Whatever they decide is evil! ** Those who do not believe in the
Hereafter set an evil example. God sets the Highest Example, for He is the
Powerful, the Wise.

60

(VIII) * If God were to take mankind to task for their wrongdoing, He
would not leave even an animal around; but He puts them off till an
appointed deadline. Once their deadline comes, they will not postpone it
for an hour nor may they advance it. * They assign to God something
they themselves dislike while their tongues mouth a lie: that the finest
things will belong to them. The Fire will absolutely be theirs and they will
be abandoned to it!

61

* By God, We have sent for nations before you, and Satan has made
their actions seem attractive to them! He is their patron today, while they
shall have painful torment. * We have merely sent the Book down to you
so you may explain to them what they are differing over, and as a guidance
and mercy for folk who believe. ** God sends water down from the sky
and revives the earth with it following its death. In that is a sign for folk
who will listen!

(IX) * You have a lesson in livestock: We let you drink what comes from
their bellies in between the cud and blood, pure refreshing milk for those
who drink it. * From the fruit of the datepalm and grapevine you derive
intoxicants as well as fine nourishment; in that is a sign for folk who
reason.

66

God's Provision

* Your Lord has inspired the **Bees**: "Set up hives in the mountains,
and in trees and on anything they may build. * Then eat some of every
kind of fruit and slip humbly along your Lord's byways."

The Bees' Instinct

From their bellies comes a drink with different colors which contains healing for mankind. In that is a sign for folk who will meditate!

Honey

** God has created you; then He will gather you (all) in. Some of you will
be sent on to the feeblest age of all, so that they will not know a thing after
once having had knowledge. God is Aware, Capable.

70

(X) * God has favored some of you over others in providing [for them].
Yet those who have been so made to excel are not going to hand over their
provision to those whom their right hands control, so they become equal
[partners] in it. Would they thus disclaim God's favor? * God has granted
you spouses from among yourselves, and granted you children and grand-

71

Class Distinction

children by means of your spouses. He has provided you with wholesome things. So will they still believe in falsehood while they disbelieve in God's favor? * Instead of God, they worship something that does not control any provision for them in any way in either Heaven or Earth, while they themselves can do nothing.

Parables:

The Slave,
the Master and
the Dumb Man

* Do not make up any parables about God; God knows while you do not know!

** God has made a comparison between a slave owned [by someone else] who cannot accomplish a thing, and someone whom We have provided for handsomely. He spends some of it privately and publicly. Are they equal? Praise be to God! Rather most of them do not know.

* God offers another comparison between two men, one of whom is dumb and cannot do a thing, and is a nuisance to his master. Wherever he sends him on an errand, he brings [him] no good. Is he equal to someone who gives proper orders and is on a Straight Road?

77

(xi) * To God belongs the Unseen of Heaven and Earth. What will the business of the [final] Hour be like, except the twinkling of an eye, or it may be even closer? God is Capable of everything!

* God has brought you out of your mothers' wombs; you knew nothing then, while He has granted you hearing, eyesight and vital organs so that you may feel thankful. * Do they not see how the birds are governed in mid air: only God holds them up! In that are signs for folk who believe.

80

** God has granted you your houses as homes to live in, and granted you the skins of livestock [to make] houses which you find so light on the day you pack them up to move elsewhere and the day you come to a halt. From their wool, their fur and their hair come furnishings and commodities for a while. * God has granted you shade out of what He has created, and granted you resorts in the mountains, and granted you garments with which to protect yourselves from the heat as well as garments to ward off your own violence.

Thus He completes His favor towards you so that you may commit yourselves to (live in) peace. * Should they still turn away, you have only to announce matters clearly. * They recognize God's favor; then they disregard it. Most of them are disbelievers.

84

(xii) * Some day We shall raise up a witness from every nation; then permission will not be granted those who disbelieve nor will they be allowed to argue back. ** When those who do wrong see the torment, it will neither be lightened for them nor will they be granted any delay.

Association
Punished

* When those who have associated [others with God] see their associates [in such worship], they will say: "Our Lord, these are our associates whom we appealed to instead of to You."

They will toss the statement back at them: "You're lying!" * They will proffer their surrender to God on that day, while anything they were inventing will leave them in the lurch. * We shall inflict torment upon torment on those who have disbelieved and obstructed God's path, because of how abusive they have acted. * Some day We shall raise up a witness from every nation against them from among themselves. We shall even bring you as a witness against such persons. We have sent the Book down to you to explain everything, and for guidance and mercy, and as good news for Muslims.

(XIII) ** God commands justice, kindness and giving [their due] to near relatives, while He forbids sexual misconduct, debauchery and insolence. He so instructs you (all) so that you may draw attention to it.

90

* Fulfil God's agreement once you have pledged to do so, and do not break any oaths once they have been sworn to. You have set God up as a Surety for yourselves; God knows whatever you do.

On Keeping Oaths

* Do not be like a woman who unravels her yarn after its strands have been firmly spun. **You use your oaths in order to snatch at advantages over one another, just because one nation may be more prosperous than another nation.** God is only testing you by means of it; so He may explain to you on Resurrection Day what you have been disagreeing about.

Exploitation

* If God had wished, He would have set you up as one community, but He lets anyone He wishes go astray, and guides anyone He wishes. You shall (all) be questioned about whatever you have been doing.

Its Responsiblity

* Do not use your oaths to take advantage of one another. Still one's foot may slip after it has felt secure, and you may taste evil for having blocked off God's way. You will have serious torment. ** Do not sell God's agreement for a paltry price; only what God has is best for you, if you only realized it. * Anything you have is temporary; while whatever God has is everlasting.
We will reward those who have been patient with their earnings according to the finest deeds they have been doing. * We shall let anyone who acts honorably, **whether it is a man or a woman**, provided he is a believer, live a happy life and reward them with their earnings for the finest deeds they have been doing.

Mutual Deceit

* **Whenever you read the Qur᾽ān, seek refuge with God from Satan the Outcast**; * he has no authority over those who believe and rely on their Lord. *** His authority rests only on those who enlist him as a patron, and who associate others with Him.

How to Read the Qur᾽ān
100

(XIV) * Whenever We shift a verse from its context in favor of another verse (God is quite Aware of what He sends down!), they say: "You are merely an impostor." Indeed most of them do not know anything! * SAY: "The Holy Spirit has brought it down as Truth from your Lord to brace those who believe, and as guidance and good news for Muslims."

101

* We already know they are saying: "It is merely a human being who is teaching him!" The tongue of the person whom they hint at is foreign, while this is clear Arabic speech. * God will never guide those who do not believe in God's signs, while they will have painful torment.

Apostasy OR
Backsliding

** Those who do not believe in God's signs are merely inventing a lie; such men are liars. * Anyone who disbelieves in God after having once made his profession of faith—except for someone who is compelled to while his heart is unwavering in its faith—but anyone who lays (his) breast wide open to disbelief will have wrath from God [descend] on him. They will have awful torment! * That is because they cherish worldly life rather than the Hereafter. God does not guide disbelieving folk.

* Those are the ones whose hearts, hearing and eyesight God has sealed off. Those are the heedless. * They will positively be the losers in the Hereafter. ** Even then your Lord—for those who have migrated after they were persecuted, then struggled and were patient—after such [trials] your Lord will be Forgiving, Merciful.

110

111

(xv) * Some day each soul will come to plead for itself, and every soul will be repaid according to whatever it has done, and they will not be wronged.

*The Disbe-
lieving Town*

* God has made up a parable about a town which had been safe, tranquil; its livelihood was brought to it comfortably from every quarter.

Yet it disbelieved in God's favors, and God let it experience a pall of hunger and fear because of what they had been producing. * A messenger came to them from among themselves and they rejected him. Torment seized them while they were doing wrong.

Food

* So eat any lawful, wholesome thing God has provided you with, and be thankful for God's favor if you have been worshipping Him. ** He has only forbidden you carrion, blood, and pork, as well as anything that has been consecrated to something besides God. Yet anyone who is obliged to do so without desiring it nor going to excess [will find] God is Forgiving, Merciful.

* Do not tell a lie about something your tongues describe (such as): "This is lawful, while this is forbidden!"; so that you fabricate a lie against God. Those who fabricate a lie about God will not prosper: * [they will have] slight enjoyment, and they shall [then] have painful punishment.

* We forbade those who became Jews what We have already told you about; We did not harm them, but they harmed themselves. * Then your Lord—for those who had done evil out of ignorance, then repented later on and reformed—your Lord was afterward Forgiving, Merciful.

120

(xvi) ** Abraham formed a community that was devoted to God since he was righteous and was no associator; * grateful for His favors, He chose and guided him to a Straight Road. * We gave him a fine thing in this world, and he will be among the honorable in the Hereafter. * Then We inspired you: "Follow the sect of Abraham the Seeker; he was no associator [of others in his worship of God]."

*The
Sabbath*

* The Sabbath was set up only for those who disagreed about it. Your Lord will pass judgment on them on Resurrection Day concerning what-

ever they have been disagreeing about. ** Invite [people] to your Lord's way with discretion and kindly instruction, and discuss [things] with them in the politest manner. Your Lord is quite Aware as to who has strayed from His path, just as He is quite Aware of those who have consented to be guided.

    * If you (all) should punish them, then do your punishing to the same extent as you have been punished. Yet if you are patient, well [things go] better for the patient. * Act patient; your patience comes only from God. Do not feel saddened because of them nor be in any anguish over how they plot. * God stands alongside those who fulfil their duty and who act kindly!

*Behavior
and
Punishment*

PART
FIFTEEN

17

The Night Journey
(Glory!; OR *The Children of Israel*)

THIS CHAPTER consists of twelve sections of 111 Meccan verses, except for vv. 26, 32-33, 37 and 73-80 (these are in sections III, IV, VIII-IX) which date from the Madinese period. It was revealed after **Stories** 28 and before the last verse in **The Cow** 2, and shortly before the Prophet's Transfer or *Hijra* to Madīna. The title *Al-Mi‹raj* in Arabic is the singular of *Al-Ma‹ārij* or 'Staircases Upward' which is the title for Chapter 70 (it is also given as *Al-Isrā›*). The celestial journey or ascension to Heaven is celebrated on the twenty-seventh night of the month of Rajab, five weeks before the fast of Ramaḍan begins. An alternative title to the chapter is **The Children of Israel** and still another is **Glory!** taken from the first word (*Subḥān*) in the chapter (and at Section x).

The style at the beginning is closely interwoven. The chapter opens with a solemn announcement of the Prophet's ascension as a lilting symphony which the Italian poet Dante was to use later on in a more elaborate form for his *Divine Comedy*. An easily obtainable description of this tradition in English is found in Jeffery's *Islam*, pp. 35-42. Its translation and interpretation are extremely difficult; Ibn-Kathīr's is probably the best.

Next there follows moral legislation, including one version of the Islamic "Do Not's" which stresses personal responsibility and the seriousness of associating others in our pure worship of God Alone (II). The treatment of parents and charity are other themes of morality (III-IV). Disbelievers are aptly described in section V. The chapter ends with a long section on how to read the Qur›ān and how to pray (IX-XII); see also I and V. In short, this is one of the most important and sustained chapters in the Qur›ān, and its beauty is inimitable.

In the name of God, the Mercy-giving, the Merciful!

Announcing the Prophet's Ascension

(I) * **Glory** be to Him Who had His servant travel by night from the Hallowed Mosque to the Further Mosque whose surroundings We have blessed, so We might show him some of Our signs! He is the Alert, the Observant!

* We gave Moses the Book and granted it as guidance for the **Children of Israel**: "Do not accept any defender except Me!" * [They were]

offspring [of those] whom We put on board with Noah; he was a grateful servant. * We decreed in the Book concerning the **Children of Israel**: "You will create havoc on earth twice, and display great haughtiness." ** When the first of both warnings came, we despatched servants of Ours to inflict severe violence upon you (all). They rampaged through [your] homes, and it served as a warning which was acted upon. * Then We offered you another chance against them, and reinforced you with wealth and children, and granted you more manpower. * If you have acted kindly, you acted kindly towards yourselves, while if you committed any evil, it was towards [yourselves] as well.

Thus the warning about the next one came along to trouble your persons, and so they would enter the Mosque just as they had entered it in the first place, so they might utterly annihilate anything they overcame. * Perhaps your Lord may show mercy to you. If you should turn back, We will go back (too) and turn Hell into a confinement for disbelievers! * This Qur'ān guides one to something that is more straightforward and reassures believers who perform honorable actions; they shall have great earnings. ** Nevertheless We have reserved painful torment for those who do not believe in the Hereafter.

10

(II) * Man appeals for evil during his appeal for good; everyman has been so hasty!

11

* We have granted night and daylight as twin signs. We blot out the sign of night, and grant the sign of daylight to see by so you may seek bounty from your Lord and know how to count the years and other such reckoning. Everything have We set forth in detail.

* We have tied everyman's fate around his neck; and We shall produce a book for him on Resurrection Day that he will find spread open; * "Read your book; today there will be none but yourself to call you to account!"

Man's Book

** Anyone who submits to guidance will be guided only so far as he himself is concerned, while anyone who strays away, only strays by himself. No burdened soul shall bear another's burden.

Personal Responsibility

We have never acted as punishers until We have despatched some messenger: * yet whenever We want to wipe out some town, We order its high-livers so they act depraved in it; thus the Sentence about it is proven to be right and We utterly annihilate it. * How many generations did We destroy since Noah? Sufficient is it for your Lord to be Informed, Observant of His servants' sins!

* For anyone who wants the fleeting present, We let whatever We wish to flit past anyone We want it to. Then We set up Hell for him; he will roast in it, condemned, disgraced. * Anyone who wants the Hereafter and makes a proper effort to achieve it while he is a believer, will have

Free Choice

20   their effort gratified. ** Each We shall supply, these as well as those, with a gift from your Lord: your Lord's gift will never be withheld.

* Watch how We have permitted some of them to get ahead of others. The Hereafter will be greater in [conferring] ranks and even greater in attainment.

The Islamic "DO NOT'S":   * Do not place any other deity alongside God, lest you sit back, condemned, forsaken.

23

Association Condemned

(III) * Your Lord has decreed that you should worship nothing except Him, and [show] kindness to your parents; whether either of them or both of them should attain old age [while they are] still with you, never say to them: "Naughty!" nor scold either of them. Speak to them in a generous fashion. * Protect them carefully from outsiders, and SAY: "My Lord, show them mercy, just as they cared for me [when I was] a little child!"

** Your Lord is quite Aware of anything that is on your minds; if you behave honorably, then He will be Forgiving towards those who are attentive.

Charity   * Render your close relative his due, as well as the pauper and the wayfarer. Yet do not squander [your money] extravagantly; * spendthrifts are the devils' brethren, and Satan has always been ungrateful towards his Lord. * Yet if you have to avoid them, seeking some mercy which you may expect from your Lord, still speak a courteous word to them. * Do not keep your hand gripping at your throat nor stretch it out as far as it

30   will reach, lest you sit back blameworthy, destitute. ** Your Lord extends sustenance to anyone He wishes, and measures it out; He is Informed, Observant about His servants.

31

Other Moral Legislation

(IV) * Do not kill your children in dread of poverty; We shall provide for both them and you. Killing them is a serious blunder!

* Do not commit adultery. It is shocking and an evil way [to behave].

* Do not kill any soul whom God has forbidden you to, except through [due process of] law. We have given his nearest relatives authority for anyone who is killed unjustly—yet let him not overdo things in killing [the culprit], inasmuch as he has been so supported.

* Do not approach an orphan's estate before he comes of age unless it is to improve it.

Responsibility   Fulfil your oaths; any promise will be checked into.

** Give full measure whenever you measure out anything, and weigh with honest scales; that is better and the finest way of acting.

* **Do not worry over something you have no knowledge about**: your hearing, eyesight and vital organs will all be questioned concerning it.

* Do not prance saucily around the earth; you can never tunnel through the earth nor rival the mountains in height.

* All that is evil with your Lord, to be hated. * Such is some of the wisdom your Lord has revealed to you.

Do not place any other deity alongside God [Alone] lest you be tossed into Hell, blamed, rejected. ** Has your Lord singled you out to have sons, while He has accepted daughters from among the angels [for Himself]? You are uttering such a serious statement!

40
*Association
Again*

(v) * We have already spelled out matters in this Reading so they will notice it, even though it only adds to their disgust.

41

* SAY: "If there were (other) gods along with Him as they say, then they would have sought a way to the Possessor of the Throne. * **Glory** be to Him! How greatly Exalted is He over anything they may say! * The Seven Heavens and Earth, as well as whoever is in them, glorify Him. Nothing exists unless it hymns His praise; yet you do not understand their glorification. Still He has been Lenient, Forgiving.

*Paganism,
Association
Once More*

** Whenever you read the Qurʾān, We place a hidden curtain between you and those who do not believe in the Hereafter. * We place wrappers over their hearts lest they comprehend it, and dullness in their ears. When you mention your Lord Alone in the Qurʾān they even turn their backs in disgust!
* **We** are quite Aware as to what they are listening for when they listen to you, and whenever they conspire together, then wrongdoers will say: "You are only following a man who is bewitched!" * Watch what sort of stories they make up about you. They have strayed away and are unable to find a way back. * They say: "When we are bones and mortal remains, will we be raised up in some fresh creation?"
** SAY: "Become stones or iron * or any creation that seems important enough to fill your breasts;" so they will say: "Who will bring us back [to life]?" SAY: "The One Who originated you in the first place."
They will wag their heads at you and say: "When will it be?" SAY: "Perhaps it is near!" * Some day He will call on you, and you will respond in praise of Him. You will assume you have lingered for only a little while.

*On Reciting
the Qurʾān*

Disbelievers

50

(vi) * Tell My servants that they should say whatever is politest. Satan stirs up trouble among them; Satan is an open enemy to man! * Your Lord is quite Aware of you (all); if He wishes, He will show you mercy, while if He wishes, He will punish you. We have not sent you as a trustee over them. ** Your Lord is quite Aware of whoever is in Heaven and Earth. We have made some prophets excel over others, and given David the Psalms.

53

Saints'
Worship

* SAY: "Invoke those whom you claim to have besides Him: they do not control any means of removing harm from you, nor for changing it." * Even those whom they appeal to, crave access to their Lord, vying to be nearest. They hope for His mercy and fear His torment. Your Lord's torment is something to beware of!

* No town exists but We shall act as its Destroyers before Resurrection Day, or as its Punishers by means of severe torment. That has been recorded in the Book. * Nothing has prevented Us from sending signs except that early men rejected them. We sent Thamūd the she-camel to open their eyes, yet they mistreated her. We merely send signs in order to

60

frighten [people]. ** Thus We told you: "Your Lord embraces [all] mankind." We granted the vision which We showed you only as a test for mankind, as well as the Tree that is cursed in the Qurʾān. We let them feel afraid; yet it only increases great arrogance in them.

61

Iblīs OR
Diabolis

(VII) * When We told the angels: "Bow down on your knees before Adam," they [all] knelt down except Diabolis. He said: "Am I to bow down on my knees before someone You have created out of clay?" * He said [further]: "Have You considered this person Yourself whom You have honored more than me? If You will postpone things for me until Resurrection Day, then I shall bring all but a few of his offspring under my mastery."

* He said: "Go away! Any of them who follows you will have Hell as your reward; it is such an ample reward! * Entice any of them whom you can with your voice. Set upon them with your cavalry and your manpower. Share wealth and children with them, and promise them anything. (Yet Satan merely promises them illusion.) ** As for My servants, you will have no authority over them; your Lord suffices as a Trustee."

* Your Lord is the One Who propels ships for you at sea, so you may seek some of His bounty. He has been so Merciful towards you! * Whenever some adversity strikes you at sea, anyone you appeal to besides Him leaves [you] in the lurch; yet whenever We bring you safely to port, you (all) turn away evasively. Man has been so thankless!

* Do you feel so safe that He will not let a slice of land cave in beneath you, or send a sandstorm down on you? Then you will find no agent to act on your behalf! * Or do you feel so secure that He will send you back for another chance at it, and drive a smashing gale against you which will drown you because you have disbelieved? Then you will not find any

70

follower in it to [help] you against Us. ** We have dignified the Children of Adam and transported them around on land and at sea. We have provided them with wholesome things and favored them especially over many of those whom We have created.

71

*Spiritual
Blindness*

(VIII) * Some day We shall call forth all mankind along with whoever has led them. Those who are given their book in their right hand, will read their book and not be harmed one bit; * while anyone who has been blind in this [life] will remain blind in the Hereafter, and go even further astray.

* They almost lure you away from what We have revealed to you, in order to invent something else against Us; then they would adopt you as a bosom friend! * If We had not braced you, you might have almost

inclined a little bit towards them. ** Then We would have made you taste a double share of life and a double one of dying; then you would not have found any supporter for yourself against Us! * They almost scare you off the earth, to exile you from it. Yet they would never survive you except for a short while.

* [Such has been] the practice with any of Our messengers whom We have sent before you. You will never find any change in Our course!

(IX) * Keep up prayer from the decline of the sun, until twilight at night;

and [observe] the Reading at daybreak, since **reading** [the Qurʾān] **at daybreak will be witnessed!**

* At night, wake up and pray during it[s reading] as an extra bonus for yourself; perhaps your Lord will raise you once again to a praise-worthy standing.

** SAY: "My Lord, let me enter through a proper entrance and leave by an honest exit! Grant me supporting authority from Your presence."

* And SAY (too):
**"Truth has come and falsehood vanished;
falsehood is so perishable!**

* We send down something from the Qurʾān [to serve] as healing and a mercy for believers, while wrongdoers are only increased in loss.

* Whenever We show man some favor, he avoids it and drifts off to one side; while whenever evil touches him, he acts desperate. * SAY: "Everyone acts according to his own disposition. Your Lord is quite Aware as to who is best guided along the Way.''

(X) ** They will ask you about the Spirit.
SAY: "The Spirit [operates] at my Lord's command, while you have been given only a smattering of knowledge." * If We so wished, We would take away anything We have inspired you with; then you would not find anyone you could rely on against Us with it * except for some mercy from your Lord. His bounty towards you has been great! * SAY: "Even if men and sprites organized to produce something like this Reading, they would never bring anything like it no matter how much assistance they lent one another." * We have set forth every [kind of] parable for mankind in this Reading; yet most men refuse to do anything except disbelieve.

** They say: "We will never believe in you unless you cause a spring to gush forth from the earth for us, * or have a garden full of datepalms and grapevines and make rivers gush forth plentifully through the midst of them, * or you cause the sky to fall in pieces on us just as you claim, or bring God and His angels to vouch for you, * or you have a luxurious house built, or soar up into the sky; we will never believe in your climbing up there until you bring down a book for us to read."

SAY: "**Glory** be to my Lord! Am I anything but a human messenger?"

78
Prayer

80

*Truth and
Falsehood*

85

*The Holy
Spirit*

90

Disbelief
OR *Skeptics*

94

*Skeptics
Again*

(XI) * Nothing prevents men from believing whenever guidance comes to them except that they say: "Has God despatched a mortal as a messenger?" ** SAY: "If there had been angels calmly walking around on earth, We would have sent an angel down from Heaven as a messenger for them."

* SAY: "God suffices as a Witness between me and you (all). He is Informed, Observant about His servants." * Anyone whom God guides, remains guided, while you will never find any sponsors besides Himself for those He lets go astray. We will summon them face down on Resurrection Day, blind, dumb and deaf; their lodging will be Hell. Every time it dies down, We will make it blaze up again for them. * Such will be their reward for disbelieving in Our signs and saying: "Once we are bones and mortal remains, will we be raised up again in some fresh creation?"

* Do they not consider that God, Who has created Heaven and Earth, is Able to create the like of them? He has set them a deadline there is no doubt about, yet wrongdoers refuse to do anything except disbelieve.

100

*** SAY: "Even if you controlled the treasures of my Lord's mercy, you would still hold them back in dread of overspending [them]. Man is so grudging!"

101

*Moses and the
Children of
Israel*

(XII) * We gave Moses nine clear signs. Ask the **Children of Israel** about how, when he came to them and Pharaoh told him: "I think you are out of your mind, Moses!", * he said: "You know that no one except the Lord of Heaven and Earth has sent these down as insights. I think you are doomed, Pharaoh!"

* He wanted to scare them away from the land, so We drowned him and everyone who accompanied him. * Later on, We told the **Children of Israel**: "Settle down in the land. When the promise about the Hereafter comes along, We will bring you in as a rabble."

*How to Read
the Qurʾān*

** We have really sent it down, and it has come down for the Truth. We have sent you only as a newsbearer and warner; * and for a Reading which We have divided up so you can read it to people in sittings. We have sent it down as a successive revelation.

*BOW
DOWN
HERE*

* SAY: "Believe in it, or do not believe in it;" those who have already been given knowledge fall down **bowing** with their faces [on the ground] whenever it is recited to them, * while they say:

"**Glory** to our Lord!
Our Lord's promise has come true!"

* They fall down with their faces [on the ground], weeping and it increases them in reverence.

110

*How to
Pray*

** SAY: "Appeal to God, or appeal to the Mercy-giving: whichever [name] you may invoke, He still has the Finest Names. Do not shout in your prayer nor say it under your breath; seek a course in between.

* SAY: ''Praise be to God Who has adopted no son and has no partner in control.'' He needs no protector against such pettiness. Magnify Him greatly!

18
The Cave

THE FOLLOWING chapter is arranged in twelve sections and consists of 110 Meccan verses. However verse 28 and verses 83-101 on Double Horns (XI) date from the Madinese period. It was revealed after **The Pall** 88 and before **Bees** 16, and it forms a series of narratives in the manner of **Joseph's** story in Chapter 12 and **Stories** 28.

The chief narration concerns the so-called "Sleepers in the Cave" who are mentioned in Edward Gibbon's *Decline and Fall of the Roman Empire* (ch. XXXIII, end) which that historian calls a legend. These sleepers were young men who were persecuted because they did not want to become associators or to worship other deities or idols. It is clear this is an allegory and that their number does not matter. It apparently refers to the difficulties of belief within the Christian church during its early centuries. This story is important since it shows how religions previous to Islam had become corrupted, and how some early Christians resisted such ideas.

Towards the end, Moses' mystic journey after Truth is related (IX-X). Double Horns may give the story of Alexander the Great which interested the Middle East as much as it did medieval Europe (XI). Most of this is allegorical, as we are clearly told at the end of the story of the Sleepers, and it should not be taken too literally; the collection of tales merely provides us with a running commentary on significant events.

Other sections deal with the sin of association, the virtue of tolerance, Hell and Heaven (IV), and charming parables like the Grateful and Ungrateful Farmers (V); Rain from Heaven (VI); and Diabolis' meeting with Adam (VII). It ends with the little gem called "The Words of the Lord" (XII). As a whole the style resembles that of Chapter 71 on **Noah** (SEE the Introduction to Chapter 72 **Sprites** on the allegorical style). Pickthall's explanation in his introduction to this chapter is also clear and easy to read.

In the name of God, the Mercy-giving, the Merciful!

(I) * Praise be to God, Who has sent down the Book for His servants and has placed no distortion in it; * [it is] straightforward, so He may warn about serious violence from Himself and give good news to believers who perform honorable deeds. They will have a handsome wage, * to bask in it for ever and ever.

* He warns those who say: "God has adopted a son." ** They have no knowledge about it, nor did their forefathers have any either. It is too serious a statement to come out of their mouths: they are merely telling a lie! * Perhaps you will fret yourself to death checking up on them, worrying lest they will not believe this report. * We have placed whatever is on earth as an ornament for it so We may test them as to which one is best in action; * and We shall turn anything on it into a barren wasteland.

10

The Sleepers in the Cave

* Have you considered how the Companions in the **Cave** and with the Tablet were such marvellous signs of Ours? ** Thus the youths sought shelter in the **Cave**, and said: "Our Lord, grant us mercy from Your presence and furnish us with some direction in our affair." * We struck them with drowsiness in the **Cave** for several years; * then We awakened them again so We might know which of the two parties would best calculate how long a stretch they had remained [there].

13

(II) * We shall relate their story to you correctly:

They were young men who believed in their Lord, and We gave them extra guidance. * We strengthened their hearts when they stood up and said: "Our Lord is Lord of Heaven and Earth. We will never appeal to any deity except Him; should we say [such a thing], then it would be an outrage. ** These people of ours have adopted other gods besides Him. If they would only bring some clear authority to support them!"

Who is more in the wrong than someone who invents a lie about God? * When you withdraw from them and whatever they serve instead of God, then seek shelter in the **Cave**. Your Lord will spread some of His mercy over you and make fitting arrangements for you in your affair.

* You should have seen how the sun as it rose, swerved away from their **Cave** toward the right; and as it set, slanted off toward the left of them, while they lay in a space in between. That was one of God's signs. Anyone whom God guides, remains guided; while anyone He lets go astray will never find any patron to set him straight.

18

(III) * You would reckon they were awake, while they [really] lay there asleep. We turned them over on the right and on the left, while their dog lay stretched out with his forepaws over the threshold. If you had chanced upon them, you would have turned and fled from them; you would have been filled with awe of them!

* Even so We raised them up again so they might question one another. One of them spoke up and said: "How long have you stayed [here]?" They said: "We have stayed a day, or part of a day." They said: "Your Lord is quite Aware of how long you have stayed [here], so send one of your men to the city with this coin of yours. Let him see which food is the most suitable and bring you [back] a supply of it. Let him act

20

discreetly and not make anyone aware of you. ** If they should find out about you, they will stone you or make you turn back to their sect. You would never succeed then!" * Thus We disclosed things to them so they might know that God's promise has come true and there is no doubt about the Hour.

So [people] debated their case among themselves, and they said: "Build a monument over them. Their Lord is quite Aware of them." Those who won out in the end said: "Let us erect a shrine for them." * They will say: "[They were] three, the fourth of them being their dog;" while [others] will say: "Five, the sixth of them is their dog," guessing at the Unseen. [Still others] say: "Seven, and the eighth of them is their dog."

SAY: "My Lord is quite Aware as to how many they were. Only a few know about them." Do not discuss them except in a discussion that is obvious, nor seek anyone else's opinion about them.

Allegory

(IV) * (Do not say about anything: "I am doing that tomorrow," * unless [you add]: "Should God so wish!" Remember your Lord whenever you might forget, and SAY: "Perhaps my Lord will guide me even closer than this to proper behavior.")

23

On Trusting God

** And they stayed in their **Cave** for three hundred years plus nine more. * SAY: "God is quite Aware as to how long they stayed [there]. He holds the Unseen in Heaven and Earth; He is quite Observant of it, and quite Alert as well. They have no patron besides Him, nor does He let anyone else share in His discretion."

* Quote whatever has been revealed to you from your Lord's book: there is no one who may change His words, nor will you ever find any sanctuary except in Him. * Restrain yourself concerning those who appeal to their Lord in the morning and evening, wanting His presence; yet do not let your eyes wander too far from them, desiring the attraction of worldly life. Do not obey anyone whose heart We allow to neglect remembering Us, so he pursues his own whim. His case results in dissipation. * SAY: "Truth comes from your Lord. Let anyone who wishes to, believe, and let anyone who wishes to, disbelieve."

Tolerance

Free Will

We have reserved a fire for wrongdoers whose sheets will hem them in. If they should ask for some relief, then water like molten brass will be showered on them to scorch their faces. How awful such a drink will be and how evil is such a couch! ** As for those who believe and perform honorable deeds, well We shall not waste the earnings of anyone whose action has been kind. * Those shall have the gardens of Eden through which rivers will flow. They will be decked out with gold bracelets there and wear green silk clothing and brocade, as they lean back on sofas in it. How superb will such a recompense be and how handsome is the couch!

Hell

30

Heaven

(V) * Set forth a comparison between two men for them: We granted two vineyards to one of them, and bordered them with datepalms and planted field crops in between. * Each garden produced its food and did not fail to yield its best; We even caused a river to spring forth in the midst of them.

* One man had fruit and told his companion while he was discussing things with him: "I am wealthier than you are, and have a bigger following!" ** He entered his garden while he was thus harming his own soul. He said: "I do not think that this will ever disappear! * I do not think the Hour is at hand; if I am ever sent back to my Lord, I shall find something better than it in exchange."

32

The Grateful and Ungrateful Farmers

Pride a Sin

* His companion told him while he was discussing things with him: "Have you disbelieved in the One Who created you from dust, then from a drop of semen; then fashioned you into a man? * However so far as we are concerned, He is God my Lord, and I do not associate anyone with my Lord! * Why, as you entered your garden, did you not say: 'Whatever God may wish; there is no strength except through God [Alone]'? Even if you see how I am less wealthy than you are and have fewer children,

40

** perhaps my Lord will still give me something better than your garden and send a reckoning down from Heaven on it, so it will eventually become a bald hilltop, * or its water will sink down some morning and you will never manage to find it again."

Punishment for Disbelief and Association

* He was caught short with his fruit, and one morning he began to wring his hands over what he had spent on it, since it had tumbled down from its trellisses. He kept saying: "It's too bad for me; I should never have associated anyone with my Lord!" * He had no party to support him against God, so he was not supported. * That is how patronage lies with the True God. He is Best as a recompense and Best in results.

45

(VI) ** Set forth an example for them about worldly life being like water We send down from the sky. The plants on the earth swell up with it; yet some morning they will become dry weeds which the winds will blow away. God is Competent to do everything!

Rain from Heaven

* Wealth and children are an attraction during worldly life. Yet honorable deeds that last for ever are better as a recompense from your Lord and even better to hope for.

The Appointment on Doomsday

* Some day We shall set the mountains travelling along and you will see the earth lying exposed. We will summon them and not one of them shall We omit; * they will be marshalled in ranks before your Lord: "You have come to Us just as We created you in the first place even though you claimed We would never make any appointment for you."

The Doomsday Book

* The Book will be produced and you will see criminals apprehensive about its contents. They will say: "It's too late for us! What does this book mean for me? It omits nothing either small nor large unless it is accounted for." They will find whatever they have done presented there, even though your Lord will not harm anyone.

50

(VII) ** When We told the angels: "Bow down on your knees before Adam," they [all] knelt down except for Diabolis; he was a sprite and acted contrary to his Lord's command. Will you (all) adopt him and his offspring as patrons instead of Myself? They are enemies of yours! How wretched is such an alternative for wrongdoers.

Diabolis and Adam

* I did not have them as witnesses at the creation of Heaven and Earth, nor even at their own creation. I am not about to adopt those who lead [others] astray as [My] attendants.

* Some day He will say: "Call on My associates whom you claim to have, and appeal to them." They will not respond to them, while We shall place a chasm between them. * Criminals will see the Fire and think they are falling into it. They will not find any way to avert it.

(VIII) * We have spelled out every sort of example for mankind in this Qur>ān, yet everyman uses it just for argument in most cases. ** What has prevented men from believing and seeking forgiveness from their Lord, once guidance has come to them, except [they may wish] that the practice of primitive people should come along with them, or that torment come face to face with them. * We have sent emissaries merely as heralds and warners while those who disbelieve idly argue away so they may refute the Truth by means of it. They treat My signs and what they are warned of as a joke!

* Who is more in the wrong than someone who has been reminded about his Lord's signs and then avoids them, and forgets anything his hands may have sent on ahead? We have placed wrappings over their hearts and dullness in their ears lest they understand it. Even if you called them to guidance, they still would never consent to be guided.

* Your Lord is the Forgiving, the Possessor of Mercy. If He were to take them to task for what they have earned, He would hasten torment for them; instead they have their appointment from which they will never find any asylum. * Such towns have We destroyed whenever they did wrong, and We fixed the time for their destruction.

(IX) ** And so Moses told his young man: "I shall not give up until I reach the place where both seas meet, even though I spend ages doing so." * So when they reached the place where they had met, they forgot their fish, which took its way to the sea as if it went out through a drain.

* When they had gone still further, he told his young man: "Bring us our lunch; we have experienced so much strain along our journey." * He said: "Did you see when we were resting by the rock, that I forgot the fish? Unless it was Satan who made me forget it so I did not remember it. It took its way through the sea like something marvellous!" * He said: "That is just what we've been searching for."

So they retraced their steps the way they had come. ** They found one of Our servants to whom We had given mercy from Ourself and taught him knowledge from Our very presence. * Moses said to him: "May I follow you so you may teach me some of the common sense you have been taught?" * He said: "You will never have any patience with me! * How can you show any patience with something that is beyond your experience?"

* He said: "You will find me patient, if God so wishes. I will not disobey you in any matter." ** He said: "If you follow me, do not ask me about anything until I tell you something to remember it by."

(X) * So they both started out until, as they boarded the ship, he bored a hole in her. He said: "Have you scuttled her to drown her crew? You have done such a weird thing!"

* He said: "Didnt I say that you would not manage to show any patience with me?" * He said: "Do not take me to task for what I have forgotten, nor weigh me down by making my case too difficult for me."

* They journeyed on until when they met a youth, he killed him. He said: "Have you killed an innocent soul without any previous murder [on his part]? You have committed such a horrible deed!"

54
*Man the
Quibbler*

60
*Moses'
Mystic
Journey*

70

71

*PART
SIXTEEN*

(x cont'd) ** He said: "Did I not tell you that you would never manage to have any patience with me?" * He said: "If I ever ask you about anything after this, do not let me accompany you. You have found an excuse so far as I am concerned."

* They both proceeded further till when they came to the people of a [certain] town, they asked its inhabitants for some food, and they refused to treat either of them hospitably. They found a wall there which was about to tumble down, so he set it straight. He said: "If you had wished, you might have accepted some payment for it."

* He said: "This [means] a parting between you and me. Yet I shall inform you about the interpretation of what you had no patience for.

* "As for the ship, it belonged to some poor men who worked at sea. I wanted to damage it because there was a king behind them seizing every ship by force. ** The young man's parents were believers, and we dreaded lest he would burden them with arrogation and disbelief. * We wanted their Lord to replace him for them with someone better than him in purity and nearer to tenderness.

* "The wall belonged to two orphan boys [living] in the city, and a treasure of theirs lay underneath it. Their father had been honorable, so your Lord wanted them to come of age and claim their treasure as a mercy from your Lord. I did not do it of my own accord. That is the interpretation of what you showed no patience for."

(xi) * They will ask you about Double Horns. SAY: "I shall render an account of him for you."

* We established things on earth for him, and gave him access to everything; ** so he followed a [certain] course * until when he reached the place where the sun sets, he found it setting in a mucky spring alongside which he (also) found some people. We said: "Double Horns, either you will punish [them] or else act kindly towards them." * He said: "Anyone who has done wrong we shall punish; then he will be sent back to his Lord, and He will punish him with horrible torment. * Anyone who believes and acts honorably will have the finest reward and we will tell him gently about our command."

* Then he followed [another] course ** until when he reached the place where the sun rises, he found it rising on a folk whom We had not granted any protection against it. * That was how We controlled information about whatever lay before him.

* Then he followed [still another] course * until when he reached two barriers, he found a folk on the nearer side of them who scarcely understood any speech. * They said: "Double Horns, Gog and Magog are ravaging the earth. Shall we pay you tribute on condition that you place a barrier between us and them?" ** He said: "Whatever my Lord has empowered me to do is even better, so help me with some [man] power: I'll place a rampart between you and them. * Bring me blocks of iron."

When he had levelled off [the space] between both cliffs, he said: "Blow on it!", until when he had built it up into a fire, he said: "Bring me molten brass so I may pour some over it." * They neither managed to climb over it nor were they able to tunnel through it. * He said: "This is a mercy from my Lord. Whenever my Lord's promise comes, he will make it crumble. My Lord's promise is true!"

* We will leave some of them surging over others on that day. The Trumpet shall be blown, and We will gather them all together. *** On that day We will spread Hell out on display for disbelievers * whose eyes have been under blinders against [seeing] My reminder. They have not even managed to hear!

(XII) * Do those who disbelieve reckon they will adopt My servants as patrons instead of Me? We have reserved Hell as a lodging for disbelievers! * SAY: "Shall We announce to you those who have lost the most through [their] actions?" * Those whose effort led them astray during worldly life, while they reckoned they were producing something fine, ** are the ones who have disbelieved in their Lord's signs and about meeting Him; their actions will prove to be useless, and We shall set up no weighing-in for them on Resurrection Day. * Such will be their reward— Hell, because of how they have disbelieved and taken My signs and My messengers for a laughingstock. * Those who believe and perform honorable deeds will have the gardens of Paradise as a lodging * to live in for ever; they will never seek any transfer from it.

> * SAY: "If the sea were an inkwell
> for the words of my Lord,
> the sea would be drained
> before my Lord's words would be spent
> even though we brought the same
> again to replenish it.

** SAY: "I am only a human being like yourselves; it has been revealed to me that your deity is God Alone. Anyone who is expecting to meet his Lord should act honorably and not associate anyone in the worship due his Lord."

Margin notes:

100

102

*Saints'
Worship
Condemned*

*The Words
of the
Lord*

110

19
Mary

THESE 98 VERSES form six sections dating from the Meccan period, except for vv. 58-71 (IV-V) which date from Madīna. This chapter was revealed after **Originator** 35 and before the next one which is called **Ṭā-Hā** 20. It furnishes us with the Islamic story about Jesus' mother, as well as his speaking as a boy from the cradle (IV-VI). It was read to the emperor of Ethiopia by the migrants or refugees to that kingdom before the classic Hijra.

The chapter also deals with the role of Abraham and other prophets (III-IV). Great emphasis is laid in this chapter on God's aspect as **The Mercy-giving** or *ar-Raḥmān*, especially by Mary. The Angels' Message in section IV is also significant. The chapter is sustained on an assonance in *-iyya* (which is interrupted between vv. 33-40 (II: end).

In the name of God, the Mercy-giving, the Merciful!

(I) * K.H.Y.E.Ṣ.

* [This is] a Reminder of your Lord's mercy towards his servant Zachariah * when he appealed to his Lord with a suppressed cry.

* He said: "My Lord, my bones are tottering for me and my head is glistening with white hair, while I have never been grumbling in my appeal to You, my Lord! ** Yet I fear for my heirs after me from Your presence * who may inherit from me, and inherit from Jacob's house. Make him someone we can approve of, my Lord!"

* "Zachariah, We bring you news about a boy whose name will be John. We have not given such a name to anyone before." * He said: "My Lord, how will I have a boy while my wife is barren and I have reached such extreme old age?" * He said: "Just as your Lord has said: 'It is a trifling thing for me [to do]. I created you before while you were still nothing!'"

** He said: "My Lord, grant me a sign!" He said: "Your sign will be that you will not speak to any people for three nights in a row." * He came forth to his folk from the sanctuary and revealed to them how they should glorify [God] both morning and evening.

* "John, hold firmly to the Book." We gave him discretion as a young boy * plus compassion from Our presence and innocence. He was conscientious * and considerate towards his parents, and was not demanding, rebellious.

> ** Peace be upon him the day he was born,
> and the day he will die,
> and the day he is raised to life again!

10

(II) * Mention in the Book how **Mary** withdrew from her people to an
Eastern place. * She chose to be secluded from them. We sent her Our
spirit, who presented himself to her as a full-grown human being. * She
said: "I take refuge with the Mercy-giving from you, unless you are
someone who does his duty."

    * He said: "I am only your Lord's messenger to bestow a clean-living
boy on you." ** She said: "How shall I have a boy when no human being
has ever touched me, nor am I a loose woman?" * He said: "Thus your
Lord has said: 'It is a simple matter for Me [to do]. We will grant him as a
sign for mankind and a mercy from Ourself.' It is a matter that has been
decided."

    * So she conceived him, and withdrew to a remote place to have
him. * Labor pains came over her by the trunk of a datepalm. She said:
"If only I had died before this, and been forgotten, overlooked!"

    * Someone called out to her from below where she was: "Dont feel so
sad! Your Lord has placed a brook at your feet. ** Shake the trunk of the
datepalm towards you so it will drop some fresh dates on you. * Eat and
drink, and refresh yourself. Should you see even a single human being,
then say: 'I have vowed to keep a fast to the Mercy-giving whereby I'll
never speak to any person today!'"

    * She carried him back to her family. They said: "Mary, you have
brought something hard to believe! * Kinswoman of Aaron, your father
was no evil man, nor was your mother a loose woman." * She pointed to
him. They said: "How shall we talk to someone who is a child in the
cradle?"

    ** He said: "I am God's servant. He has given me the Book and made
me a prophet. * He has made me blessed wherever I may be, and
commissioned me to pray and [pay] the welfare tax so long as I live; * and
[to act] considerate towards my mother. He has not made me domineering,
hard to get along with. * Peace be on the day I was born, and the day I
shall die and the day I am raised to life again!"

    * Such was Jesus, the son of Mary; [it is] a true statement which they
are still puzzling over. ** It is not God's role to adopt a son. Glory be to Him!
Whenever He determines upon some matter, He merely tells it: "Be!", and
it is. * God is my Lord and your Lord, so worship Him [Alone]. This is a
Straight Road [to follow].

    * Factions have differed among themselves, yet how awful will it be for
those who disbelieve when it comes to the spectacle on such a dreadful
day! * Listen to them and watch for the day when they will come to Us;
though wrongdoers are in obvious error even today. * Warn them of the
Day of Regret when the matter will be decided; they act so heedless and
still do not believe. ** It is We Who will inherit the earth plus anyone on
it; to Us shall they return!

(III) * Mention Abraham in the Book. He was a truthful prophet * when
he told his father: "My father, why do you worship something that neither
hears nor perceives [anything], and does not benefit you in any
way? * My father, I have been given some knowledge which has not
come to you, so follow me: I'll guide you along a Level Road. * My

16
Mary

20

30
Jesus'
Speech
As a
Child

40

41
Abraham

father, do not serve Satan! Satan was defiant towards the Mercy-giving. ** My father, I fear lest some torment from the Mercy-giving should afflict you, and you become a partisan of Satan."

    * He said: "Do you dislike my gods, Abraham? If you do not stop, I'll cast you out. Leave me alone as soon as you can!"

*His
Farewell*

    * He said: "Peace be upon you!
I'll seek forgiveness for you from my Lord;
He has been so Gracious towards me.
* I'll move away from you (all)
and from anything you appeal to
instead of God. I shall appeal to my Lord;
perhaps I'll not feel quite so miserable
with my Lord's appeal."

50

    * When he moved away from them and what they worshipped instead of God, We bestowed Isaac and Jacob on him. Each We made a prophet. ** We bestowed some of Our mercy on them and granted them a sublime tongue for telling truth.

51

*Other
Prophets*

(IV) * Mention Moses in the Book. He was sincere, and was a messenger, a prophet. * We called out to him from the right side of the Mountain, and brought him close to confide in. * We bestowed his brother Aaron on him as a prophet through Our mercy.

    * Mention Ishmael in the Book. He kept true to the Promise, and was a messenger, a prophet. ** He used to order his people to pray and [pay] the welfare tax; he was approved by his Lord.

    * Mention Idrīs in the Book. He was a truthful prophet; * We raised him to a lofty place.

*BOW
DOWN
HERE*

    * Those are some of the prophets from Adam's offspring whom God has favored, and some of those We transported along with Noah, and some of Abraham's and Ishmael's offspring, as well as some (others) We have guided and chosen. Whenever the Mercy-giving's signs are recited to them, they **drop down on their knees** and weep!

60

*The
Garden*

    * Descendants have replaced them who neglected prayer and followed [their own] passions. They shall meet with aimlessness ** except for anyone who turns around (in repentance) and believes, and acts honorably; those will enter the Garden and not be harmed in any way— * —the gardens of Eden which the Mercy-giving has promised His servants even though [they are still] Unseen. So far as He is concerned, His promise has already been fulfilled. * They will hear no nonsense in it, only: "Peace!" (as a greeting); they will have their provision there both morning and evening. * Such is the Garden which We bequeath to those of Our servants who have been pious.

*The Angels'
Message:
God's
Vastness*

    * We never descend except at your Lord's command. He owns whatever is in front of us and whatever is behind us, and whatever lies in between. Your Lord is not forgetful, ** [for He is] the Lord of Heaven and Earth and whatever lies in between them! So serve Him and persevere in His worship. Do you know of any other title for Him?"

(v) * Everyman says: "When I die will I be brought forth alive   66
[again]?" * Does man not recall that We already created him once when
he was nothing? * By your Lord, We shall summon both them and the
devils; then We shall parade them forth to crouch around Hell! * Next   *Hell*
We shall drag those away from every sect who have been the most insolent
towards the Mercy-giving. ** Thus We are quite Aware as to who are the   70
closest to roasting in it; * there is not one of you but he will be led up to
it. That is a decree determined by your Lord. * Then We shall save those
who have heeded and leave the wrongdoers crouching inside.

* Whenever Our clear signs are recited to them, those who disbelieve
say to those who believe: "Which group is better in status and a finer club
to join?" * How many generations have We wiped out before them who
were even finer in equipment and appearance!

** SAY: "May the Mercy-giving extend an opportunity to anyone who
has been in error so that when they see what they are threatened with,
whether it is torment or even the Hour, they will know who is in a worse
plight and has the weakest following.

* God increases guidance for those who have consented to be guided,
while honorable deeds that endure are best with your Lord as a
recompense and yield the best returns.

* Have you seen someone who disowns Our signs and says: "I shall still be
given wealth and children"? * Has he probed the Unseen or made a pledge
with the Mercy-giving? * Not at all! We shall write down anything he says
and extend a chance of torment to him; ** We will inherit anything he   80
says, and he will come to Us as an individual. * They have adopted other
deities instead of God, so they will mean [more] influence for them. * Not   *False*
at all! The [false gods] will reject their own worship and pit themselves   *Gods are*
against them.   *Futile*

(VI) * Have you not seen how We send devils to disbelievers, to provoke   83
them to fury? * So do not act hasty towards them; We are only counting
out so much [time] for them. ** Some day We shall summon the heedful
in a delegation before the Mercy-giving, * and drive criminals in a drove
towards Hell. * They will possess no power of intercession except for
someone who has already accepted a pledge from the Mercy-giving.

* They say: "The Mercy-giving has adopted a son!" * You have
brought up something monstrous! ** The heavens almost burst apart   90
from it, while the earth splits open and the mountains fall down with a
crash * that anyone should ascribe a son to the Mercy-giving! * It is   *God Needs*
not proper for the Mercy-giving to adopt a son.   *No Son*

* Everyone who is in Heaven and Earth comes to the Mercy-giving merely
as a servant; * He numbers them and counts them up. ** Each of them is
coming to Him on Resurrection Day as an individual. * The Mercy-giving
will grant affection to those who believe and perform honorable deeds.

* We have made it easy for your tongue
so you may announce good news about it
to those who do their duty,
and warn headstrong folk by means of it.

* How many generations have We wiped out before them? Do you find
any trace of even one of them, or hear a murmur from them?

20

ṬĀ-HĀ (or Ṭ. H.)

T HIS CHAPTER of eight sections is made up of 135 Meccan verses, although vv. 130 and 131 (in Section VIII) are Madinese. It was revealed after the previous one on **Mary** 19 and before **The Inevitable** 56. The title comes from its opening letters, which are now used as a man's name, as in the case of the similar title **Yā-Sīn** 36.

It begins with the story of Moses (I-II), narrated in a conversational style, full of vivid word pictures. The initial rhyme and rhythm are very soothing. Then we are told how to read the Qurʾān and about Adam's fall (VI); while the chapter ends with a section on prayer (VIII). Its sections are long and the message comes in a very narrative style, which provides relief for the Prophet's troubles in his native city. Some have called it the best of the Meccan chapters.

In the name of God, the Mercy-giving, the Merciful!

(I) * Ṭ.H.

* We have not sent the Qurʾān down to you in order to upset you, * but only as a Reminder for someone who acts cautiously; * [it is] a revelation from the One Who created the earth and the highest heavens, ** the Mercy-giving [Who is] settled on the Throne. * He owns whatever is in Heaven and whatever is on Earth, as well as whatever lies in between them, and what lies underneath the sod.

> * No matter whether you speak out loud,
> He still knows your secrets
> and what is even more suppressed.
> * God, there is no deity except Him!
> His are the Finest Names!

* Has Moses' story ever reached you? ** Once he saw a fire and told his family: "Wait here; I have glimpsed a fire. Maybe I can bring you a live coal from it, or find some guidance at the fire."

    * As he came up to it, [a voice] called out: "Moses, * I am your Lord! Take off your sandals; you are in the sacred valley of Ṭuwà. * I have chosen you, so listen to whatever is revealed: * I am God [Alone]! There is no deity except Myself, so serve Me and and keep up prayer to remember Me by. ** The Hour is coming! I am keeping it hidden so that each soul may be rewarded for whatever it accomplishes. * So do not let anyone who does not believe in it and follows his own passion, bar you from it so that you perish!

10
Moses'
Story

Disbelievers'
Victims

* "What do you have in your right hand, Moses?" * He said: "It is my staff. I lean on it, and beat down fodder for my sheep and goats with it; and I have still other uses for it." * He said: "Toss it down, Moses."

20

** So he threw it down, and just imagine, it became a snake that crawled along! * He said: "Pick it up, and do not be afraid. We shall return it to its original shape. * And stick your hand under your armpit: it will come out white without [showing] any blemish, as another sign * so that We may show you some of Our greatest signs! * Go to Pharaoh; he has been so arrogant."

25

(II) ** He said:

Moses'
Prayer

"My Lord, ease my breast for me!
* Make my affair easier for me,
* and loose a knot from my tongue
* so they may understand whatever I say.
* Grant me a helpmate from my own people,

30

** Aaron, my brother.

* "Back me up by means of him
* and let him share in my affair
* so that we may glorify You frequently
* and mention You often, ** since You
have been Observant of us."

* He said: "You have been granted your request, Moses. * We endowed you another time * when We revealed whatever was revealed to your mother: * 'Cast him into the chest, and toss it into the river. The current will throw him up on the shore where an enemy of Mine as well as an enemy of his will pick him up.'

"I have lavished love of My own on you so that you might be made

40

into My darling. ** So your sister was walking along, and said: 'Shall I lead you to someone who will take care of him?' Thus We returned you to your mother to comfort her and so she would not feel so sad.

"You killed a soul and We saved you from grief. We tested you severely, and you stayed among the people of Midian for years. Then you came just as fate [decreed], Moses. * I have produced you for Myself. * Take My signs away, both you and your brother, and do not neglect to mention Me. * Go to Pharaoh; he has been so arrogant. * Speak a soft word to him so that he may be reminded or even feel afraid."

** They both said: "Our Lord, we fear lest he crack down on us or that he should act arrogant." * He said: "Do not fear; I am with you both. I both hear and see. * Go to him and say: 'We are both messengers from

The Greeting
to non-Muslims

your Lord. Send the Children of Israel away with us and do not torment them. We have brought you a sign from your Lord, and may **"Peace be upon whoever follows guidance**." * As for us, it has been revealed to us that torment is due anyone who says it is a lie and turns away!'"

50

* He said: "Who is Lord for both of you, Moses?" ** He said: "Our Lord is the One Who has given everything its own constitution; then

guided it." * He said: "So what was the attitude during earlier centuries?" * He said: "Knowledge concerning them rests in a Book with my Lord. My Lord neither misses anything, nor does He forget, * [since he is the One] Who has laid out the earth as a carpet for you and has traced highways on it for you, and sent down water from the sky. We have brought forth every sort of plant with it, of various types. * Eat and pasture your livestock [on it]; in that are signs for men of accomplishment.

(III)   ** "From it We have created you   55
and We will return you to it,   *A Burial*
and from it shall We bring you forth   *Prayer*
for another chance."

* Yet We showed him all Our signs, and he said they were lies and rejected them! * He said: "Have you come to us to turn us out of our land through your magic, Moses? * We will bring magic to match it, so make an appointment between us and you in some convenient place which neither we nor you will break." * He said: "Your appointment will be on Decoration Day so that people may be summoned early in the morning."

** So Pharaoh turned away and put his plan together; then he came   60
[back]. * Moses told them: "Watch out for yourselves! Dont invent any lie about God lest He blot you out through torment. Anyone who invents things will be disappointed." * They debated their case among themselves and kept the discussion secret. * They said: "These are both magicians who want to expel you from your land by means of their magic, and do away with your exemplary ways. * Get together for your scheme; then come all lined up. Whoever comes out on top today will prosper!"

** They said: "Moses, either you will cast [something] or shall we be   *The*
the first to cast [a spell]?" * He said: "Rather you throw [first]."   *Tournament*
You should have seen their ropes and rods! It appeared to him as if   *of Magic*
they were moving around because of their magic, * so Moses conceived a fear within himself. * We said: "Do not act afraid: you will come out on top! * Throw down what is in your right hand so it will swallow up anything they have produced. What they have produced is only some magician's trick, and no magician succeeds no matter where he goes."

** So the magicians threw themselves down on their knees. They said: 70
"We believe in the Lord of Aaron and Moses." * He said: "Have you believed in Him before I permit you to? He must be your chief who has taught you magic! I'll cut your hands and feet off on opposite sides, and have you crucified on the trunks of datepalms, so you may know which of us is harsher with torment and going to last longer."

* They said: "We will never choose you before explanations have come to us nor ahead of the One Who originated us. Decide anything you may decide; you are no judge: You will only decide during this worldly life. * We believe in our Lord, so He may forgive us our mistakes as well as for any magic you have compelled us to perform. God is Better and more Enduring."

* Anyone who comes to his Lord as a criminal will have HELL [as his reward]; **he will neither die in it, nor yet will he live [a decent life]**. ** Whoever comes to Him as a believer has performed honorable deeds; those will have the highest ranks, * the gardens of Eden through which rivers flow, to live in for ever. That will be the reward for anyone who becomes purified.

77

(IV) * We inspired Moses [as follows]: "Travel with My servants at night and open up a dry road through the sea for them. Do not fear being overtaken nor dread anything." * Pharaoh had them pursued by his troops, and the flood overwhelmed them as only it could overwhelm them. * Pharaoh led his folk astray and did not guide [them].

80

** Children of Israel, We saved you from your enemy and made an appointment for you on the right side of the Mountain, and sent down manna and quail for you. * "Eat some of the wholesome things We have provided you with and do not act arrogantly while doing so, lest My anger light upon you; anyone My anger lights upon will surely collapse. * Yet I am quite Forgiving towards anyone who turns (in repentance) and believes, and acts honorably; then he will be guided."

* "Whatever made you hurry away from your people, Moses?" * He said: "They were close upon my tracks, while I have hastened to You, my Lord, so You may feel pleased." ** He said: "We have tested your folk in your absence and the Samaritan has led them astray."

* Moses returned to his people angry, sorrowful. He said: "My folk, did your Lord not make you a handsome promise? Did the agreement seem too long in reaching you, or did you want anger from your Lord to settle upon you, so that you broke the appointment to meet Me?" * They said: "We did not break your appointment of our own accord, but we had to carry loads of the people's ornaments and toss them [into a furnace]. That is what the Samaritan suggested." * He produced a calf for them in the shape of a body that mooed. They said: "This is your god, the god of Moses; he has forgotten [it]."

* Did they not consider it would not talk back to them, nor control any harm or advantage for them?

90

(V) ** Now Aaron had already told them: "My people, you are only being tested by means of it. Your Lord is the Mercy-giving, so follow me and obey my command!" * They said: "We will never quit being devoted to it until Moses returns to us."

* He said: "Aaron, what prevented you, when you saw they had strayed * from having them follow me? Did you disobey my order?" * He said: "My (blood) brother, do not seize me by my beard nor by my head! I dreaded you would say: 'You have brought dissension to the Children of Israel and did not observe what I said.'"

** He said: "What have you been trying to do, O Samaritan?" * He said: "I noticed something they do not notice, so I snatched a handful from the messenger's footprints and flung it away. Thus my soul has lured me on."

* He said: "Go away! During your lifetime you will say: 'Dont touch [me]!' You have an appointment [for your torment] which will not be broken. Look at your god which you have become so devoted to: we shall burn it up, then scatter its remains in the flood." *The Samaritan Untouchable*

> * Your God is God [Alone];
> there is no other deity
> than Him! He is Vaster
> than everything in knowledge.

* Thus We relate some news to you about what has occurred previously; We have even brought you a Reminder from Our very presence. *** Anyone who evades it will bear a burden on Resurrection Day * which he will remain with. Evil will be such a load for them on Resurrection Day, * the day when the Trumpet shall be blown. We shall summon bleary-eyed criminals on that day. * They will mutter to one another: "Did you only stay away ten [days]?" * We are quite Aware of what they will say when the best behaved among them will say: "You have only stayed away a day!" **100**

(VI) ** They will ask you about the mountains, so SAY: "My Lord will crumble them into powder * and leave them as flat as a prairie. * You will see no rough spots nor any unevenness on them. * On that day they will follow the Crier who has no crookedness in him either; their voices will be hushed before the Mercy-giving and you will hear only [people] shuffling past. **105** *Resurrection Day*

* On that day intercession will only benefit someone whom the Mercy-giving has permitted to enjoy it, and whose statement has pleased Him. ** He knows what lies in front of them and what is behind them, while they do not embrace any knowledge about Him. * Faces will seem downcast before the Living, the Eternal, and anyone who carries a load of harm will have blundered, * while anyone who has performed honorable deeds and is a believer will need fear no harm nor any injustice. **110**

* Thus We have sent it down as an Arabic reading and set forth some of the Threat in it so that they may do their duty, or so it will arouse them to remember. * Exalted is God, the True Controller!

Do not hurry while reading [the Qurʾān] before its revelation has been accomplished for you, and [rather] SAY: **"My Lord, increase me in knowledge!"** *How to Read the Qurʾān*

** We had already made a pledge with Adam which he forgot. We found he had no determination. *Adam's Fall*

(VII) * When We told the angels: "Bow down on your knees before Adam," they [all] knelt down except for Diabolis; he refused [to do so]. * We said: "Adam, this is an enemy for both you and your wife. Do not let him turn either of you out of the Garden, so you will regret it. * You have so much in it that you need go neither hungry nor naked; * you will neither thirst there nor feel sunstruck." **116**

120

** Satan whispered to him; he said: "Adam, shall I lead you to the Tree of Immortality and such control as will never disappear?" * So they both ate some of it, and their private parts became apparent to them. They set to patching themselves over with leaves from the Garden. Adam had disobeyed his Lord and was misled!

* Later on his Lord chose him, and He relented towards him and guided [him]. * He said: "Clear out of here, both of you together! Some of you [will become] enemies of others. Should guidance ever come to you from Me, no one who follows My guidance shall ever stray away nor regret it; * while anyone who fails to remember Me will have a meager living and We shall summon him as a blind person on Resurrection Day. ** He will say: 'My Lord, why have you summoned me as a blind person when I was sighted?' * He will say: 'Thus did Our signs come to you, and you forgot them; that is why you have been forgotten today.'"

* Thus We reward anyone who overdoes things and does not believe in his Lord's signs. Torment in the Hereafter will be even more severe and everlasting. * Did it not guide them [to see] how many generations We had wiped out before them whose dwellings they walk around in? In that are signs for persons who are wary.

129

(VIII) * If word had not already gone ahead from your Lord, it would have been made compulsory and a deadline set.

130

Times for Prayer

** So be patient about anything they may say and hymn your Lord's praise before the sun's rise and before its setting, and in the small hours of the night. Hymn it as well at the ends of the day so that you may meet approval.

* Do not strain your eyes towards what We let some types of them enjoy, the blossoming of worldly life, so We may test them by means of it. Your Lord's provision is better and more lasting.

Family Worship

* Order your household to pray and to discipline themselves by means of it. We do not ask you for any provision; yet We will provide for you, and the outcome rests on doing your duty.

* They say: "If he would only bring us some sign from his Lord!" Has not evidence already reached them about what was in the early scriptures? * If We were to wipe them out ahead of time with torment, they would say: "Our Lord, if You had only sent us a messenger, we would have followed Your signs before we were humbled and disgraced." ** SAY: "Everyone lives in expectation, so be on the lookout! * You will know who are [your] companions along the Level Road and who has been guided.

PART SEVENTEEN

2 1

Prophets

T HIS CHAPTER of 112 Meccan verses arranged in seven sections was
revealed after the one on **Abraham** 14 and before **Believers** 23 and
[**Soul-**]**Snatchers** 79.   It is full of important philosophy beginning in
Section II which deals with the essential Oneness of God. We are also told
that the God of everyman allows for no intercession (II).

The next theme concerns a prophet's gifts, and it states that
Muḥammad was a messenger rather than a poet (IV). We learn how
Abraham dealt with images or idols (V), while the roles of David and
Solomon are also discussed (VI), a section that is somewhat parallel to
38:III-IV. The theme becomes inspiring in the face of the Prophet's trials,
and at the end it becomes almost apocalyptic.

In the name of God, the Mercy-giving, the Merciful!

(I) * Men turn aside through indifference even though their reckoning
approaches. * No fresh reminder ever comes to them from their Lord
except they listen to it as they play away, * their hearts distracted. Those
who do wrong consult together privately; "Isnt this [man] just a human
being like yourselves? Will you succomb to magic while you can see it
happening?"

* SAY: "My Lord knows whatever is spoken in Heaven and Earth; He
is Alert, Aware." ** "Rather", they say, "it's a jumble of dreams! In fact,
he has made it all up! Indeed, he's a poet. Let him bring us a sign such as
the first men were sent with."

* No town that ever believed before have We wiped out. Will they
believe? * Before you We have sent only men whom We inspired. Ask
people with [long] memories if you do not know it already. * We did not
grant them bodies which did not eat food, nor were they immortal.
* Then We confirmed the Promise for them, and saved them as well as
anyone We wished to, and wiped out those who were dissipated. ** We
have sent down a Book to you which contains your Reminder. Will you
not use your reason?

                           10

(II) * How many a town which had been doing wrong did We demolish,   I I
and raise up other folk in its stead? * When they felt Our might
[approaching], they rushed headlong away from it!

* Do not rush away; return to what you were luxuriating in and your
dwellings, so that you may be questioned. * They say: "Alas for us! We
have been doing wrong." ** Such an appeal as theirs will never cease until

We leave them withered away like a crop in need of harvesting. * We did not create Heaven and Earth and whatever lies in between them while just playing around.

Creation is Serious

* If We had wanted to adopt it as a pastime, We would have adopted it within Our very presence, had We ever done so. * Rather **We hurl Truth against falsehood, so it knocks it down. Then it disappears**. You are the ones [who need] to worry because of what you are describing.

The God of Everyone

20

* He owns whoever is in Heaven and Earth. Anyone who is with Him is never too proud to do Him service, nor are they even wearied; ** they celebrate [Him] night and day; they never pause. * Or have they taken gods from earth who will raise the dead?

God's Transcendence

* **If there were other gods in either [Heaven or Earth] besides God [Alone], they would both dissolve in chaos**.

Glory be to God, Lord of the Throne, beyond what they describe! * He will not be questioned about what He does, while they shall be so questioned.

* Yet do they still adopt other gods instead of Him? SAY: "Bring on your proof! This is a Reminder for anyone who is with me, as well as a Reminder for whoever came before me." Instead, most of them do not recognize the Truth, so they avoid it.

** We did not send any messenger before you unless We inspired him with the fact there is no deity except Me, so serve Me!

Intercession

* They say: "The Mercy-giving has adopted a son." Glory be to Him! Rather they are honored servants; * they do not try to speak ahead of Him, while they act at His command. * He knows what lies in front of them and what is behind them; while they do not intercede except for someone who has been approved. They are apprehensive and hence in awe of Him. * Should any of them say: "I am a god as well as He," that person We shall reward with Hell. Thus We reward wrongdoers!

30
Creation

(III) ** Have not those who disbelieve seen how Heaven and Earth were once one solid mass which We ripped apart? We have made every living thing out of water. Will they still not believe? * We have placed headlands on earth lest it should sway while they are on it, and have placed mountain passes on it as highways so they may be guided. * We have placed the sky as a roof which is held up even though they shun its signs! * He is the One Who has created night and daylight, and the sun and the moon; each floats along in an orbit.

* We have not granted immortality to any human being before you; so if you should die, will they become immortal?

** **Every soul shall taste death**. We will test you (all) with something bad and something good as a trial; then to Us will you be returned!

Immortality; Death

* Whenever those who disbelieve see you, they never accept you unless it is to ridicule you: "Is this the person who mentions your gods?", while they disown any mention of the Mercy-giving!

> * Man has been created from impatience.
> I will show you My signs
> so do not try to hurry Me up.

* They say: "When will this promise be, if you are (all) so truthful?" * If those who disbelieve only knew about the time when they will not fend the Fire off from their faces nor from their backs, nor will they be supported. ** Rather it will come upon them suddenly and dumbfound them; they will not manage to cast it off nor will they be allowed to wait. * Messengers have been ridiculed before you, till whatever they were sneering at swept in around those who had been ridiculing them."

40

(IV) * SAY: "Who shields you night and day from the Mercy-giving?" Indeed they are evasive about mentioning their Lord! * Or do they have gods who can defend them from Us? They can neither assist themselves nor yet are they accompanied by Us. * Rather We have let such persons and their forefathers enjoy themselves until life seems to last too long for them. Do they not see how We come to the earth to clip it off along its borders? Will they turn out to be the winners?

** SAY: "I am warning you only through inspiration." The deaf will not hear the Appeal even when they are warned [directly]; * if a breath from your Lord's torment should ever touch them, they would say: "It's too bad for us! We have been doing wrong." * We shall set up scales for justice on Resurrection Day, and no soul will be dealt with unjustly in any way. Even if the weight of a mustard seed should exist, We would bring it along; sufficient are We as Reckoners!

42

* We brought Moses and Aaron the Standard and radiance, plus a Reminder for the heedful, * [all those] who dread their Lord even though [He is] Unseen. They are (also) anxious about the Hour. ** This is a blessed Reminder We have sent down; so why are you (all) so distrustful concerning it?

A Prophet's Gifts

50

(v) * We gave Abraham his integrity long ago, and We were (fully) Conscious of him * when he told his father and his folk: "What are these images which you are so devoted to?" * They said: "We found our forefathers serving them." * He said: "You and your forefathers have been in such obvious error."

51

Abraham and Idols

** They said: "Have you brought us the Truth, or are you just a trifler?" * He said: "Rather your Lord is the Lord of Heaven and Earth, and the One Who originated them, while I am another witness for that. * By God, I am planning to confound your idols once you have turned your backs!"

* So he broke them into fragments except for the biggest one of them, so that they might return to [question] it. * They said: "Who did this to **60** our gods? He must be some wrongdoer!" ** They said: "We heard a young man mentioning them; he is called Abraham." * They said: "Bring him before the people's eyes so they may witness it."

* They said: "Is it you who has done this to our gods, Abraham?" * He said: "Rather this biggest one of them did it. Ask them, if they are able to speak up."

* They turned to one another and said: "You yourselves are the wrongdoers!" ** Then they hung their heads: "You knew those things do not utter [a word]." * He said: "So do you worship something instead of God that neither benefits you in any way nor does it harm you? * Shame on you and on whatever you worship instead of God [Alone]! Dont you use your reason?" * They said: "Burn him up and support your gods if you must be doing something!"

70 * We said: "Fire, be cool, and safe for Abraham!" ** They wanted to outwit him, so We made them lose the most. * We rescued him and Lot, [bringing them] to a land which We had blessed for [everyone in] the Universe. * We bestowed Isaac and (then) Jacob on him as an additional boon; each We made into honorable men. * We made them leaders who guided (others) by Our command and We inspired them to perform good deeds, keep up prayer, and pay the welfare tax. They have been serving Us.

* And Lot We gave discretion and knowledge, and saved him from the town which had been performing wicked deeds. They had been such evil folk, perverts. ** We admitted him into Our mercy; he was such an honorable man!

76

Noah

(VI) * When Noah had cried out previously, We responded to him, and saved him and his family from serious distress. * We delivered him from a folk who had rejected Our signs. They had been such evil folk that We drowned them all.

David and Solomon

* And when David and Solomon both passed judgment on the field where some people's sheep had strayed to pasture there at night, We acted as Witnesses for their decision. * We made Solomon understand it. Each We gave discretion and knowledge, and We let David develop the mountains and the birds which celebrate [Us]. We were Active [in **80** this]. ** We taught him how to manufacture coats [of mail] for you, to protect you from your own violence. Yet are you ever grateful?

* Solomon had wind as a storm which blew at his command over the earth which We had blessed. We were Conscious of everything. * Some devils there were who dived for him and performed other work besides that. We acted as Guardians over them.

* And Job, when he cried out to his Lord: "Adversity has afflicted me while You are the most Merciful of the Mercy-granting!", * We responded to him and removed any adversity he was facing, and We gave him his

household and the same as them besides, as a Mercy from Our presence and a Reminder for worshippers.

** And Ishmael, Idrīs and [Ezekiel] with the Commission—were all patient. * We admitted them to Our mercy; they were honorable. * And the Man in the Whale when he stormed off angrily, and thought We would never have any power over him; yet he cried out in the darkness: "There is no deity except You! Glory be to You! I have been a wrongdoer." * We responded to him and saved him from grief. Thus We save believers.

Other Prophets

* And Zachariah when he cried out to his Lord: "My Lord, do not leave me childless, even though You are the Best of heirs." ** We responded to him and bestowed John on him, and restored his wife [to childbearing] for him. They had always competed in doing good deeds and appealed to Us eagerly yet reverently. They were so humble towards Us. * And she who guarded her chastity, so We breathed some of Our spirit into her, and set both her and her son up as a sign for [everyone in] the Universe.

90

Mary

* This community of yours [forms] one nation, while I am your Lord, so worship Me. * They have carved up their own affair among themselves; yet everyone will be returning to Us.

(VII) * Anyone who performs some honorable deeds while he is a believer will never have his effort spurned. We will be Writing it down for him. ** Yet a ban has been placed on any town We have wiped out; they shall not return * until when things are opened up for Gog and Magog and they come swarming down from every hillside * and the true Promise is approaching: then behold it will be staring into the eyes of those who have disbelieved: "Alas for us! We have been so heedless concerning this. Indeed we were wrongdoers."

94

The Final Promise

* You and anything you worship instead of God [will serve as] pavement for Hell! You are being led to it; * if those had been gods, they would not have been led there; yet everyone will remain in it for ever. *** They will [find people] moaning in it while they will not [be able to] hear in it.

False Gods

100

* Those whose finest deeds have preceded them will be sent far away from it by Us; * they will not hear it even as a rustle while they will live for ever in what they themselves have been longing for. * The greatest dismay will not sadden them while angels will welcome them with: "This is your Day which you have been promised!"

* [It will be] a day when We shall roll up the sky just as a scroll for books is rolled up; just as We began with the first creation, so We shall do it all over again as a promise binding on Us which We have been Acting on. ** We have written in the Psalms following the Reminder; "My honorable servants shall inherit the earth." * In this is a proclamation for folk who are worshipful.

* We have merely sent you as a mercy
for [everybody in] the Universe.

110

* SAY: "It has only been revealed to me that your god is God Alone. Are you committed to [live in] peace?" * If they should turn away, then SAY: 'I have announced it to you all alike. If I only knew whether what you are promised is near or far away!' ** He knows anything one says out loud and He (also) knows whatever you conceal. * If I only knew whether it may mean a trial for you as well as enjoyment for a while."

* He said: "My Lord, judge with Truth," and "Our Lord is the Mercy-giving Whose help is sought against what you describe."

22
Pilgrimage

T HIS CHAPTER of ten sections contains 78 verses from Madina, except for vv. 52-55 (in section VII), which were revealed on the road between Mecca and Madina during the Prophet's *Hijra* or Transfer to the latter city in the year 622 A.D. It comes after **Light** 24 in the order of revelation, and before **Hypocrites** 63.

The first section contains a beautiful description of how each individual is created. It then proceeds to the matter of the Pilgrimage, the sin of association, and polytheism (IV). Self-defence is permitted Muslims (VI), and the matter of retaliation is discussed (VIII). The chapter ends with the parable of "The Fly" (X) and an impassioned plea for sincere worship.

In the name of God, the Mercy-giving, the Merciful!

(I) * O mankind, heed your Lord! The quaking at the Hour will be a serious matter. * On the day when you see it, every nursing mother will neglect whatever she is nursing and every pregnant female will miscarry. You will see men drunk while they have not been drinking. However God's torment is severe!

* Some men argue about God without having any knowledge, and they follow every wilful Satan. * It has been written down concerning anyone he befriends that he shall mislead him and guide him to the torment of the Blaze.

** O men, if you have ever been in doubt about rising again, well We (first) created you from dust; then from a drop of semen; then from a clot; then from a lump of tissue either shaped or else shapeless, so We might explain [things] to you. We cause anything We wish to rest in wombs for a stated period; then We bring you forth as infants; eventually you reach full growth. Some of you will pass away [early in life], while others of you will be sent back to the feeblest age of all, so that he will not know a thing after once having had knowledge.

Man's Creation

You see the barren earth when We send water down upon it, stirring, sprouting and producing every sort of lovely species. * That [comes about] because God is the Truth: He revives the dead and is Capable of everything!

* The Hour is coming, there is no doubt about it. God will raise up whoever are in [their] graves. * Yet some men argue about God without having any knowledge or guidance, nor any enlightening Book, * twisting things around in order to lead [others] astray from God's way. Such a man will have disgrace in this world while We shall let him taste the torment of

10 burning on Resurrection Day. ** "That is because of what your hands have sent on ahead." Yet God is no One to harm [His] worshippers.

11 (II)* Some men serve God along the fringes: if some good should happen to him, he accepts it calmly, while if some trial should strike him, he turns over on his face [in despair]. He loses both this world and the Hereafter. That is such an obvious loss! * He appeals to something that neither harms him nor yet benefits him, instead of to God. That is extreme error; * he appeals to someone whose harm is closer than his benefit. How wretched is such a patron; how wretched is such a colleague!

* God will show those who believe and perform honorable deeds into gardens through which rivers flow; God does anything He wants.

** Let anyone who has been thinking that God will never support him in this world as well as in the Hereafter, [try to] stretch a tent-rope up to the sky; then cut it off. Let him see whether his scheme will take away whatever is irritating him.

* Thus We have sent it down as clear signs. God guides anyone He wants to.

* God will sort out those who believe, as well as those who have become Jews, Sabeans, Christians, Magians, from those who associate [others with Him], on Resurrection Day. God is a Witness for everything. * Have you not seen how whoever is in Heaven and whoever **is on earth drops down on his knees** before God, as well as the sun, moon and stars, the mountains, trees and animals, and many people, even some [of those] deserving torment? Anyone whom God weakens will have no one to honor him. God does anything He wishes.

BOW DOWN HERE

* Both [sets of] these opponents debate about their Lord. Those who disbelieve will have garments tailored out of fire for them; over their heads scalding water will be poured. ** Anything in their stomachs as well as their skins will be melted by it. * They will have iron goads: * every time they may want to leave because of [their] gloom, they will be sent back to it: "Taste the torment of burning!"

20

23 (III)* God will show those who believe and perform honorable deeds into gardens through which rivers flow; there they will be decked out with gold and pearl bracelets while their clothing will be [made of] silk. * They have been guided to a wholesome way of talking as well as guided along the Praiseworthy's road.

** Those who disbelieve and obstruct God's way and (block) the Hallowed Mosque which We have granted to mankind on the same footing—whether the one devoted to it[s care] or the nomad—yet We shall let anyone who wants to misuse it wrongfully, taste some painful torment.

26 (IV)* Thus We settled Abraham at the site of the House [saying]:

"Do not associate anything with Me,

"and purify My house for those who walk around it, and those who stand there [praying], and those who bow down on their knees in worship.

* "Proclaim the **Pilgrimage** among mankind: they will come to you on foot and on every lean [beast of burden];

"let them come from every deep ravine, * to bear witness to the advantages they have, and to mention God's name on appointed days over such heads of livestock as He has provided them with.

"So eat some of it and feed the needy pauper. * Then let them attend to their grooming, fulfil their vows, and circle round the Ancient House."

** That is [how it should be], and it will be best with one's Lord for anyone who emphasizes God's restrictions. You are permitted livestock except for those which have been listed for you. Avoid the filth of idols and refrain from deceptive speech, * seeking righteously after God, nor associating anything with Him. Anyone who associates anything with God [will feel] as if he had fallen out of the sky and the birds had snatched him away, or the wind had blown him to some faroff place.

* That is [how it is]. Anyone who emphasizes God's ceremonies should do so from heartfelt heeding; * you have advantages in them for a fixed period, then their place shall be at the Ancient House.

(v) * To every nation We have granted ritual so they may mention God's name over any heads of livestock He has provided them with. Your God is **God Alone, so commit yourself to Him peacefully and proclaim good news to the meek,** ** whose hearts tremble whenever God is mentioned and are patient with anything that may happen to them, and those who keep up prayer and spend something out of whatever We have provided them with.

* Animals' bodies [to be sacrificed] We have granted to you as some of God's symbols. They contain good for you, so mention God's name over them as they are lined up [for slaughter]. Once they slump down on their sides, then eat some of them and feed both the [poor man who is] carefree and the one who insists on it. Thus We have subjected them to you so that you may be thankful.

> * Neither their meat nor their blood ever reaches God,
> but **heedfulness on your part does reach Him**.

Thus He has subjected them to you, so that you may magnify God because He has guided you, and proclaim good news to those who act kindly. * God defends those who believe; God does not love every thankless traitor.

(VI) * Those who have been wronged are permitted to fight [back]—since God is Able to support them— ** any who have been driven from their homes unjustly, merely because they say: "Our Lord is God [Alone]." If it were not because God repels some men by means of others, cloisters,

The Pilgrimage Proclaimed

30

Association and Idolatry (**OR** *Polytheism*)

34

The True Meaning of Sacrifice

39
Self Defence
40

churches, synagogues and mosques where God's name is mentioned frequently would have been demolished.

God supports anyone who supports Him—God is Strong, Powerful— * those who, if We established them in the land, would keep up prayer and pay the welfare tax, command what is proper and forbid debauchery. God holds the destiny of things! * If they should reject you, well Noah's folk and ʿĀd's and Thamūd's (all) rejected [messengers] before them, * and [so did] Abraham's folk and Lot's folk, * —and the inhabitants of Midian; even Moses was rejected!

Destiny

I put up with disbelievers; then I seize them, and how [awful] is My repudiation! ** How many towns have We wiped out while they were doing wrong? Their rafters have fallen in, their wells have been abandoned, and [many an] impressive palace as well. * Have they not travelled around the earth so they may acquire hearts to reason with or ears to listen with? It is not their eyesight which is blind, but their hearts in their breasts which are blind. * They try to make you hurry up the torment! God will never go back on His promise; a day with your Lord is like a thousand years such as those you count by. * How many towns have I put up with while they were doing wrong! Then I have seized them, and towards Me lay the Goal!

49 50

(VII) * SAY: "Mankind, I am merely a clear warner for you ** and for those who believe and perform honorable deeds; they shall have forgiveness and generous provision, * while those who work against Our signs in order to frustrate them, will become the inmates of Hades."

* We have never sent any messenger nor any prophet before you unless Satan interfered with his desire even while he desired something. God will cancel out whatever Satan tampers with; then God will decide on His signs. God is Aware, Wise, * so He may set up anything Satan has proposed as a trial for those whose hearts contain malice and whose hearts are hardened—wrongdoers are in such extreme dissension— * and so those who have been given knowledge should know that it means Truth from your Lord and they may believe in it, and their hearts yield to it. God acts as a Guide towards a Straight Road for those who believe.

** Those who disbelieve will remain in a quandary concerning it until the Hour comes upon them suddenly or the torment of a desolate day reaches them. * Control will belong to God on that day; He will judge between them, and those who believe and perform honorable deeds will be in the gardens of Bliss. * Those who disbelieve and deny Our signs will have humiliating torment.

58

(VIII) * God will provide handsomely for those who migrate for God's sake, then are killed or die. God is the Best Provider! * He will show them through an entrance they will be pleased with. God is so Aware, Lenient.

60

Retaliation

** Such will it be. **God will support anyone who retaliates insofar as he has suffered**, then is set upon again; for God is Pardoning, Forgiving.

* That is because
God merges night into daylight
and merges daylight into night.
God is Alert, Observant.

* That is because God is Truth,
while anything they appeal to
instead of Him is false.
God is the Sublime, the Great.

* Have you not seen how God sends down water from the sky, so the earth becomes verdant next morning? God is so Gracious, Informed. * He holds whatever is in Heaven and whatever is on Earth; God is the Transcendent, the Praiseworthy!

(IX) ** Have you not seen how God has subjected whatever is on earth to you, and the ships that sail at sea by His command? He holds back the sky from falling down on the earth except with His permission. God is so Gentle, Merciful towards mankind. * He is the One Who gives you life, then causes you to die; next He will revive you. Yet man is so ungrateful!

65

* Each nation have We granted ritual they are devoted to, so do not let anyone argue with you about the matter. Appeal to your Lord; for you are following straight guidance. * If they should dispute with you, then say: "God is quite Aware as to what you are doing; * God will judge between you on Resurrection Day concerning what you (all) have been disagreeing about."

** Do you not know that God knows whatever is in Heaven and Earth? That is [contained] in a Book; such a thing is easy for God! * Yet instead of God they worship something for which no authority has been sent down, and about which they have no knowledge. There is no supporter for wrongdoers. * Whenever Our clear signs are recited to them, you will recognize the disgust on the faces of those who disbelieve; they almost pounce upon those who recite Our verses to them!

70

SAY: "Shall I announce something even worse than that to you? The Fire!" God has promised it to those who disbelieve. How awful is such a goal!

(X) * O mankind, a parable has been composed, so listen to it!

73

The Fly

Those whom you appeal to other than to God will never create a **fly**, even though they combined together to do so.

Yet if the **fly** should snatch anything away from them, they would not even know how to recover it from it. *How weak the seeker is, and anything he seeks!*

* They cannot measure God according to His true power. God is Strong, Powerful. ** God selects messengers from both angels and from mankind; God is Alert, Observant. * He knows what lies in front of them and what stands behind them; to God do (all) matters return.

* You who believe, **bow down and kneel** before [Him], and worship your Lord; and do good, so that you may succeed. * Strive for God's sake, the way He should be striven for. He has picked you out and has not placed any constraint upon you concerning [your] religion, the sect of your forefather Abraham.

He has named you Muslims both previously and right now, so the Messenger may be a witness for you, and you may act as witnesses for mankind.

Keep up prayer and pay the welfare tax, and cling firmly to God; He is your Protector. What a splendid Protector, and what a splendid Supporter!

23
Believers

T HIS CHAPTER of six sections contains 118 late Meccan verses, all in fact
except for the very last one. It was revealed after **Prophets** 21 and
before **Worship** 32 and **The Inevitable** 56. It takes its name from the first
sentence in the chapter (NOTE that Chapter 40 has an alternate title, **The
Believer**, with the same noun used in the singular).

The mood here is somewhat poetic with its initial vision of creation and
man's reproduction; then it relates God's transcendent care in providing for
mankind and the Universe. Noah's mission is mentioned next (II), followed
by a description of the final reward in an inspiring scene (IV). Then one
follows on God in all His Oneness (V), which continues to the end of the
chapter.

In the name of God, the Mercy-giving, the Merciful!

PART
EIGHTEEN

(I) * **Believers** will succeed!

* [This means] those who are reverent in their prayer, * who refrain
from idle talk, * who are active in [promoting] public welfare ** and
who guard their private parts * except with their spouses and whomever
their right hands may control, since then they are free from blame.
* Those who hanker after anything beyond that are going too far! * And
those who preserve their trusts and their pledge, * and who attend to their
prayers, ** will be the heirs * who shall inherit Paradise to live there for
ever.

*The True
Believer*

10

* We created man from an extract of clay; * then We placed him as a
drop of semen in a secure resting-place. * Then We turned the semen
into a clot; next We turned the clot into tissue; and then We turned the
tissue into bones and clothed the bones with flesh.

Then We reproduced him as a fresh creation. Blessed be God, the
Best of Creators!

** Then later on you shall die. * Next you will be raised up again
on Resurrection Day.

*Creation and
Reproduction*

* We have created seven orbits above you; We have not been heedless
about creation. * We send down water from the sky in due measure, and
let it trickle into the earth. We are even Able to make it disappear. * We
have produced date groves and vineyards on it for you; from which you
have much fruit to eat, ** as well as a tree growing on Mount Sinai which

*God's
Care*

20

produces oil and seasoning for those who [want to] eat. * You have [still another] lesson in livestock: We let you drink what is in their bellies, and you have many [other] uses in them; some of them you eat, * while on them and on shipboard are you transported.

23

Noah

(II) * We sent Noah to his folk, and he said: "My people, worship God; you have no other deity except Him. Will you not do your duty?" * The elders among his folk who disbelieved said: "This is only a human being like yourselves who wants to attain some superiority over you. If God had wished, He would have sent down angels [instead]. We never heard about this from our early forefathers. ** He is only a man possessed by some sprite, so try to catch him off guard for a moment." * He said; "My Lord, support me in view of how they have rejected me!"

* So We inspired him: "Build the ship under Our eyes and through Our inspiration. When Our command comes and the reservoir bursts open, send two out of every species on board as well as your own family, except for any of them against whom the Sentence has already been pronounced. Do not lecture Me about those who have done wrong: they will be drowned. * When you and anyone else who is with you have boarded the ship, then SAY: "Praise be to God, Who has saved us from such wicked folk!" * And (also) SAY:

"My Lord, land me through a blessed landing;
You are the best Harbormaster!"

30

Unnamed Messengers

** In that there were signs: We are always Testing (people)."
(* Then We produced a generation of others after them; * We sent a messenger around from among themselves: "Serve God; you have no other deity except Him! Will you not do your duty?")

33

(III) * The elders among his people who disbelieved and denied there would be any meeting in the Hereafter, even though We had granted them every luxury during worldly life, said: "This is only a human being like yourselves; he eats what you eat, and drinks what you drink. * If you obey a human being just like yourselves, you will then turn out to be losers. ** Does he promise you that when you die and have become dust and bones, that you will be brought forth again? * Away, off with whatever you are threatened with! * There exists only our present life; we die even as we live, and shall not be raised up again. * He is only a man who has invented some lie about God, and we do not believe in him." * He said: "My Lord, support me because they have rejected me!"

40

** He said: "Some morning soon they will feel regretful." * The Blast really caught them and We turned them into rubbish. Away with such wicked folk! * Then We raised up other generations after them. * No nation may anticipate its deadline nor will they ever postpone it.

* Then We sent Our messengers one after another. Each time its messenger came to some nation, they rejected him, so We followed some of them up with others and turned them into conversation pieces. Away with any folk who will not believe!

** Next We sent Moses and his brother Aaron with Our signs and clear authority * to Pharaoh and his courtiers, and they acted too proudly and were such haughty folk. * So they said: "Are we to believe in two human beings like ourselves while their people are slaving for us?" * They rejected them both, and so eventually were wiped out. * Yet We had given Moses the Book so that they might be guided.

** We set up the son of Mary and his mother as a sign, and sheltered them both on a hilltop where there was both lodging and a spring.

(IV) * O messengers, eat wholesome things and act honorably; I am Aware of anything you do. * This nation of yours [forms] one community while I am your Lord, so heed me! * Yet they carve up their business into cartels among themselves, each faction happy with whatever lies before them. * Leave them in their excitement for a while.

** Do they reckon that We have only afforded them wealth and children because of it? * We hurry good things up for them, yet they do not even notice it! * Those who feel anxious out of awe for their Lord, * and those who believe in their Lord's signs, * and those who do not associate anything with their Lord, ** and those who give away anything they may give while their hearts feel wary lest they should return to their Lord; * [all] those compete in doing good deeds and they will soon attain them.

* **We only assign a soul something it can cope with**. Before Us lies a Book which speaks up for Truth; they will not be dealt with unjustly. * Instead their hearts are full of excitement because of this. They have other deeds besides those which they are committing, * so that whenever We seize their high-livers with torment, just imagine how they bellow! ** "Do not roar [so loud] today; you will not be supported by Us. * My signs have already been recited to you while you proudly turned on your heels * away from it, sitting up nights to chatter on and on about it."

* Have they not reflected on the Sentence, whether something that never reached their earliest forefathers may not have come to them? * Or do they not recognize their Messenger and are disgusted with him? ** Or do they say: "Some [mad] sprite possesses him!"?

Rather he has brought them the Truth, while most of them hate the Truth. * If Truth had followed their whims, Heaven and Earth would have collapsed in chaos, along with anyone who is in them. Rather We have brought them their Reminder, yet they keep avoiding their Reminder.

* Or are you asking them [to make] some outlay? Your Lord's tribute is best, for He is the Best Provider! * You are calling them to [follow] a Straight Road * while those who do not believe in the Hereafter go swerving off the Road. ** Even if We showed them mercy and removed any trouble that worries them, they would still blindly persist in their arrogance. * We had already seized them with torment yet they did not surrender to their Lord nor beseech [Him] * until just as We opened up a gate for them leading to severe torment, why they were dumbfounded by it!

78

God's
Presence

80

(v) * He is the One Who has furnished you with hearing, eyesight and vital organs; yet how seldom are you grateful!

    * He is the One Who has scattered you over the earth, and to Him shall you be summoned.

    ** He is the One Who gives life and brings death; He controls the alternation between night and daylight. Will you not reason?

* Instead they say the same thing as the first men said; * they say: "When we have died and become dust and bones, will we be raised up again? * This was promised us and our forefathers long ago. These are only legends [made up] by primitive people!"

    * SAY: "Who owns the earth and anyone on it, if you know [anything]?" ** They will say: "It is God's." SAY: "Will you not bear it in mind?"

    * SAY: "Who is Lord of the Seven Heavens and Lord of the splendid Throne?" * They will say: "They are God's." SAY: "Will you not do your duty [by Him]?"

    * SAY: "In Whose hand lies sovereignty over everything? He protects, while against Him there is no protection, if you but realized it." * They will say: "It is in God's." SAY: "How is it you act so

90

bewildered?" ** Rather We have brought them the Truth while they deny it.

* God has not adopted any son, nor is there any [other] deity alongside Him, otherwise **each god would carry off whatever it has created**, and some of them would gain the upper hand over others.

> **Glory be to God**
> beyond what they describe!
> * Knower of the Unseen and the Visible:
> Exalted is He over anything
> they may associate [with Him]!

93

(VI) * SAY: "My Lord, will you show me what they are threatened with? * My Lord, do not place me among such wrongdoing folk!"

    ** We are Able indeed to show you whatever We are threatening them with! * **Repay evil with something that is finer;** We are quite Aware of anything they describe.

    * SAY: "My Lord, I seek refuge with You from the devils' promptings. * I seek refuge with you, my Lord, lest they accompany

IOO

me, * since whenever death comes to any one of them, he says: 'My Lord, send me back *** so I may act honorably with anything I may have left behind'"

    Indeed not! It is merely a remark he is making. Beyond them there lies

The Last
Trumpet

a barrier till the day when they will be raised up again. * Once the Trumpet is blown, no ties of kinship will exist between them on that day, nor may they question one another. * Those whose scales are heavy will be prosperous; * while those whose scales are light will be the ones who have lost their souls; they will remain in Hell. * The Fire will scorch their faces while they will glower away in it. ** "Were My signs not recited to you as you (all) were rejecting them?"

* They will say: "Our Lord, our misery has overwhelmed us and we were errant folk. * Our Lord, get us out of here! If we ever should return [to disobedience], then we would indeed be wrongdoers." * He will say: "Sink down into it, and never speak to Me! * A group of My servants used to say: 'Our Lord, we believe, so forgive us and have mercy on us; You are the Best One to show mercy!' ** You took them for a laughing-stock until they made you forget to remember Me since you had been laughing so hard at them. * I have rewarded them today for how patient they have been; they are triumphant."

110

* He will say [further]: "How many years did you stay on earth?" * They will say: "We stayed a day or part of a day. Ask the timekeepers." * He will say: "You only lasted a little while, if you only realized it. ** Did you reckon We have created you just for fun and that you would never be returned to Us?"

Life is not Frivolous

> * Exalted is God, the true King!
> There is no deity except Him,
> Lord of the Noble Throne!

* Anyone who appeals to any other deity along with God (Himself), has no proof for it. His reckoning rests only with his Lord. Disbelievers will not succeed.

> * SAY: "My Lord, forgive and show mercy!
> You are the Best One to show mercy!"

24
Light

THIS CHAPTER forms one of the great treasures of the Qurʾān, chiefly because of the lyrical hymn to **Light** found in section v. It contains 64 Meccan and Madinese verses arranged in nine sections. The chapter dates from before **Pilgrimage** 22, while v. 64 was revealed after **Banishment** 29. NOTE the elevated style and the frequent use of the adverb *abadan* or 'never' throughout this chapter.

The beginning contains advice or **"light"** on sex, etiquette and personal modesty, and states that marriage is desirable (IV); it also warns against committing slander and perjury. The middle portion consists of the great hymn to "Light" which gives the chapter its title, and from which much illumination and mysticism arise in Islam. Proof of God follows (VI). The end concerns etiquette and protocol in connection with public business, as Islamic society began to need rules to live by and for its own government. Old maids and eating in public are other topics which are discussed in VIII.

In the name of God, the Mercy-giving, the Merciful!

(1) * [This is] a chapter We have sent down and ordained.
We send clear signs down in it
so that you (all) may be reminded.

Sexual Offences

* Flog both the adulterous woman and the adulterous man with a hundred lashes, and do not let any pity for either party distract you from [complying with] God's religion if you believe in God and the Last Day. Have a group of believers witness their punishment. * An adulterous man may only marry an adulterous woman or one who associates [others with God]; while an adulterous woman may only be married to an adulterous man or one who associates [others with God]. Such [conduct] is forbidden to believers.

Perjury Punished

* Flog those who cast things up at honorable matrons with eighty lashes unless they bring four witnesses, and never accept their testimony from them [again]. Those are Immoral; ** except for the ones who repent later on and reform. God is Forgiving, Merciful.

* Any persons who accuse their spouses yet have no witnesses except themselves for it, should offer testimony by swearing four times before God that he is telling the truth, * plus a fifth [time] that God's curse will rest on him if he is a liar. * It will avert the punishment from her if she swears four times before God that he is a liar, * plus a fifth that God's anger will rest on her if he has been truthful. ** How would it be without God's bounty and mercy towards you (all)? God is the Receiver of Repentance, Wise.

10

(II) * Those who have brought up such slander form a clique among you. Do not reckon it is a bad thing for you; rather it will be good for you: every last man of them shall be charged with whatever he has committed in the way of an offence, while whoever has assumed his leadership over them [through such gossiping] will have serious torment.

* If you believing men and believing women had only thought of something good by yourselves when you heard it, and said: "This is an obvious falsehood!" * If they had only brought four witnesses to [prove] it! When they did not bring any witnesses, those were liars before God. * If it had not been for God's bounty towards you, as well as His mercy in this world and the Hereafter, some serious torment might have afflicted you because of the talk you had indulged in.

** When you encountered it on your tongues and said something with your own mouths that you had no knowledge about, you reckoned it was trifling although it was serious with God. * If you had only said as you heard it: "We ought not to talk about this. Glory be to You! This is serious slander."

* God cautions you never to repeat anything like it again if you are believers. * God explains signs to you; God is Aware, Wise. * Those who love to spread shocking news around concerning those who believe will have painful torment in this world and the Hereafter. God knows while you (all) do not know. ** If God's bounty and mercy had only rested on you; for God is Gentle, Merciful!

(III) * You who believe, do not follow in Satan's footsteps. Satan orders anyone who follows in his footsteps to commit acts of sexual misconduct as well as dishonor. If it had not been for God's bounty and mercy towards you, not one of you would have ever been pure; but God purifies anyone He wishes. God is Alert, Aware. * Those among you possessing resources and [other] means should not fail to give [something to] near relatives, paupers and those who are refugees for God's sake; let them act forgivingly and show indulgence. Do you not like God to pardon you? God is Forgiving, Merciful.

* Those who cast things up at heedless [yet] believing matrons will be cursed in this world and the Hereafter. They will have severe torment * on a day when their tongues, their hands and their feet will testify against them concerning whatever they have been doing. ** On that day God will repay them with their rightful due; they will realize that God means obvious Truth.

* Bad women are for bad men, and bad men are for bad women; while good women are for good men, and good men are for good women. The latter are absolved from anything they may say; they will have forgiveness and generous provision.

(IV) * You who believe, do not enter any houses except your own homes unless you act politely and greet their occupants; that is best for you so you may remember. * If you do not find anyone in them, still do not enter them until permission has been granted you. If you are told: "Get out!", then turn back; it is more fitting for you. God is Aware of anything you do. * It will not be held against you, however, for entering any houses which are not inhabited, for some property belonging to you. God knows anything you show and anything you hide.

30
Modesty

** Tell believers to avert their glances and to guard their private parts; that is chaster for them. God is Informed about anything they may produce. * **Tell believing women** to avert their glances and guard their private parts, and not to display their charms except what [normally] appears of them. **They should fold their shawls over their bosoms and show their charms only to their husbands, or their fathers** or their fathers-in-law, or their own sons or stepsons, or their own brothers or nephews on either their brothers' or their sisters' side; or their own womenfolk, or anyone their right hands control, or male attendants who have no sexual desire, or children who have not yet shown any interest in women's nakedness. Let them not stomp their feet in order to let any ornaments they may have hidden be noticed. Turn to God, all you believers, so that you may prosper!

*Marriage is
Desirable*

* Marry off any single persons among you, as well as your honorable servants and maids. If they are poor, God will enrich them from His bounty. God is Boundless, Aware. * **Yet let those who do not find [any way to] marry, hold off** until God enriches them out of His bounty.

Should those whom your right hands control desire their freedom, then draw up such a writ for them if you recognize anything worthwhile in them. **Give them some of God's wealth which He has given you.** Do not force your girls [whom you control] into prostitution so that you may seek the display of worldly life, if they want to preserve their chastity. Anyone who forces them (to do otherwise) [will find] God is Forgiving, Merciful, even after forcing them to. * We have sent you down clarifying signs and an example in those who have passed on before you, as well as instruction for the heedful.

35

*God as
the Light
of the
World*

(v) ** God is the **Light** of Heaven and Earth!
His **light** may be compared to a niche
in which there is a lamp; the lamp
is in a glass; the glass
is just as if it were a glittering star
kindled from a blessed olive tree,
[which is] neither Eastern nor Western,
whose oil will almost glow though fire
has never touched it. **Light** upon **light**,
God guides anyone He wishes to His **light**.
God composes parables for mankind;
God is Aware of everything!

*Houses of
Worship*

* There are houses God has permitted to be built
where His name is mentioned; in them
He is glorified morning and evening
* by **men whom neither business nor trading
distract from remembering God,**
keeping up prayer, and paying the welfare tax.

They fear a day when their hearts and eyesight
will feel upset * unless God rewards them
for the finest things they may have done,
and gives them even more out of His bounty.
God provides for anyone He wishes
without any reckoning!

    * Those who disbelieve [will find] their deeds
[will disappear] like a mirage on a desert:
the thirsty man will reckon it is water
till, as he comes up to it,
he finds it is nothing.
Yet **he finds God [stands] beside him**
and he must render Him his account;
God is Prompt in reckoning!

    ** Or like darkness on the unfathomed sea: 40
one wave covers up another wave,
over which there [hang] clouds;
layers of darkness, one above the other!
When he stretches out his hand,
he can scarcely see it. Anyone
whom God does not grant **light** to
will have no **light**!

(VI) * Have you not seen how everyone in Heaven and Earth glorifies God,   41
even to the birds lined up (in flight)? Each knows its prayer and how to   *Proof*
glorify Him. God is Aware of whatever they do. * God holds control over   *of God*
Heaven and Earth; towards God lies the goal!
    * Have you not seen how God drives along the clouds, then masses
them together, next piles them into layers? You see a downpour coming
from inside of them; He sends down mountainous masses from the sky
with cold hail in them, and pelts anyone He wishes with it and wards it off
from anyone He wishes. A flash from His lightning almost takes one's sight
away!

    * God alternates night and daylight;
in that there lies a lesson
for those possessing insight.

    ** God has created every animal out of water; some of them walk on
their belly, while others walk on two legs and still others walk on four. God
creates anything He wishes; God is Able [to do] everything! * We have
sent clarifying signs down, and God guides anyone He wishes to a Straight
Road. * They will say: "We believe in God and the Messenger, and we
obey." Then a group of them will turn away even after that; those are not
believers. * Whenever they are invited to [come to] God and His
messenger so He may judge among them, watch how a group of them will
shunt it aside. * Yet if they have the Truth on their side, they come to it
voluntarily.

50 ** Does some malice lurk in their hearts? Either they act skeptical, or else they fear that God and His messenger will cheat them. In fact such persons are wrongdoers!

51 (VII) * The only statement believers should make when they are invited to [meet with] God and His messenger, so He may judge among them, is: "We have heard, and are at your orders!" Those persons will be successful. * Those who obey God and His messenger, and dread God and heed Him, will be triumphant.

* They swear before God with their most solemn oaths that they would go forth if you ordered them to. SAY:

> "Do not swear so; obedience will be recognized.
> God is Informed about anything you do."

* SAY: "Obey God and obey the Messenger." If you should turn away, he is responsible only for what he has been commissioned with while you are responsible for what you are commissioned with. If you obey him, you will be guided; the Messenger has only to announce things clearly. ** God has promised to appoint those of you who believe and perform honorable deeds as [His] representatives on earth, just as He made those before them into (such) overlords, and to establish their religion for them which He has approved for them, and to change their fear into confidence. They serve Me [Alone] and do not associate anything else with me. Those who disbelieve later on will be perverse. * Keep up prayer, pay the welfare tax, and obey the Messenger so that you may receive mercy. * Do not reckon those who disbelieve can ever frustrate things on earth; their lodging will be the Fire, and how wretched is such a goal!

58

Good Manners at Home

(VIII) * You who believe, have those whom your right hands control and those of you who have not yet reached puberty, ask permission from you on three occasions: before the daybreak prayer; when you take off your clothes at noon [for a siesta]; and after the late evening prayer. You have three times for privacy.

There is no objection for you nor for them outside those times as they move around you so some of you may wait on others. Thus God explains signs to you; God is Aware, Wise. * Whenever any children of yours reach puberty, let them ask permission just as those before them have had to ask for such permission. Thus God explains His signs to you; God is Aware, Wise.

60

Unmarried Women (Old Maids)

On Eating Out

** Those [elderly] women sitting around [after their menopause] who no longer expect to marry will meet with no objection if they take off their [outer] clothing, though without displaying their charms. Yet it is best for them to act modestly. God is Alert, Aware.

* It should not be held against the blind nor against the lame, nor against the sick nor against yourselves, for your eating in your own homes or at your fathers' or your mothers' homes, or your brothers' or your sisters' homes, or at your uncles' or aunts' homes on your father's side, or your uncles' or aunts' on your mother's side, or those whose keys you have in your custody, or with some friend of yours. There is no objection to

your eating either together or separately. Whenever you enter any houses, greet one another with a blessed, wholesome greeting by invoking God. Thus God explains [His] signs to you so that you may reason things out.

(IX) * Believers are merely those who believe in God and His messenger. Whenever they are with the latter on some collective errand, they should not leave until they have asked him for permission to do so. Those who do ask you for such permission are the ones who believe in God and His messenger.

62

Protocol with Public Business; Manners in Public

Whenever they ask you for permission [to attend] to some affair of their own, then give anyone of them you may wish, leave to do so, and seek forgiveness from God for them. God is Forgiving, Merciful.

* Do not treat the Messenger's bidding you [to do something] just as if one of you were calling out to someone else. God knows which of you try to slip away, aiming to get out of something. Let anyone who opposes his order beware lest some trial afflict them or some painful torment should befall them! * God possesses whatever is in Heaven and Earth! He knows what you (all) stand for, while He will notify them about whatever they have done on the day they are returned to Him. God is Aware of everything!

25
The Standard
(OR *The Criterion*)

HIS RATHER long chapter of six sections consists of 77 Meccan verses, and vv. 68-70 in section VI which date from Madīna. It was revealed after **Yā-Sīn** 36 and before **Originator** 35. The purpose of its message is to make associators reflect on the future.

The **Standard** mentioned refers to man's intellectual faculties and his power of distinguishing right from wrong. It begins with a statement directed against those associators who accused Muḥammad of copying others and not being a Prophet in his own right, and likewise against their objects of worship (I-II). It ends in a long hymn to God's creation, His power, and the parable of "The Two Seas" (V).

In the name of God, the Mercy-giving, the Merciful!

(I) * Blessed is the One Who has sent down the **Standard** to His servant so he may [act as] a warner for [everyone in] the Universe, * the One Who holds control over Heaven and Earth, Who has not adopted any son nor has He any associate in control. He has created everything and measured it out precisely.

Associators
　　　　* Instead of Him, they have taken on (other) gods which do not create anything while they themselves have been created. They control no harm nor do they control death nor life, nor even rebirth. * Those who disbelieve say: "This is only some swindle he has invented; other folk have helped him at it." They have trumped up something wrong and counterfeit. ** They say: "He has had legends by primitive men written down; they are dictated to him in the early morning and evening!"

　　　　* SAY: "The One Who knows the secrets of Heaven and Earth has sent it down. He is Forgiving, Merciful."

Muḥammad's Personality
　　　　* Yet they say: "What sort of messenger is this? He eats food and walks through the markets! If only some angel were sent down to him, to act as a warner alongside him! * Or a treasure were offered him, or a garden belonged to him from which he might eat." Wrongdoers say: "You are only following a man who is bewitched." * Watch what sort of stories they make up about you; they are lost and cannot find any way back.

10
　　　　(II) ** Blessed is the One Who may grant you something even better than that if He so wishes: gardens through which rivers flow. He may even grant you palaces!

* Yet they even deny the Hour. We have prepared a Blaze for anyone who denies the Hour; * when it appears to them from afar off, they will hear it raging and moaning. * When they are flung all hitched together into a narrow part of it, they will plead to be blotted out there. * "Do not plead to be blotted out today once and for all: plead for annihilation many times over!"

** SAY: "Is that best, or the Garden of Immortality which has been promised the heedful?" They are both a reward and a goal for them. * They will have anything they may wish for in it eternally; it is a promise your Lord will be held responsible for.

* Some day He will summon them along with whatever they have been worshipping instead of God. He will say: "Were you the ones who led these servants of Mine astray, or did they stray away by themselves?" * They will say: "Glory be to You! We would never take on any patrons besides You! However you let them and their forefathers enjoy things until they forgot the Reminder and became a worthless folk."

* They will reject you in anything you (all) may say, so you will not manage to avert it nor find any support. We shall let any of you who does any wrong taste great torment. ** We have never sent any emissaries before you unless they ate food and walked around the markets. We have placed some of them as a trial for others. Will you be patient while your Lord is Observant?

Meddlers

20

PART NINETEEN

21

(III) * Those who do not expect to meet Us say: "Why arent angels sent down to us, or we are allowed to see our Lord?" They act too proud of themselves, and strut around quite insolently!

* Some day they shall see the angels! There will be news for criminals on that day and they will say: "Oh, for a stonewall built to protect [us]!" * We shall advance upon whatever action they have performed and turn it into scattered dust. * The inhabitants of the Garden will have the best residence and finest lodging on that day, ** on a day when the sky will split open along with its clouds, and the angels will be sent right on down. * True control will belong to the Mercy-giving on that day.

It will be a harsh day for disbelievers, * a day when the wrongdoer will gnaw away at his hands. He will say: "It's too bad for me! If I had only taken a pathway alongside the Messenger! * It's too bad for me! If I had not adopted So-and-So as a close friend! * He led me astray from the Reminder even after it had reached me. Satan is such a turncoat with man."

** The Messenger will say: "My Lord, my folk assume this Reading is out-of-date. * Thus have We granted every prophet an enemy among criminals. Yet your Lord suffices as a Guide and Supporter. * Those who disbelieve say: "Why has not the Qurɔān been sent down to him in one single piece?"

[It has been done] like that so your vitals may be braced by it; We have phrased it deliberately. * They will not come to you with any example

Doomsday

30

unless We will bring you the Truth and something even finer as a commentary. * Those who are dragged off face down to Hell will be in a worse plight and farthest off the track.

35

(IV) ** We gave Moses the Book, and placed Aaron alongside him as a helpmate. * We said: "Go off to a folk who have denied Our signs." We utterly destroyed them!

* So when Noah's folk rejected the messengers, We let them drown and set them up as a sign for mankind. We reserve painful torment for wrongdoers * such as ʿĀd and Thamūd and the companions at the Well and many generations in between. * We have made up parables for each,

40

and each We followed up with doom. ** They have come to the town on which an evil rain poured down. Had they not seen it? Indeed they had not expected to be reborn.

* Whenever they see you, they merely treat you as a laughingstock: "Is this the person whom God has sent as a messenger? * He almost led us away from our gods, if we had not acted so patient towards them." They will know who is furthest off the track when they see the torment!

* Have you seen someone who has taken his own passion as his god? Would you act as a trustee for him? * Or do you reckon that most of them do hear or even use their reason? They are just like livestock—indeed, they are even further off the track!

45

God's Power

(V) ** Have you not seen how your Lord
lengthens shadows? If He so wished,
He would make them stand still.

Then We placed the sun as an indicator for them;
* next **We gradually pulled them toward Us**.
* He is the One Who has placed night
as a garment for you, and sleep for repose;
He makes daytime for rising again.

* He is the One Who has sent the winds
as heralds announcing His mercy.
We send pure water down from the sky,
* so We may bring life to a dead land,
and let everything We have created
drink from it, such as livestock
and men aplenty.

50

** We have spelled it out for them
so they may bear it in mind; yet most men
refuse [to do] anything
except disbelieve (in it).

* If We had so wished, We might have despatched a warner into every town. * Do not obey disbelievers and struggle seriously with them concerning it.

The Two Seas

* He is the One Who has cut off both seas,
this one being sweet, fresh, while the other is salty, briny.
He has placed an isthmus in between them
plus a barrier to block them off.

* He is the One Who created humanity out of water; and He has granted them blood ties as well as in-laws. Your Lord has been so Capable! ** Yet instead of God they worship something that neither benefits nor hurts them. The disbeliever will be a backer [for anything] against his Lord!

Creation

* We have only sent you as a herald and a warner. * SAY: "I do not ask you for any payment for it except that anyone who wishes to may accept a way unto his Lord. * Rely on the Living One Who never dies. Hymn His praise! Sufficient is it for Him to be Informed about His servants' offences, * since He is the One Who created Heaven and Earth as well as whatever lies in between them, in six days. Then the Mercy-giving mounted on the Throne. Ask any informed (person) about Him."

God is Living

** When they are told: "**Bow down on your knees** before the Mercy-giving," they say: "What is the Mercy-giving?" Are we to bow down on our knees just because you order us to?" It merely increases their disdain.

60
BOW DOWN HERE
61

(VI) * Blessed is the One Who has placed constellations in the sky and set a beacon in it, plus a shining moon!

* He is the One Who has granted night and daytime in succession for anyone who wants to reflect (on it) or wants [to show] gratitude,

* and the Mercy-giving's servants who walk modestly on earth and peacefully say: "How do you do!" whenever ignorant men address them;

God's Servants OR *Worshippers*

* who spend the night bowing down on their knees and standing before their Lord;

** and who say:

> "Our Lord, ward off Hell's torment
> from us! Its torment is atrocious;
> * it is such an evil residence
> and station;"

* who when they spend, give neither too lavishly nor yet hold back, and keep to a happy medium;

Charity Described

* who do not appeal to any other deity besides God [Alone]; nor kill any soul whom God has forbidden [them to] except through [due process of] law; nor misbehave sexually.

Murder and Sexual Misconduct Forbidden

Anyone who does so will incur a penalty. * Torment will be doubled for him on Resurrection Day and he will remain disgraced for ever in it, ** except for someone who repents and believes, and acts in an honorable manner. God will replace their evil deeds with fine ones, since God is Forgiving, Merciful.

Sin is Punished
70

* Anyone who repents and acts honorably should turn to God in repentance,

* and those who will not bear false witness, and **when they pass by [people] gossiping, pass by in a dignified manner,**

* who whenever they are reminded of their Lord's signs, do not fall down deaf and blind [when thus reminded] of them;

Gossip

* and [rather] who say: "Our Lord, bestow the comfort of our eyes
on us in our spouses and our offspring. Make us a model for those who
do their duty."

Paradise   ** Those will be rewarded with the Mansion because they have been so
patient, and welcomed there with greetings as well as "Peace [be on
you]!", * to live there for ever. How fine is such a residence and status!
        * SAY: "My Lord will never care about you unless you appeal to Him.
Yet since you have rejected [Him], something else will be necessary.

26
Poets

T HIS CHAPTER of eleven sections and 227 mostly Meccan verses was
revealed after **The Inevitable** 56 and before the next chapter on **The
Ants** 27. Verse 197 however and vv. 224-226 at the end of the final section
(XI) date from the Madinese period.

The next four chapters display a different style, being rather long but
using short verses; thus they form a special unit. One notices how each
prophetic parallel and refrain mentioned brings home the fact that while
prophets may use poetic utterances, this illustrates the patterns they need,
so as to show mankind how history and man's fate should be understood.
Moses (II), then Abraham's attitude toward idols, plus his prayer (V), are
first presented: Noah (VI), then the early Arabian messengers Hūd (VII),
Ṣāliḥ or Methusaleh (VIII), Lot (IX), and Shuꜥayb (X) follow.

This motif in fact sounds like that of a symphony as it moves along and
is gradually worked out, or like the *kharja* or refrain in an Andalusian
choral lyric. The concern is directed toward God as the Lord of the
Universe. The chapter ends with a dramatic description of how early
Arabian poets went "staggering around in every river valley".

In the name of God, the Mercy-giving, the Merciful!

(I) * Ṭ.S.M.
* These are verses from the Clear Book.
* Perhaps you are fretting your soul away because they are not
believers. * If We so wished, We might send a sign down to them from
Heaven so they would bow their heads submissively before it. ** No
Reminder ever comes to them as a renewal from the Mercy-giving except
they shun it. * They have just rejected [it], so news of what they have been
ridiculing will soon come to them. * Have they not looked at the earth [to
see] how many generous species We have grown on it?

> * In that is a sign; though *most of them*
> *are not believers.* * Yet your Lord
> is the Powerful, the Merciful.

(II) ** So your Lord summoned Moses: "Go to the wrongdoing
folk, * Pharaoh's folk! Will they not heed?" * He said: "My Lord, I fear
they will reject me, * and my breast feels cramped while my tongue will
not loosen up. Send for Aaron! * They have [laid] a charge against me; so
I fear they will kill me." ** He said; "Indeed not; let both of you go off

10

Moses'
Story

with Our signs. We will be listening along with you. * Go to Pharaoh and say: 'We are messengers from the Lord of the Universe. * Send the Children of Israel off with us!'"

* He said: "Did we not rear you as a child among us and you spent several years of your life with us? * Yet you committed the deed you did: You are so ungrateful!" ** He said: "I did it while I was misguided. * I fled from you (all) because I feared you. Still my Lord has bestowed discretion on me and set me up as an emissary. * Is this some favor you have shown me—that you have enslaved the Children of Israel?"

* Pharaoh said: "What is the Lord of the Universe?" * He said: "The Lord of Heaven and Earth and whatever [lies] in between them, if you will be convinced." ** He said to those around him: "Arent you listening?" * He said: "Your Lord and the Lord of your very first forefathers."

* He said: "Your messenger who has been sent to you is crazy!" * He said: "[He comes from] the Lord of the East and West, and whatever lies in between them, if you know how to reason." * He said: "If you should adopt any god besides me, I shall make you a prisoner." ** He said: "Even if I bring you something obvious?" * He said: "Bring it, if you are telling the truth!"

* So he cast his staff down and imagine, it was clearly a snake! * He pulled out his hand [from his shirtfront], and imagine, it was white to the spectators!

(III) * He told the councilmen around him: "This is some clever magician ** who wants to drive you out of your land through his magic. What do you order?" * They said: "Make him and his brother wait, and send recruiters out into the cities * who will bring you in every clever magician."

* So the magicians were gathered for the appointment on a certain day, * and the people were told: "Are you assembling ** so that we may follow the sorcerers once they have won out?"

* When the sorcerers came, they said to Pharaoh: "Will we have any payment if we are the winners?" * He said: "Yes, you will then become courtiers."

* Moses told them: "Throw down whatever you are going to throw." * So they threw their ropes and their staffs, and said: "By Pharaoh's majesty, we will be the winners!" ** So Moses cast his staff, and imagine, it swallowed up what they were shamming about!

* The sorcerers dropped down on their knees; * they said: "We believe in the Lord of the Universe, * the Lord of Moses and Aaron!" * He said: "Have you believed in Him before I permit you to? He is your chief who has taught you magic. You will know! I'll cut your hands and feet off on opposite sides and crucify you all! ** They said: ''It won't hurt! We will be sent home to our Lord; * we long for our Lord to forgive us our mistakes so we may be the first among believers.''

(IV) * We inspired Moses as follows: ''Travel with My servants at night: you will be pursued!''

* Pharaoh sent ;ecruiters into the cities: * "Those are a few dissidents; ** they are agitating against us. * We are completely forewarned."

* Yet We drove them out of (their) gardens and springs, * treasures and a splendid position. * The same We let the Children of Israel fall heirs to.

** They followed after them at sunrise. * When both groups sighted each other, Moses' companions said: "We have been overtaken!" * He said: "Not at all! My Lord stands by me; He will guide me!"

* So We inspired Moses as follows: "Strike the sea with your staff!" It opened up and each section was like a huge cliff. * We brought the others up next, ** and saved Moses and all those who were with him. * Then We let the rest drown.

> * In that is a sign; though *most of them*
> *are not believers.* * Yet your Lord
> is the Powerful, the Merciful.

(v) * Recite Abraham's news to them ** when he said to his father and his folk: "What are you worshipping?" * They said; "We worship idols, and are utterly devoted to them." * He said; "Do they hear you when you call, * or benefit you or harm [you]?" * They said: "Rather we found our fathers doing so."

** He said: "Have you ever seen what you have been worshipping, * you and your forefathers, the oldtimers? * They are enemies of mine, except for the Lord of the Universe * Who created me. He guides me * and is the One Who feeds me and gives me something to drink. ** Whenever I fall ill, He heals me; * [He is] the One Who will cause me to die, then bring me back to life [again]; * the One Who I expect will forgive me my mistakes on the Day for Repayment.

* "My Lord, bestow discretion on me and acquaint me with honorable men! * Grant me a truthful reputation among later men. ** Grant me an inheritance in the Garden of Bliss. * Forgive my father even though he may be [considered] lost. * Do not disgrace me on the day they are raised up again, * the day when neither wealth nor children will benefit anyone * except for someone who comes to God with a sound heart."

** The Garden will be brought near for those who did their duty; * while Hades will appear for the straying * and someone will say to them: "Where is whatever you were serving * instead of God? Will they support you, or even support themselves? * So they will be toppled into it, both they and the misguided ones, ** as well as all of Diabolis' armies. * They will say while they quarrel away in it: * "By God, we were in such obvious error * when we put you (all) on the same footing as the Lord of the Universe! * It has only been criminals who have led us astray; *** We have no intercessors * nor any bosom friend. * If we only had another chance, we would then be believers!"

> * In that is a sign, though *most of them*
> *are not believers.* * Yet your Lord
> is the Powerful, the Merciful.

60

69 70
*Abraham
and Idols*

*God's
Care*

80

*Abraham's
Prayer*

90

Doomsday

100

105

Noah

110

(VI) ** Noah's folk rejected the emissaries * when their brother Noah said to them: "Will you not do your duty? * I am a trustworthy messenger for you, * so heed God and obey me. * I do not ask you for any payment for it; my payment only concerns the Lord of the Universe. ** So heed God and obey me!"

* They said: "Are we to believe in you while the meanest people follow you?" * He said: "What knowledge do I have about what they have been doing? * Their reckoning only concerns my Lord, if you will only notice it! * I do not intend to drive any believers away; ** I am merely a plain warner."

* They said: "If you do not stop, Noah, you will become an outcast." * He said: "My Lord, my folk have rejected me! * Decide the case between me and them, and rescue me as well as any believers who may be with me!" * So We rescued him and anyone who was with him on the

120

laden ship. ** Then later on We let those who remained drown.

* In that is a sign, *though most of them
are not believers.* * Yet your Lord
is the Powerful, the Merciful!

123

Hūd

(VII) * ʿĀd rejected the emissaries * when their brother Hūd said to them: "Will you not do your duty? ** I am a trustworthy messenger for you, * so heed God and obey me. * I do not ask you for any payment for it; my payment only concerns the Lord of the Universe.

130

* "Are you building a sign on every hill just so you may fool around? * Are you setting up workshops so that you may live for ever? ** Whenever you assault anyone, you pounce on them like bullies. * So heed God and obey me; * heed the One Who has furnished you with whatever you know. * He has furnished you with livestock and children, * gardens and springs. ** Yet I fear the torment of a terrible day for you!"

* They said: "It's all the same for us whether you lecture [us] or are not lecturing. * This is only a fabrication [made up] by primitive men; * we are not going to be punished. * They rejected him, so We wiped them out.

140

In that is a sign; though *most of them
are not believers.* ** Yet your Lord
is the Powerful, the Merciful!"

141

Ṣāliḥ

(VIII) * Thamūd rejected the emissaries * when their brother Ṣāliḥ said to them: "Will you not do your duty? * I am a trustworthy messenger for you, * so heed God and obey me. ** I do not ask you for any payment for it; my payment only concerns the Lord of the Universe.

150

* "Will you be left securely in what you have here, * among gardens and springs, * crops and datepalms with slender stalks? * You skillfully hew houses out of the mountains. ** Heed God and obey me; * do not obey the order of extravagant people * who corrupt [things] on earth and never reform." * They said: "You are merely someone deluded; * you are only a human being like ourselves! Bring a sign if you are so truthful."

** He said: "This is a she-camel. She has drinking rights while you have drinking rights on a fixed day. * Do not touch her so that you hurt her, lest the torment of an awful day may seize you!"
  * Yet they mistreated her, and one morning they felt remorseful about it. * Torment overtook them.

> In that is a sign, though *most of them*
> *are not believers.* * Yet your Lord
> is the Powerful, the Merciful.

(IX) ** Lot's folk rejected the emissaries * when their brother Lot said to them: "Will you not do your duty? * I am a trustworthy messenger [sent] to you, * so heed God and obey me. * I do not ask you any payment for it; my payment only concerns the Lord of the Universe. ** Do you approach males among [everyone in] the Universe, * and ignore any wives whom your Lord has created for you? Indeed you are such defiant folk!"
  * They said; "If you do not stop, Lot, you will become an exile." * He said: "I am someone who detests your behavior. * My Lord, save me and my family from what they are doing!"
  ** So We saved him and his whole family * except for an old woman among those who stayed behind. * Then We annihilated the rest; * We sent a rain down upon them. How evil was such a rain for those who had been warned!

> * In that is a sign; though *most of them*
> *are not believers.* ** Yet your Lord
> is the Powerful, the Merciful.

(x) * The dwellers in the Forest rejected the emissaries * when Shuʿayb said to them: "Will you not perform your duty? * I am a trustworthy messenger [sent] to you, * so heed God and obey me! ** I do not ask you for any payment for it; my payment only concerns the Lord of the Universe.
  * "Give full measure and do not cause [people] any losses. * Weigh with honest scales; * do not undersell people to cheat them of their things nor storm around the earth in order to spoil matters. * Heed Him Who created you and the character of the earliest men."
  ** They said: "You are merely someone bewitched. * You are only a human being like ourselves, and we think you are a liar. * Let a piece fall out of the sky on us if you are so truthful." * He said: "My Lord is quite Aware of what you are doing."
  * So they rejected him, and the torment of a gloomy day gripped them; it was the torment of a terrible day!

> ** In that is a sign, though *most of them*
> *are not believers.* * Yet your Lord
> is the Powerful, the Merciful!

160
Lot

170

176
Shuʿayb
180

190

192 (XI) * It is a revelation from the Lord of the Universe.
* The Faithful Spirit has brought it down * for your heart, so you may be a warner ** in a clear Arabic tongue. * It [can be found] in the Psalms of early men. * Do they not have a sign since the scholars from the Children of Israel knew about it? * If We had sent it down to some outsider * and he had read it to them, they would never have believed in it.

200 *** Despite that, We slip it into criminals' hearts. * They will not believe in it until they see painful torment; * it will come upon them suddenly while they least suspect it, * and so they say: "Will we be allowed to wait?"
* Are they trying to hasten up Our torment? ** Have you seen how We let them enjoy themselves for years, * then whatever they have been threatened with, comes to them? * Whatever they have been enjoying will never benefit them.
* We never wipe out any town unless it has had its warners * to

210

Devils are Helpless

remind [it]. We have never been unfair. ** The devils did not descend with it: * it does not suit them to, nor can they manage it; * they are too withdrawn to even hear it. * Do not appeal to any other deity along with God, lest you be tormented. * Warn your nearest kinfolk; ** lower your [protecting] wing over any believers who may follow you. * If they are opposed to you, then SAY: "I am innocent of whatever you are doing." * Rely on the Powerful, the Merciful * Who sees you whenever you stand up [in prayer] * as well as how you move around among those

220 who are bowing down on their knees. ** He is the Alert, Aware.

The Poets Themselves

* Shall I tell you who are the ones on whom the devils descend? * They come down upon every bluffing sinner. * They even try to eavesdrop, since most of them are liars; * and **poets** are followed around by them bewildered.
** Do you not see them staggering around in every river-valley? * They preach what they never practise, * except for those who believe and perform honorable deeds, remember God often, and protect themselves once they have been wronged. Those who do wrong shall know what sort of upsets they may expect to face!

27
The Ants

THIS CHAPTER of seven sections consists of 92 Meccan verses. It was revealed following the previous chapter on **Poets** 26 and before the next one on **Stories** 28. The chapter consists of fables or allegories which give it a narrative quality somewhat like **The Cave** 18.

It begins with the story of Moses (ɪ) and then describes King Solomon's knowledge and his meeting with the Queen of Sheba (ɪɪ), which thus creates a beautiful allegory on that king's campaigns. The title to the chapter comes from the **ants** he meets on one such campaign. Thamūd's ancient Arabian messenger, Ṣāliḥ or Methusaleh and Lot are also mentioned (ɪv). The grave sin of Association is next discussed in section v, which leads into a splendid hymn to God Alone.

The chapter ends with consolation for Muḥammad despite the apparent thanklessness of the Prophet's mission, for it assures him that God will take care of everything he has been worrying over. The final section (vɪɪ) offers a description of the fate awaiting rejectors.

In the name of God, the Mercy-giving, the Merciful!

(ɪ) * Ṭ. S.

These are verses from the Qur»ān and a clear Book * [offered] for guidance and as good news for believers * who keep up prayer and pay the welfare tax while they feel certain about the Hereafter. * We have made those who do not believe in the Hereafter feel their actions are attractive even though they are (really) groping around. ** Those are the ones who will have the worst torment, while they will be the greatest losers in the Hereafter. * Yet you have been profferred the Qur»ān by Someone [Who is] Wise, Aware.

* Thus Moses told his household: "I've glimpsed a fire. I'll bring you some news from it, or I'll bring you a glowing ember so that you may warm yourselves."

* When he came up to it, [a voice] called out: "Blessed be Whoever is in the Fire, and whoever stands around it! Glory be to God, Lord of the Universe! * O Moses, I am God, the Powerful, the Wise. ** Throw down your staff!"

When he saw it wriggling as if it were possessed, he turned his back on it and tried to run away. "Moses, do not fear. Emissaries do not fear in My presence * except for someone who has done wrong.　Then, should he change to something finer after [committing] evil, I will be Forgiving,

Moses

10

Merciful. * Put your hand into your shirtfront; it will come out white without [causing any] evil. There will be nine signs for Pharaoh and his folk. They have been such immoral people."

* When Our signs came to them so plain to see, they said: "This is sheer magic!" * They repudiated them wrongfully and haughtily even though they themselves felt certain about it. See how the outcome was for mischief makers.

15

Solomon's Knowledge

(II) ** We gave David and Solomon knowledge, and they both said: "Praise be to God, Who has made us excel over many of His believing servants." * Solomon fell heir to David, and he said: "O mankind, we have been taught the speech of birds, and been given [a little] of everything. This is manifest bounty."

* His armies of sprites, men and birds were drawn up before Solomon; they paraded forth * until, when they came to the Valley of **the Ants**, an ant said: "O **ants**, enter your dwellings lest Solomon and his armies crush you without even noticing it."

* So he smiled, laughing at its statement, and said: "My Lord, arrange things for me so I shall act grateful for Your favor which You have bestowed upon me and my parents, and so I may act so honorably that You will approve of it. Admit me through Your mercy among Your honorable servants."

20

** He inspected the birds, and said: "What's wrong with me that I do not see the plover? Or could it be absent? * I shall punish it severely or slaughter it, unless it brings me some clear authority."

The Queen Of Sheba

* It was not long in coming, and said: "I have just acquired some information you have not picked up, for I bring you reliable news from Sheba. * I found a woman ruling over them, and she has been given everything and has a splendid throne. I found both her and her people bowing down on their knees to the sun instead of to God [Alone]. Satan has made their actions seem attractive to them, and diverted them from the [proper] Way.

BOW DOWN HERE

They are not guided ** so they do not **bow down** on their knees before God,

> Who brings forth what is concealed
> in Heaven and Earth, and knows
> anything you hide as well
> as anything you display.
> * God, there is no deity except Him,
> Lord of the splendid Throne!

* He said: "We shall see whether you have been truthful or are a liar. * Take this letter of mine and deliver it to them. Then leave them, **and see what [answer] they send back."

30

* She said: "Councilmen, an important letter has been delivered to me. ** It is from Solomon and it [reads]: "*In the name of God, the Mercy-giving, the Merciful*! * Do not act haughtily towards me, and come to me committed to [live at] peace."

(III) * She said: "Councilmen, give me your opinion concerning my affair: 32
I have never settled any matter unless you were present with me." * They
said: "We possess strength and can be extremely violent, while authority
rests with you; so attend to whatever you will command."

* She said: "Whenever any kings enter a town and plunder it, they turn
the most important men among its people into the lowest. Thus they
act. ** I am sending them a gift and shall be watching for whatever the
emissaries bring back."

* When it reached Solomon, he said: "Will you furnish me with
wealth? What God has given me is better than what He has given you;
nevertheless you seem quite happy with your gift. * Go back to them, for
We shall come to them with armies they can never resist. We shall expel
them from it just like the meanest people, and they will be humiliated."

* He said: "Councilman, which of you will bring me her throne before
they come to me committed to [live at] peace?" * An imp among the
sprites said: "I'll bring it to you before you even rise up from your place. I
am strong enough to be entrusted with it." ** Someone who had some   40
knowledge about the Book said; "I shall bring you it in the twinkling of an
eye!"

When he saw it set before him, he said: "This is some of my Lord's
bounty, so He may test me whether I am thankful or thankless. Anyone
who is thankful gives thanks only on his own behalf, while with anyone
who is thankless, well my Lord is Transcendent, Generous." * He said:
"Disguise her throne for her; let us see whether she is guided or is one of
those who are not guided."

* When she came, someone said: "Is your throne like this?" She said:
"It seems to be similar." (We were given knowledge before she was, and
have become Muslims. * What she had been worshipping instead of God
distracted her; she belonged to disbelieving folk.)

* Someone (else) said to her: "Enter the hall." When she saw it, she
reckoned it was a pool [of water] and [tucked up her skirt and] bared the
calves of her legs. He said: "It is a hall paved with glass slabs." She said:
"My Lord, how I have wronged myself! I commit myself peacefully, along
with Solomon, to God, Lord of the Universe!"

(IV) ** We sent Thamūd their brother Ṣāliḥ: [who said]: "Worship God   45
[Alone]!"   *Thamūd*

Nonetheless they became two quarreling factions. * He said: "My
people, why do you hasten towards evil rather than something fine? If you
only sought forgiveness from God, you might find some mercy." * They
said: "Shall we take it as an omen from you and from someone who is with
you?" He said; "Your fate depends on God; in fact, you are a folk who will
be tested."

* There was a gang of nine persons in the city who caused trouble on
earth and never improved matters. * They said: "Let's all swear by God
that we shall catch him and his family some night. Then we shall tell his
next of kin: 'We did not witness the slaughter of his family. We are telling
the truth!'"

50   ** They plotted away while We plotted too, and they did not even
notice it. * See what was the outcome of their plotting! We annihilated
them and their folk completely! * Those used to be their houses — [now]
empty because of the wrong they had committed! In that is a sign for folk
who know. * We saved the ones who believed and had been doing their
duty.

Lot   * When Lot told his folk: "Do you indulge in sexual misconduct with
your eyes open? ** Do you approach men passionately instead of
women? Indeed you are folk who act out of ignorance!"

*PART
TWENTY*

56   (IV cont'd) * His folk's answer was merely to say: "Run Lot's family out of
your town; they are people who try to keep clean!" * So We saved him
and his family, except for his wife; We destined her to be one of those who
stayed behind. * We sent a rain down upon them; how evil was such a
rain for those who had been warned!

59   (V) * SAY: "Praise be to God, and peace on those servants of His whom He
Association   has selected. Is God Better, or whatever they associate [with Him]?
60   ** "Who created Heaven and Earth and has sent down water from the
sky for you, so We have caused lovely gardens to grow by means of it? You
have no other way to make their trees grow."

*A Hymn to
God Alone*
            Is there any (other) deity alongside God?
            Rather they are people
            who dodge the facts.
                * Who set the earth up as a residence,
            laced it with rivers and planted headlands on it,
            and laid an isthmus between both seas?
                Is there any (other) deity alongside God?
            Rather most of them do not know.

                * Who answers the distressed man
            when he appeals to Him, and removes evil,
            and makes you overlords on earth?
                Is there any deity alongside God?
            How seldom do you reflect [on this]!

                * Who guides you through darkness
            on land and at sea, and Who sends out winds
            as heralds for His mercy?
                Is there any deity alongside God?
            Exalted is God over anything
            they may associate [with Him]!

                * Who begins with creation,
            then performs it all over again?
            Who provides for you
            from Heaven and Earth?
                Is there any deity alongside God?

SAY: "Bring on your proof
if you have been so truthful!"

** SAY: "No one in Heaven or Earth
knows the Unseen except God!"

*True
Knowledge*

They do not even realize when they will be raised up again; * nor does
their knowledge grasp the Hereafter. Rather they are in doubt about it;
indeed they are blind concerning it!

(VI) * Those who disbelieve say: "When we and our forefathers have
become dust, shall we be brought forth again? * We and our forefathers
were promised this before; these are only legends [made up] by primitive
men."
　　* SAY: "Travel around the earth and see what the outcome for criminals
was like." ** Do not worry about them nor feel any anxiety over whatever
they are plotting. * They are saying: "When will this promise be, if you are
so truthful?" * SAY: "Perhaps part of what you are trying to hurry up will
catch you from behind!"
　　* Your Lord possesses bounty for mankind, although most of them are
not thankful; * yet your Lord does know anything your breasts conceal as
well as anything they display. ** There is nothing elsewhere in either
Heaven or Earth unless it appears in a plain Book. * This Reading tells
the Children of Israel most of what they have been differing over; * it
serves as guidance and a mercy for believers.
　　* Your Lord will judge between them through His discretion; He is the
Powerful, the Aware! * So rely on God, since you hold manifest
Truth. ** You cannot make the dead hear, nor even the deaf hear the
Appeal once they turn around to escape. * You are no one to guide the
blind out of their error; you will only cause someone who believes in Our
signs to listen, for they are committed to [live in] peace. * Whenever the
Sentence prevails against them, We shall bring forth a monster from the
earth for them who will speak to them, because mankind has not been
convinced by Our signs.

(VII) * Some day We shall summon a troop from every nation which has
rejected Our signs, and they will be paraded forth * until, when they come
[before God], He will say: "Did you reject My signs and not grasp any
knowledge concerning them? What have you been doing?"
　　** The Sentence will prevail against them because of the wrong they
have committed. They will not utter [a word]. * Have they not considered
how We have made night so they may rest in it, and daylight so they can
see? In that are signs for folk who believe.
　　* Some day the Trumpet will be blown and startle whoever is in
Heaven and whoever is on Earth, except for anyone God may wish.
Everyone will come to Him abjectly. * You will see the mountains, which
you reckoned were solid, slip away just as clouds slip away, through the
handiwork of God Who consummates everything. He is Informed about
whatever you are doing.
　　* Anyone who comes with a fine deed will have something better than
it and they will be safe from that day's terror; ** while anyone who comes

67

70

80

83

Doomsday

90

with an evil deed will be flung face down into the Fire: "Arent you rewarded with just what you've been doing?"

The Prophet's Orders

* I have only been ordered to serve the Lord of this region which He has hallowed. He possesses everything. I have been ordered to be a Muslim, * and to recite the Qurʾān. Anyone who is guided, will be guided only for his own sake, while tell anyone who strays away: "I am merely a warner."

God's care

SAY: "Praise be to God!
He will show you His signs
so you may recognize them.
Your Lord is not overlooking
anything you do!"

28
Stories

THIS NINE-SECTION chapter consists of 88 late Meccan verses, except for vv. 52-55 (in section VI) which date from Madīna. The whole chapter was revealed after **The Ants** 27 which immediately precedes it, and before **The Night Journey** 17, during the Transfer from Mecca to Madīna in the year 0 / 622.

The reader should gather all of these tales about Moses and the proud rich man, Qārūn (VIII), together, and try to understand them; they are similar to the comparisons found in **Poets** in Chapter 26.

Moses previously appears in Midian in connection with the Burning Bush (I-IV), and we are once more shown God and His light in VII. The chapter ends with solace for Muḥammad and believers, and relief for the Prophet's worries as they all contemplate God's face (IX).

In the name of God, the Mercy-giving, the Merciful!

(I) * Ṭ.S.M.

* These are verses from the clear Book!

* We shall recite in all truth to you some information about Moses and Pharaoh for folk who believe.

Moses and Pharaoh

* Pharaoh had acted haughtily on earth and split his people into factions, seeking to weaken a group of them. He slaughtered their sons and let their women live; he was so depraved! ** Yet We wanted to endow those who were considered inferior on earth, and make them into leaders and make them [Our] heirs. * We established them on earth and showed Pharaoh and Haman as well as their troops how they should beware of them.

* We inspired Moses' mother [as follows]: "Nurse him. If you should fear for him, then cast him into the river. Do not fear nor feel sad; We will return him to you, and appoint him as a missionary."

* Pharaoh's household took him in, so that he became an enemy and [a source of] sadness for them. Pharaoh and Haman as well as their troops were so mistaken! * Pharaoh's wife said: "[He'll be] a comfort for me and for you. Do not kill him! Perhaps he'll benefit us, or we'll adopt him as a son." They did not suspect [a thing].

** Next morning the vitals of Moses' mother felt empty; she almost revealed who he was, if We had not bound up her heart so she would be a believer. * She told his sister: "Keep track of him."

10

So she watched out for him from a distance while they did not notice it. * We kept him from nursing at first, and so she said: "Shall I lead you to a family who will look after him for you? They will take good care of him." * Thus We restored him to his mother so he might comfort her and she would not feel so sad, and so she would know that God's promise is true, even though most of them do not realize it.

14

(II) * When he reached maturity and came of age, We gave him discretion and knowledge. Thus We reward those who act kindly.

** He entered the city at a time when its people were lax, and found two men fighting there, one from his own sect and the other from his enemy's. The one who was from his own faction appealed for his assistance against the one who was from his enemy's. Moses punched him and he finished him off!

Moses'
Soliloquy

He said: "This is some of Satan's work; he is such an enemy, a plain misleader." * He said: "My Lord, I have wronged my own soul. Forgive me!" So He forgave him; He is the Forgiving, the Merciful. * He said: "My Lord, since You have shown me such favor, I shall never back up any criminals [again]."

* Yet he felt fearful next morning in the city; he was on the alert, when the man he had tried to support the day before called out to him for help [again]. Moses told him: "You are clearly a trouble-maker." * When he wanted to catch the one who was an enemy to them both, he said: "Moses, do you want to kill me just as you killed another person yesterday? You only want to become a bully on earth; you do not want to be a reformer."

20

** A man came hurrying up from the further end of the city; he said: "Moses, the councilmen are deliberating about you, whether they should execute you. Clear out! I am giving you sincere advice." * He left it fearfully, on the alert. He said: "My Lord, save me from such wrongdoing folk!"

22

Moses in
Midian

(III) * As he made his way towards Midian, he said: "Perhaps my Lord will guide me along some level path." * When he approached the water of Midian, he found a company of people watering [their flocks] there, and found two women besides them, holding theirs off at a distance. He said: "What's the matter with you?" They both said: "We may not draw any water until the herdsmen move on. Our father is an elderly gentleman."

* So he did the watering for them. Then he went off to [rest in] the shade, and said: "My Lord, I am poor enough to accept anything You may grant me." ** One of the girls came up to him, walking bashfully. She said: "My father invites you, in order to reward you with some [sort of] payment since you have done the watering for us."

When he came up to him, he told him the **stories**. He said: "Do not fear; you have escaped from wrongdoing folk."

* One of the two (girls) said: "My father, hire him! The best man you can hire is someone who is strong, trustworthy." * He said: "I want to marry you to one of these daughters of mine, provided you hire yourself out to me for eight seasons. If you should complete ten, then that will be your own affair. I do not want to be hard on you; you will find me an

honorable man, if God so wishes." * He said: "That is up to you and me; whichever term I may serve out, there will be no injustice done to me. God is a Trustee for anything we say."

(IV) * When Moses had completed the term [that he had promised to work] and was travelling away with his family, he glimpsed a fire on a slope of Mount [Sinai]. He told his family: "Stay here! I've glimpsed a fire. Perhaps I may bring you some news from it, or an ember from the fire so you may warm yourselves."

29
The Burning Bush

** So when he came up to it, someone called out to him from the tree in the blessed hollow on the right bank of the valley: "Moses, I am God, Lord of the Universe!" * And then: "Throw down your staff."

30

When he saw it twitching as if it were possessed, he turned around and tried to escape. "Moses, come closer and do not act afraid. You will be safe! * Slip your hand into your shirtfront; it will come out white without being harmed. And gather up your courage against any apprehension. These will be two proofs from your Lord for Pharaoh and his councillors; they have been such immoral folk.''

Other Signs

* He said: "My Lord, I killed a person among them, and fear they may execute me. * My brother Aaron is more convincing with his tongue; send him along with me to back me up and vouch for me. I fear they will talk me out of it." ** He said: "We shall strengthen your arm by means of your brother and grant both of you authority so they will not overtake either of you. Because of Our signs, you both will win out, as well as anyone who follows you."

* When Moses brought them Our clear signs, they said: "This is only some contrived magic. We have not heard of this through our early forefathers." * Moses said: "My Lord is quite Aware as to who brings guidance from His presence and who will attain the Home in the end. Wrongdoers do not succeed."

* Pharaoh said: "Councilmen, I have not known any god for you except myself. Light [a kiln] for me, Haman, for some clay, and build me a tower so I may climb up to Moses' god. Still I think he's a liar!"

Pharoah's Tyranny

* Both he and his troops acted overproud on earth without any right [to be so]. They thought they would never return to Us. ** We seized him and his troops and hurled them into the deep. See how the outcome was for wrongdoers! * We turned them into leaders who invite [men] to the Fire. On Resurrection Day they will not be supported. * We shall let a curse follow them in this world, while on Resurrection Day they will look hideous.

40

(V) * We gave Moses the Book after We had wiped out the earliest generations [to serve] as insights for mankind, and for guidance and mercy so they might bear it in mind. * You [Muḥammad], were not (present) on the western slope when We settled the matter for Moses, nor were you a witness; ** but We raised up some generations, and [their] lifetime was prolonged for them. Nor were you a resident among the people of Midian, reciting Our signs to them, but We were [to send] emissaries.

43

* You were not on the slope of Mount [Sinai] when We called out, but [have been sent] as a mercy from your Lord so you might warn a folk whom no warner had come to before you, so that they might bear it in mind. * If only some calamity would strike them because of what [evil] their hands have sent on ahead, and so they would say: "Our Lord, if only you had sent us some messenger, we should have followed Your signs and been believers!"

* Yet when the Truth did come to them from Our presence, they said: "If he were only given the same as Moses was given!" Still had they not already disbelieved in what Moses was given? They say: "Double magic, to back each other up!" And they say: "We disbelieve in everything."

50 * SAY: "Bring a book from God's presence which will be a better guide than either of them so I may follow it if you are that truthful." ** If they do not respond to you, then know they are merely following their own whims. Who is more misguided than someone who follows his own whim without having any guidance from God? God does not guide wrongdoing folk."

51

Early
Believers

(VI) * We have conveyed the Statement to them so they might keep it in mind. * The ones We gave the Book to previously believe in it; * whenever it is recited to them, they say: "We believe in it; it is the Truth from our Lord! We have already committed ourselves to [live in] peace."

> * Those will be given their payment twice over because of what they have endured; they ward off evil with good and spend some of what We have provided them with.
>
> ** Whenever they hear any gossip, they shun it and say: ''We hold to our actions while you have your actions.'' Peace be upon you! We do not hanker after ignorant people.
>
> * **You do not guide someone you love,**
> **but God guides anyone He wishes.**
> He is quite Aware as to who are guided.

* They say: "If we followed guidance along with you, we'd be swept out of our land." Yet have We not established a safe haven for them where produce of every sort is brought from Our presence as sustenance? However most of them do not realize it.

* How many towns have We wiped out who were reckless in their way of living? Those dwellings of theirs have been inhabited only occasionally since then. We have been [their] heirs! * Your Lord has never been the destroyer of any towns unless He had despatched a messenger to their capital city who recited Our signs to them. Nor did We ever destroy any 60 towns unless their people became wrongdoers. ** Anything you have been given is for enjoyment and as an attraction during worldly life. Yet what God has is better and more lasting. Will you not use your reason?

61 (VII) * Is someone We have made a handsome promise to and who will receive it, like someone whom We have allowed to enjoy worldly life, then will be made to appear on Resurrection Day?

* Some day He will call out to them and say: "Where are My associates whom you have been claiming?" * The ones against whom the Sentence will be pronounced will say: "Our Lord, those are the people whom we have misled! We misled them just as we ourselves went astray. We absolve ourselves before You; it was not we whom they worshipped."

God Needs No Associates

* Someone will say: "Appeal to your associates!" So they will appeal to them, yet they will not answer them. They will see the Torment—if only they had accepted guidance!

** Some day He will call out to them and say: "How did you answer the emissaries?" * The news will seem confusing to them on that day, and they will not [be able to] question one another. * Yet anyone who has repented, believed and acted honorably may possibly be among those who are successful.

> * Your Lord creates and chooses
> anything He wishes;
> while they have no choice.
> Praise be to God; Exalted is He
> over anything they may associate with Him!
> * Your Lord knows anything their breasts conceal
> and anything they may disclose.

God the Lord

> ** He is God [Alone];
> there is no deity except Him!
> Praise belongs to Him from the very first
> as well as in the Hereafter.
> Discretion is His, and to Him
> will you (all) return.

70

* SAY: "Have you considered, if God should lay perpetual night over you until Resurrection Day, what deity besides God would bring you any radiance? Will you not listen?"

God's Light

* SAY: "Have you considered whether if God should lay perpetual daylight over you until Resurrection Day, what deity other than God would bring you night wherein you might find rest? Will you not observe [these things]?

> * "Out of His mercy He has granted you night and daytime so you may rest in the one and seek some of His bounty [in the other], and so that you may feel grateful."

Night and Day

* Some day He will call out to them and say: "Where are My associates whom you have been claiming?" ** We shall drag a witness out of every nation and We shall say: "Bring on your proof!" They will realize that Truth belongs to God while whatever they were inventing has left them in the lurch.

(VIII) * Qārūn belonged to Moses' folk, and he acted insolently towards them. We gave him such treasures that his keys [alone] would have overburdened a squad of strong men. So his people told him: "Dont act so happy, for God does not love people who are too happy. * Seek a home

76

Qārūn OR *Koran*

in the Hereafter through whatever God has given you. Do not neglect your share in this world, and **act kindly**, just as God has treated you kindly. Do not aim to cause mischief on earth; God does not love mischief makers."

* He said: "I have been given it only because of some knowledge I possess." Did he not realize that God had wiped out generations before him who were stronger than he and possessed even greater resources? Will not criminals be questioned concerning their offences?

* He went forth to his folk [dressed] in his finery. Those who wanted worldly life said: "If we only had the same as Qārūn has been given! He has been extremely lucky!" ** However those who had been given knowledge said: "It will be too bad for you! God's recompense is better for anyone who believes and acts honorably. Yet only the patient will encounter it."

* Then We let the earth swallow up him and his home. He did not have any party to support him against God; he was not supported. * Those who longed to be in his place the day before, said the next morning: "Since it is God Who extends sustenance to anyone He wishes from among His servants and measures it out, it would have swallowed us up too if God had not cared for us." It seems that disbelievers do not prosper.

80

83

Comfort for the Heedful

(IX) * That home in the Hereafter will We grant to those who want neither haughtiness nor any corruption on earth. The outcome belongs to those who do their duty. * Anyone who brings a fine deed will have something even better than it, while anyone who comes with an evil deed [will find that] those who perform evil deeds will not be rewarded except for whatever they have been doing.

** The One Who has charged you with the Reading will return you to [your] destination. SAY: "My Lord is quite Aware as to who has brought guidance and who is in plain error." * You did not expect that the Book would be delivered to you except as a mercy from your Lord.

Do not back up disbelievers! * Do not let it distract you from [observing] God's signs once they have been sent down to you. Invite [people to meet] your Lord and do not be an associator; * do not appeal to any other deity along with God: there is no god except Him.

God's Face

Everything is perishable except His face!
Discretion belongs to Him, and to Him
will you (all) be returned.

29
The Spider

THIS CHAPTER of seven sections consists of 69 middle Meccan verses, except for the first eleven and the very last one, which date from Madīna. It was revealed after **The [East] Romans** (OR **The Byzantines**) 30, the chapter which follows this one, but before **The Cheats** 83.

The title comes from the fable on **the Spider** contained at the end of section IV which demonstrates how flimsy it is to associate anything else in our worship of God. It begins with an admonition on the treatment of parents (I), then mentions Noah, Abraham and offers a philosophy of history (II). Lot (III) and other prophets follow (IV). It ends with a passage on the duty of *Jihād* or striving for God's sake (VII).

In the name of God, the Mercy-giving, the Merciful!

(I) * A.L.M.

* Do people reckon that they will be left alone just because they say: "We believe," and they will not be tested? * We have tested the ones who preceded them. God knows the ones who are truthful and He will recognize liars. * Or do the ones who perform evil deeds reckon they will get ahead of Us? How badly do they judge!

** God's deadline is coming for anyone who has been expecting to meet God! He is the Alert, Aware. * Anyone who strives, strives only for his own soul's sake. God is Transcendent, beyond [any need of] the Universe! * We will overlook their evil deeds, and reward them with the finest of whatever they have been doing.

* We have instructed everyman to treat his parents kindly. Yet if they should strive to make you associate anything with Me which you have no knowledge of, do not obey them! To Me shall be your return, and I will notify you about anything you have been doing. * We will let the ones who believe and perform honorable deeds enter in among honorable people.

Treatment of Parents

** There are some people who say: "We believe in God"; yet whenever they suffer abuse for God's sake, they maintain that any trials by mankind are like God's torment. If any support should come from your Lord, they would say: "We have stood alongside you." Is God not quite Aware of what is on the minds of [everybody in] the Universe? * God does recognize those who believe and He (also) recognizes hypocrites.

10

* Those who disbelieve tell those who believe: "Follow our course and we will assume [responsibility for] your mistakes." **They will not assume**

their mistakes in any way: they are such liars! * However they will carry their own loads and others' loads besides their own. They will be questioned on Resurrection Day about what they have invented.

14

Noah

(II) * We sent Noah to his folk. He remained among them for a thousand years less fifty twelvemonths. The Flood seized them while they were doing wrong. ** However We saved him and the companions in the ship, and made it into a sign for [everyone in] the Universe.

Abraham and Image Worship

* Next Abraham told his folk: "Serve God and heed Him. That will be best for you if you only realized it. * You serve only images instead of God, and create a sham. The ones you serve instead of God do not control any sustenance for you, so seek sustenance from God Himself and serve Him; act grateful towards Him; to Him will you be returned.

Philosophy of History

20

* "Yet if you should deny it—and nations before you have already denied such—the Messenger has only to deliver [his message] clearly. * Have they not seen how God begins with creation, then performs it all over again? That is so easy for God [to do]!" ** SAY: "Travel around the earth and see how He began with creation; later on God raises up fresh growth. God is Capable of everything! * He punishes anyone He wishes to and shows mercy to anyone He wishes; to Him will you be restored. * You cannot prevent anything [from happening] on earth nor in Heaven; you have no patron nor any supporter besides God."

23

Abraham's Test

(III) * Those who reject God's signs and [any hope of] meeting Him despair of My mercy; those will have painful torment.

* There was no answer from his folk except they said: "Kill him or burn him up!" Yet God saved him from the fire; in that are signs for folk who believe. ** He said: "You have merely adopted images instead of God, out of affection for one another during worldly life. Then on Resurrection Day some of you will disown one another while others of you will curse each other. Your refuge will be the Fire; you will have no supporters!"

* Lot believed in him and he said: "I will move elsewhere for my Lord's sake. He is the Powerful, the Wise." * We bestowed Isaac and Jacob on him, and granted prophethood and the Book to his offspring. We gave him his payment in this world while in the Hereafter he will be among the **honorable**.

Lot

* So Lot told his folk: "You indulge in such sexual misconduct as no one in the Universe has attempted before you. * You even accost men and intercept [them on] the highway! You commit such a horrible thing in your clubs." His folk's answer was merely to say: "Bring us God's torment if you are so truthful!" ** He said: "My Lord, support me against such degenerate folk!"

30

31

(IV) * When Our messengers brought Abraham the good news, they said: "We'll destroy the people of this town. Its people have been doing wrong." * He said: "Yet Lot is in it!" They said: "We are quite aware as to who is in it. We'll save both him and his household, except for his wife; she is one of those who will stay behind."

* When Our messengers came to Lot, he felt wretched because of them, for [his] ability to protect them was so slender. They said: "Do not fear nor feel so sad. We shall save you and your family, except for your wife; she will be one of those who will stay behind. * We are sending a blight down from Heaven upon the people of this town because they have been acting so depraved." ** We have left some of it as a clear sign for folk who will [use their powers of] reason.

* To Midian [was sent] their brother Shuᶜayb. He said: "My folk, serve God and await the Last Day. Do not cause such mischief that it will ruin the earth." * They rejected him, so the Tremor seized them, and one morning they lay cowering in their home. * Both ᶜĀd and Thamūd have been explained to you by means of their [empty] dwellings; Satan made their actions seem attractive to them and he diverted them from the Way even though they had been granted insight. *Other Prophets*

* [In the case of] Qārūn, Pharaoh and Haman, Moses brought them explanations and they [still] acted overbearing on earth; yet they could never get ahead [of Us]. ** Each We seized for his offence; some of them We sent a hailstorm against, some the Blast overtook, others of them We let the earth swallow up, while still others We drowned. It was not God Who wronged them, but they had already wronged themselves. 40 *Different Punishments*

* Those who enlist other patrons instead of God may be compared to the **Spider**, who adopts a house for himself. The flimsiest house is the **Spider's** house, if they only realized it! *The Spider's Web*

* God knows anything they may appeal to besides Himself; He is the Powerful, the Wise.

* These are parables We make up for mankind, though only the learned will use their [powers of] reason. * God created Heaven and Earth in [all] Truth; in that is a sign for believers!

(v) ** Recite whatever has been revealed to you from the Book, and **keep up prayer: prayer restrains one from sexual misconduct and debauchery**. Yet mentioning God is even more important, for God knows whatever you produce. 45 *The Aim of Prayer*

PART TWENTY-ONE

(v, cont'd) * **Do not argue with the People of the Book unless it is in the politest manner**, except for those of them who do wrong. SAY: "We believe in what has been sent down to us and what has been sent down to you. Our God and your God is [the Same] One, and we are committed to [observe] peace before Him. 46 *Debating and Handling Arguments*

* Thus We have sent you down the Book. The ones whom We have given the Book to believe in it. Some of those are [people] who believe in it; only disbelievers repudiate Our signs. * You had not been reciting any book previously nor did you copy it down with your right hand; otherwise quibblers would suspect it. * Rather it exists as clear signs in the breasts of those who have been given knowledge. Only wrongdoers repudiate Our *The Book*

50   signs. ** They say: "If only some signs were sent down to him from his
Lord!"

SAY: "Signs rest only with God; I am merely a plain warner." * Is it not
sufficient for them that We have sent you down the Book to be recited to
them? In that lies mercy plus a Reminder for folk who believe.

52   (VI) * SAY: "God suffices as a Witness between (all of) you and me." He
knows whatever exists in Heaven and Earth while those who believe in
falsehood and disbelieve in God will be the losers. * They try to make you
hurry up torment. If it had not been for a specific deadline, torment would
already have come to them. It will come upon them suddenly while they do
not even notice it.

* They try to have you hurry up torment! Hell will engulf
disbelievers. ** Some day torment will cover them from both above and
from underneath their feet, and He will say: "Taste what you have been
doing!"

> * O My servants who believe,
> My earth is vast,

Mortality

> so Me should you worship!
> * Every soul will be tasting death;
> then to Us shall you return.

* We shall lodge the ones who believe and perform honorable deeds in
the Garden with mansions by which rivers will flow, to live there for
ever. How splendid will be the earnings of the workers * who are
patient and rely on their Lord!

60

*God the
Provider*

** How many animals do not carry their own provision! God
provides both for them and for you. He is the Alert, the Aware.

* If you should ask them Who created Heaven and Earth, and has
regulated the sun and moon, they would say: "God." So why do they shrug
[things] off? * God extends sustenance to any of His servants whom He
wishes and measures it out for him. God is Aware of everything. * If you
should ask them Who sends water down from the sky and revives the earth

Pagans

with it after it has died, they would say: "God." SAY: "Praise be to God!"
Nevertheless most of them do not use their reason.

64   (VII) * What is this worldly life except an amusement and a game? Yet the
final Home will mean [real] living, if they only realized it! ** Whenever
they sail on board a ship, they appeal to God sincerely; religion (then)
belongs to Him. Yet whenever He lands them safely, then they associate
[others with Him]. * Let them disbelieve in whatever We have given them,
and let them enjoy themselves; they soon shall know!

* Have they not seen how We have granted a safe sanctuary while men
are being kidnapped all around them? Yet they still believe in falsehood
and disbelieve in God's favor! * Who is more in the wrong than someone

who invents a lie about God and rejects the Truth even when it has come to him? Will there not be room in Hell for [such] disbelievers?

* We shall guide the ones who strive for Us along Our ways. God stands by those who act kindly!

Jihād OR *Striving*

30

The [East] Romans
(OR The Byzantines)

THIS CHAPTER was revealed after **Splitting Open** 84 and before the previous chapter on **The Spider** 29. It consists of six sections with 60 verses in all; 59 are Meccan, while one, v.17, dates from Madīna. The term *Ar-Rūm* refers to Europe in its imperialistic phase, even recently in North Africa.

A clear consciousness of history is displayed here, as it was in the previous chapter; the reference is to the current wars then being waged between the Byzantine or Eastern Roman Empire and the Persian Empire in the days of the Prophet. The chapter also has some lyric passages on the glory of God (II) and His signs (III). Marriage is discussed, and also differences in speech and race. Associates or partners must always be watched carefully, we are warned (IV).

In the name of God, the Mercy-giving, the Merciful!

(I) * A.L.M.

* The Byzantines have been defeated * on the nearest front! Following their defeat they shall conquer * a few years later. With God lies command, both before and later on. On that day believers will be glad ** of God's support. He supports anyone He wishes, and is the Powerful, the Merciful. * [Such is] God's promise; God does not break His promise even though most men do not realize it. * They recognize the outer show of worldly life, while they are heedless about the Hereafter.

* Have they not reflected about themselves? God has only created Heaven and Earth and whatever lies in between them for the Truth and till a specific deadline. Yet many men disbelieve about meeting their *Philosophy of History* Lord. * Have they not travelled around the earth and seen what the outcome was for those who existed before them? They were even stronger than they are: they cultivated the earth and developed it more than they have ever developed it. Their messengers brought them explanations; it was not God who wronged them, but they wronged themselves.

10

** Then **how evil was the outcome for those who practised evil,** simply because they denied God's signs and kept on making fun of them!

11
The Hour

(II) * God begins with creation, then He performs it all over again; then to Him will you return. * Some day when the Hour has been

established, criminals will feel stunned. * They will have no intercessors
from among their own associates; they will even deny they were their
associates! * Some day when the Hour has been established, on that day
they will be dispersed. ** Those who believe and have performed
honorable deeds will rejoice in a park, * while those who disbelieve and
reject both Our signs and meeting in the Hereafter will be presented with
torment.

> * Glory be to God when you reach evening
> and when you arise in the morning!
> * Praise belongs to Him throughout Heaven and Earth,
> and after supper and when you are at your noonhour.

*Glory
to God*

> * He brings forth the living from the dead
> and brings forth the dead from the living,
> and He revives the earth following its death.
> Thus shall you (all) be brought forth [again].

(III) ** **Among His signs** is [the fact] that he has created you from
dust; then you were propagated as human beings.

20
*God's
Signs*

* **Among His signs** is [the fact] that He has created spouses for
you from among yourselves so that you may console yourselves
with them. He has planted affection and mercy between you; in
that are signs for people who think things over.

Marriage

* **Among His signs** are the creation of Heaven and Earth, as
well as the diversity in your tongues and colors. In that are signs
for those who know.

*Differences
in Speech
and Race*

* **Among His signs** are your sleeping at night and by day, and
your pursuit of His bounty. In that are signs for any folk who
listen.

* **Among His signs** is how He shows you lightning for both
fear and anticipation. He sends water down from the sky so He
may revive the earth with it following its death. In that are signs
for folk who use their reason.

** **Among His signs** are [the fact] that the sky and earth hold
firm at His command. Then whenever He calls you forth out of the
earth once and for all, you will (all) come forth! * Anyone who is
in Heaven and Earth belongs to Him; all are subservient to Him.

* He is the One Who starts out with creation; then He
performs it all over again. It is quite simple for Him [to do]. He
sets the Supreme Example in Heaven and Earth; He is the
Powerful, the Wise!

(IV) * He offers you an example from among yourselves. Do you have
any partners for what We have provided you with among those whom
your right hands control? Do you [feel] the same in such a case so that
you fear [these servants] just as you fear one another? Thus We spell out
signs for folk who will use their reason. * Rather the ones who do
wrong follow their own whims without having any knowledge. Who will

28
*Sharing
Control*

guide someone whom God has let go astray? They will have no supporters.

30

Correct Religion

** So keep your face set enquiringly towards the [true] religion, God's natural handiwork along which lines He has patterned mankind. There is no way to alter God's creation. That is the correct religion, though most men do not realize it * even as they turn towards Him. Heed Him and keep up prayer, and do not be one of those who associate [others with Him], * such as the ones who split up their religion and form sects. Each party is happy with whatever lies before them. * Whenever some trouble afflicts mankind, they appeal to their Lord, turning towards Him; then when He lets them taste some mercy from Himself, a group of them will associate others with their Lord, * so as to disbelieve in whatever We have given them. So enjoy yourselves, for you shall know!

** Or have We sent down some authority to them which speaks to them about what they are associating with Him? * Whenever We let mankind taste mercy, they are glad about it; yet if any evil should strike them because of what their hands have sent on ahead, then they feel despondent. * Have they not seen how God extends sustenance to anyone He wishes, and budgets it? There are signs in that for folk who believe.

* So give the near relative his due, and the needy and the wayfarer; that will be best for the ones who want [to see] God's face. Those will be prosperous. * Any usury you farm out so it will be increased from (other) people's wealth will never increase so far as God is concerned; while those of you who pay something as welfare tax while you seek

40

God's face, will have it multiplied. ** God is the One Who has created you, then provided for you; next He will cause you to die, then revive you. Are there any of your associates who can perform anything like that? Glory be to Him; Exalted is He over anything they may associate [with Him]!

41

(v) * Pollution has appeared on land and at sea because of what man's hands have accomplished, so He may let them taste something of what they have earned, in order that they will turn back [in repentance]. * SAY: "Travel around the earth and see what the outcome was for those who [lived] before. Most of them were associators [of others in their worship of God]."

* Keep your face set toward the established religion before a day comes from God which cannot be fended off. On that day they will be dispersed! * Anyone who disbelieves must assume [responsibility for] his disbelief, while whoever acts honorably will have things adjusted for themselves, ** so He may reward the ones who have believed and performed honorable deeds out of His bounty. He does not love disbelievers.

* **Among His signs** is [the fact] that He sends the winds to bring news so He may let you taste some of His mercy, and so ships may sail at His command, in order that you may seek some of His bounty and so that you may act grateful. * We have sent

messengers to their folk before you; they brought them explanations and We were avenged on those who had committed any crimes. It is right for Us to support believers!

* God is the One Who sends the winds to blow the clouds along. He spreads them out in the sky just as He wishes, and breaks them up into patches so you see a shower coming from inside them. When He strikes any of His servants whom He wishes with it, they are overjoyed, * even if before it fell on them, they had felt disheartened.

** Look at the traces of God's mercy, how He revives the earth following its death. Such is the Reviver from the dead; He is Capable of everything! * Even if We sent a wind so they might see it turning things yellow, they would still keep on disbelieving even after it. * You cannot make the dead hear, nor even make the deaf hear the Appeal once they have turned their backs on it. * You are no one to guide the blind out of their error: only someone who believes in Our signs will listen; since they are committed to (live in) peace.

(VI) * God is the One Who has created you out of weakness; then He has granted strength following [your] weakness; later on He has granted weakness and grey hairs in place of strength. He creates whatever He wishes; He is the Aware, the Capable. ** Some day the Hour will be established when criminals will swear they have been hanging around for only an hour. Thus they have (always) shrugged things off!

* The ones who have been given knowledge and faith will say: "You have hung around until the Day of Rebirth according to God's book. Now is the Day for Rebirth, but you are such that you do not know it!" * On that day no excuse of theirs will benefit those who have done wrong nor will they be allowed to argue back.

* We have set forth every sort of example for men in this Qurʾān. Yet even if you brought them some sign, those who disbelieve would still say: "You (all) are only trifling!" * Thus God seals off the hearts of those who will not know. ** Be patient; God's promise is true. Do not let those who will not be convinced treat you lightly!

50

54

The Final Hour

60

31
Luqmān

THIS CHAPTER was revealed after (**Drawn Up In) Ranks** 37 and before **Sheba** 34. It consists of four sections which embrace 34 Meccan verses (except that the poem on "God's Words" in section III dates from a later period in Madīna).

Among the Arabs Luqmān was a spiritual associate and possible grandnephew of the Old Testament prophet Job, and similar to the fable-teller and wise man of Greece called Aesop. He is in fact the traditional Arab sage who fills much the same place in Arab folklore as Aesop (OR the 'Ethiopian') did among the Greeks.

From now on the chapters become shorter. This one is full of fine thoughts, including a Polonius-style speech to the wiseman's son. Towards the end, it also has two hymns, one on "God's Words" (III) and the other on "God the All-Knowing" (IV).

In the name of God, the Mercy-giving, the Merciful!

(I) * A.L.M.

> * These are verses from the Wise Book, * [offered] as guidance and mercy for those who act kindly, * who keep up prayer, pay the welfare tax and are convinced about the Hereafter. ** Those hold on to guidance from their Lord; such will be prosperous.

* Some men buy up sporting tales to mislead [others] from God's way without having any knowledge, and they take it [all] as a joke. Those shall have shameful torment. * Whenever Our verses are recited to him, he turns around disdainfully as if he had not even heard them, just as if both his ears were hard of hearing. Announce painful torment to him!

* The ones who believe and perform honorable deeds will have gardens of Bliss * to live in for ever. * God's promise is true, and He is the

10

Powerful, the Wise. ** He has created the heavens without any visible support. He has cast headlands on the earth lest it sway with you, and dispersed all kinds of animals throughout it. We send water down from the

The Skeptic's Challenge

sky with which We grow every type of noble species. * This is God's creation. Show me what those others besides Him have created! Indeed, wrongdoers are in obvious error.

12

(II) * We gave **Luqmān** wisdom:
"Give thanks to God. Anyone who gives thanks, merely gives

thanks for his own sake; while anyone who is ungrateful [will find] God is Transcendent, Praiseworthy."

* Thus **Luqmān** told his son as he was instructing him: "My dear son, do not associate anything [in your worship] of God [Alone]. Association is such a serious wrong!"

* (We have commissioned (every)man to [look after] his parents: his mother bears him with one fainting spell after another fainting spell, while his weaning takes two years. Thank Me as well as your parents; towards Me lies the Goal! ** Yet if either of them should strive to make you associate anything with Me which you have no knowledge about, do not obey them although you should (still) keep company with both of them properly during [their life in] this world. Follow the way of anyone who feels concerned about Me. Then to Me will be your return and I shall notify you about whatever you have been doing.)

* "My dear son, if there existed the weight of a mustard seed, and it lay in some boulder in either Heaven or Earth, God would still bring it forth. God is so Gracious, Informed.
   * "My dear son, keep up prayer, command what is proper and forbid dishonor. Endure patiently whatever may afflict you; for that shows determination in [handling] matters. * Do not sneer down your cheek at other men nor walk brashly around the earth: God does not love every swaggering boaster. * Act modestly in the way you walk, and lower your voice:

   "The ugliest sound is a donkey's voice!"

(III) ** Do you not see how God has harnessed whatever is in Heaven and whatever is on Earth for you? He has lavished His favor on you both publicly and privately. Yet some men will still argue about God without having any knowledge or guidance, nor any enlightening Book! * Whenever they are told: "Follow whatever God has sent down," they say: "Rather we follow what we found our forefathers doing." Even though Satan has been inviting them to the torment of the Blaze?
   * Anyone who commits his person peacefully to God and acts kindly has grasped the Firmest Handle! Towards God lies the destiny of matters.
* No matter who disbelieves, do not let his disbelief sadden you; to Us will be their return and We shall notify them about whatever they have done. God is Aware of what is on people's minds. * We will let them enjoy themselves for a little while; then We will drive them along to stern torment.
   ** If you should ask them who created Heaven and Earth, they would say: "God." SAY: "Praise be to God!" However most of them do not realize it. * God owns whatever is in Heaven and Earth; God is Transcendent, Praiseworthy.

   * If only the trees on earth were pens
   and the [inky] sea were later on

Luqmān's Advice to His Son

Association is a Serious Sin

Respect for Parents

Social Conduct

20

Tolerance Towards Disbelievers

God's Words

replenished with seven other seas,
God's words would never be exhausted;
God is Powerful, Wise!

* Your creation and your rebirth
[happen] only as with a single soul.
God is Alert, Observant.
* Have you not seen how God
wraps night up in daylight
and wraps daylight up in night?
He regulates the sun and moon:
each runs along on a fixed course.
God is Informed about anything you do!
30 ** That is because God is the Truth
while anything they appeal to
instead of Him is false.
God is the Sublime, the Great!

31
The Sea

(IV) * Have you not seen ships sailing along at sea because of God's favor, so He may show you some of His signs? In that are signs for every [person who is] persevering, grateful.

* Whenever waves cover them like awnings, they appeal to God sincerely; religion belongs to Him! Yet once He delivers them to land, some of them act disinterested. It is only every ungrateful swindler who repudiates Our signs.

* Mankind, heed your Lord and dread the day when no parent will make amends for his child nor will any offspring make amends in any way for his parent. God's promise is true, so do not let worldly life deceive you, nor even let the Deceiver deceive you concerning God.

God the
All-Knowing

* God has knowledge about the Hour.
He sends down showers and knows
whatever wombs contains. **Yet no person knows
what he will earn tomorrow,
nor does any person know
in what land he will die.**
Still, God is Aware, Informed!

32
Worship OR *Adoration*
(Bowing Down On One's Knees)

THIS CHAPTER WAS revealed after **Believers** 23 and before **The Mount** 52. The act of kneeling in worship or prostration is mentioned in II, 15:III, and 41:V. However I do not care for the term 'prostration' that has often been given as a translation for the title since it has neurotic overtones in contemporary English. Islamic worship requires more reverence.

This is the last chapter initialed with the letters A.L.M. (these have already appeared in Chapters 2, 3, 29, 30, & 31). It consists of 30 Meccan verses arranged in three sections, except for vv. 16-20 in section II which date from Madīna. Creation and man are the initial themes heard in section I.

In the name of God, the Mercy-giving, the Merciful!

(I) * A. L. M.

   * The revelation of the Book which contains no doubt [has been accomplished] through the Lord of the Universe.

* Or do they say: "He has invented it!"? Rather, it is the Truth from your Lord so you may warn a folk to whom no warner has come before you, so that they may be guided.

   * God is the One Who created Heaven and Earth as well as whatever lies in between them, in six days. Then He mounted on the Throne. You (all) have no patron nor any intercessor besides Him. Will you not bear this in mind?   *Creation*

   ** He organizes the matter from Heaven [down] to Earth; then it will soar back up to Him on a day whose measure is a thousand years according to the way you count. * Such is the Knower of the Unseen and the Visible, the Powerful, the Merciful * Who makes everything He creates so fine!

   He started out by creating man from clay; * then He made his progeny   *Man*
from an extract of discarded liquid; * next He completed him and
breathed some of His own spirit into him. He has granted you hearing,   10
eyesight and vital organs. Yet small thanks do you give for it! ** They
say: "When we have sunk deep into the earth shall we [take part] in some
fresh creation?" Indeed they disbelieve about meeting their Lord! * SAY:
"The Angel of Death who has been given charge of you will gather you in.
Then you will (all) be returned to your Lord.

12

BOW
DOWN
HERE

20

23

30

(II) * If you only could see how criminals will hang their heads before their Lord: "Our Lord, we have observed and heard; so send us back! We will act honorably; we are convinced!" * If We had so wished, We might have given each soul its own guidance, but the Sentence [passed] by Me has been confirmed: "I shall fill Hell with sprites and men all together! * So have a taste, since you have forgotten about meeting on this day of yours! We have likewise forgotten you. Taste the torment of eternity because of what you have been doing."

** The only ones who believe in Our signs are those who drop down **kneeling [in worship]** whenever they are reminded of them, and hymn their Lord's praise. They do not act so proudly. * They slip quietly away from their beds to appeal to their Lord in fear and anticipation, and spend [charitably] whatever We have provided them with. * No soul knows what comfort is hidden from their eyes as a reward for what they have been doing.

* Is someone who is a believer like someone who has been acting immorally? They are not on the same footing! * Those who believe and perform honorable deeds will have gardens with living quarters to relax in because of what they have been doing. ** Those who have been immoral will have the Fire as their lodging; every time they may want to leave it, they will be returned to it. They will be told: "Taste the torment of the Fire which you have been denying!"

* Still We shall let them taste worldly torment rather than supreme torment, so they may yet turn back. * Who is more in the wrong than someone who has been reminded of his Lord's signs, then shuns them? We shall be Avenged on criminals!

(III) * We gave Moses the Book, so do not be in any doubt about meeting it. We granted it to the Children of Israel for guidance. * We even set some of them up as leaders to guide [people] at Our command, once they were patient and convinced about Our signs. ** Your Lord will sort them out on Resurrection Day concerning whatever they have been differing over.

* Does it not guide them [when they notice] how many generations We have wiped out before them whose dwellings they now walk around in? That contains signs, so will they not listen? * Have they not seen how We drive along water for the parched earth and bring forth crops with it so your livestock and they themselves may eat by means of it? Will they not observe?

* They say: "When will this victory be if you are so truthful?" * SAY: "On the day of victory their [profession of] faith will not benefit those who have disbelieved, nor will they be allowed to wait. ** Shun them and wait; they will be waiting too!"

33
The Coalition
(OR *The [Combined] Forces*)

THIS SLIGHTLY longer chapter was revealed after **The House of** ʿImrān 3 and before **Examining Her** 60. It contains 73 verses arranged in nine sections, all of which were revealed in Madīna. This thus represents a break in the diminishing sequence of chapters.

The Jews and pagan Arabs around Madīna had risen 10,000 strong in a conspiracy directed against the nascent Islamic state at this point (the year 5 / 626-7), and the chapter bears witness to the difficulties existent in this developing society. The troubles which Muḥammad faced in Madīna in the year 5 / 626-7 were different from the ones he had met with in Mecca. We hear graphic portrayals of meddlers and slackers who, for instance, gave rise to recruiting and defence problems (II). Salmān the Persian had a trench dug so the Madīnese could withstand a siege. Following this success, the Prophet began to achieve the hegemony of Arabia and control over the trade routes to Syria.

The Prophet's wives appear again (IV & VI), plus rules for divorce (VI) and modesty (VIII). There is also a section on protocol in connection with affairs of state (VII). The chapter ends with a statement on the philosophy of history (VIII) plus a vivid picture of how God's trust was offered to the mountains, but they were prudent enough to reject it (IX).

In the name of God, the Mercy-giving, the Merciful!

(I) * O Prophet, heed God and do not obey disbelievers and hypocrites. God is Aware, Wise. * Follow whatever you are inspired with by your Lord; God is Informed about what you (all) are doing. * Rely on God; God suffices as a Trustee.

* God has not placed two hearts in any man's body. Nor has He granted you wives whom you may back away from, to act as your mothers, nor has He granted your adopted sons to be your own sons. That is your own statement made by your own mouths. God states the Truth and He guides one along the Way. ** Call them after their own fathers; it is fairer so far as God is concerned. If you do not know who their fathers were, then [call them] your **brothers in religion** and your wards.

What you may have slipped up on already will not be held against you, but only something your hearts have done intentionally. Yet God is Forgiving, Merciful.

* The Prophet is closer to believers than even they themselves are, and his wives are [like] their mothers. Yet blood relatives are closer to one another in God's book than are believers and the Refugees, except that you should act in a proper manner towards your wards. That has been underlined in the Book.

* When We made an agreement with the prophets, with you and with Noah, Abraham, Moses and Jesus the son of Mary, We pledged a solemn agreement with them * so He might question sincere persons concerning their sincerity. He has prepared painful torment for disbelievers!

*Divine
Intervention*

9

10

(II) * You who believe, remember God's favor upon you when the armies charged at you! We sent a wind and even armies you did not see against them. God was Observant of what you were doing, ** as they came at you both from above you and from below you, and your eyesight faltered and your hearts leaped up into your throats, and you entertained certain thoughts about God; * there believers were tested and severely shaken as if in an earthquake. * Thus hypocrites and those whose hearts contain malice said: "God and His messenger have only promised us something to lure us on."

*Recruiting
Problems*

* So when a faction of them said: "O people of Yathrib, there is no room for you, so return!", a group of them took leave of the Prophet, saying: "Our houses lie exposed." They were not defenceless; they merely wanted to run away. * If a raid had been made on them from [all] its quarters, then they had been asked to rise up in dissension, they would have done so and yet not lasted very long. ** Still they had already pledged to God that they would not turn their backs! Any oath [made] to God will be asked about.

* SAY: "Fleeing will never help you: if you should flee from death or slaughter, then you will still enjoy (life) only briefly." * SAY: "Who is there to shield you from God if He should want any ill for you or wants mercy for you?" They will find they have no patron nor any supporter besides God.

* God knows the meddlers among you and the ones telling their brethren: "Come over to our side!" They only take part in conflict for a little while, * skimping towards you (all). Whenever fear comes over them, you will see them looking at you, their eyes rolling around like someone whom death has almost seized. Once fear leaves them, they will lash out at you (all) with [their] sharp tongues, yet skimping about [doing] any good. Those persons do not believe, so God has foiled their actions. That is so

20

easy for God [to do]. ** They reckon the **Coalition** will not go away. If the **Coalition** should come [again], they would like to be wandering around far away among the [desert] Arabs, asking for news about you. Yet even if they were among you, they would only fight a little.

21

(III) * In God's messenger you have a fine model for someone who looks forward to [meeting] God and the Last Day, and mentions God frequently. * When believers saw the **Coalition**, they said: "This is what God and His messenger have promised us. God and His messenger have told the truth." It merely increased them in faith and submission. * Some believers are men who are sincere in what they pledge to God, while others have already fulfilled their mortal duty, and still others are waiting [their chance]; they have not changed in the least, * so God may reward the truthful for their truthfulness and punish hypocrites if He so wishes, or else relent towards them. God is Forgiving, Merciful.

** God sent the ones who disbelieved back in their fury; they did not accomplish any good. God spares believers the trouble of fighting; God is Strong, Powerful! * He has tossed some People of the Book who had backed them up, out of their strongholds and cast panic into their hearts; one group you killed while you captured another group. * He let you inherit their land, their homes and their property, plus a land you have not yet set foot on. God is Capable of everything!

(IV) * O Prophet, tell your wives: "If you are wanting worldly life and its attraction, then come on! I'll let you enjoy them and dismiss you in a handsome fashion. * However if you have been wanting [to see] God and His messenger, as well as having a home in the Hereafter, well God has prepared splendid payment for the kindly women among you. ** O wives of the Prophet, anyone of you who commits some flagrant act of misconduct shall have [her] punishment doubled twice over. That is easy for God [to do].

28
The Prophet's Wives
30

PART TWENTY-TWO
31

(IV cont'd) * "Yet We will give any of you who is devoted to God and His messenger, and acts honorably, her earnings twice over. We have reserved a generous provision for her. * O wives of the Prophet, you are not like any other women! If you do your duty, then do not act too deferential while talking [to others] lest someone whose heart contains malice may thereby be encouraged. Employ suitable speech. * Remain in your homes and do not dress up fancily the way they used to dress during [the time of] primitive Ignorance. Keep up prayer and pay the welfare tax, and obey God and His messenger. God merely wants to remove any blight from you [since you are] People of the [Prophet's] House, and to cleanse you thoroughly. * Remember any of God's verses and wisdom which are recited in your homes. God is Gracious, Informed."

(v) ** Muslim men and Muslim women, believing men and believing women, devout men and devout women, truthful men and truthful women, patient men and patient women, reverent men and reverent women, charitable men and charitable women, fasting men and fasting women, and men who safeguard their private parts and women who safeguard [theirs], and men who remember God often and women who remember [Him]—for [all of] them God has prepared forgiveness and a splendid wage.

35

* No believing man nor any believing woman should exercise any choice in their affair once God and His messenger have decided upon some matter. Anyone who disobeys God and His messenger has wandered off into manifest error.

* Thus you told someone whom God had favored and whom you yourself have favored: "Hold on to your wife, and heed God," while you kept to yourself what God had disclosed and you dreaded people['s opinion], although it is more correct for you to dread God. Once Zayd had accomplished his purpose with her, We married her off to you so that there would be no objection for believers in respect to their adopted son's wives once they have accomplished their purpose with them. God's command must be done! * The Prophet is not to be reproached for [doing] what God has stipulated for him to do. God's practice has been such with those who have passed on already—God's command is a pre-ordained decree—
* for those who transmit God's messages and dread him, while **they do not dread anyone else than God**. God suffices as a Reckoner.

40
Muḥammad the Last Prophet

** Muḥammad is not the father of any of your men, but [he is] **God's messenger and the Seal of the Prophets**. God is Aware of everything!

41
Piety

(VI) * You who believe, remember God often. * Celebrate him morning and evening; * He is the One Who accepts prayers from you, as do His angels, to lead you out of darkness into Light. He is Merciful with believers. * Their greeting on the day they meet Him will be: "Peace!" He has prepared generous payment for them.

** O Prophet, We have sent you as a witness, herald and warner, * and as someone who invites people to [know] God by His permission, and as a shining lamp. * Proclaim to believers how they will have great bounty from God.

* Do not obey disbelievers and hypocrites. Disregard their annoyance and rely on God: God suffices as a Trustee.

Divorce

* You who believe, whenever you marry believing women, and then divorce them before you have touched them, you have no number [of months] to count in their case. Provide for them and release them in a handsome manner.

50
Muḥammad's Wives (again)

** O Prophet, We have permitted you [to deal with] your wives whom you have given their allotments to, and anyone your right hands control from what God has furnished you [as captives], and your paternal uncles' and aunts' daughters, and your maternal uncles' and aunts' daughters who have migrated along with you, and any believing woman who bestows herself upon the Prophet, provided the Prophet wants to marry her; such is exclusively for you and not for [other] believers. We know what We have stipulated for them concerning their wives and anyone their right hands control, so it will not be held against you. God is Forgiving, Merciful.

* You may make any one of them you wish wait, and let any one you wish approach you. It will not be held against you concerning anyone you may desire among those whom you have set aside. That is more suitable so that you may comfort them and they will not be saddened, and [instead] pleased with anything you may give them all. God knows what is in your hearts; God is Aware, Lenient.

* No [other] women will be lawful for you later on nor may you exchange them for other wives, even though their beauty may entice you, except for someone your right hand controls. God is an Observer over everything.

(VII) * You who believe, do not enter the Prophet's [private] quarters unless an invitation has been extended to you for a meal, though still without watching how it is prepared. However once you have been invited, then go on in; and once you have been fed, then disperse, not indulging in conversation. That has been disturbing the Prophet and he feels ashamed [to tell] you so. Yet God is not ashamed [to raise] the Truth.

Whenever you ask (his wives) for any object, ask them for it from behind a curtain. That will be purer for your hearts as well as for their hearts. It is not proper for you to annoy God's messenger, nor ever to marry his wives after him; that would be serious with God! * Whether you reveal anything or hide it, God is Aware of everything.

** There is no objection to their [appearing before] their fathers, their sons nor their brothers, nor their brothers' and sisters' sons, nor their own womenfolk, nor anyone their right hands control. Heed God (you women); God is a Witness for everything!

* God and His angels accept prayers for the Prophet. You who believe, **pray for him (too) and greet him** properly. * God will curse those who [try to] annoy God and His messenger in this world and the Hereafter, and will prepare shameful torment for them. * Those who annoy believing men and believing women without their having deserved it, will assume [the guilt of] slander and [commit] a clear offence against themselves.

(VIII) * O Prophet, tell your wives and daughters, and believers' wives as well, to draw their cloaks close around themselves. That is more appropriate so they may be recognized and not molested. God is Forgiving, Merciful. ** If hypocrites and those whose hearts contain malice do not stop, as well as the agitators in Madīna, We shall stir you up against them. Then they will live alongside you as neighbors for only a little while [longer]; * cursed wherever they are encountered, they will be seized and completely routed. * [Such is] God's practice with those who have passed on before; you will never find any change in God's practice.

* People will ask you about the Hour. SAY: "Knowledge about it rests only with God." What will make you realize that perhaps the Hour is near! * God will curse disbelievers and prepare a Blaze for them ** to remain in for ever. They will not find any patron nor supporter; * on a day when their faces will be twisted by the Fire, they will say: "If we had only obeyed God and obeyed the Messenger!" * They will (also) say: "Our Lord, we have obeyed our superiors and our great men, and they led us off from the Way. * Our Lord, give them double torment and curse them with a great curse!"

(IX) * You who believe, do not be like those who abused Moses. God cleared him of what they said. He became outstanding with God. ** You who believe, heed God and speak straight to the point; * He will improve

53
Etiquette;
Affairs
of State

On
Greeting
the
Prophet

59
Rules for
Modesty
60

Philosphy
of History

69
70

your actions for you and forgive you your sins. Anyone who obeys God and His messenger will achieve a splendid Triumph.

God's Trust;
The Human
Dilemma

        * We offered the trust to Heaven and Earth,
        and to the mountains too,
        yet they refused to carry it,
        and shrank back from it.
        However man accepted it:
        he has been unfair [to himself], ignorant!

* Still God will punish hypocritical men and hypocritical women and associating men and associating women. However God relents with believing men and believing women. God is Forgiving, Merciful!

34
Sheba

THIS CHAPTER comes after **Luqmān** 31 and before **Throngs** 39 in the chronological order of revelation. It consists of 54 Meccan verses arranged in six sections; only v.6 dates from later in Madīna. This also marks the first of six chapters in a new series.

It begins with an exordium on God's omniscience. Then the message warns against the effects of luxury and of associating others in our pure worship of God (III). It also recounts the story of King David, his wise son Solomon, and their war against Sheba (II), which lay in Yaman far to the south of the Ḥijāz. It ends with a vivid picture of how knowledge must be pursued carefully (VI).

In the name of God, the Mercy-giving, the Merciful!

(I) * Praise be to God, Who holds
whatever is in Heaven and whatever is on Earth!
Praise will be His in the Hereafter;
He is the Wise, the Informed.

* He knows what penetrates the earth
and what issues from it,
and what falls down from the sky
and what soars up into it.
He is the Merciful, the Forgiving.

A Doxology

God's Knowledge

* Those who disbelieve say: "The Hour will not come upon us!" SAY: "Of course, by my Lord, it will come to you through the Knower of the Unseen." No atom's weight in either Heaven nor on Earth nor anything less than that nor larger ever escapes Him, unless it is in a clear Book, * so He may reward the ones who believe and perform honorable deeds. Those will have forgiveness and generous provision, ** while the ones who work against Our signs in order to defeat them will have painful torment from a blight.
* Those who have been given knowledge see that what has been sent down to you from your Lord is the Truth, and guides [us] along the Road to the Powerful, the Praiseworthy; * while those who disbelieve say: "Shall we introduce you to a man who will notify you, once you have been utterly torn to pieces, that you will [reappear] in some fresh creation? * Has he invented a lie about God or has he some sprite within him?"
Rather the ones who do not believe in the Hereafter will be in torment and extreme error. * Have they not considered whatever lies before them

from the sky and earth, and what is behind them? If We wished, We would let the earth swallow them up or a patch of sky drop down on them. In that is a sign for every penitent servant.

10
David

(II) ** We gave David bounty from Ourself: "O mountains, echo back [God's praises] along with him! And [so may] the birds." We softened iron for him: * "Make suits of armor and measure out the links in mail, and act honorably; I am Observant of anything you do."

Solomon

* Solomon possessed the wind; it would blow for a month in one direction and then blow back for [another] month. We melted down a font of brass for him. There were some sprites who worked in front of him by his Lord's permission, and We let any of them who wavered from Our command taste torment from the Blaze. * They worked away for him just as he wished on shrines and images, bowls as big as troughs and built-in cauldrons: "Give thanks, O House of David!" Yet few of My servants are grateful.

* When We determined he should die, nothing indicated his death to them except a worm from the earth which was eating away at his cane. When he fell down, the sprites realized clearly that if they had known the Unseen, they would not have had to continue in such humiliating torment.

Sheba
Itself

** There had been a sign for **Sheba** in their dwelling: two gardens, to the right and left: "Eat some of your Lord's provision and thank Him. Such a good land and forgiving Lord!"

* They spurned [it], so We sent a torrent from the dam upon them, and We changed both their gardens for them into two gardens yielding bitter food, tamarisk and a very few hawthorns. * That is how We rewarded them for the way they disbelieved. Should We reward only the ungrateful person?

* We placed towns in plain view between them and the towns which We had blessed, and We measured out travel between them: "Travel safely between them by night and day." * They said: "Our Lord, lengthen the distance between our stops!" They wronged themselves so We turned them

20

into legends; We scattered them into every [possible] fragment. In that are signs for every patient, grateful person. ** Diabolis proved his idea was sound about them: they (all) followed him except for a group of believers. * Yet he held no authority over them, except so We might distinguish someone who believes in the Hereafter from someone who is in any uncertainty about it. Your Lord acts as an Overseer for everything.

22
Intercession
is Useless

(III) * SAY: "Appeal to those whom you claim to instead of to God; they do not control even an atom's weight in either Heaven nor on Earth." They have no share in either, nor has He any backer among them. * Intercession does not benefit anyone so far as He is concerned except for someone He grants it to, until when [panic] is driven from their hearts, they say: "What did your Lord say?" They will say: "The Truth!" He is the Sublime, the Great!

Individual
Respon-
sibility

* SAY: "Who provides for you out of Heaven and Earth?" SAY: "God [Alone].'' Are either we or you closer to guidance, or else in obvious error? ** SAY: ''You will not be questioned about what we have

perpetrated nor shall we be questioned about what you have done." * SAY: "Our Lord will gather us in together; then things will be opened up in all Truth for us. He is the Opener, the Aware."

* SAY: "Show me the ones you have connected with Him as associates. It cannot be; rather He is God, the Powerful, the Wise." * We have not sent you [Muḥammad] except as a newsbearer and warner to every single human being, even though most men do not realize it, * and they say: "When will this promise be if you (all) have been so truthful?" ** SAY: "You hold an appointment for a day which will be neither postponed nor advanced by so much as an hour."

The Universal Message

30

(IV) * Those who disbelieve say: "We'll never believe in this Reading nor in the one which [came] before it." If you could only see how, when wrongdoers are stationed before their Lord, they will toss the statement back and forth at one another. Those who had been despised as weaklings will tell those who acted overbearing: "If it were not for you, we'd be believers."

31

* Those who were overbearing will tell those who acted like weaklings: "Did we block you off from guidance once it came to you? Rather you yourselves were guilty!" * Those who had been despised will tell those who were overbearing: "Rather there was plotting night and day when you ordered us to disbelieve in God and we set up rivals to him." They will conceal their regret once they see the torment; We will place fetters around the necks of those who disbelieve. Will they not be rewarded for just what they have been doing?

* We have sent no town a warner unless its high-livers said: "We are disbelievers in what you have been sent with." ** They say: "We have more wealth and children, and will not be tormented!" * SAY: "My Lord extends sustenance to anyone He wishes and budgets it, even though most men do not realize it."

(V) * It is not your wealth nor your children that will bring you close to Us in patronage; only someone who believes and acts honorably (will do so). Those will have a double reward because of what they have done. They will feel secure in mansions * while those who were attempting to thwart Our signs will be paraded forth into torment.

37

* SAY: "My Lord extends sustenance to anyone He wishes among His servants and He budgets it out. He will compensate you for anything you have spent since He is the best Provider." ** Some day He will summon them all together; then He will say to the angels: "Are those the ones who were worshipping you?" * They will say: "Glory be to You! You are our Patron rather than they. Instead they have been worshipping sprites; most of them even believe in them!"

40

* Some day when some of them will not control any advantage nor harm for others, We will tell those who have done wrong: "Taste the torment of Fire which you have been denying!" * When Our clear verses are recited to them, they will say: "This is only a man who wants to discourage you from [worshipping] what your forefathers have been worshipping." They will say: "This is only some invented sham." Those

Ancestor Worship is Wrong

who disbelieve will say about Truth, once it comes to them: "This is nothing but sheer magic!"

* We did not bring them any books to study from nor send them any warner before you. ** Those who [lived] before them denied it and did not achieve a tenth of what We gave them. They even rejected My messengers, so [imagine] how [real] was My disgust!

46 (VI) * SAY: "I preach only one thing to you: that you stand up in pairs or singly for God; then consider how there is no madness in your companion. He is only a warner [sent] to you in the face of stern torment."

* SAY: "What I ask you in payment is merely something for yourselves. My own payment lies only up to God; He is a Witness for everything."

* SAY: "My Lord, the Knower of Unseen things, aims at the Truth."

> * SAY: **"Truth has come,**
> **while falsehood neither originates**
> **nor does anything over again**."

50 ** SAY: "If I have strayed, I have only led myself astray; while if I have been guided, then it is because of what my Lord has inspired in me. He is Alert, so Near!"

*The
Pursuit
of Faith*

* If you could see when they are startled and there is no escape, and they are seized from a place near at hand, * how they will say: "We believe in it!" Yet have they any way to snatch it up at such a distance? * They have already disbelieved in it, and aimed at [knowing] the Unseen from a distance. * Something will intervene between them and whatever they crave to have, just as was done with their [different] sects long before. They have [lived] in such suspicious doubt!

35
Originator
(OR *The Angels*)

THESE FORTY-FIVE verses are arranged in five sections; they were revealed after **The Standard** 25 and before **Mary** 19. The chapter bears two titles, **Originator**, as well as **The Angels**; both words appear in verse 1. It is a late Meccan revelation.

This chapter contains a statement concerning the futility of intercession (III), as well as comfort for the Prophet in his role as a warner. "Fresh and Salt Water" (or "The Two Seas") is a parable also set in this chapter (II).

In the name of God, the Mercy-giving, the Merciful!

(I) * Praise be to God, **Originator** of Heaven and Earth, Who appoints **the Angels** as winged messengers in pairs, and in threes and fours. He increases anything He wishes through creation; God is Capable of everything! * There is no withholding any mercy that God may open up for mankind; while neither is there any [means of] sending anything later on once He has withheld it. He is the Powerful, the Wise.

* Mankind, remember God's favor towards you. Is there any creator besides God who provides for you out of the sky and earth? There is no deity except Him; yet you shrug Him off! * If they should reject you, well, messengers before you have already been rejected. To God are matters referred.

** Mankind, God's promise is true; do not let worldly life lure you on nor let the Deceiver deceive you concerning God. * Satan is an enemy of yours, so treat him as an enemy: he only calls his party to become inmates of the Blaze. * Those who disbelieve will have severe punishment while those who believe and act honorably will have forgiveness and great earnings.

(II) * Does anyone exist whose evil action seems so attractive to him that he regards it as fine? God lets anyone He wishes go astray while He guides whomever He wishes. Do not let yourself go around pitying them; God is Aware of what they are producing.

8

* God is the One Who sends the winds to blow the clouds along. We drive them on to a dead land, and revive the earth by means of them after it has died. Such is regeneration. ** For anyone who has been wanting glory, God holds all glory: towards Him do wholesome words ascend while honorable action He exalts. Those who plot evil deeds will have severe

God's Role

10

punishment while their very plotting will collapse. * God has created you from dust, then from a drop of semen; then He divided you into couples. No female conceives nor gives birth unless He knows it. No elderly person grows even older nor has anything shortened from his life unless it is [written down] in some book. That is easy for God [to do]!

Fresh and Salt Water ("The Two Seas")

* **Both seas** are not alike: this one is sweet, fresh, refreshing to drink, while the other is salty, briny. From each you eat fresh meat and extract jewelry you wear. You see ships sailing along on it so you may seek His bounty and so that you may feel thankful.

* He wraps night up into daytime and wraps daytime up in night, and regulates the sun and moon; each runs along on a stated course. Such is God, your Lord! Control belongs to Him; while the ones whom you appeal to instead of Him do not control a wisp. * If you should appeal to them, they will not hear your appeal; while even though they heard it, they would not respond to you. On Resurrection Day they will disown your associating [them with God]. No one notifies you in the way that someone Who is Informed does.

False Gods are Futile

(III) ** Mankind, you are so poor as far as God is concerned, while God is Transcendent, Praiseworthy. * If He so wished, He could take you away and bring some fresh creation; * that would not be impossible for God to do. * **No burdened [soul] may bear another's burden**: if some overladen soul should call out for someone else to carry his load, no one would bear any part of it even though he were a near relative. You can only warn those who dread their Lord although [He is] Unseen, and keep up prayer. Anyone who purifies himself, only purifies his own soul. Towards God should lie one's goal.

15

Intercession is Void

Dualities

20

* The blind and the sighted are not equal,
** nor are darkness and light,
* nor a shady nook and a heatwave.
* The living and the dead are not alike.
God lets anyone He wishes listen, while you
will not make those in their graves hear.

* **You are nothing but a warner**;
* We have sent you as an announcer
and a warner about the Truth.
**No nation exists unless some warner
has passed among them.**

** Yet if they should reject you, well the ones before them rejected [their messengers too]; their messengers brought them explanations, the Psalms, and an enlightening Book. * Then I seized the ones who disbelieved. How great was My displeasure!

27

(IV) * Have you not seen how God sends water down from the sky? We produce different colored fruits with it. From the mountains come white and red marbling in different shades as well as black obsidian. * Some men, wild beasts and livestock are of different colors as well. Yet only His learned servants dread God [Alone], even though God is Powerful, Forgiving.

* The ones who recite God's book, keep up prayer and spend something both secretly and publicly from whatever He has provided for them, can hope for a business which will never slacken, ** so He may repay them their earnings and grant them even more out of His bounty. He is Forgiving, Appreciative.

* What We have revealed to you from the Book is the Truth confirming what has preceded it. God is Informed, Observant concerning His servants. * Then We allow some of Our servants whom We have singled out to inherit the Book. One of them may harm his own soul while another is lukewarm, and still another vies in performing good deeds with God's permission.

It [will mean] great bounty: * gardens of Eden will they enter. They will be allowed to wear gold and pearl bracelets there while their clothing will be [made of] silk. * They will say: "Praise be to God Who has lifted sadness from us! Our Lord is Forgiving, Appreciative, ** the One Who has settled us in the Everlasting Home because of His bounty. No toil will ever touch us there nor will any weariness affect us in it."

* The ones who disbelieved will have Hell fire. It will be neither finished off for them so that they may [really] die; nor will its torment be lightened for them. Thus We reward every ingrate. * They will scream away in it: "Our Lord, take us out! We'll act honorably, so differently from the way we have been acting!"

Did We not let you live on and on so anyone who bears things in mind might remember (them) during its course? The Warner came to you. So have a taste! Wrongdoers will have no supporter.

(v) * God is the One Who knows the Unseen in both Heaven and Earth. He is Aware of whatever is on your minds. * He is the One Who has set you up as [His] representatives on earth. Anyone who disbelieves is responsible for his own disbelief. Their disbelief merely increases disbelievers in loathing towards their Lord; their disbelief involves disbelievers in even greater loss.

** SAY: "Have you ever seen your associates whom you appeal to instead of to God? Show me what part of earth they have created. Have they any partnership in Heaven? Or have We given them a book? Have they come upon any explanation from it? Rather wrongdoers merely promise one another delusion.

* God grasps both Heaven and Earth lest either one should slip out of place. If either should slip out of place, no one else would hold on to them besides Him. God is Lenient, Forgiving.

* They have sworn before God by their most solemn oaths that if a warner should ever come to them, they would be better guided than any other nation. Yet whenever a warner has come to them, it only increased their aversion * because of how proud they had acted on earth and plotted evil. Plotting evil engulfs the people who practise it.

Philosophy
of History

Are they only waiting for what happened to primitive people? Yet **you will never find any change in God's practice**, nor will you ever find any substitute for God's practice. * Have they not travelled around the earth and observed how the outcome went for those who preceded them? They were much stronger than they are.

> God will not be thwarted by anything in Heaven nor on Earth; He is Aware, Capable. ** If God should take mankind to task for whatever they have been earning, He would not leave any creature on its surface; but He puts them off for a specific period. Once their deadline comes, God will indeed be Observant of His servants.

36
Yā-Sīn (Y.S.)

T HIS CHAPTER is often called the "Heart" of the Qurʾān and sometimes it bears the alternate title of **The Sprites**. It is frequently read for solace in times of stress such as one faces with death or illness. It is traditionally recited at funerals.

The entire chapter consists of five sections with 83 middle Meccan verses, all except for v. 45 which dates from Madīna. It was revealed just before **The Standard** 25. The full name of the initials occurring in the title is said to stand for "*Yā insān!*" OR "O Man!", or "Everyman", but these letters have become traditional and like those of another title, Ṭā-Hā 20, are now a common man's name.

"The Town Which Was Warned" (II) and "The Last Trumpet" (III) are two parables contained in it. Towards the end of the chapter is an apocalyptic description of how the world will end.

In the name of God, the Mercy-giving, the Merciful!

(I) * Y.S.

> * By the Wise Reading, * you are an emissary * [sent] along a Straight Road ** with a revelation from the Powerful, the Merciful, * so you may warn a folk whose forefathers have not been warned, and hence they are unaware.

* The statement has been proven to be true about most of them, yet they still will not believe. * We have placed fetters around their necks which reach up to their chins till they seem to be out of joint. * We have placed a barrier before them and another barrier behind them, and have covered them up so they do not notice anything.

Fate and Destiny

** It is all the same for them whether you warn them or do not warn them; they still will not believe. * You will only warn someone who follows the Reminder and dreads the Mercy-giving even though He is Unseen. Proclaim forgiveness and generous payment to him. * We revive the dead and write down whatever they have sent on ahead and [left] as traces; We calculate everything in an open ledger.

10

(II) * Compose a parable for them about the inhabitants of the town when emissaries came to them. * When We sent them two, they rejected them both, so We reinforced them with a third. They said: "We have been sent to you as emissaries." ** They said: "You are only human beings like ourselves. The Mercy-giving has not sent anything down; you are only

13

The Town Which Was Warned

lying!" * They said: "Our Lord knows that we have been [sent] to you as emissaries. * We have only to proclaim things clearly."

* They said: "We sense something unlucky about you; so if you will not stop, we'll expel you, and painful torment from us will afflict you." * They said: "The bad luck you sense lies within yourselves. Will you not be reminded? Indeed you are such dissipated folk!"

20   ** A man came hurrying up from the further end of the city. He said: "O my people, follow the emissaries! * Follow someone who does not ask for any payment while they are being guided."

PART
TWENTY-THREE

22   (II cont'd) * "Why should I not worship the One Who has fashioned me and to Whom you will (all) return? * Should I adopt other gods instead of Him? If the Mercy-giving should want any harm [to happen] to me, their intercession would never help me out in any way nor would they rescue me: * I'd then be completely lost! ** I believe in your Lord, so hear me!"

* He was told: "Enter the Garden." He said: "If my people only knew * how my Lord has forgiven me and placed me among the honored ones!"

* We did not send any army down from Heaven to his folk after him, nor do We ever send any down. * There was only a single Blast, and

30   imagine, they [lay] shrivelled up! ** What a pity it is with such worshippers! No messenger has ever come to them unless they made fun of him. * Have they not seen how many generations We have wiped out before them who will never return to them? * Each will be arraigned so they all stand before Us.

33   (III) * The dead earth serves as a sign for them; We revive it and bring forth grain from it which they may eat. * We have placed date groves and

God's Signs   vineyards on it, and make springs flow forth from it ** so they may eat its fruit. Their own hands did not produce it. So, will they not give thanks? * Glory be to the One Who has created every kind of species such as the earth grows, their own kind, and even some things they do not know!

* Another sign for them is night; We strip daylight off from it so they are plunged into darkness! * The sun runs along on a course of its own. Such is the design of the Powerful, the Aware! * And We have designed phases for the moon so it finally appears again like an old palm

40   frond. ** The sun dare not overtake the moon nor does night outpace the day. Each floats along in its own orbit.

* Another sign for them is how We transported their offspring on the laden ship. * We have created something like it for them on which they may sail. * If We so wished, We might even let them drown and they would have no one to cry out to, nor would they be rescued * except as a mercy from Us and to enjoy things for a while.

** When they are told: "Heed what lies in front of you and what's behind you so that you may find mercy," * not one of their Lord's signs has come to them except they tried to avoid it. * When they are (also) told: "Spend something God has provided you with," the ones who disbelieve tell those who believe: "Should we feed someone whom God would feed if He so wishes? You are quite obviously in error!"

* They say: "When will this promise occur if you are so truthful?"
* They need only wait for a single Blast to catch them while they are arguing away. ** They will not even manage to draw up a will, nor will they return to their own people.

(IV) * The Trumpet will be blown and then they will swarm forth from their tombs to meet their Lord. * They will say: "It's too bad for us! Whoever has raised us up from our sleeping quarters? This is what the Mercy-giving has promised; the emissaries have been telling the truth."

* There will be only a single Blast and then they will all be assembled in Our presence. * On that day no soul will be harmed in any way, and you will be rewarded only for what you have been doing. ** The inhabitants of the Garden will be happily at work on that day. * They and their spouses will relax on couches in shady nooks; * they will have fruit there and they shall have anything they request. * "Peace!" will be a greeting from a Merciful Lord.

* "Step aside today, you criminals! ** Did I not contract with you, O children of Adam, not to serve Satan? He is an open enemy of yours. * And to worship Me [Alone]! This is a Straight Road. * He has led a numerous mob of you astray. Havent you been reasoning things out? * This is Hell, which you were threatened with. * Roast in it today because you have disbelieved!"

** That day We shall seal their mouths up while their hands will speak to Us and their feet bear witness about what they have been earning. * If We so wished, We would put their eyes out so they must grope along the Road. Yet how will they ever notice [anything]? * If We wished, We would nail them to the spot so they would not manage to keep on going nor would they ever return.

(V) * Anyone We grant long life to, We switch around within creation. Will they not use their reason?

* We have not taught him any poetry nor would it be fitting for him. It is merely a Reminder and a clear Reading ** so he may warn anyone who is alive and the Sentence may be confirmed against disbelievers.

* Have they not considered how We have created livestock for them out of what Our own hands have made, and they are masters over them? * We let them tame them: some of them are to be ridden, while others they eat; * they receive benefits and drinks from them. Will they not act grateful?

* Yet they have adopted [other] gods instead of God [Alone], so that they may be supported. ** They still cannot achieve their support; yet they stand up for them like an army in their presence! * Do not let their statement sadden you; We know what they are keeping secret and what they are disclosing.

* Has not man considered how We created him from a drop of semen? Yet he is an open adversary! * He makes something up to be compared with Us and forgets how he was created. He even says: "Who will revive [our] bones once they have rotted away?"

The Last Trumpet
50

51

Paradise

60
Satan a Hindrance

68

70
Muhammad no Poet

80   * SAY: "The One Who raised them up in the first place will revive them. He is Aware of all creation, ** the One Who grants you fire from green trees. Notice how you kindle a fire from them. * Is not Whoever created Heaven and Earth Able to create the same as them?"

Of course [He is]! He is the Creator, the Aware. * Once He wishes anything, **His command only needs to tell it: "Be!"; and it is!** * Glory be to Him Whose hand holds sovereignty over everything! To Him will you return.

37
(Drawn up in) Ranks

T HIS CHAPTER contains five long sections arranged in 182 Meccan verses. It was revealed after the chapter on **Livestock** 6 and before **Luqmān** 31.

Here we find a vivid description of what men can expect to meet after **Doomsday** (I): eternal bliss, or the Infernal Tree (II). We also hear the story of several prophets in rapid narrative: Noah, Abraham and Isaac (III): Moses, Aaron, Elijah and Lot (IV); and finally Jonah (V), each summed up by a unifying refrain: "Thus We reward those who act kindly..."

The angels **"drawn up in ranks"** finally speak out in v. 165, and we are told at the very end that God is not a father (V). The word *Jahīm* is used rather consistently for 'Hades', and not *Jahannim* or 'Hell', in an alliterative effect. The whole chapter provides a very moving picture.

In the name of God, the Mercy-giving, the Merciful!

(I) * As the **Ranks** are **drawn up**,
* rebuking with restraint
* and reciting a Reminder,
* your God is One [Alone],
** Lord of Heaven and Earth
and whatever lies between them,
plus Lord of the Eastern parts!

   * We have beautified the worldly sky
with the splendor of stars
* plus a safeguard against every stubborn devil
so they may not listen to the supreme council
and are hurled forth on every side.
* Driven away, they will have lingering torment
** except for someone who tries to eavesdrop
so that a blazing meteor follows him.

10

* Ask their opinion whether they or someone We created have been created stronger. We created them from sticky clay. * Rather you have been surprised as they sneered; * yet whenever they are reminded, they do not recall anything. * Whenever they see some sign, they make fun of it ** and say: "This is just sheer magic! * When we have died and become dust and bones, will we be raised up again? * Along with our earliest forefathers?''

Doomsday
20

* SAY: "Yes, and you yourselves abashed." * There will only be a single rebuke and then, they shall see! ** They will say: "How awful it is for us: this is the Day for Repayment! * This is the day for sorting things out which you have been denying."

22

The Road
to Hades

(II) * Summon the ones who have done wrong plus their spouses, and anything they have been worshipping * instead of God; lead them along the road towards Hades. * Stop them! They must be questioned: ** "What's wrong with you that you do not support each other?"

30

* Rather today they are surrendering. * Some of them will step forth to question one another. * They will say: "You used to come at us from the right." * They will say: "Rather, you were not believers! ** We have no authority over you. Instead you have been such arrogant folk. * Our Lord's sentence has been confirmed against us; we are indeed tasting it! * We lured you on; we were seducers."

* They will become partners in torment on that day. * Thus We deal with criminals! ** They have acted so proudly whenever: "**There is no deity except God [Alone]**" was said to them, * and they were saying: "Should we abandon our gods for a crazy poet?"

* Rather he has brought the Truth and vouches for the emissaries. * Yet you will taste painful torment * and only be rewarded for what you

40

Bliss

have been doing, ** except for God's sincere servants. * Those will have an acknowledged provision * of fruit, and will be honored * in gardens of Bliss * facing one another on couches. ** A cup will be passed around for them from a clear spring * [which will be] delicious for anyone who drinks from it! * There will be no hangover from it nor will they feel exhausted by it. * With them will be bashful women whose eyes will sparkle * as if they were hidden [like hatching] eggs.

50

** Some of them will step forward to question one another. * Someone among them will speak up and say: "Once there was a soulmate of mine * who used to say: 'Have you become convinced? * When we have died and become dust and bones, will we be called to account?' " * He will say: "Will you (all) just take a look?"

Hades
Again

60

** "So he did look down and saw he was [standing] in the midst of Hades! * He said: 'By God, you have almost ruined me! * If it were not for my Lord's favor, I'd have been made to appear. * Arent we mortal * except for our first death? Will we not be punished? ** This is the splendid Achievement!'"

The
Infernal
Tree

* For such as this let workers toil. * Is that a better welcome or is the Infernal Tree? * We have placed it as a trial for wrongdoers. * It is a tree that rises from the depths of Hades. ** Its cluster [of fruit] looks like devils' heads; * they will eat some of it and fill their stomachs with it. * Then on top of it, they will have a concoction made from bathwater [to drink].

70

* Then their return must be to Hades. * They discovered their forefathers had been misled ** and yet they went scurrying along in their footsteps. * Most primitive men went astray before them, * even though We had sent warners out among them; * yet see what the outcome was for those who were warned, * except for God's sincere servants.

(III) ** Noah called out to Us, and how favored are those [like him] who   75
respond! * We saved him and his family from serious grief, * and set his   *Noah*
offspring up as survivors. * We left [mention] of him among later men:
* "Peace be upon Noah throughout the Universe!"

        ** Thus We reward those who act kindly: 80
        * he was one of Our believing servants.

* Then We let the rest drown.

    * To his sect belonged Abraham * when he came to his Lord with a   *Abraham*
sound heart ** as he said to his father and his people: "What are you
worshipping? * Is it some sham; do you want (other) gods instead of God
[Himself]? * What is your opinion concerning the Lord of the Universe?"

    * So he took a glance at the stars * and said: "I feel heartsick!"
** They turned their backs on him: * so he shifted [his attention] to their   90
(false) gods, and said: "Dont you eat? * What is wrong with you that you
dont utter a word?" * He aimed a blow at them with his right hand.

    * They quickly pounced on him. ** He said: "Do you worship
something you have been carving, * while God created you and whatever
you make?" * They said: "Build him a pyre and cast him into
Hades!" * They wanted to plot against him, so We made them come out
on the shorter end of things.

    * He said; "I am going away to [meet] my Lord; He will guide
me! *** My Lord, bestow some honorable men on me!" * So We gave   100
him news about an even-tempered boy.

    * When [the son] reached the stage of working alongside him, he said:
"My son, I saw in my sleep that I must sacrifice you. Look for whatever   *His*
you may see [in it]." He said: "My father, do anything you are ordered to;   *Sacrifice*
you will find me to be patient, if God so wishes."

    When they both had committed themselves peacefully [to God] and he   *The*
had placed him face down, * We called out to him: "Abraham, ** you   *Supreme*
have already confirmed the dream!" * Thus We reward those who act   *Test*
kindly. * This was an obvious test. * We ransomed him by means of a
splendid victim, * and left [him to be mentioned] among later men: "Peace
be upon Abraham!"

        ** Thus We reward those who act kindly.   110
        * He was one of Our believing servants.

* We announced to him that Isaac would become a prophet who was
honorable. * We blessed both him and Isaac; some of their offspring have   *Isaac*
acted kindly while others have clearly wronged themselves.

(IV) * We endowed Moses and Aaron ** and saved both them and their   114
people from serious distress. * We supported them and they became   *Moses and*
victorious; * and We gave them both the clarifying Book. * We guided   *Aaron*
them along the Straight Road * and left [mention] of them among later
men; ** "Peace be upon Moses and Aaron!"   120

        * Thus We reward those who act kindly.
        * They were both Our believing servants.

Elijah

* Elijah was an emissary * when he told his folk: "Will you not do your duty? ** Do you appeal to Ba‹al and ignore the Best Creator, * God your Lord, and your earliest forefathers' Lord?" * They rejected him, yet they were made to appear, * except for God's sincere servants. * We left

130

[mention] of him among later men: ** "Peace be upon Elijah!"

> * Thus We reward those who act kindly;
> * he was one of Our believing servants.

Lot

* Lot was an emissary * when We saved him and his entire family ** except for an old woman who lagged behind. * Then We annihilated the rest; * You still pass by them in the morning * and at night. Will you not use your reason?

139 140

(v) * Jonah was an emissary ** when he deserted to the laden ship, * gambled and was one of those who lost out. * The fish swallowed

Jonah

him while he was still to blame. * If he had not been someone who glorified [God], * he would have lingered on in its belly until the day when they will be raised up again. ** We flung him up on the empty shore and he [felt] heartsick. * We made a gourd tree grow up over him * and sent him off to a hundred thousand [people] or even more. * They believed so **We let them enjoy themselves for a while**.

God is   150
Not a
Father

> * Ask their opinion as to whether your Lord has daughters while they have sons; ** or did We create the angels as females while they were looking on? * Are they not saying something they have trumped up with [the statement that]: * ''God has fathered something!''

Pagans

They are such liars! * Would He select daughters ahead of sons? * What is wrong with you? How do you make decisions? ** Will you not be reminded? * Or do you have some clear authority? * Bring on your scripture if you are so truthful! * They have even placed a tie of kinship between Him and the sprites. Yet the sprites well know that they too will be made to appear.

160

> * Glory be to God over whatever they describe ** except for God's loyal servants! * You and anything you serve * cannot incite anyone against Him * except for someone who will roast in Hades.

* There is none of us but he has an acknowledged status. ** We are **drawn up in ranks**. * We are those who glorify [God]. * There were some [people] saying: * ''If we only had a reminder from early men * we should have become God's loyal servants.''

170

** They have disbelieved in Him so they soon shall know! * Our word has already gone on ahead to Our servants who were sent forth; * they will indeed be supported. * Our army will be victorious over them! * Turn aside from them for a while; ** watch them, for they too will be made to watch.

* Do they seek to hasten Our torment? * Whenever it settles down into their courtyard, how dismal will be the morning for those who have

been forewarned! * Turn aside from them for a while; * watch, for they too will have to watch.

> ** Glory be to your Lord,
> the Lord of Grandeur,
> beyond what they describe!
> * Peace be on the emissaries!
> * Praise be to God,
> Lord of the Universe!

180

A Deathbed Prayer

38
(The Letter) ṢĀD
(Ṣ)

THIS FIVE-SECTION chapter contains 88 early Meccan verses; it was revealed after **The Moon** 54 and before **The Heights** 7. Its revelation occurred during a period of intense trial for the Prophet.

The title refers to the unvoiced velarized sibilant, or the letter 'ṣ' which here may stand for *aṣ-Ṣādiq* or 'the Truthful [God]' or 'the friend' (who tells you everything, whether you want to hear it or not); thus it means our voice of conscience or power of discretion.

One of David's judgments is described in a dramatic manner (II); Solomon then appears (III); next Job and other prophets (IV). Soon we have a description of Heaven and Hell (IV) and the chapter ends with Diabolis' fall (V). Sections III-IV are somewhat parallel to those of 21:V-VI.

In the name of God, the Mercy-giving, the Merciful!

(I) * Ṣ.
By the Qurʾān so full of renown!

* Rather those who disbelieve [are toying] with prestige and dissension. * How many generations have We wiped out before them? They called out, and the time for escape had lapsed. * They are surprised that a warner should come to them from among themselves. Disbelievers say: "This is some lying magician! ** Has he made [all] the gods into One God? This is such an amazing thing!"

* The elders among them sound off: "Walk around and be patient concerning your gods. This is something to be desired. * We have not heard any of this among any latterday denomination; this is merely a fabrication. * Has a Reminder been revealed just to him among us?"

Indeed they are in doubt about My reminder; rather they have not yet tasted any torment! * Or do they have treasures from the mercy of your Lord, the Powerful, the Bountiful? ** Have they control over Heaven and Earth and whatever [lies] between them? Let them haul themselves up on ropes. * What a partisan army will be routed there! * Noah's folk and ʿĀd's rejected [Me] before them, * and [so did] Pharaoh who [impaled men] on stakes, and Thamūd, Lot's folk, and the inhabitants of the Forest. Those were all partisans; * every last one rejected the messengers, so My punishment was justified.

10

(II) ** Those persons only await a single Blast which will [allow for] no delay. * They will say: "Our Lord, hasten our doom for us before the Day of Reckoning!" * Endure what they are saying and remember how Our servant David commanded assistance; he was attentive [to God]. * We forced the mountains to glorify [God] with him at evening and sunrise * —and the birds were summoned and each was [made] attentive to him. ** We strengthened his control and gave him wisdom and distinction as an orator.

    * Has news of the litigants ever reached you, when they climbed over the wall into the sanctuary? * Thus they burst in upon David so he was startled by them. They said: "Dont be afraid: [we are] two litigants, one of whom has injured the other; so judge correctly between us and do not act too stern. Guide us along the Level Road.

    * "This is my brother; he has ninety-nine ewes while I have but a single ewe. He has said: 'Turn her over to me,' and has spoken harshly to me." * He said: "He has wronged you by asking for your ewe [to be added] to his own ewes. Many partners try to take advantage of one another, except for those who believe and perform honorable deeds. Such are few indeed."

    David suspected that We were merely testing him, so he sought **forgiveness from his Lord and dropped down on his knees** [in worship], and repented. ** So We forgave him that. He enjoys precedence with Us and the finest retreat. * David, We have placed you as an overlord on earth, so judge among men correctly and do not follow any whims which will lead you away from God's path. Those who stray from God's path will have severe torment because they have forgotten the Day of Reckoning!

(III) * We did not create Heaven and Earth and whatever [lies] in between them to no purpose. That is the opinion of those who disbelieve. Those who disbelieve should beware of the Fire! * Shall We treat those who believe and perform honorable deeds just like mischief-makers on earth? Or should We treat those who do their duty, like lawbreakers? * We have **sent down a Book to you that is blessed, so prudent men may ponder** over its verses and thereby be reminded.

    ** We bestowed Solomon on David. How favored was such a servant; he was so attentive! * When the thoroughbreds were led out to prance before him in the evening, * he said: "I have loved good things instead of remembering God," until the [sun] was concealed behind the veil [of night again]. * "Bring them back to me!" [he said], and he started to stroke their legs and necks.

    * We tested Solomon and dropped a[nother] body on his seat; then he repented. ** He said: "My Lord, forgive me and bestow control on me such as will not suit anyone after me. You are the Bountiful!" * So We subjected the wind to him: it blew gently at his command wherever he directed it; * and the devils, every builder and diver, * as well as others hitched together in a chain gang. * Such are Our gifts; grant them freely or hold them back, without any [further] reckoning." ** He holds precedence with Us and the finest retreat.

15

David

20

His Judgment

Partnership; Cooperation

BOW DOWN HERE

27

30

Solomon's Trials

40

41

Job

(IV) * Remember Our servant Job when he called upon his Lord: "Satan has afflicted me with toil and torment." * "Stomp your foot; this is a cool spring to wash in and for drinking (too)." * We restored his family to him and the like of them besides, as a mercy from Us and a Reminder for prudent persons. * "Take a bundle [of twigs] in your hand and beat [your wife] with it, and do not break your word." We found him to be patient; how favored was such a servant. He was so attentive!

Other Prophets

** Remember Our servants Abraham, Isaac and Jacob, who possessed both might and insight. * We dedicated them specifically as a reminder for the Home; * some of them were selected from the very best by Us. * Remember Ishmael, Elisha and [Ezekiel] with the Commission; each [came] from the very best.

50

Heaven

* This is a Reminder; those who do their duty shall have a fine retreat, ** gardens of Eden whose gates will swing open for them! * Relaxing there, they will call for much fruit and drink in them. * With them there will be bashful mates equal in age to them. * This is what you were promised on the Day of Reckoning; * this is Our provision which will never be used up.

Hell

** Such will it be, while the arrogant will have the worst retreat— * Hell! They will roast in it, and on an awful couch! * Here it is; let them taste it: scalding water and bitter cold; * and others of its sort to match. * Here comes a troop rushing at you! They have no welcome here, for they must roast in the Fire. ** They will say: "Indeed you have no welcome either. You have prepared it for us; what an awful plight!"

60

* They will say: "Our Lord, whoever prepared this for us? Give him double torment in the Fire!" * They will say: "What is the matter with us that we do not see any men whom we used to consider were evil persons? * Did we take them for laughingstocks or has our eyesight failed to notice them?" * That is true: the people in the Fire will just argue away.

65

(v) ** SAY: "I am only a warner, and there is no deity except God Alone, the Irresistible, * Lord of Heaven and Earth and whatever [lies] in between them, the Powerful, the Forgiving!" * SAY: "It is a fateful message * you are shunning. * I have no knowledge about the supreme council such as they claim to have. ** It has been revealed to me only that I am a plain warner."

70

Diabolis' Fall

* Once your Lord told the angels: "I am about to create a human being out of clay. * When I have fashioned him and breathed some of My spirit into him, drop down on your knees before him." * The angels all bowed down on their knees together * except for Diabolis; he was too proud and a disbeliever besides.

** He said: "Diabolis, what prevents you from kneeling down before something I have created with My own hands? Have you become too proud, or are you overbearing?" * He said: "I am better than he is: You created me from fire while You created him from clay." * He said: "Clear out of here! You are an outcast; * upon you My curse will rest until the Day for Repayment."

80

* He said: "My Lord, let me wait until the day when they will be raised up again." ** He said: "You are one of those who may wait * till a day in

known time." * He said: "Through Your influence, I'll seduce them all * except for those among them who are Your sincere worshippers." * He said: "Such is the Truth, and the Truth do I speak: ** I shall fill Hell with you and any of them who follows you!"

* SAY: "I do not ask you (all) for any payment for it. Nor am I standing on ceremony; * it is only a Reminder to [everyone in] the Universe, so you may know its message after a while."

39
Throngs

T HIS RAPIDLY moving chapter was revealed after **Sheba** 34 and before the next one called **The Believer** OR **The Forgiving [God]** 40. It consists of eight sections of 75 Meccan verses, except for vv. 52-54 (V-VI) which may date from Madīna.

The chapter begins with an admonition against the sin of associating anything or anyone in our pure worship of God (I), and then it shows how such intercession is void (V). A majestic picture paints God's role in the world (VI). Watch for its dramatic ending which describes Heaven and Hell as the **"Throngs"** march there in two separate companies, the saved and the damned (VIII).

In the name of God, the Mercy-giving, the Merciful!

(I) * The revelation of the Book [occurs] through God, the Powerful, the Wise! * We have sent the Book down to you with the Truth, so serve God sincerely: religion belongs to Him.

Association

* Pure religion belongs to God [Alone]! The ones who take on [other] patrons instead of Him [claim]: "We do not serve them except to bring us closer to God in homage." God will judge among them about whatever they have been differing over; God does not guide anyone who is a disbelieving liar. * If God had wanted to adopt a son, He would select anyone He wished from what He has created.

> Glory be to Him! He is God Alone,
> the Irresistible! ** He has created
> Heaven and Earth for Truth.
> He wraps night up in daytime,
> and wraps daytime up in night.
> He regulates the sun and moon:
> each runs along on a specific course.
> Is He not the Powerful, the Forgiving?

* He has created you (all) from a single soul; then made its mate from it. He has sent down eight types of livestock for you. He creates you in your mothers' wombs, one creation following upon another creation in three [stages of] darkness. Such is God, your Lord. Control belongs to Him; there is no god except for Him. Yet you disregard [Him]!

* Even if you disbelieved, God could still dispense with you. He does not approve of disbelief among His servants; however if you act grateful, He will approve of you. No burdened [soul] may bear another's burden. Soon your return will be unto your Lord; then He will notify you about anything you have been doing. He is Aware of everything that is on your minds.

The Atonement Rejected

* Whenever any trouble afflicts a man, he appeals to his Lord, showing his concern for Him; then when He confers some favor on him from Himself, he forgets what he had already been appealing to Him about, and sets up rivals for God so he may mislead [people] from His way. SAY: "Enjoy your disbelief for a little while; you will [soon] be an inmate of the Fire!"

* Who is so prayerful during the small hours of the night, bowing down on his knees [in worship], standing on his guard about the Hereafter, and hoping for his Lord's mercy?

The Prophet at Prayer

SAY: "Are those who know, to be considered equal to those who do not know? Only prudent men reflect [on this]."

(II) ** SAY: "My servants who believe, heed your Lord. Those who act kindly in this world will have kindness [as their reward]. **God's earth is vast!** Surely the patient will be paid their wages without any reckoning."

10

* SAY: "I have been ordered to serve God sincerely, [making] religion exclusively His. * I have been ordered to be the first of those who are committed to [live in] peace.

* SAY: "I fear the torment of an awful day if I should disobey my Lord." * SAY: "God do I worship sincerely; my religion belongs to Him. ** So worship anything you wish to instead of Him!" SAY: "The losers will be those who have lost their own souls as well as their families' on Resurrection Day. That will be an obvious loss! * They will have sheets of fire above them and sheets beneath them." That is how God frightens His servants: "My servants, heed Me!"

* The ones who turn aside from the arrogant ones lest they serve them, and turn toward God, will have good news: proclaim such to My servants * who listen to the Statement and follow the best in it. Those are the ones whom God has guided; those are prudent persons. * Against whom has the sentence of torment been carried out? Will you save someone who is [already] in the Fire?

** Still the ones who heed their Lord will have mansions placed above it, with rooms constructed underneath through which rivers flow, as God's promise. God never breaks any appointment. * Have you not seen how God sends down water from the sky and lets it trickle through the earth into springs? Then He produces crops of different colors by means of it; next it withers away so you see it yellowed; then he turns it into stubble. In that is a Reminder for prudent persons.

20

22 (III) * Anyone whose breast God has opened up to Islām will [receive] light from his Lord. It will be awful for those whose hearts have been hardened against remembering God! Such people are in obvious error. * God has sent down the finest report in a consistently duplicated Book. The skins of those who dread their Lord tingle with it; then their skins and hearts are softened up for remembering God. Such is God's guidance; He guides anyone He wishes by means of it, while anyone whom God lets go astray will have no one to guide him.

* Who is it who wards off the worst torment from his person on Resurrection Day? Wrongdoers will be told: "Taste what you have been earning!" ** The ones who preceded them denied it, so torment came at them from somewhere they did not notice. * God lets them taste disgrace during worldly life while torment in the Hereafter will be even greater if they only realized it! * We have made up every sort of comparison for mankind in this Reading so that they may be reminded by * an Arabic Qurʾān possessing no ambiguity so that they may do their duty.

Getting Along Socially

* God has compared one man who has quarrelsome partners with another man dealing peacefully with [still another] man. Are either of them comparable? Praise be to God! Yet most of them do not realize it.

30 ** You are mortal and they are mortal [too]. * Still on Resurrection Day you (all) will argue it out before your Lord.

PART TWENTY-FOUR

32 (IV) * Who is more in the wrong than someone who lies about God and denies the facts even though they have come to him? Is there not room in Hell for such disbelievers? * Those who bring the facts and confirm them are heedful. * They will have anything they wish from their Lord; that is the reward for those who act kindly.

** God will erase the worst that they have done for them: He will reward them by paying them for the finest part of anything they have been doing. * Is not God Sufficient for His servant? They frighten you with the ones [they worship] instead of Him, while anyone whom God lets go astray will have no guide. * No one can mislead anyone whom God guides. Is God not Powerful, the Wielder of Retribution?

Proof of God

* If you should ask them who created Heaven and Earth, they would say: "God." SAY: "Have you (all) ever seen what you appeal to instead of to God [Alone]? If God wanted [to cause] me any trouble, would such females ever remove His trouble? Or if He wants some mercy for me, will such females hold back His mercy?" SAY: "God is [the Means] by Which I reckon; on Him do the reliant rely."

40 * SAY: "My people, act according to your situation. I am so acting, and you shall know ** who will be given such torment as will disgrace him, and on whom lasting torment will settle down." * We have sent you down the Book with Truth for mankind. Anyone who is guided, will

be so for his own sake, while anyone who goes astray will only stray because of it as well. You are not set up as any guardian over them.

(v) * God recalls souls at the time of their death, and those who have not died, during their sleep. He holds on to anyone whom death has been decided for, and sends the others back for a specific period. In that are signs for folk who meditate.

42
Death and Sleep

* Or do they adopt intercessors instead of God? SAY: "Even though they do not control a thing and cannot even reason?" * SAY: "Intercession belongs entirely to God. He holds control over Heaven and Earth; soon you will return to Him." ** Whenever God Alone is mentioned, the hearts of those who do not believe in the Hereafter shudder, while when others are mentioned instead of Him, why, they are overjoyed! * SAY: "O God, the Originator of Heaven and Earth, Knowing the Unseen and the Visible! You will judge among Your servants concerning whatever they may have been differing about."

Intercession is Futile

* Even if those who do wrong had absolutely everything on earth and the like of it besides, with which to redeem themselves from the worst torment on Resurrection Day, something they had not been figuring on will be shown them by God: * the evil deeds they have earned will appear before them, and whatever they were joking about will sweep in around them.

Retribution

* Whenever any trouble afflicts man, he appeals to Us; then when We confer some favor from Ourself on him, he says: "I was given it only because I knew [enough]." ** Rather it is a test, even though most of them do not realize it. * Those who preceded them said so, yet whatever they had earned did not help them out. The evil deeds they will have earned will alight upon them, and the evil deeds they have earned will strike those who have done wrong, so they will not escape it. * Do they not know that God extends sustenance to anyone He wishes, and budgets it out? There are signs in that for folk who believe.

50

(vi) * SAY: "My servants who have acted extravagantly against themselves still do not despair of God's mercy. God forgives all offences; He is the Forgiving, the Merciful. * Turn in repentance towards your Lord and commit yourselves peacefully to Him before torment comes to you; then you will not be supported. ** Follow the finest part of whatever has been sent down to you from your Lord before torment comes upon you suddenly while you do not notice it, * lest some soul should say: "O pity me, since I have been so lax so far as God is concerned, and because I was a scoffer." * Or he may say: "If God had only guided me, I'd have been more heedful." * Or he may say as he sees the torment: "If I only had another chance, then I'd be someone who acts kindly!"

53
Repentance

* Of course My signs came to you, yet you rejected them and acted proudly, and were a disbeliever! ** On Resurrection Day you will see how the faces of the ones who have lied about God will be blackened. Is there not room in Hell for the overbearing? * God will deliver the ones who have done their duty, to their place of achievement; evil will not touch them nor will they be saddened. * God is the Creator of everything; He is in Charge of everything. * He holds the controls for

60
God's Role in the World

Heaven and Earth while those who disbelieve in God's signs will be the losers.

64

Resurrection Day

70

71

Hell

Heaven
OR
Paradise

(VII) * SAY: "Are you ordering me to worship somebody besides God, you know-nothings? ** Yet there has been inspired in you as well as in those before you: 'If you associate [anything with God], your action will collapse and you will be a loser.' * Rather you should worship God [Alone] and act grateful."

* They have not valued God the way He should be valued. The whole earth will lie within His grasp on Resurrection Day, while Heaven will be folded up in His right hand. Glory be to Him; Exalted is He over anything they may associate [with Him]! * The Trumpet will be sounded and whoever is in Heaven and whoever is on Earth will be stunned, except for someone God may wish. Then another [blast] will be blown and behold, they will stand there watching! * The earth will shine through its Lord's light and the Book will be laid open. Prophets and witnesses will be brought in, and judgment will be pronounced among them formally, and they will not be harmed. ** Every soul will be repaid for whatever it has done; He is quite Aware of what they are doing.

(VIII) * The ones who disbelieve will be driven along to Hell in **throngs** until, just as they come up to it, its gates will swing open and its keepers will say to them: "Did not messengers come to you from among yourselves reciting your Lord's verses to you and warning you about meeting [Him] on this day of yours?" They will say: "Of course!" But the Sentence about torment has still come due for disbelievers. * Someone else will say: "Enter Hell's gates to remain there. What an awful lodging will it be for the overbearing!"

* The ones who have heeded their Lord will be driven along to the Garden in **throngs** until just as they come up to it, its gates will swing open and its keepers will tell them: "Peace be upon you! You have been good, so enter it to remain there." * They will say: "Praise be to God Who has held True to His promise for us and let us inherit the earth! We shall settle down anywhere we wish to in the Garden. How favored are such workers' wages!"

** You will see the angels clustering around the Throne hymning their Lord's praise. Judgment will be pronounced on them formally, and someone will say: "Praise be to God, Lord of the Universe!"

40
The Believer;
(OR *The Forgiving* [*God*])

THIS CHAPTER was revealed after the previous one on **Throngs** 39, and before the next, [**Signs**] **Spelled Out** 41. It initiates a fresh series of seven chapters, each of which bears the initials Ḥ.M. as its opening. Chapter 40 is laid out in nine sections arranged in 85 late Meccan verses, except for vv. 56-57 (in section VI) which may be from Madīna. The title is derived from the "believing man" in Pharaoh's court who appears in v. 28 & 30 (IV) or alternately, from **Forgiving**, the first word in v. 3 (and last in v. 41).

In the name of God, the Mercy-giving, the Merciful!

(I) * Ḥ.M.

    * The revelation of the Book [comes] through God, the Powerful, the Aware, * **Forgiving** sin and Receiving Repentance, Stern in punishment, Wielder of Influence. There is no deity except Him; towards Him lies the Goal.

* Only those who disbelieve will argue about God's signs; do not let their activity throughout the land deceive you. ** Noah's folk denied it even before them, and [so did] the coalition later on. Every nation worried about their own messenger, how to catch him [off guard]. They argued with him in vain to refute the Truth. So I caught up with them and how [awful] was My punishment! * Thus your Lord's word will be confirmed against those who disbelieve; they [will become] inmates of the Fire.

    * The ones who uphold the Throne and anyone surrounding it hymn their Lord's praise and believe in Him. They seek forgiveness for those who believe: "Our Lord, You embrace everything through mercy and knowledge. **Forgive** those who repent and follow Your path: shield them from the torment of Hades. * Our Lord, show them into the gardens of eternity which You have promised them, and whoever among their forefathers, spouses and off-spring have acted honorably. You are the Powerful, the Wise! * Shield them from evil deeds. You will show mercy on that day to anyone You shield from evil deeds. That will be the supreme **Achievement!**"

(II) ** The ones who disbelieve will be addressed [as follows]: "God's disgust will be even greater than your own disgust is towards one another when you are called upon to believe and [still] disbelieve." * They will say:

10

Disbelievers in Hell

"Our Lord, You have let us die twice and have revived us twice, and so we [now] acknowledge our sins. Is there no way to escape from here?"
    * This has happened because you disbelieved when God was invoked in His Oneness, while if others were associated with him, you would believe.

Discretion belongs to God, the Sublime, the Great. * He is the One Who shows you His signs and sends you down sustenance from the sky. Yet only someone who repents will bear this in mind. * So appeal to God sincerely; religion belongs to Him even though disbelievers may hate [to admit] it. ** Lofty in rank, Possessor of the Throne, He drops the Spirit of His bidding on any of His servants He may wish, so he may warn about the day of the Meeting, * the day when they will [all] emerge. Nothing concerning them is hidden from God.

Who holds control today? God Alone, the Irresistible holds it! * Today each soul will be rewarded for whatever it has earned. There will be no wrong [done] on that day; God is Swift in reckoning!

Doomsday

20

* Warn them about the day of the Approach [of Doom], when hearts will leap up into their throats, to choke them. Wrongdoers will have no bosom friend nor any intercessor who will be obeyed. * He recognizes the furtive glance in their eyes and whatever is concealed in their minds. ** God judges correctly while those they appeal to instead of Him do not decide a thing. God is the Alert, the Observant.

21

Philosophy of History

(III) * Have they not travelled around the earth and seen what the outcome was for those who preceded them? They were even stronger than they are and left more remains on earth. God seized them because of their sins and there was no one to shield them from God. * That was because their own messengers were sent to them with explanations and they still disbelieved. So God seized them; He is Strong, Stern in punishment.

Moses

* We sent Moses with Our signs and clear authority * to Pharaoh, Hāmān and Qārūn. They said: "[He's] a lying magician!" ** When he brought them the Truth from Our presence, they said: "Kill the sons of those who have believed along with him, and let their women live." Yet disbelievers' plotting only goes astray. * Pharaoh said: "Let me kill Moses! Let him appeal to his Lord! I fear he will change your religion or cause havoc to appear on earth." * Moses said: "I take refuge with my Lord and your Lord against every overbearing man who does not believe in the Day of Reckoning."

28

(IV) * A man from Pharaoh's court who was a **believer** and had been hiding his faith said: "What, will you kill a man for merely saying: 'My Lord is God'? He has brought you explanations about your Lord. If he is a liar, then his lie falls upon himself; while if he is truthful, some of what he threatens you with will afflict you. God does not guide anyone who is a preposterous liar. * My folk, you hold control today as masters do on earth. Who will support us against God's might if it should ever come to us?"

Pharaoh said: "I am only showing you what I see myself; I am only guiding you along the path of normal behavior." ** **The man who believed** said: "My folk, I fear the same for you as [happened] on the day of the Coalition, * the same as in the case of Noah's folk, and ʿĀd's and Thamūd's, as well as those who came after them. God wants no injustice to happen to [His] servants. * My people, I fear the day of the Summons for you, * the day when you will (all) turn around to retreat. You will not have any defender against God; anyone whom God lets go astray will have no guide.

*   30

* "Joseph brought you explanations before, yet you continued to suspect what he had brought you until when he perished, you said: 'God will never despatch a messenger after him!' Thus God lets any extravagant doubter stray away; ** the ones who argue about God's signs without any authority to do so having been brought them, incur the greatest disgust so far as God is concerned and so far as those who believe are concerned. Thus God seals off every overbearing oppressor's heart."

* Pharaoh said; "Hāmān, build me a tower so that I may reach the means of access, * the access to Heaven, so I may climb up to Moses' God. Still I think he is a liar." Thus his evil action was made to seem attractive to Pharaoh, and he was hampered along the Way. Pharaoh's plot only meant (his own) downfall.

(v) * The **believing man** said: "My folk, follow me; I'll guide you along the path of common sense. * My folk, this worldly life is to be enjoyed only [briefly]; the Hereafter is the Home to settle down in. ** Anyone who commits some evil deed will merely be rewarded with something else like it, while someone who acts honorably, whether it is a man or a woman, provided he is a **believer** will enter the Garden. He [or she] will be provided for there without any reckoning.

*   38

*   40
Responsibility is Rewarded

* "My people, why am I inviting you to salvation while you are inviting me to the Fire? * You invite me to deny God and to associate something with Him I have no knowledge about, while I invite you to [meet] the Powerful, the **Forgiver**. * You are merely inviting me to [worship] someone who has positively no way of being invoked in this world nor in the Hereafter. Our ultimate appeal will be to God, while the dissipated will become inmates of the Fire. * You must remember what I am telling you! I shall entrust my affair to God, for God is Observant of [His] worshippers."

** God shielded him from the evil deeds they plotted while the worst torment engulfed Pharaoh's court, * the Fire! They will be exposed to it morning and evening, while on the day when the Hour is set up [there will be heard]: "Send Pharaoh's court into the harshest torment!"

* As they quarrel away inside the Fire, the weaklings will tell those who acted proudly: "We were your following. Wont you spare us from a portion of the Fire?" * The ones who acted so proudly will say: "We are all in it together! God has judged among [His] servants!" * Those who are inside the Fire will tell the guards of Hell: "Appeal to your Lord to reduce the torment for us by just a day!" ** They will say: "Did not your messengers bring you explanations?" They will say: "Of course!" They will

*   50

say: "Well, make [your own] appeal then!" Yet the disbelievers' appeal will only go astray.

51   (VI) * We will support Our messengers and those who believe, both during worldly life and on the day when witnesses will stand up, * the day when their excuse making will not benefit any wrongdoers. They shall have the Curse; they will have the worst home!

* We gave Moses guidance and let the Children of Israel inherit the Book * for guidance and as a Reminder to prudent persons, ** so be patient: God's promise is true! Seek forgiveness for your offence and hymn God's praise at evening and in the morning hours. * Those who argue about God's signs without their having any authority to do so, only feel pride within their breasts; they shall never achieve anything. Take refuge with God; He is the Alert, the Observant.

* To create Heaven and Earth is greater than creating mankind, though most men do not realize it. * A blind and a sighted person are not equal, nor are those who believe and perform honorable actions, and an evildoer. How seldom do you keep it in mind! * The Hour is coming,
60   there is no doubt about it; yet most men will not believe. ** Your Lord has said: "Appeal to Me; I shall respond to you. The ones who are too proud to worship Me will enter Hell abjectly."

61   (VII) * God is the One Who has granted you night so you may rest in it, and daylight to see your way around. God possesses bounty for mankind, even though most men are not grateful for it.

A Hymn
to God
            * Such is God your Lord,
            the Creator of everything.
            There is no deity except Him;
            yet how you shrug things off!
            * Thus those who have repudiated God's signs
            just shrug them off!

* God is the One Who has granted you the earth to settle down on and the sky built above you, and has shaped you. He has made your shapes handsome and provided you with wholesome things.

            Such is God, your Lord;
            so blessed is God
            Lord of the Universe!
            ** He is the Living;
            there is no deity except Him,
            so appeal to Him sincerely,
            [making] religion exclusively His.
            Praise be to God,
            Lord of the Universe!

* SAY: "I have been forbidden to worship those you appeal to instead of to God [Alone], since explanations have reached me from my Lord, and I have been ordered to commit myself peacefully to the Lord of the Universe.

* "He is the One Who created you from dust, then from a drop of semen, then from a clot. Next He brings you forth as a child, then lets you reach maturity. Then you will grow elderly, even though some of you may pass away even earlier, and you will reach an appointed deadline so that you may use your reason. * He is the One Who gives life and brings death. Whenever He has decided on some matter, He merely tells it: 'Be!'; and it is."

Man's Stages

(VIII) * Have you not considered how the ones who argue about God's signs actually disregard them? ** Those who reject the Book and anything We have sent along with Our messengers shall know * when fetters as well as chains are placed around their necks. They will be hauled along * into scalding water; then they will be scorched in the Fire. * Next they will be told: "Where are the [false gods] you have been associating with * instead of God [Alone]?" They will say: "They have left us in the lurch. In fact we did not appeal to anything previously."

69
70

Thus God lets disbelievers go astray. ** That is because you went around the earth rejoicing without having any right to and because you felt so elated. * Enter Hell's gates to remain there; how wretched will the lodging of the overbearing be. * Yet be patient: God's promise will come true whether We show you part of what We promise them or recall you to Us; to Us they (too) will be returned.

* We have sent messengers before you, some of whom We have told you about, while We have not told you about others. No messenger may bring any sign unless it is with God's permission. Once God's command comes, [matters] will be decided correctly, and that is where the quibblers will lose out!

Other Messengers

(IX) * God is the One Who has granted you livestock so you may ride on some and eat from others. ** You receive benefits from them so that by means of them, you may satisfy any need you have in mind; on them and on shipboard are you transported. * He shows you His signs, so which of God's signs will you disregard?

79
80

* Have you not travelled around the earth and observed what the outcome has been for those who preceded them? They were more numerous and stronger than they are, and they [left greater] remains on earth. Yet whatever they had accomplished did not help them out: * when their messengers brought them explanations, they were happy with the knowledge they already possessed; so what they had been making fun of swept in around them. * However once they saw Our might, they said: "We believe in God Alone, and disbelieve in what we used to associate with Him."

Eleventh Hour Conversion

** Their [sudden] faith did not benefit them once they saw Our might; [such is] God's practice which He has already used with His servants. The disbelievers lost out right there!

41

[*Signs*] *Spelled Out*
(OR *Ḥā-Mīm on Worship– Bowing Down on One's Knees*)

THIS CHAPTER of 54 Meccan verses is arranged in six sections. It was revealed in sequence after the previous one called **The Believer** 40 and before the next one on **Consultation** 42. When the Prophet's uncle ʿUtbah ibn-Hishām heard this, he is said to have exclaimed: "By God, I have heard a recitation such as I have never heard before! It is neither poetry, nor magic, nor divination... Leave this man alone," referring of course to his nephew.

The chapter deals with creation (II) and what one may expect as a reward for his actions. The role of the prophets who were sent to the ancient Arabian peoples of ʿĀd and Thamūd is mentioned (II); the Golden Rule in its Islamic context is also stated (V); and then at the very end, the Qurʾān itself is described. The alternate title for the chapter is "**Ḥā-Mīm on Worship**".

In the name of God, the Mercy-giving, the Merciful!

(I) * Ḥ.M.

> * [It is] a revelation from the Mercy-giving, the Merciful, * a Book whose verses have been **spelled out**, as an Arabic reading for folk who know, * [sent down] as good news and a warning. Yet most of them avoid it and will not listen.

** They say: "Our hearts are [covered] with wrappers against what you invite us to; in our ears there [rings] a dullness while a curtain [hangs] between us and you. So act, for we (too) are acting!"

* SAY: "I am only human like yourselves. It has been revealed to me that your god is God Alone. So go straight towards Him and seek His forgiveness; how awful will it be for associators * who pay no welfare tax while they disbelieve in the Hereafter! * The ones who believe and perform honorable deeds will have payment which will never be withheld from them."

9

(II) * SAY: "How can you disbelieve in Someone Who created the earth in two days? You even set up rivals to Him!"

Yet such is the Lord of the Universe! ** He has placed headlands
towering above it and blessed [whatever is] on it, and measured out its
types of nourishment for it in four seasons, equally [within reach] for those
who ask for it. * Then He soared up to Heaven while it was still a haze,
and told both it and the earth: "Come, either obediently or reluctantly."
They both said: "We shall come willingly!" * He determined there should
be seven heavens [constructed] within two days, and inspired its own order
in each heaven. We have beautified the lowest heaven with lamps and a
safeguard. Such is the design of the Powerful, the Aware!

        * If they avoid it, then say: "I have warned you of a thunderbolt like
ᶜĀd's and Thamūd's thunderbolt." * When messengers came at them from
both before and behind them [saying]: "Serve no one except God!"; they
said: "If our Lord had so wished, He would have sent angels down, so we
are disbelievers concerning whatever you have been sent with."

        ** As for [the people of] ᶜĀd, they acted proudly on earth without any
right [to do so], and they said: "Who is stronger than we are?" Did they not
see that God, Who created them, is much Stronger than they were? They
had disregarded Our signs. * We sent a howling gale against them during
some disastrous days, so We might let them taste the torment of
humiliation during worldly life. Yet torment in the Hereafter will be even
more humiliating, and they will never be supported.

        * As for Thamūd, We guided them too, yet they preferred blindness to
guidance. [Another] thunderbolt seized them with shameful punishment
because of what they had been earning. * Yet We saved the ones who
believed and had been doing their duty.

(III) * On the day when God's enemies are summoned to the Fire, they will
be paraded forth ** so that when they come up to it, their hearing,
eyesight and their skins will testify against them concerning anything they
have been doing. * They will say to their skins: "Why have you testified
against us?"

        They will say: "God, Who grants speech to everything, has given us
speech. He created you in the first place, and to Him are you returning.
* Even though you tried to disguise yourselves, lest your hearing, eyesight or
your skins would still testify against you, did you suppose that God does
not know so much about whatever you are doing? * That supposition of
yours which you conceived about your Lord has ruined you, so you have
awakened among the losers."

        * Even if they are patient, the Fire will still be a lodging for them, while
if they want their case to be reviewed, they will not be granted any
review; ** We have assigned them soulmates who have made anything
that lies before them and anything behind them seem attractive to them.
The Sentence has been confirmed against them just as it was with the
nations of sprites and humankind who passed away before them. They
have been the losers!

(IV) * Those who disbelieve will say: "Do not listen to this Reading, and
chatter away while it is [being recited], so you will drown it out." * We
will let those who disbelieve taste severe torment; We will reward them for

10

ᶜĀd

Thamūd

19
20
*What
Retribution
Means*

26

the worst which they have done. * Such will be the reward for God's enemies: the Fire! They will find a home there for ever as a reward because they have repudiated Our signs. * The ones who disbelieve will say: "Our Lord, show us which sprites and humans have misled us; we shall trample on both [types] of them with our feet so they will become underdogs."

30   ** The ones who say: "Our Lord is God [Alone];" then keep straight on ahead, will have angels alight on them [saying]: "Do not fear nor feel saddened, and rejoice in word about the Garden which you have been promised! * We are your sponsors during worldly life and in the Hereafter; during it you shall have whatever your souls may crave. You will have whatever you request in it * as hospitality from Someone [Who is] Forgiving, Merciful."

33

The Islamic Golden Rule

(v) * Who speaks in a finer way than someone who appeals to God, acts honorably and says: "I am a Muslim!"?

* A good deed and an evil deed are not alike: **repel [evil] with something (that is) finer**, and notice how someone who is separated from you because of enmity will become a bosom friend!

** Yet only those who discipline themselves will attain it; only the very luckiest will achieve it!

* Nevertheless if some impulse from Satan should prompt you, then seek refuge with God; He is the Alert, Aware!

BOW DOWN HERE

* **Among His signs** are night and daylight, and the sun and moon. Do not bow down on your knees to the sun nor the moon: **bow down on your knees** before God [Alone], Who created them, if you have been worshipping Him. * Even though they may act proud, those who are with your Lord still glorify Him night and day; they never weary of it.

40

* **Among His signs**, you see how desolate the earth is; yet whenever We send water down upon it, it stirs and sprouts. The One Who revives it is the Reviver of the dead; He is Capable of everything! ** The ones who distort Our signs are never hidden from Us. Is someone who will be cast into the Fire better, or someone who will come safely through on Resurrection Day? Do whatever you (all) may wish: He is Observant of anything you do. * Such are those who disbelieve in the Reminder when it has come to them; it is such a splendid Book! * No falsehood shall approach it from either in front of it or behind it, since it is a Revelation from Someone [Who is] Wise, Praiseworthy.

The Qurʾān is Unassailable

* Anything that has been told you is merely what was told [other] messengers before you. Your Lord is the Master of Forgiveness as well as the Wielder of Painful Punishment. * If We had set it up as some foreign Reading, they would still say: "If its verses were only **spelled out in detail!**" Must it be foreign while [he speaks] Arabic? SAY: "It means guidance and healing for such people as believe, while the ones who do not believe are merely hard of hearing and it [implies] blindness on their part as well. Those people [act as if they] are being called to from a long distance off."

45

(VI) ** We gave Moses the Book, yet differences have arisen over it. If word had not gone on ahead from your Lord, things would have already been settled concerning them. They are in such disquieting doubt about it. * Whoever acts honorably, does so for his own soul's sake; while anyone who commits evil, merely does so against his own interests. Your Lord is never unjust towards His servants.

(VI, cont'd) * To Him should knowledge about the Hour be referred: no fruit comes forth from its blossom and no female conceives nor gives birth without His knowledge. The day when He calls out to them: "Where are My associates?", they will say: "We assure You there is not a witness [for them] among us." * Whatever they were appealing to previously will leave them in the lurch; they will think they have no way to escape.

> * **Man never tires of appealing for good,**
> while if some evil ever afflicts him,
> he becomes desperate, disheartened.

** If We let him taste some mercy from Ourself after some hardship has afflicted him, he is sure to say: "This is mine! I do not think the Hour is at hand. Even if I were sent back to my Lord, I would still [receive] the finest [treatment] from Him!"

We shall notify those who disbelieve about whatever they have done; We will let them taste fierce torment. * Whenever We show man some favor, he spurns it and drifts off to one side. Then when any evil afflicts him, he appeals [to Us] both loud and long. * SAY: "Have you considered whether it [came] from God? Yet even then you (all) disbelieved in Him!" Who wanders further off the track than someone who is in extreme disagreement?

* We will show them Our signs on [all] the horizons as well as within themselves, until it becomes clear to them that it is the Truth. Does your Lord not suffice as a Witness for everything?

> * Still they [remain] in a quandary
> about meeting their Lord!
> Yet He is the One
> Who embraces everything!

42
Consultation

THIS CHAPTER WAS revealed in sequence after the previous one on [Signs] Spelled Out 41 and before the next, **Luxury** 43. It consists of five sections of 53 late Meccan verses, except for vv. 23-24 and v. 27 which are all in section III, and date from Madīna.

The **consultation** referred to in v. 38 (IV(C) gives us a basis for democratic action which is often quoted even though it is not a full guide for parliamentary procedure. God's attributes (I) should become clear to those who associate others with Him (II). Morals and ethics form another theme (IV), especially in cases of self defence and protection. The final paragraph describes the process of divine inspiration.

In the name of God, the Mercy-giving, the Merciful!

(I) * Ḥ.M.
      * O.S.Q.

* Thus God the Powerful, the Wise, inspires you as well as those preceding you. * He owns whatever is in Heaven and whatever is on earth; He is the Sublime, the Almighty! ** The heavens almost burst apart above them as the angels hymn their Lord's praise and seek forgiveness for whoever is on earth. Indeed God is the Merciful Forgiver!

* Those whom they adopt as patrons instead of Him will still have God as an Overseer, while you are no agent [set up] over them. * Thus We have inspired you with an Arabic reading so you may warn the Mother Town and anyone around her, and warn about the Day of Gathering there is no doubt will take place. A group will be in the garden while another group will be in the Blaze.

* If God had so wished, He would have set them up as a single community, but He admits anyone He wishes into His mercy while wrongdoers will have no patron nor any supporter.

God's Attributes

* Why, have they adopted other patrons instead of Him? God is the [Only] Patron; He revives the dead; He is Capable of everything!

10

(II) ** No matter what you (all) may have differed over in any way, its jurisdiction still [remains] up to God.

A Hymn to God

> Such is God, my Lord;
> on Him have I relied
> and to Him do I refer.

* Originator of Heaven and Earth,
He has granted you spouses
from among yourselves,
as well as pairs of livestock
by means of which He multiplies you.

There is nothing like Him!
He is the Alert, the Observant.
* He holds the controls over Heaven and Earth;
He extends sustenance and measures it out
to anyone He wishes.
He is Aware of everything!

* He has instituted the [same] religion for you [Muslims] as He recommended for Noah, and which We have inspired in you and recommended for Abraham, Moses and Jesus: "Maintain religion and do not stir up any divisions within it."

What you invite them to do seems unacceptable for associators. God chooses anyone He wishes for Himself and guides to Himself anyone who repents. * They only separated after knowledge had come to them, because of envy towards one another. If word from Your Lord had not already gone on ahead till a specific period, things would already have been determined among them.

Associators Will Not Listen

Those who inherited the Book after them feel a suspicious doubt concerning it. ** Therefore appeal [to them] and keep straight on just as you have been ordered to; do not follow their whims, and say [instead]: "I believe in whatever God has sent down [in the form] of a Book, and have been commanded to deal justly with you (all). God is our Lord as well as your Lord. We have our actions while you have your actions; no quarrel exists between us and you. God will bring us (all) together; towards Him lies the goal! * The ones who argue about God after He has responded to them will have their arguments refuted by their Lord. On them anger will fall and they will have severe torment.

* God is the One Who has sent down the Book as well as the Scales for Truth. What will make you realize that perhaps the Hour may be near? * The ones who do not believe in it would like to hurry it along, while the ones who do believe are apprehensive about it for they know it is the Truth. Are not those who want to discredit the Hour [acting] in extreme error? * God is Gracious towards His worshippers. He sustains anyone He wishes; He is the Strong, the Powerful!

(III) ** For anyone who has been wanting a harvest in the Hereafter, we will increase his harvest; and We shall give some of it to anyone who has been wanting a worldly harvest, while he will not have any share in the Hereafter. * Or do they have associates who legislate for them about religion in matters which God would not sanction? If it were not for a decisive statement, things would have been decided among them. Wrongdoers will have painful torment! * You will see wrongdoers apprehensive about what they have earned even while it is bound to happen to them. The ones who believe and perform honorable deeds will

20

be in parks inside the Gardens; they will have anything they wish from their Lord. That will be the great boon. * That is what God proclaims to those servants of His who believe and perform honorable deeds.

SAY: "I do not ask you any payment for it except affection towards your relatives." We shall add to its fineness for anyone who acquires a fine deed. God is Forgiving, Appreciative. * Or do they say: "He has made up a lie about God?" If God wished, He might seal off your heart: God blots out falsehood and verifies the Truth through His own words. He is Aware of

God's Omniscience

anything that is on your minds. ** He is the One Who accepts repentance from His servants and overlooks [their] evil deeds. He knows anything you do. * He responds to those who believe and perform honorable deeds, and adds even more for them out of His bounty, while disbelievers will have severe torment.

* If God were to expand sustenance for His servants, they would act outrageously on earth; but He sends down anything He wishes in [due] measure. He is Informed, Observant concerning His worshippers. * He is the One Who sends down showers after they have lost hope, and scatters His mercy abroad. He is the Praiseworthy Patron! * Among His signs is the creation of Heaven and Earth, as well as any animals He has propagated in either of them. He is Capable of gathering them in whenever He wishes.

30

(IV) ** Any disaster that happens to you will [occur] because of what your own hands have earned. Yet He overlooks a great deal. * You (all) will not frustrate anything on earth nor do you have any patron nor supporter besides God. * Among His signs are the vessels that loom up at sea like landmarks. * If He so wished, He would hush the wind so they would lie becalmed on its surface. In that are signs for every disciplined, grateful person. * Or He would wipe them out because of what they have earned, even though He overlooks a great deal. ** Yet those who argue about Our signs realize they have no escape.

Morals and Ethics; Legislation

Self-Defence

40

Handling Oppression and Injury

* Anything you are given is for enjoyment during worldly life; while what God possesses is better and more enduring for those who believe and rely on their Lord, * who refrain from the greatest misdeeds and sexual offences, and forgive whenever they become angry, * and who respond to their Lord and keep up prayer; and whose business is [conducted] through mutual **consultation** among themselves, and spend some of what We have provided them with, * and who protect themselves whenever any outrage happens to them. ** The reward for an injury should be an injury proportionate to it.

Yet anyone who overlooks things and becomes reconciled shall receive his payment from God; He does not love wrongdoers! * Those who defend themselves after being wronged will have no way open against them; * a way [to blame them] is open only against those who mistreat [other] people and behave outrageously on earth without having any right to do so. Those will have painful torment. * Yet anyone who acts patiently and forgives, [shows] perseverance in [handling] matters.

(v) * Anyone whom God lets go astray will have no patron beyond Him; you will see wrongdoers saying, once they have seen the torment: "Is there any way to turn back?" ** You will see them solemnly trying to avoid it because of the disgrace they feel as they steal furtive glances at it. The ones who believe will say: "The losers are the ones who have lost their own souls plus their families' on Resurrection Day. Will wrongoders not [live] in lasting torment? * They did not have any patrons to support them besides God. Anyone whom God lets go astray will have no [other] way [to go]."

   * Respond to your Lord before a day comes along that will not be fended off; you will not find any refuge from God on that day nor will you have [any chance] to reject it. * If they should still evade it, We did not send you as any guardian over them; you have only to state things plainly. Whenever We let man taste some mercy from Ourself, he acts overjoyed by it, while the moment some evil deed strikes them because of something their own hands have prepared, man [acts so] thankless.

   * God holds control over Heaven and Earth; He creates anything He wishes. He bestows a daughter on anyone He wishes and bestows a son on anyone He wishes; ** or marries them off, both male and female, and makes anyone He wishes barren. He is Aware, Capable.

* It is not [fitting] for God to speak to any human being except through inspiration or from behind a curtain, or by sending a messenger anything He wishes to inspire [mankind] with, through His permission. He is Sublime, Wise. * Thus We have revealed a spirit from Our bidding for you. You did not know what either the Book or Faith were, but We have set it up as a Light by means of which We guide any of Our servants whom We wish. You are guiding [men] toward a Straight Road, * the Road to God, Who owns whatever is in Heaven and whatever is on Earth. Matters (all) end up with God!

44

50

*Divine
Inspiration*

43
Luxury

THIS CHAPTER was revealed in sequence after the previous one on **Consultation** 42 and before the next one on **Smoke** 44. It consists of 89 late Meccan verses arranged in seven sections; only v. 54 (in section v) dates from Madīna.

The chapter leads off with a description of God in His roles as Creator (I) and the Mercy-giving (II-IV); then it tells about Moses (V), and ends with an explanation of Jesus' place as a prophet (VI). God has no son, we are assured, nor does He need any associates (VII).

The title is found in verse 35 (III), where luxurious houses are described, and at the beginning of section VII where we also find a picture of Paradise. The word *zukhruf* can be variously translated as 'glitter', 'ornament(s', 'gilding' or 'glamor'.

In the name of God, the Mercy-giving, the Merciful!

(I) * H.M.

* By the Clear Book, * We have set it up as an Arabic reading so that you may (all) use your reason. * It is [comprised] in the Mother of the Book [which exists] in Our presence, so lofty, wise! ** Should We quietly slip the Reminder away from you since you have been such dissipated folk? * How many prophets have We sent to early men? * No prophet ever came to them unless they made fun of him. * We have wiped out more valiant people than they were, and the same has already occurred with early men.

10

God the Creator

* If you should ask them who created Heaven and Earth, they would say: "The Powerful, the Aware has created them, ** the One Who has placed the earth as a cradle for you, and traced highways for you on it so that you may feel guided, * Who has sent down water from the sky in due measure." Just so have We raised up a dead land with it; thus you (all) will come forth too! * [He is] the One Who has created all [sorts] of species, and granted you ships and livestock to ride on, * so you may mount on their backs. Then once you have mounted (or boarded) them, remember your Lord's favor and say:

"Glory be to Him
Who has subjected these to our [use];
we (ourselves) would never achieve it!
* We shall be sent home to our Lord."

** Still they have assigned a portion of His own servants to Him; man is so obviously thankless!

(II) * Or should He adopt daughters from what He creates and single   16
out sons for you? * Whenever one of them is notified about the same as
he imputes concerning the Mercy-giving, his face becomes dark with
gloom and he feels like choking. * Is someone who is set up just to look
pretty while he is unable to discuss things clearly [worth worshipping]?
* They even pretend the angels who are the Mercy-giving's servants are
females! Were they present at their own creation? Their testimony will be
written down and they will be questioned about it.

   ** They say: "If the Mercy-giving had so wished, we would not have   20
worshipped them." No matter what knowledge they may have about that,
they are still merely guessing. * Or have We given them a book already
which they try to hold on to?

   * Moreover they say: "We found our forefathers following such a   *Tradition*
community and we are merely being guided along their tracks." * Just the   *Can Be*
same We have not sent any warner into a town previous to you unless its   *Wrong*
highlivers said: "We found our forefathers with such a community, and are
merely being led along their tracks." * He said: "Even if I should bring
you better guidance than what you found your forefathers had?", they
would say: "We reject anything you are sent with!"

   ** We have been avenged on them; see what the outcome was for those
who denied [it all]!

(III) * Thus Abraham told his father and his folk: "I am innocent of what   26
you are serving. * Only the One Who originated me will guide me!" * He   *Abraham*
left it as an enduring word with his posterity so they might return (to it).

   * Indeed I have let those (men) as well as their forefathers enjoy things
until Truth and a plain messenger should come to them. ** Yet whenever   30
Truth did come to them, they said: "This is magic! We disbelieve in
it!" * They said: "If this Reading were only sent down to some important
man from either town!"

   * Are they dividing up your Lord's mercy? We divide up their
livelihood among them during worldly life, and raise some of them higher
in rank than others so that some of them may take advantage of the labor
of others. Your Lord's mercy is better than what they are collecting. * If it
were not that mankind has been a single nation, We would grant anyone
who disbelieves in the Mercy-giving silver roofs for their houses and
staircases to climb up on, * and doors for their houses and couches to
recline on ** and [similar] **luxury**! All that means nothing except
enjoyment during worldly life while those who do their duty will [spend]
the Hereafter with your Lord.

(IV) * We assign anyone who fails to remember the Mercy-giving at   36
nightfall, a devil who will become a soulmate for him. * They divert them
from the [right] way while they may reckon they are guided, * until when
he comes up to Us, he says: "Alas, if the distance between the two Easts
only lay between you and me! He's such an awful soulmate!"

40

* It will never benefit you today to have any partners in torment since you have already gone wrong. ** Will you make the deaf hear or guide the blind, as well as anyone else who is in obvious error? * Even should We take you away, We will still be avenged on them. * Or shall We show you what We have promised them? We are Competent to deal with them!

* Hold on to whatever has been revealed to you; you are on a Straight Road. * It is a Reminder for you and your folk, and you will (all) be questioned. ** Question any of Our messengers We have sent before you: "Did We set up any [other] gods they should serve instead of the Mercy-giving?"

46

Moses

(v) * We sent Moses with Our signs to Pharaoh and his courtiers, and he said: "I am a messenger from the Lord of the Universe." * When he brought them Our signs, they merely laughed at them! * Yet We did not show them any sign unless it was even greater than the one that had preceded it. We afflicted them with torment so that they might return. * They said: "Mr. Magician, appeal to your Lord for us concerning what He had pledged to you; we will act as if we are guided."

50

** Yet once We removed torment from them, why they broke their word! * Pharaoh announced it among his people; he said: "My people, do I not hold control over Egypt and these rivers flowing by me? Do you not notice anything? * Surely I am better than this wretch who can scarcely explain a thing! * If he were only presented with gold bracelets or some angels came along hitched up with him!"

* He sneered at his folk, yet they obeyed him; they were such immoral folk. ** When they provoked Us [sufficiently], We took revenge on them and let them all drown; * We left them as has-beens and an example for later men.

57

Jesus

(vi) * When Mary's son is quoted as an example, why, your people resist him! * They say: "Are our gods better, or is he?" They quote him to you only for the sake of argument; indeed they are such quarrelsome folk!

> * He was only a servant whom We favored
> and offered as an example
> to the Children of Israel.

60

** If We had so wished, We might have made angels out of some of you who would replace you on earth. * It will be because of knowledge about the Hour. Do not puzzle over it and follow Me; this is a Straight Road. * Do not let Satan hamper you; he is an obvious enemy of yours.

* When Jesus came with explanations, he said: "I have brought you wisdom, so that I may explain something to you about what you have been differing over. So heed God and obey me! * God is my Lord and your Lord, so serve Him. This is a Straight Road."

** Factions have disagreed among themselves. It will be too bad for the ones who have done wrong as [they face] torment on a painful day! * Are they merely waiting for the Hour to come upon them suddenly while they do not even notice it? * On that day even bosom friends will become one another's enemies, unless they have done their duty.

(VII) * My servants, you have no need to fear today nor should you feel   68
saddened; * [tell] those who believe in Our signs and are committed to
[live in] peace: ** "Enter the Garden rejoicing, both you and your   70
spouses!"

   * Gold platters and cups will be passed around among them containing
anything (their) souls may hanker for and (their) eyes delight in. You will
live there for ever. * Such is the Garden which you will inherit because of   *Paradise*
what you have been doing. * You will have plenty of fruit to eat in it.

   * Yet criminals will remain in Hell's torment; ** it will not be eased
for them and they will feel confounded in it. * Still We will not harm
them but rather they have already harmed themselves. * They will cry out:
"Master, have your Lord put an end to us!"

   He will say: "You must stay on here! * We brought you the Truth
even though most of you detest the Truth." * Or have they tried to use
some scheme [against you]? Well, We will try something too! ** Or do   80
they reckon that We do not hear their secrets nor how they conspire
together? Of course Our messengers are writing it (all) down in their very
presence!

   * SAY: "If the Mercy-giving had a son, I would be the first to worship   *God Has*
[him]." * Glory be to the Lord of Heaven and Earth, Lord of the Throne,   *No Son*
ahead of what they ascribe [to Him]! * Leave them to speculate and play
around until they face their day which they have been promised.

> * He Alone is God in Heaven
> and God on Earth; He is the Wise, Aware.
> ** Blessed is He Who holds control
> over Heaven and Earth,
> and anything in between them.
> He has knowledge of the Hour
> and to Him will you be returned.

   * The ones whom they appeal to instead of Him control no intercession   *Associates*
except for someone who testifies concerning the Truth, and they realize   *Cannot*
it. * If you should ask them Who created them, they would say: "God   *Intercede*
[Alone]"; and yet they shrug Him off!

   * So he says: "My Lord, those are folk who do not believe."
   * Disregard them, and say: "Peace [be on you!" instead]. They will
realize it eventually.

44
Smoke

THIS CHAPTER contains 59 middle Meccan verses arranged in three
sections which were again revealed in sequence, after the previous
chapter on **Luxury** 43 and before the next one on **Crouching** 45. The title
comes from the reference in v. 10 (I) to the smoke or haze which will
announce the drought preceding Doomsday. It ends with another
description, first of Hell, and then of Heaven (III).

In the name of God, the Mercy-giving, the Merciful!

(I) * Ḥ.M.
  * By the Clear Book * which We sent down on a blessed night We
have been warning about! * In it every wise matter is set forth ** as a
command from Our presence; We have been sending * mercy from your
Lord. He is the Alert, Aware, * Lord of Heaven and Earth and anything
in between them, if you will be convinced. * There is no deity except Him;
He gives life and brings death, your Lord and the Lord of your earliest
ancestors.

10
*Eleventh-
Hour
Belief*

  * Instead they play around with doubt. ** Watch out for the day
when the sky will bring obvious **smoke** * to envelop mankind; this will
mean painful torment: * "Our Lord, remove the torment from us; we are
believers!"
  * Yet they had the Reminder, and an obvious messenger had already
come to them. * Then they turned away from him and said: "He has been
taught it; [he's] so crazy!"
  ** Were We to lift the torment for a while, you would still revert [to
it]! * Some day We will kidnap everyone in the greatest operation; We
shall be Avenged!

*Pharaoh's
People*

  * We tested Pharaoh's folk before them, and a noble messenger came
to them: * "Hand over God's servants to me. I am a trustworthy
messenger for you. * Do not act so haughtily concerning God: I bring you

20

clear authority. ** I have sought refuge with my Lord and your Lord, lest
you cast me out. * If you do not believe in me, then keep away from
me." * So he appealed to his Lord: "These are criminal folk!"
  * "Travel with My servants at night for you will be followed. * Leave
the sea parted; they are an army who will be drowned." ** How many
gardens and fountains have they left behind! * And crops and a splendid
position * and a life of ease they were delighted with. * Even so We let
other folk inherit it from them. * Neither Heaven nor Earth wept over
them, nor were they allowed to wait.

(II) ** So We saved the Children of Israel from shameful torment, * from   30
Pharaoh, who was haughty, so dissipated. * We chose them knowingly
ahead of [anyone in] the Universe; * and gave them signs which contained
an obvious test. * Yet the latter kept on saying: ** "There is only this
first death of ours; we will not be raised again. * Bring on our forefathers
if you have been truthful."

* Are they any better than the people of Tubba‹ and the ones before   *Life is*
them whom We wiped out? They were such criminals! * We did not create   *Serious*
Heaven and Earth and anything in between them just by playing
around. * We have created them both only [to reveal] the Truth, even
though most of them do not realize it. ** The Day for Sorting things out   40
will mean an appointment for everyone, * a day when no patron will be
able to help a favorite out in any way nor will they be supported * except
for someone whom God has shown mercy to. He is the Powerful, the
Merciful.

(III) * The infernal tree * will be food for the sinner; ** like molten   43
copper, it will seethe inside (their) bellies * like a bathhouse boiler: *Hell*
* "Take him and drag him into the midst of Hades! * Then pour some
torment of scalding water over his head: * 'Taste it; you were such a
powerful noble!' " ** This is what you (all) were puzzling over!   50

* The heedful will be in a safe position * among gardens and   *Heaven*
springs. * They will wear satin and brocade as they sit facing one
another, * just like that; and We will wed them to dark-eyed
damsels. ** They will call confidently for every kind of fruit in it. * They
will not taste death there except for the very first death [they had]. He will
shield them from the torment of Hades * as a boon from your Lord; that
will be the supreme Achievement!

> * We have made it easy for your tongue [to recite]
> in order that they may bear this in mind.
> * So watch out: they too are watching!

45
Crouching

THIS CHAPTER was revealed after the previous one called **Smoke** 44 and before the next one, **The Dunes** 46, thus continuing the sequence. It contains four sections of 37 late Meccan verses, except for v. 14 which dates from the Madinese period. The title is to be found in v. 28 (IV). There is much moral teaching in this chapter, especially in section II.

In the name of God, the Mercy-giving, the Merciful!

(I) * H.M.

* The revelation of the Book [happens] through God, the Powerful, the Wise; * there are signs in Heaven and Earth for believers. * In your own creation as well as how animals are propagated there are signs for folk who are convinced. ** The alternation of night and daylight, and any sustenance God sends down from the sky with which He revives the earth after its death, and the wheeling of the winds are signs for folk who use their reason. * Those are God's signs which We recite to you for the Truth, so in what report will you believe if not in God and His signs?

* How awful will it be for every shamming sinner * who hears God's signs recited to him, then proudly persists as if he had never heard them. Announce some painful torment to him! * Whenever he learns anything about Our signs, he takes them as a joke.

10 Those shall have shameful torment: ** beyond them there lies Hell. Anything they have earned will not help them out at all, nor will anything they have adopted as patrons instead of God. They will have awful torment! * This means guidance, while those who disbelieve in your Lord's signs will have painful punishment as a blight.

12 (II) * God is the One Who has subjected the sea to you, so that ships may sail on it at His command and you may seek His bounty and even feel grateful. * He has subjected whatever is in Heaven and whatever is on Earth to you; it all comes from Him. In that are signs for folk who think things over. * Tell those who believe to forgive the ones who do not expect [to see] God's days, so He may reward a folk according to whatever it has earned. ** Anyone who acts honorably, acts on his own behalf; while whoever commits evil will find it stands against him; then to your Lord shall you (all) return.

The Children of Israel * We already gave the Children of Israel the Book, discretion and prophethood, and We provided them with wholesome things and let them excel over [everyone in] the Universe. * We gave them explanations about the Matter. They only disagreed after knowledge had come to them, out of envy towards one another. Your Lord will judge among them on Resurrection Day concerning anything they may have been differing over.

 * Next We placed you on a highroad [to receive] the command, so follow along it and do not follow the whims of those who do not know. * They will never help you out in any way against God; some wrongdoers act as patrons for others, while God is Patron of those who do their duty. ** These are insights for mankind, as well as guidance and mercy for folk who are convinced. * Or do those who commit evil deeds reckon that We will treat them exactly like those who believe and perform honorable actions, just as if their mode of living and their way of dying were equivalent? How lamely do they judge!

 20

 (III) * God has created Heaven and Earth for a true purpose, and so every soul may be rewarded for whatever it has earned, and they will not be harmed. * Have you seen someone who has taken his passion as his god? God knowingly lets him go astray and seals off his hearing and his heart, and places a covering over his eyesight. Who will guide him instead of God? Will you not reflect [on this]?

 22

> * They say: "Nothing exists except our worldly life! We die and live, and only fate destroys us."

Secularism

They have no knowledge about that; they are only supposing. ** Whenever Our clear verses are recited to them, their argument is merely to say: "Bring back our forefathers if you are so truthful." * SAY: "God gives you life; then brings you death. Next He will bring you (all) together on Resurrection Day; there is no doubt about it." Yet most men do not realize it.

 (IV) * God holds control over Heaven and Earth, and the day when the Hour will take place. On that day, quibblers will lose out! * You will see every nation **crouching**; each nation will be called [to appear] before its book: "Today you will be rewarded for whatever you have been doing. * This book of Ours will pronounce the Truth about you; We have been recording whatever you have been doing."

 27

The Final Hour

The Doom of Nations

 ** Their Lord will admit those into His mercy who believe and perform honorable deeds; that will be the clear Achievement. * As for the ones who disbelieve: "Were not My signs recited to you, and yet you acted proudly and were such criminal folk? * When someone said that God's promise is true and there is no doubt about the Hour, you (all) said: 'We do not know what the Hour is. We are only making a conjecture, and we are not convinced!'"

 30

 * The evil deeds they have committed will appear before them while whatever they were joking about will sweep in around them. * Someone will say: "Today we shall forget you just as you forgot about a Meeting on this day of yours. Your lodging will be the Fire; you have no supporters! ** That is because you took God's signs for a joke. Worldly life has lured you on."

Today they will not be allowed to leave there nor will they be permitted to argue back.

> * Yet God merits praise as Lord of Heaven and Lord of
> Earth; even as Lord of the Universe! * He holds
> greatness in Heaven and Earth; He is the
> Powerful, the Wise!

46
The Dunes

THIS CHAPTER was revealed after the previous one entitled **Crouching** 45 and forms the last of the Ḥā-Mīm series. It is dated prior to **Winnowing [Winds]** 51 and consists of 35 late Meccan verses arranged in four sections, except for vv. 10, 15 & 35, which date from Madīna. Verse 21 (III) mentions the dunes in the country of ᶜĀd in southern Arabia which provide the chapter with its title.

Here the Prophet is heard pleading with the disbelievers in Mecca. The chapter also discusses how to treat one's parents (II). "Sprites and the Qurʾān" is a graphic tale to be found at the end of the chapter (IV).

In the name of God, the Mercy-giving, the Merciful!

PART
TWENTY-SIX

(I) * Ḥ.M.

     * The revelation of the Book [occurs] through God, the Powerful, the Wise. * We have only created Heaven and Earth, and whatever lies between them for the Truth and for a specific period, while those who disbelieve are dodging what they have been warned about. * SAY: "Have *Association* you ever seen what you appeal to instead of to God? Show me what part of earth they have created! Have they any partnership in Heaven? Bring me a book previous to this one or any other trace of knowledge if you are so truthful."

     ** Who is further off the track than someone who appeals to *False* something which will not respond to him until Resurrection Day, instead *Gods* of to God [Alone]? They are oblivious [of the fact] that they are being appealed to. * When mankind is summoned, they will become enemies of theirs and renounce their own worship. * When Our clear signs are being recited to them, those who disbelieve will remark about the Truth once it comes to them: "This is sheer magic!" * Or do they say: "He has invented it"?

     SAY: "Even if I have invented it, yet do you control anything from God for me? He is quite Aware of what you are engaged in; He suffices as a Witness between me and you. He is the Forgiving, the Merciful." * SAY: "I am no upstart among messengers. I do not know what will happen to me nor to you. I only follow what has been inspired in me, and am merely a plain warner."

     ** SAY: "Have you considered whether it [comes] from God's presence, while you disbelieve in it? A witness from the Children of Israel has

IO

testified concerning something similar to it; he has believed while you are too proud to. God does not guide wrongdoing folk."

I I

(11) * The ones who disbelieve tell the ones who believe: "If it were any good, they would not have gotten so far ahead of us on the way toward it." Yet since they are not guided by it, they will say: "This is an old swindle!"

* Before it, Moses' book served as a model and a mercy, while this is a Book which confirms such in the Arabic tongue, so as to warn those who do wrong, and [it forms] an announcement to those who act kindly. * The ones who say: "Our Lord is God [Alone]," then proceed straight ahead, will find no fear afflict them nor will they ever be saddened. * Those will become inhabitants of the Garden, remaining there forever as a reward for what they have been doing.

Treatment of Parents

** We have instructed everyman to be kind to both his parents. His mother bears him with reluctance, and gives birth to him painfully. Bearing him and weaning him last thirty months, until when he attains his full growth and reaches forty years [of age], he says:

A Prayer

> "My Lord, train me to be grateful
> for Your favor which you have shown to me
> and to both my parents, and to act honorably
> so You may approve of it.
> Improve my offspring for me:
> I have turned toward You (in repentance)
> and am one of those who are committed
> to (live in) peace [with God and society]."

* Those are the ones from whom We will accept the best out of whatever they do, while We will overlook their evil deeds since it concerns the occupants of the Garden, as a true promise which has been made to them.

* Anyone who says to his parents: "Phooey on you! Do you promise me that I'll come forth [from my grave] while generations have passed on before me?",—and while they both implore God's help: "It will be too bad for you! Believe: God's promise will come true," he merely says: "These are only legends about primitive men." * Those are the ones among the nations of sprites and humans who have passed away before them, against whom the Sentence will be justified. They will be the losers. * Each will have rank according to whatever they have done, so He may repay them

20

for their actions and they will not be harmed. ** On the day when those who disbelieve are exposed to the Fire [they will be told]:

"You used up your wholesome things during worldly life, and enjoyed them. Today you will be rewarded with humiliating punishment because of how proudly you acted on earth without any right to do so, and because you were misbehaving."

21

ʿĀd by the Dunes

(111) * Remember ʿĀd's brother when he warned his folk by the **Dunes** (warners have passed away both before and after him): "Will you worship only God? I fear the torment of an awful day for you!" * They said: "Have you come to us to turn us against our gods? Bring us what you threaten us with, if you are so truthful." * He said: "Knowledge rests only

with God. I am communicating to you what I have been sent with, even though I see you are a folk who act out of ignorance."

* When they saw it as a disturbance advancing on their valleys, they said: "This is some storm which will bring us rain." Rather it was what you sought to hasten up for yourselves, a wind containing painful punishment, ** which would demolish everything at its Lord's command. They were found next morning with only their dwellings still visible. Thus We reward criminal folk! * We had set them up with something We have not established you with, and granted them hearing, eyesight and vital organs; yet their hearing, eyesight and vital organs did not help them out at all. Once they repudiated God's signs, what they had been making fun of engulfed them.

(IV) * We have wiped out some towns around you; while We have arranged signs so that they may return. * If only those whom they have adopted as gods in order to gain access [to Heaven] instead of [trusting] God, had supported them! Instead they left them in the lurch. That was because of their shamming and of what they had invented.

27

* Once We detailed a platoon of sprites for you so they might listen to the Qur〉ān. When they were present at it, they said: "Hush!"

When it was finished, they went back to their folk as warners. ** They said: "Our people, we have just heard a Book sent down after Moses to confirm what came before it. It guides one to Truth and to a Straight Road. * Our people, answer God's herald and believe in him! He will forgive you some of your offences and protect you from painful torment."

Sprites and the Qur〉ān

30

* Anyone who does not answer God's herald will never escape on earth, nor will he have any patrons besides Him. Such people are in obvious error.

* Have they not considered that God, Who created Heaven and Earth, has not been worn out through creating them since [He is] Able to revive even the dead? Indeed He is Capable of everything!

* Some day when those who disbelieve are exposed to the Fire [and asked]: "Is this not real?"; they will say: "Indeed, by our Lord!" He will say: "Well, taste torment since you were disbelieving."

** Be patient just as those messengers who were steadfast were patient. Do not try to hurry [things] up for them, since they will seem to have lingered for only an hour of daylight on the day when they shall see what they have been promised! [It is] a decree! Yet will only immoral folk be wiped out?

47
Muḥammad;
(OR *Fighting)*

THIS CHAPTER was revealed after **Iron** 57 and before **Thunder** 13, and
following the victory at Badr. It consists of four sections in 38 verses
from Madīna, except for v. 18 (II) which was revealed during the Transfer
or Hijra in the year 622 A.D., and possibly v. 3 which came six years later
during the truce at Ḥudaybiyya in the year 6/628. Its rhythm is sustained
or punctuated by means of assonance.

The chapters in the Qurɔān now are becoming noticeably shorter. The
name of the Prophet as a title is found in v. 2 (I), while "fighting" is
mentioned in v. 20 (III); these form the alternate titles to the chapter. The
topic discussed is the problem of conduct during warfare (I).

In the name of God, the Mercy-giving, the Merciful!

(I) * God will let the actions of those who disbelieve and obstruct His way
miss their mark, * while He will cancel out the evil deeds and improve the
attitude of those who believe, perform honorable deeds and believe in what
has been sent down to **Muḥammad**—for it is the Truth from their
Lord. * That is because the ones who disbelieve follow falsehood while
those who believe follow the Truth from their Lord. Thus God makes up
their comparisons for mankind.

*Conduct
in War*

* Whenever you encounter the ones who disbelieve [during war], seize
them by their necks until once you have subdued them, then tie them up as
prisoners, either in order to release them later on or also to ask for ransom,
until war lays down her burdens. Thus shall you do—; yet if God so
wished, He might defend Himself from them—in order that some of you
may be tested by means of one another. The ones who have been killed in
God's way will never find their actions have been in vain; ** He will guide
them and improve their attitude * and admit them to the Garden He has
acquainted them with.

* You who believe, if you support God, He will support you and
steady your footsteps, * while the ones who disbelieve will feel wretched
and their actions will miss the mark. * That is because they have hated
anything God has sent down and so their actions have miscarried.

10

** Have they not travelled around the earth and seen what the outcome
was for those who came before them? God annihilated them, while
disbelievers will have the same as they did. * That is because God is the
Protector of those who believe, while disbelievers have no protector.

(II) * God will admit the ones who believe and perform honorable deeds into gardens through which rivers flow, while those who disbelieve will enjoy themselves and eat just as livestock eat, and the Fire will be a lodging for them. * How many towns have We wiped out which were much stronger than your own town which has expelled you? They had no supporter. * Is someone who holds on to evidence from his Lord like someone else whose evil action seems attractive, while they follow their own whims?

12

** [Here] is what the parable of the Garden which the heedful have been promised will be like: it will have rivers of never stagnant water and rivers of milk whose flavor never changes, and rivers of wine so delicious for those who drink it, and rivers of clarified honey. They will have every [sort of] fruit in it, as well as forgiveness from their Lord. Are they like someone who will remain for ever in the Fire and they will be given scalding water to drink so it rips into their bowels?

Rivers in the Garden

* Some of them listen to you until once they have left your presence, they tell those who have been given knowledge: "What did he say just now?" Those are the ones whose hearts God has sealed off; they follow their own whims. * Yet He increases guidance for those who consent to be guided and grants them their sense of duty.

Hypocrites

* Are they just waiting for the Hour to come upon them suddenly? Its tokens have already come. Yet how will they [recognize] their Reminder once it comes to them? * Know that **there is no deity except God [Alone]**, and beg forgiveness for your offence, as well as for believing men and believing women. God knows how you (all) bustle about on your business and where you settle down.

(III) ** Those who believe say: "If a chapter were only sent down!"; yet whenever some decisive chapter is sent down and **fighting** is mentioned in it, you will see the ones whose hearts contain malice looking at you as if they were going to faint from [fear of] death. It would be more fitting for them * to [offer their] obedience and use decent speech; when some matter is resolved, it would be better for them if they acted sincerely towards God.

20

* Would you by any chance, if you assumed power, cause havoc on earth and fight with your own flesh and blood? * Those are the ones whom God has cursed; He has made them deaf and blinded their eyesight. * Will they not meditate on the Qurɔān, or do they have locks on their hearts? ** Satan has seduced the ones who turned their backs after guidance had been explained to them, and he is dictating to them. * That is because they tell the ones who hate what God has sent down: "We will obey you (only) in part of what you order." Yet God knows their secrets!

Civil War Condemned

* How will it be when the angels gather them up, beating them on their faces and their backs? * That is because they have followed something that exasperates God and they hate to please Him, so He lets their actions miscarry.

29
30

(IV) * Or do those whose hearts contain malice reckon that God will never expose their grudges? ** If We so wished, We would point them out to you so you might recognize them by their features. You will still recognize them by their tone in speaking, while God knows your own actions. * We will test you till We know those who strive among you as well as those who are patient. We will test your reactions.

* The ones who disbelieve and obstruct God's way, and oppose the Messenger even after guidance has been explained to them, will never injure God in any way while He will let their actions founder. * You who believe, obey God and obey the Messenger and do not leave your actions useless. * God will never pardon those who disbelieve and obstruct God's way, then die while they are disbelievers.

Apostasy

** So do not waver, and appeal for peace while you hold the upper hand. God is with you and will never let you be cheated in your actions. * Worldly life is only a game and an amusement. If you believe and do your duty, your wages will be given you while your wealth will not be requested of you. * If He should ask you for it, and even dun you, you would act miserably and your grudges would become apparent. * Here you are, those who are called upon to spend in God's way, even though some of you are miserly!

*Greediness
Does Not
Pay*

Anyone who acts niggardly
is miserly only so far as his own soul
is concerned. God is Transcendent
while you are poor. If you should turn away
[from the call of duty and belief],
He will replace you with some other folk
who then will not be like you at all!

48
Victory (OR *Conquest*)

THIS CHAPTER of 29 verses arranged in four sections was revealed in the interval after the truce made at the tree of Ḥudaybiyya in the sixth year following the Hijra, or during 628 A.D.; thus it belongs to the Madinese period. It was revealed after **Friday** (OR **Congregation**) 62, when we consider the sequence of the chapters within the Qurʾān itself.

The chapter mentions political difficulties in section II, while a mob scene is described in section III. Ultimate victory is promised the Prophet and believers in section IV, which also contains the fable of "The Sturdy Plant". One great problem facing the early Muslims was how to divide up or dispose of booty that fell to them in battle; the Prophet did not want any followers who joined his forces merely in order to acquire it. This chapter reinforces the Muslim's sense of duty.

In the name of God, the Mercy-giving, the Merciful!

(I) * We have opened up a clear **victory** for you * so God may forgive you for any offence of yours you have committed previously or whatever you may do later on, complete His favor toward you and guide you along a Straight Road, * and so God may support you in a mighty success! * He is the One Who sends down Serenity on believers' hearts so they may add faith to the faith they already have.

God [commands] the armies of Heaven and Earth; God is Aware, Wise, ** so that He may admit believing men and believing women into gardens through which rivers flow, to live there for ever, and to cancel out their evil deeds for them. That will be a supreme Achievement with God, * so He may punish hypocritical men and women as well as associating men and women who conjecture such evil about God; on them will fall an evil turn of fortune. God has become angry with them, and has cursed them and prepared Hell for them. How evil is such a goal!

* God [commands] the armies of Heaven and Earth. God is Powerful, Wise! * We have sent you as a witness, herald and warner, * so you may (all) believe in God and His messenger, and revere and honor Him, and glorify Him morning and evening. ** The ones who swear allegiance to you merely swear allegiance to God. God's hand rests above their hands, so anyone who breaks his word, only breaks it at his own peril, while We will pay a splendid fee to anyone who fulfils what he has pledged [to do] before God.

10
Swearing Allegiance in Islam

11

(II) * Those desert Arabs who have held back will tell you: "Our property and our families have kept us busy. Seek forgiveness for us!" They say something with their tongues that is not in their hearts.

SAY: "Who controls anything for you against God, if He should want to cause you any harm, or wants to offer you some advantage? Rather God is Informed about whatever you are doing! * Instead you (all) thought that the Messenger and believers would never come home to their families. That [conduct] seemed attractive to your hearts while you thought such evil thoughts and were a worthless folk."

* We have reserved a Blaze for disbelievers, [such as] anyone who will not believe in God and His messengers. * God holds control over Heaven and Earth. He forgives anyone He wishes and punishes anyone He wishes; God is Forgiving, Merciful.

** The ones who held back will say, once you have set out to take some prizes: "Allow us to follow you!" They want to change God's word. SAY: "You will never follow us! God has already told you so." Next they will say: "Rather you envy us." Instead they only understand a little.

* Tell those desert Arabs who have held back: "You will be called upon to fight against a folk who are extremely violent; you will fight them unless they surrender. If you obey, God will pay you a handsome fee, while if you turn away just as you turned away before, He will punish you with painful torment." * There is no objection for the blind nor is there any objection for the lame, nor any objection for the sick [if they do not fight]. He will show anyone who obeys God and His messenger into gardens through which rivers flow, while He will punish anyone who turns away with painful torment.

18

(III) * God was pleased with believers as they swore allegiance to you under the tree. He recognized what was in their hearts and sent down Serenity upon them, and compensated them with a nearby **victory** * as well as many prizes they still may take. God is Powerful, Wise.

20

** God has promised you will take many prizes; he furnished these promptly for you and fended men's hands off from you so it might serve as a sign for believers and guide you along a Straight Road; * God has already included other things you do not yet have in your possession. God is Capable of everything. * If those who disbelieve should ever fight you, they will still turn their backs [and run away]; then they will not find any patron nor supporter, * according to God's practice which has occurred before.

You will never find any change in God's practice! * He is the One Who fended off their hands from you and your hands from them in the centre of Mecca after He let you vanquish them. God is Observant of anything you do. ** They are the ones who disbelieved and blocked you from [reaching] the Hallowed Mosque so the offerings were hindered from reaching their destination. If it had not been for some men who believed and some women who believed whom you did not recognize and would have trampled down, an outrage would have afflicted you because of them without [your] even knowing it, so that God will show anyone He wishes into His mercy.

*A Mob Scene
at Mecca*

If they had dispersed, We would still have punished those of them who disbelieved with painful torment. * While those who disbelieved were setting up fanaticism, the fanaticism of Ignorance in their own hearts, God sent His serenity down upon His messenger and on believers, and obliged them to respect the formula of heedfulness. They were truer to it and much more entitled to it. God is Aware of everything!

Doing One's Duty

(IV) * God has indeed verified the vision for His messenger, so you may enter the Hallowed Mosque safely, if God wishes, with your heads shaven and clipped. Do not fear: He knows what you do not know and grants besides that, **a victory** nearby. * He is the One Who has sent His messenger with guidance and the True Religion so He may have it prevail over all (other) religion. God suffices as a Witness!

27

Ultimate Victory

* **Muhammad is God's messenger** while those who are with him should be strict with disbelievers, merciful among themselves. You will see them bowing down, kneeling, craving bounty and approval from God. Their sign [shows] on their faces from the trace of bowing down on their knees [in worship].

Muhammad and Believers

Such is their description in the Torah, while their description in the Gospel is like a field crop which puts forth its shoots so it swells up, till it grows thick enough to stand straight on its stalk in the way farmers admire, so that disbelievers are exasperated by them. God has promised forgiveness and a splendid fee to any of those who believe and perform honorable deeds.

"The Sturdy Plant"

49
The [Inner] Apartments

THIS IMPORTANT chapter tells a great deal about the Prophet's private life and his growing concerns of state. It was revealed during the so-called "Year of Delegations" in 9/630, when all of Arabia was finally united in a political federation, and some sort of protocol had to be set up. Muḥammad's own house in Madīna where he had apartments for his numerous family, was becoming the center for this activity, and his household had to be protected from unexpected incidents and intruders. (It is now the site for the great mosque with the Green Dome in Madīna.)

The chapter consists of only 18 longer Madinese verses arranged in two sections. They were all revealed after **The Pleading Woman** 58 and before **Prohibition** 66. Here we meet the Prophet as a man with great cares of state and clearly in need of privacy.

The chapter also deals with social relationships between individual Muslims, and how to handle gossip and rumor, and to patch up quarrels (I). The next section furnishes more rules on social behavior and etiquette (II). Finally we receive recommendations on budding foreign policy and international law, which at this stage were quite embryonic. Nevertheless these details are all important.

In the name of God, the Mercy-giving, the Merciful!

Etiquette

(I) * You who believe, do not press forward in the presence of God and His messenger. Heed God: God is Alert, Aware. * You who believe, do not raise your voices over the Prophet's voice nor shout at him while [you are] speaking just as you shout at one another, lest your actions miscarry while you do not even notice it. * The ones who lower their voices in the presence of God's messenger are those whose hearts God examines for heedfulness. They will have forgiveness and a splendid fee. * Most of those who call out to you from outside the **apartments** do not use their reason; ** if they would wait patiently until you came out to [see] them, it would be better for them. God is Forgiving, Merciful.

Handling Gossip and Rumor

* You who believe, if some scoundrel should come up to you with some piece of news, clear up the facts lest you afflict some folk out of ignorance, and some morning feel regretful for what you may have done. * Know that God's messenger is among you. If he obeyed you in too much of such business, you would fall into discord; but God has so endeared faith for you that it seems attractive within your hearts, and made you hate disbelief, immorality and rebelliousness. Such persons are sensible * through bounty and favor from God. God is Aware, Wise.

* Whenever two factions of believers fall out with one another, try to reconcile them. If one of them should oppress the other, then fight the one which acts oppressively until they comply with God's command. If they should comply, then patch things up again between them in all justice, and act fairly. God loves those who act fairly. ** **Believers merely form a brotherhood**, so reconcile your brethren and heed God so that you may find mercy.

Patching Up Quarrels

10

(II) * You who believe, do not let one [set of] people make fun of another set; perhaps they are better than they are. Nor let any women [mistreat other] women; perhaps they are even better than they are themselves. Nor should you criticize one another, nor insult one another by using nicknames; it is bad to use a dirty name instead of one you can believe in. Those who do not turn away from it are wrongdoers.

11
More On Etiquette OR *the Rules for Social Conduct*

* You who believe, refrain from conjecturing too much: even a little suspicion forms a vice.

Gossip

Do not spy on one another, nor let any of you backbite others. Would one of you like to eat his dead brother's flesh? You would loathe it! Heed God, for God is Relenting, Merciful!

* O mankind, We have created you from a male and female, and set you up as nations and tribes so you may recognize [and cooperate with] one another. **The noblest among you with God is that one of you who best performs his duty;** God is Aware, Informed.

Foreign Policy; International Law

* The desert Arabs say: "We believe." SAY: "You have not yet believed, but say [instead]: 'We commit ourselves to [live in] peace'. Yet belief has not penetrated your hearts. If you obey God and His messenger, He will not slight you in any of your actions. God is Forgiving, Merciful!"

** **Believers** are merely the ones who believe in God and His messenger; then never doubt and **strive for God's sake with their property and persons**. Those are reliable.

Who Are Believers

* SAY: "Would you [presume to] teach God something concerning your religion? God knows whatever is in Heaven and whatever is on Earth. God is Aware of everything!"

* They want you to feel flattered because they have entered Islam. SAY: "You do not flatter me with your commitment to [live in] peace; rather God flatters you, provided you are loyal, since He has guided you to faith. * God knows the Unseen part of Heaven and Earth. God is Observant of anything you do."

50
(The Letter) QĀF
(OR Q)

THIS CHAPTER was revealed after **[Winds] Sent Forth** 77 and before **This Countryside** 90. It consists of 45 middle Meccan verses arranged in three sections, except for v. 38 (III) which dates from the period in Madīna. Some persons recommend that this chapter be recited on Fridays.

Here we begin a fresh group of seven chapters which date from the Meccan period. This one deals with man's lack of responsibility, God's care for him (II), and what will happen on Doomsday (II). It ends with recommendations concerning the times for prayer (III). The illustrations offered are apocalyptic and intended to shock disbelievers into thinking about the advantages presented by Islam.

In the name of God, the Mercy-giving, the Merciful!

(I) * Q.

By the majestic Qurʼān!

* Indeed they are astonished that a warner should come to them from among themselves. Disbelievers say: "This is an astonishing thing! * Why, when we have died and become dust, that will mean such a long way to return!"

* We well know how the earth hems them in, and We (also) have a Book to record it in. ** Rather they denied the Truth when it came to them, so (now) they are in a confused state. * Have they not seen how We have built the sky above them and made it seem attractive? There are no flaws in it. * And We have spread the earth out and cast headlands upon it, and grown every sort of lovely species on it * as a token and Reminder for every repentant worshipper. * We have sent down blessed water from the sky and We grow gardens with it as well as grain to be harvested, ** and soaring palms which have compact clusters * as sustenance for worshippers. We have revived a dead countryside with it; thus will (your) reappearance be.

10

* Before them, Noah's folk denied it, and the companions at the Well, and Thamūd, * ʿĀd, and Pharaoh, as well as Lot's brethren, * the inhabitants of the Forest, and the people of Tubbaʿ; each rejected messengers, so My warning was confirmed. ** Were We worn out by the first creation? Yet they are in a quandary about any fresh creation!

(II) * We have created man and know
what his soul is whispering within him.
**We are Closer to him
than his jugular vein!**
    * When both encountering [angels] meet,
seated to the right and to the left,
* he will utter no statement
unless he has an observer on hand
ready to note it down.

16

God's Care

* The agony of death will come [and confront you] with the Truth; that is
what you have been trying to escape! ** The Trumpet shall be blown: that
will be the day of the Threat!

Doomsday
20

    * Every soul shall come along; each will have a driver and a
witness: * "You have been so heedless of this, that We have removed your
blinders from you so your sight may be keen today!" * His soulmate will
say: "All this lying before me needs to be checked into; * let us both toss
every stubborn disbeliever into Hell, ** [since he is] hindering good,
aggressive, suspicious, * someone who has set up some other deity
alongside God! Toss him into severe torment!"
    * His soulmate will say: "Our Lord, I did not make him act arrogantly,
but he was gone too far astray." * He will say: "Do not argue in My
presence! I had already sent the Threat ahead to you (all)! * The sentence
will not be changed within My presence, nor am I unjust towards My
worshippers."

(III) ** On the day We shall say to Hell: "Are you filled up?", it will say:
"Are there any more to be added?"

30

Paradise

    * The Garden will be brought up a short distance from the heedful;
* "This is what you have been promised, for everyone who turns to observe
it, * who lives in awe of the Mercy-giving, even though [He is] Unseen,
and comes with a repentant heart. * Enter it peacefully; that is the day
that will last for ever." ** They will have anything they wish in it, and
more besides [when they are] in Our presence.
    * How many generations have We wiped out before them? They were
much braver than they are and stormed through the land. Yet had they any
escape? * In that is a Reminder for anyone who has a heart or lends an
ear while he [also] acts as a witness.

    * We created Heaven and Earth and whatever lies in between them in
six days, while no weariness ever affects Us. * So be patient about
anything they may say, and hymn your Lord's praise before the sun's rising
and before its setting, ** and at night. Glorify Him whenever you finish
bowing down on your knees.

*Times of
Prayer*

40

    * Listen for the day when the Crier will call out from a nearby
place, * a day when they will really hear the Blast; that will be the day
to reappear in! * It is We Who give life and bring death, and toward
Us lies the goal * on a day when the earth will split open quickly
because of them. Such a mustering will be easy for Us.

** We are quite Aware of what they say: you should not be too demanding on them. Remind anyone who fears My warning by means of the Qurɔān.

51
Winnowing [Winds]

HIS HIGHLY mystic chapter, as the title suggests, deals with Abraham and other prophets. It contains 60 early Meccan verses in three sections, and was revealed after **The Dunes** 46 and before **The Pall** 88.

The end (III) concerns divine worship and our duty towards God. SEE also Chapter 77 on **[Winds] Sent Forth** and **The Chargers** 100 for similar apocalyptic pictures. The shorter verses are now very apparent.

In the name of God, the Mercy-giving, the Merciful!

(I) * By the **Winnowing [Winds]**
* and those bearing a burden
* and the ones blowing gently
* and those delivering a command,
** whatever you are promised
    is certain! * Doom
    is about to occur!

Doomsday

* By the sky full of orbits, * you (all) have different ways of saying things, * to brush off anyone who may be brushed off. ** Damned will be guessers * who are dazed with excitement.

10

* They ask: "When will Doomsday be?" * Some day they will be tested over the Fire: * "Taste your test! This is what you wanted to hurry up."

** The heedful will be in gardens and by springs * partaking of whatever their Lord has given them. They had acted kindly even before that; * they used to slumber only a portion of the night * while in vigils towards dawning they sought forgiveness. * The beggar and the destitute had some right to their wealth.

The Heedful (Those Who do their Duty)

** On earth there are signs for the convinced, * and even within yourselves; do you not notice them? * In the sky is your sustenance and whatever you are promised; * so by the Lord of Heaven and Earth, it is the Truth just the same as you have been uttering!

20

(II) * Has the report of Abraham's honored guests ever come to you, ** when they entered his home and said: "Peace [be upon you]!"? He said: "[On you be] peace!" [even though] they were people he did not know. * So he slipped off to his family and fetched a fattened calf, * and brought it up to them. He said: "Will you not eat?"

24

Abraham

30

* He felt a fear concerning them. They said: "Dont be afraid," and gave him the news of a clever lad. * His wife came up sighing, and struck her face and said: "[I'm] a barren old hag!" ** They said: "Even so did your Lord say. He is the Wise, the Aware!

PART
TWENTY-SEVEN

31

(II cont'd) * He said: "Yet what is your errand, O emissaries?" * They said: "We have been sent to a criminal folk, * to launch clay pellets on them * marked by your Lord for the dissipated." ** So We brought out anyone there who were believers, * though We found only one house with Muslims in it. * We left a sign there for those who fear painful torment.

* And with Moses when We sent him off with clear authority to Pharaoh, * who turned away with his warlords and said: "[He's either] a magician or a madman!" ** We seized him and his troops and hurled them into the deep while he was to blame.

40

*Moses and
Other
Prophets*

* And with ʿĀd, when We loosed a devastating wind on them: * it left nothing that it chanced upon without turning it into rubble. * And with Thamūd when someone told them: "Enjoy things for a while!" * They strutted around against their Lord's command, as the Thunderbolt caught them while they were looking on. ** They were unable to withstand it nor were they supported. * And Noah's people had already been such immoral folk.

47

50

(III) * The sky We have built firmly and We are extending it. * The earth have We spread out; how Blissful is the One Who has smoothed it off! * With everything We have created pairs so that you may be reminded; ** so flee to God: "I am a plain warner to you from Him!"

* "Do not place any other deity alongside God [Alone]: I am a plain warner to you from Him. * Thus no messenger ever came to those who preceded them unless they said: '[He's] a magician or a madman!' * Do they recommend it to one another? Yet they are such arrogant folk. * Turn away from them; you are not to blame! ** Remind, for reminding benefits believers."

*Man's Duty
Towards
God*

60

* I have only created sprites and men so they may worship Me; * I do not want any sustenance from them nor do I need them to feed me. * God is the Provider, wielding sturdy strength. * The ones who do wrong have offences just like their companions' offences, so do not let them ask Me to hurry things up. ** It will be too bad for those who disbelieve on their day which has been promised them!

52
The Mount

THIS CHAPTER of 49 Meccan verses is arranged in two sections. It was revealed after **Worship (Bowing Down on Your Knees)** 32 and before **Control** 67.

Its chief quality lies in its poetic mood which describes both Doomsday and Bliss (I), plus offering a long and direct challenge to disbelievers. This includes Muḥammad's classic rebuttal (II)—for which SEE Chapter 21 on **Prophets** as well. The Prophet himself said that this chapter helps one believe in God and also in either His punishment or His favor.

In the name of God, the Mercy-giving, the Merciful!

(I) * By **the Mount** * and a Book recorded
* on unrolled parchment,
* and the thriving House
** with the roof raised [over it],   *Doomsday*
* and the swollen sea,
* your Lord's torment is bound to happen!
   *. No one will avert it
* on a day when the sky will shift about
** and the mountains travel around.   10

* It will be too bad on that day for rejectors * who play around with speculation, * on the day they will be pushed firmly towards Hell fire: * "This is the Fire which you have been denying. ** Is this magic or dont you notice anything? * Roast in it! Whether you act patient or impatient, it will be all the same for you; you are merely being rewarded for what you have been doing."

* The heedful will be in gardens and bliss, * delighted with whatever   *Bliss* OR
their Lord has given them. Their Lord has shielded them from the torment   *Delight*
of Hades: * "Eat and drink at leisure because of what you have been
doing." ** Relaxing on couches all lined up, We will pair them off with   20
dark-eyed damsels!.

* We shall unite those who believe and whose offspring have followed them in faith with their offspring. We will not deprive them of any action of theirs in any way; **each man is a pledge for whatever he has earned**. * We will spread out any fruit and meat for them such as they may desire. * They will compete for a cup there in which no idle talk nor any faultfinding lurks. * Young men of theirs will pass around among them as if they were treasured pearls.

** Some of them will step forward to question one another; * they will say: "We were anxious about our family previously, * yet God has compensated us and shielded us from the torment of [Hell's] scorching breath. * We have long since appealed to Him; He is the Virtue-granting, the Merciful!"

29
30
*Muḥammad's
Rebuttal
to Skeptics*

(II) * Remind, for by your Lord's favor, you are no fortune-teller nor any madman. ** Or do they say: "[He's] a poet! We'll wait for some quirk of fate to [upset] him." * SAY: "Lie in wait; for I am waiting along with you."

* Do their fancies order them to do this or are they arrogant folk? * Or do they say: "He has talked it all up"? Rather they do not believe. * Let them bring a report like it if they are so truthful.

** Or were they created out of nothing, or are they their own creators? * Or did they create Heaven and Earth? Rather they will never be convinced.

* Do they hold on to your Lord's treasures, or are they even in charge of them? * Or have they some ladder from which to eavesdrop? Let their eavesdropper bring some clear authority!

40

* Or has He daughters while you have sons? ** Or are you asking them for some fee so they will feel weighted down with debt? * Do they have the Unseen which they are writing down? * Or do they want [to hatch] some plot, while those who disbelieve are themselves being plotted against?

* Or do they have some other deity instead of God [Alone]? Glory be to God ahead of anything they may associate [with Him]!

* If they ever saw some object falling out of the sky, they would say: "Some clouds have been piled up."

** Leave them alone till they encounter their day in which they will be stunned, * a day when their plotting will not help them out at all nor will they be supported. * The ones who act unjustly will have torment beyond that, even though most of them do not realize it.

*Times of
Prayer*

* Act patiently towards your Lord's discretion since you are under Our eyes. Hymn your Lord's praise whenever you arise, * and at night glorify Him occasionally, and as the stars fade away.

53
The Star

THIS CHAPTER was revealed after **Sincerity** (OR **[God's] Oneness**) 112, and before **He Frowned!** 80. It consists of three sections containing a total of 62 early Meccan verses, except for v. 32 which dates from Madīna. The star referred to is variously stated to be either the morning and evening star which is called Venus in Western terminology, or else the dogstar or Sirius mentioned in III, or perhaps the cluster of the Pleiades.

This chapter too is mystical and soaring in spirit, for it concerns the *Miʿraj* or Ascension of the Prophet which is also described at the beginning of **The Night Journey** 17 (I). The first section announces Muḥammad's call to prophethood and explains how intercession is of no avail; while the second emphasizes that God is Just. The complete vision is superb and should be studied carefully for inspiration.

In the name of God, the Mercy-giving, the Merciful!

(I) * By **the Star** as it sets, * your companion
has neither strayed nor is he misguided.
* He does not speak from some whim;
* it is merely inspiration
that is revealed [to him].

    ** Someone firm in strength has taught him,   *The Sublime*
* someone possessing such ability   *Vision*
that he soared up * and stood,
poised at the highest [point on the] horizon.
* Then he approached and came right down,
* and stood two bow-lengths off
or even closer. ** He inspired   10
whatever he inspired in His servant.
* His vitals did not deny whatever he saw.
* Yet will you (all) distrust him
about what he [actually] saw?

    * He saw him in another descent
* near the Hawthorn on the Boundary
** alongside the Garden of Repose.
* When whatever covered the Hawthorn
covered it, * his eyesight did not falter
nor was it carried away. * He saw
some of his Lord's greatest signs!

20
Futile
Goddesses

* Have you (all) considered al-Lāt and al-ʿUzzà, ** and Manāt the other [who ranks] in third place? * Do you have sons while He has daughters? * That would then be an unfair attribution! * They are only some names which you and your forefathers have called them; God has not sent down any authority for them. They merely follow conjecture and something their souls fancy.

Yet guidance has already reached them from their Lord. * Or may man have anything he hankers for? ** Yet God still holds the Last as well as the First!

26
Intercession
Does Not
Help

(II) * How many angels are there in Heaven whose intercession does not help in any way except after God permits it, for whomever He wishes and approves of? * The ones who do not believe in the Hereafter call the angels by the names of females. * Yet they have no knowledge about it; they only follow guesswork. Conjecture will not help out in any way against the Truth, * so shun anyone who avoids mentioning Us and only wants [to enjoy] worldly life; ** that will be their range of knowledge.

30

God is
Just

Your Lord is quite Aware as to who has strayed from His path, just as He is quite Aware as to who is guided; * God possesses whatever is in Heaven and whatever is on Earth, so He may reward the ones who commit evil according to whatever they have done while He rewards the ones who act kindly with [equal] kindness.

* Those who refrain from the greatest vices and sexual offences, except for oversights [will find] your Lord is Boundless when it comes to forgiveness.

He was quite Aware of you when He produced you from the earth and when you were still embryos in your mothers' wombs. Do not try to justify yourselves; He is quite Aware as to who has done his duty.

33

(III) * Have you seen someone who turns away? * He has given little, and even skimps at that! ** Has he such knowledge about the Unseen that he can (actually) see [it]? * Or has he not been notified about what was on Moses' scrolls * and on Abraham's, who always kept his word:

* "That no burdened soul shall bear another's burden.
* That everyman receives only what he makes an effort for:

40

Moses' and
Abraham's
Message:
Cause and
Effect

** so his effort shall be noticed;
* then he will be rewarded to the fullest extent.

* "And that towards your Lord lies the final End; * and He makes (us) both laugh and cry; * He brings death and grants life. ** He has created both sexes, male and female, * from a drop of semen which has been ejected. * On Him [rests your] next appearance.

* "He grants wealth and riches;
* He is even Lord of the Dogstar!

50

** "Yet He wiped out the first [nation] of ʿĀd * and Thamūd, and left nothing over, * and even Noah's folk previously, who had been most

unjust and arrogant. * And he fell upon the Overthrown [Towns], * and
covered them up with whatever covered them."

** So which of your Lord's benefits will you distrust? * This is a
warner just like the early warners. * What is imminent is approaching;
* there is nothing besides God to remove it!

* Are you amazed at this report? ** You laugh, and do not
weep * while you hold your heads so high!
* **Bow down** on your knees to God
and worship [Him]!

60

*BOW DOWN
HERE*

54
The Moon (OR *The Hour Approaches)*

THIS CHAPTER was revealed after **The Nightcomer** 86 and before (**The Letter**) **Ṣād** 38. It consists of three sections of 55 early Meccan verses, except for vv. 44-46 in section III which date from Madīna. A prevailing rhyme uses -*r* as a final consonant. The chapter moreover bears the haunting refrain which is first stated in vv. 16-17: "How were My torment and My warnings!"

This refrain underlines how prophets like Noah, Hūd (I), Ṣāliḥ and Lot (II) were rejected by their own people in times past, Hūd by ʿĀd, and Ṣāliḥ by Thamūd. Thus Muḥammad should take comfort for himself. The fate of Pharaoh is also mentioned in the final section (III), which ends in an apocalyptic description of the final Hour which is intended to shock disbelievers and associators into meditating on their errors.

In the name of God, the Mercy-giving, the Merciful!

(I) * **The Hour approaches** and **the Moon** is splitting apart! * Yet if they see any sign, they avoid it and say: "It's constant magic!" * They deny [it all] and follow their own whims, even though every matter has been settled.

* News has come to them containing a rebuke, ** as eloquent wisdom, even though warners can get nowhere. * So turn away from them on the day when the Crier will call out about a horrible event. * Their eyes cast down, they will issue forth from their tombs as if they were scattered grasshoppers * dashing along towards the Crier. Disbelievers will say: "This is such a hard day!"

Noah
10

* Noah's folk denied it long before them; they rejected Our servant and said: "[He's] crazy!", and he was rebuffed. ** He appealed to his Lord: "I have been overpowered, so support [me]!" * So We opened Heaven's gates for water to pour down. * We drilled the earth full of springs and the waters met at a command which had been decreed. * We transported him on something built with planks and caulking * which sailed on before Our eyes, as a reward for someone who had been rejected. ** We left it as a sign; yet will anyone bear it in mind?

    * How were My torment, and My warnings?
    * **We have made the Qurʾān easy to memorize**;
      yet will anyone [bother to] memorize it?

* ʿĀd rejected it. How were My torment, and My warnings? * We sent a howling gale against them on a day full of continuous misfortune ** which snatched men up as if they were hollow palm trunks.

    ʿĀd

    20

    * How were My torment, and My warnings!
    * We have made the Qurʾān easy to memorize;
      yet will anyone memorize it?

(II) * Thamūd rejected My warnings too * and they said: "Are we to follow a single human being from among ourselves? We would then be in error and frenzy. ** Has the Reminder been delivered merely to him among Us? Instead he is a brash liar."

    23

    Thamūd
    and Ṣāliḥ

    * Tomorrow they will know who the brash liar is! * We are sending them a she-camel as a test, so watch them and act patient. * Announce to them how water must be shared among them; each will have his own special time to drink. * They called out to their companion; and he assumed the task and hamstrung [her].

    ** How were My torment, and My warnings?
    * (We sent a single Blast against them
    so they [lay] like dry stalks
    caught in a fence corner.)
    * We have made the Qurʾān easy to memorize;
      yet will anyone [bother to] memorize it?

    30

* Lot's people rejected the warnings. * We sent a sandstorm against them, except for Lot's own household whom We saved at daybreak ** as a favor from Ourself; thus We reward anyone who acts grateful. * He had warned them of Our onslaught, yet they discredited the warnings. * They tried to coax his guests away from him, so We dazzled their eyes: "Taste My torment and My warnings!" * Early one morning, unavoidable torment dawned upon them.

    Lot and
    Sodom

    * "Taste My torment and My warnings!"
    ** We have made the Qur'ān easy to memorize;
      yet will anyone memorize it?

    40

(III) * Warnings came to Pharaoh's court. * Yet they rejected Our signs completely, so We seized them the way a Powerful, Competent person would seize [them]. * Are your disbelievers any better than those men were, or have you some dispensation [to be found] in the Psalms? * Or do they say: "We all support one another"?

    41

    Pharaoh

    ** They will all be defeated together and turn their backs [to run away]. * Indeed the Hour has been promised them; the Hour will be quite disastrous and most bitter. * Criminals will be lost in error and frenzy. * Some day they will be dragged face down through the Fire: "Experience the sense of scorching!"

    The Hour
    of Bitter
    Disaster

    * We have created everything in due proportion. ** Our command comes only once, in the twinkling of an eye! * We wiped out your adherents; does no one recall it? * Everything they did is [to be found] in the Psalms; * everything small or great has been recorded. * The heedful will be by gardens and a river ** in a sure position under a Competent Sovereign.

    50

55
The Mercy-Giving

T HIS APOCALYPTIC chapter containing 78 verses was completed after **Thunder** 13 and before **Everyman** (OR This Day and Age) 76. It may possibly be an early Meccan revelation. God in His role as *ar-Raḥmān* or 'The Mercy-giving' is also expounded in Chapter 19 on **Mary**.

Another unifying refrain similar to that in Psalm 136 and its refrain on how the Lord's ''mercy endureth for ever'' runs through this chapter: ''So which of your Lord's blessings will both of you deny?'' This is repeated 31 times, carried along on rhyme or assonance (in -*ān*) in a strophic form. The measured prose is very effective; the chapter is in fact a long poem dealing with proofs of God's favors. Duals or pairs give it another special figure which is difficult to bring out through English verbs or nouns.

Its inspiring message also describes the future life which is offered the faithful, while there is a passage on Creation at the end of section I. Hell (II) and Heaven (III) are likewise pictured.

In the name of God, the Mercy-giving, the Merciful!

(I) * The **Mercy-giving**, * has taught the Reading,
* created man, * taught him self-expression.

Natural Phenomena

     ** The sun and moon [move along] like clockwork,
* shrubs and trees both bend in worship;
* while He has raised the sky up
and placed scales [there]
* so you may not skimp in weighing.
* Always measure accurately with [all] fairness
and do not give short weight!

10

     ** The earth has He laid out for humanity,
* offering fruit, datepalms bearing blossoms,
* grain wrapped up in husks, and fragrant herbs.
     * So which of your Lord's benefits
will both of you deny?

Creation

* He created man from ringing clay
just as a potter does, ** while He created
sprites from the glow in fire.
     * So which of your Lord's benefits
will both of you deny?

* Lord of both Easts and Lord of both Wests!
  * So which of your Lord's benefits
  will both of you deny?

* He has loosed both seas
which still come together;
** between them lies an isthmus
which neither tries to cross.   20
  * So which of your Lord's benefits
  will both of you deny?

* He produces pearls and coral from them both;
  * so which of your Lord's benefits
  will both of you deny?

* His are the vessels looming up
like landmarks on the sea;
  ** so which of your Lord's benefits
  will both of you deny?

(II) * Everyone upon it will disappear   26
* while your Lord's face will remain
full of majesty and splendor.
  * So which of your Lord's benefits
  will both of you deny?

* Everyone in Heaven and Earth
asks for something from Him;
each day He is [Busy] at some task.
  ** So which of your Lord's benefits   30
  will both of you deny?

* We shall finish off both loads for you;
  * so which of your Lord's benefits
  will both of you deny?

* O company of sprites and humankind,
if you can manage to penetrate
beyond the realms of Heaven and Earth,   Exploring
then pass beyond them! Yet you will only   Space
penetrate them through some authority.
  * So which of your Lord's benefits
  will both of you deny?

** A flare of fire and sparks
will be loosed against you, from which
neither of you will be protected;   Hellfire
  * so which of your Lord's benefits
  will both of you deny?

* When the sky splits open and becomes
like a rose [painted] by some artist,

* so which of your Lord's benefits
will both of you deny?

* On that day, no man nor any sprite
will be questioned about any offence of his;
 ** so which of your Lord's benefits
will both of you deny?

40

* Criminals will be recognized by their features,
and seized by their forelocks and feet;
 * so which of your Lord's benefits
will both of you deny?

* Such is Hell, which criminals
deny exists. * They will circle around
between it and a seething bath.
 ** So which of your Lord's benefits
will both of you deny?

46
Paradise

(III) * Yet anyone who fears to stand
before his Lord will have **two gardens;**
 * so which of your Lord's benefits
will both of you deny?

* Both containing many sorts of things;
 * so which of your Lord's benefits
will both of you deny?

50

** Each will have two flowing springs;
 * so which of your Lord's benefits
will both of you deny?

* Each will have a pair
for every kind of fruit;
 * so which of your Lord's benefits
will both of you deny?

* They will recline on couches
upholstered in brocade
while the harvest from both orchards
droops nearby;
 ** so which of your Lord's benefits
will both of you deny?

* Bashful maidens will be there
whom no human being has tampered with
previously, nor any sprite.
 * So which of your Lord's benefits
will both of you deny?

* They will be like rubies and coral;
  * so which of your Lord's benefits
  will both of you deny?

** Is there any reward for kindness   60
except kindness itself?
  * So which of your Lord's benefits
  will both of you deny?

* Besides both of these, there will be   Two Extra
two extra gardens;   Gardens
  * so which of your Lord's benefits
  will both of you deny?

 * Both densely shaded;
  ** so which of your Lord's benefits
  will both of you deny?

* Each will have two splashing fountains;
  * so which of your Lord's benefits
  will both of you deny?

* Both will have fruit,
datepalms and pomegranates;
  * so which of your Lord's benefits
  will both of you deny?

** In them there will be the best,   70
the fairest women!
  * So which of your Lord's benefits
  will both of you deny?

 * Bright-eyed damsels sheltered in pavilions;
  * so which of your Lord's benefits
  will both of you deny?

* Whom no human being has tainted
previously, nor any sprites!
  ** So which of your Lord's benefits
  will both of you deny?

* They will lean back on green cushions
and handsome carpets;
  * so which of your Lord's benefits
  will both of you deny?

  * **Blessed be your Lord's name,
  Possessor of Majesty and Splendor!**

56
The Inevitable

HIS CHAPTER was revealed after **Ṭā-Hā** 20 and before **Believers** 23 and **Poets** 26. It forms the last of the seven early Meccan chapters to be found in this present grouping. All of its 96 verses date from Mecca, except for vv. 81-82 (in section III) which are from Madīna.

An urgent message and strophic form underlies the chapter's rhythm. The poetic vision here suggests that life is a race, and it speaks of future rewards. We meet three groups: first the "Pioneers"; then "Those on the Right" (I); and finally "Those on the Left" (II). In the last section (III) the Qurʾān itself is discussed.

In the name of God, the Mercy-giving, the Merciful!

The Last
Judgment

(I) * When the **Inevitable** arrives
* no one will deny its happening,
* humbling, exalting!

* The earth will be rocked with a jolt ** and the mountains crumble to pieces * and become dust that is scattered about. * You will form three groups: * the Companions on the Right (What do the Companions on the Right [mean]?); * the Companions on the Left (What do the Companions on the Unlucky side [mean]?); ** and the Pioneers will be out there leading!

The
Pioneers
10

Paradise

* Those will be the nearest * in gardens of bliss, * a multitude from early men * and a few from later ones ** on couches set close together, * leaning back on them, facing one another. * Immortal youths will stroll around them * with glasses, pitchers, and a cup from a fountain * which will not upset them nor dull their senses; ** and any fruit that they may choose, * and the meat from any fowl they may desire; * and bright-eyed damsels [chaste] * just like treasured pearls, * as a reward for what they have been doing. ** They will not hear any idle talk there nor any fault-finding, * merely people saying: "Peace! Peace!"

20

Those on
the Right
30

* The Companions on the Right—what about the Companions on the Right? * [They will be] among hawthorns trimmed of their thorns, * and bananas piled bunch on bunch, ** with their shade spread out, * water pouring forth, * and plenty of fruit * which is neither rationed nor forbidden, * and padded furniture raised [off the floor]. ** We have produced special women * and made them (ever) virgins, * easy to get along with and of their same age, * for the Companions on the Right, * a multitude from early men ** as well as a multitude from later ones.

40

(II) * The Companions on the Unlucky side, what about the Companions   41
on the Left? * In a scorching wind, scalding water, * and the shade of   *Those on*
pitch-black smoke, * which is neither cool nor refreshing. ** They had   *the Left*
been luxuriating before that happened * and persisted in awesome
blasphemy, * and kept on saying: "When we have died and become dust
and bones, will we be raised up again? * Along with our earliest
forefathers?"

    * SAY: "The earlier and the later ones ** will be gathered together for   50
an appointment on a well-known day. * Then you mistaken rejectors
* will be eating something from the Infernal Tree, * filling (your) bellies
with it * and drinking scalding water in addition, ** lapping it up, the   God's
way thirsty [camels] drink."   Role in
    * Such will be their fare on the Day for Repayment! * We created   Reproduction
you, if you would only acknowledge it. * Have you ever considered what   60
you emit? * Did you create it, or are We its Creators? ** We have
ordained death for (all of) you; no one will get ahead to prevent
Us * from changing your attributes, and transforming you into something
you would never recognize.
    * You know about the first transformation, if you will only recall
it. * Have you considered what you plant as crops? * Do you farm it or
are We the Farmers? ** If We so wished, We would turn it into chaff so
you would do nothing but exclaim: * "We are debt-ridden; * in fact, we
are destitute!"
    * Have you ever considered the water you drink? * Do you pour it
down from the rainclouds or are We its Pourers? ** If We so wished, We   70
might make it brackish. If you would only act grateful!
    * Have you considered the Fire you kindle? * Are you the ones who
grow its trees [for firewood] or are We their Growers? * We have granted
it as a Reminder and enjoyment for those living in the wilderness.

        * So celebrate your Lord's almighty name!

(III) ** Yet I swear by the stars' positions * (it is a serious oath, if you   75
only knew it!) * that it is a **Noble Qur'ān** * [kept] as a treasured   The Qur'ān
Book * which **none but the purified may touch**, ** something sent down   80
by the Lord of the Universe.
    * Are you (all) trying to dodge this report? * **Are you making [the
fact] that you reject it into your means of livelihood**? * Why not

    —when [your soul] leaps to your throat [at death] * and you are then   *The*
    observing, ** (We are even Nearer to it than you are, even though you   *Arrogant*
    do not notice it)—   *Challenged*

* provided you are not under any obligation, * answer back if you are so
truthful...!
    * Thus if he is one of those who are drawn close * [he will have]
contentment, fragrance, and a garden of bliss— ** while if he is one of the   90
Companions on the Right! * ''Peace be on you'' [will be the greeting] from
the Companions on the Right.
    * However if he is one of the mistaken rejectors * a welcome of
scalding water * plus a roasting in Hades [will await him]. ** This is the
absolute Truth;

        * **So celebrate your Lord's almighty name!**

57
Iron

THIS CHAPTER containing 29 verses in four sections from the Madinese period was revealed after **The Earthquake** 99 and before **Muḥammad** 47. It is composed in a different style from those immediately before and after it, because its verses are longer, like those found in other chapters composed in Madīna.

It begins in a lyric mood with a hymn to God's omnipresence (I) and then presents a picture of hypocrites begging for light to guide them (II). Other subjects discussed are showers of rain (III), different prophets (IV), monasticism and finally God's bounty or grace. **Iron**, which gives the chapter its title, is mentioned as the source of physical power (III).

In the name of God, the Mercy-giving, the Merciful!

*A Hymn
to God*

(1) * Whatever is in Heaven and Earth
celebrates God. He is
the Powerful, the Wise!

   * He holds control
over Heaven and Earth.
He grants life and brings death;
He is Capable of everything!

*God's
Omnipresence*

* He is the First and the Last,
the Outward and the Innermost.
He is Aware of everything!

   * He is the One Who created
Heaven and Earth in six days;
then He mounted on the Throne.
He knows what penetrates the earth

*and
Omniscience*

and what issues from it,
and what comes down from the sky
and what soars up into it.
He is with you (all) wherever you may be!
God is Observant of anything you do.

   ** He holds control
over Heaven and Earth;
unto God do matters return.
* He wraps night up in daytime;
and wraps daytime up in night.
He is Aware of whatever is on our minds.

* Believe in God and His messenger, and spend something out of whatever He has let you inherit [from anyone else]. Those of you who believe and spend [on charity and in public service] will have an even larger fee. * What is wrong with you that you do not believe in God and the Messenger? He invites you (all) to believe in your Lord; He has made an agreement with you, provided you are believers.

     * He is the One Who has sent down clear signs upon His servant, so he may lead you out of darkness into Light. God is so Gentle, Merciful with you. ** What is wrong with you that you do not spend anything for God's sake? God holds the heritage of Heaven and Earth. Those among you who have spent and fought before the victory are not equal: those stand higher in rank than the ones who spent and fought later on. God has promised each one the very finest. God is Informed about whatever you do.

(II) * Who is the one who will advance God a handsome loan? He will double it for him so he [will receive] a generous fee. * Some day you will see believing men and believing women with their light streaming on ahead of them and off to their right: "Your good news today [consists of] gardens through which rivers flow, to live in for ever!" That will be the splendid Achievement.

     * Some day hypocritical men and hypocritical women will tell the ones who believe: "Wait for us; we need to borrow a light from you!" Someone will say: "Go on back the way you came, and request a light [somewhere else]!"

     So a wall will rise up between them which will have a door in it; inside there will be mercy while outside facing it there will be torment. * They will call out to them: "Were we not with you?"

     They will say: "Of course, but you tempted one another, and let yourselves waver and doubt. [Your saying] 'Amens' [to everybody] has deceived you till God's command came along. The Deceiver has even deluded you concerning God! ** So today no redemption will be accepted from you nor from those who disbelieve: your lodging shall be the Fire; it is your patron and how awful is such a goal!"

     * Is it not high time for the hearts of those who believe to submit to God's reminder and any truth that has been sent down? Let them not act like the ones who were given the Book previously: the waiting period seemed too long for them, so their hearts were hardened, and many of them became immoral. * Know that God revives the earth following its death. We have explained signs to you so that you may use your reason.

     * Charitable men and charitable women who have advanced God a handsome loan will have it doubled for them; they shall have a generous fee. * Those who believe in God and His messengers act sincerely, and serve as witnesses for their Lord, will have their earnings plus their own light, while those who disbelieve and reject Our signs will become the inmates of Hades.

(III) ** Know that worldly life is merely a sport and a pastime [involving] worldly show and competition among yourselves, as well as rivalry in wealth and children. It may be compared to showers where the plantlife amazes the incredulous: then it withers away and you see it turning yellow; soon it will be just stubble. In the Hereafter there will be both severe torment and forgiveness as well as approval on the part of God. Worldly life means only the enjoyment of illusion.

* Compete for forgiveness from your Lord, and a garden broader than the sky plus the earth, which has been prepared for those who believe in God and His messenger. Such is God's bounty which He gives to anyone He wishes. God possesses splendid bounty!

Predesti-
nation

* No disaster ever happens on earth nor to yourselves unless it is [contained] in a Book even before We brought it into existence. That is easy for God [to do], * so that you should not feel sorry about what may have escaped you, nor yet rejoice in what He has given you. God does not love every conceited boaster * who is miserly and orders people to be miserly. For anyone who turns away from it, God is Transcendent, Praiseworthy.

Human
Behavior

** We have sent Our messengers with explanations, and sent the Book and the Balance down along with them, so that mankind may conduct themselves with all fairness. We have sent **iron** down laden with grim violence as well as (other) benefits for mankind, so that God may know who supports Him and His messengers even though [He is] Unseen. God is Strong, Powerful.

26

Other
Prophets

Christians
and
Monasticism

(IV) * We sent Noah and Abraham, and granted prophethood and the Book to the offspring of them both. Some of them have accepted guidance while many of them have been immoral. * Then We made Our messengers follow along in their footsteps and We followed them up with Jesus the son of Mary. We gave him the Gospel and placed compassion and mercy in the hearts of those who have followed him, as well as **monkhood; yet they initiated it:** We did not prescribe it for them—except through (their) aspiring for God's approval. They do not observe it in the way it should be observed. We gave their earnings to those of them who believe; yet many of them are immoral.

God's
Bounty OR
Grace

* You who believe, heed God and believe in His messenger; He will give you double shares in His mercy and grant you a light to walk by as well as forgive you. God is Forgiving, Merciful, * so let the People of the Book know they can do nothing about God's bounty, since bounty lies [entirely] in God's hand. He gives it to anyone He wishes. God possesses such tremendous grace!

58
The Pleading Woman
(OR *God Has Heard...*)

THIS CHAPTER of 22 verses arranged in three sections dates from
Madīna, like the previous one. It was revealed after the one on
Hypocrites 63 and before **The [Inner] Apartments** 49. This thus makes it
the second of the two Madinese chapters which are placed here, as one can
see with its longer verses and more involved paragraphs. Its theme
condemning arrogant conduct likewise gives it an affinity to the beginning
of Chapter 24 **Light** (sections I-III).

The woman referred to was Khawlaʾ bint-Thaʿlaba, and the incident
refers to her domestic problems. The mock divorce of the pagan Arabs
which bound the rejected wife to her household chores is condemned at the
very beginning of the chapter (I). The chapter also contains some lyrical
passages concerning God's awareness of everything, especially of intrigue.
Manners at meetings and parliamentary procedure are discussed in section
II.

PART
TWENTY-EIGHT

In the name of God, the Mercy-giving, the Merciful!

(1) * **God has heard** the speech of **the woman pleading** with you about
her husband, and complaining to God. God hears whatever you both
discuss; God is Alert, Observant.

* Those among you who back away from their wives even though they
are not their mothers (their mothers are only the ones who have given birth
to them) are making a dishonorable statement as well as twisting things
around. Yet God is Pardoning, Forgiving. * The ones who back away
from their wives [as if they were their mothers], then retract whatever they
have said, should free a captive before either of them may touch one
another [again]. That you are instructed to do; God is Informed about
anything you do. * Whoever does not find such [a captive to free], should
then fast for two consecutive months before either of them may touch one
another. Anyone who is still unable [to conform] should then feed sixty
paupers.

Mock
Divorce
Condemned

That is [laid down] so you may believe in God and His messenger; such
are God's limits. Disbelievers will have painful torment! ** The ones who
want to limit God and His messenger will be restrained just as those before
them were restrained. We have sent down clear signs: disbelievers will have

disgraceful torment. * Some day God will raise them all up again and notify them about anything they have done. God has calculated it while they have forgotten it. God is a Witness for everything!

7

Intrigue

God is Everywhere

(II) * Have you not considered how God knows whatever is in Heaven and whatever is on Earth? No private conversation ever takes place among three [persons] unless He is their Fourth, nor among five unless He is their Sixth, nor [any number] less than that nor greater unless He is with them, wherever they may be. Then on Resurrection Day, He will notify them about whatever they have been doing. God is Aware of everything!

* Have you not considered the ones who, even though they have been forbidden to [carry on any] intrigue, still go back to what they have been forbidden to do and conspire out of sin and enmity, and in defiance of the Messenger? Whenever they come to you, they greet you the way God never greets you, and tell themselves: "Should God not punish us for what we say?"

Hell will be enough for them; they shall roast in it, for it is such an awful goal to have. * You who believe, whenever you confer with one another, do not conspire out of sin and enmity, and in defiance of the Messenger: confer virtuously and through a sense of duty. Heed God, before whom you will appear.

10

** Intrigue comes only from **Satan**, so he may sadden those who believe. Yet **he will not harm them in any way except with God's permission;** so on God let believers rely.

* You who believe, whenever someone tells you to make room at (any) sessions, then make room; God will make room for you [elsewhere]. When it is said: "Move on ahead!", then move on up. God will raise those of you who believe, in rank, as well as the ones who are given knowledge. God is Informed about anything you do.

Manners at Mettings; Parliamentary Procedure

* You who believe, whenever you confer with the Messenger, offer some sort of charity before you confer [with him]; that will be better for you, and purer [besides]. Yet if you do not find anything [to give], God is still Forgiving, Merciful. * Are you worried about proffering some charity before your consultation? If you do not do so, God still turns towards you, so keep up prayer and pay the welfare tax, and obey God and His messenger. God is Informed about anything you do.

14

Hypocrites

(III) * Have you not considered those who make friends with a folk whom God is angry with? They are neither on your side nor yet on their own, and they perjure themselves while they know it. ** God has prepared severe torment for them; with them, anything they do is evil. * They have taken their faith as a disguise and obstructed God's way. They will have disgraceful torment; * neither their wealth nor their children will help them out in any way with God. Those will become inmates of the Fire; they will remain there for ever.

* Some day God will raise them all up together and they will swear to Him just as they have sworn to you; they reckon they will get something out of it. They are such liars! * Satan has won them over and made them forget to mention God; those are Satan's party. Yet Satan's side will be the losers! ** Those who would limit God and His messenger are the vilest sort.

* God has written: "I shall prevail, both I Myself and My messengers!" God is Strong, Powerful. * You will not find any people who believe in God and the Last Day showing affection for anyone who places limits on God and His messenger, even though they are their own fathers, their sons, their brothers or anyone from their family connection. With those He will engrave faith on their hearts, assist them with a spirit from Himself, and will show them into gardens through which rivers flow, to live there for ever. God will approve of them while they will be pleased with Him. Those are on God's side. God's party are those who shall be successful!

59
Banishment

T HIS CHAPTER of 24 verses which are arranged in three sections was revealed at Madīna after **Evidence** 98. It deals with the expulsion of the Jewish clan called the Banū-Naḍīr who lived three miles outside of Madīna, and how to distribute the booty resulting from the campaign in which they had been defeated (I). This incident occurred six months after the battle of Uḥud in the year 4 / 625.

In the final section (III), the description of how, if the Qurʾān should be delivered to a mountain, it would shudder at receiving such a burden gives us a graphic picture, while the concluding passage forms a beautiful doxology, in praise of the Deity.

In the name of God, the Mercy-giving, the Merciful!

(I) * Whatever is in Heaven
and whatever is on Earth
celebrates God. He is
the Powerful, the Wise!

The Banū-Naḍīr

* He is the One Who turned those People of the Book who disbelieved, out of their homes in the first **banishment.**

You (all) did not think that they would leave, while they thought that their strongholds would keep God away from them. Yet God came at them from where they did not anticipate it and cast such panic into their hearts, that they tore their houses down with their own hands as well as through believers' hands: so learn a lesson, you who have any insight! * If God had not prescribed expulsion for them, He would still have punished them in this world. They shall have the torment of Fire in the Hereafter. * That is because they have broken off with God and His messenger. Anyone who breaks with God [finds out] that God is Stern in punishment.

Distribution of Spoils in War

** Any nursery stock you cut down or leave standing on their roots, is with God's permission so He may disgrace such immoral people, * as well as any [property] of theirs that God has assigned to His messenger, since none of you spurred along any horses or riding camels to get it; however God gives His messenger authority over anyone He wishes. God is Capable of [doing] everything. * Anything from townsfolk which God has assigned to His messenger belongs to God and the Messenger, as well as near relatives, orphans, the needy and the wayfarer, so that it will not be traded around merely among the rich men you have.

Accept anything the Messenger may give you, and keep away from anything he withholds from you. Heed God [Alone]: God is Stern with punishment.

* [It is also] for those poor refugees who have been expelled from their homes and property, while they are seeking bounty and approval from God and are supporting God and His messenger; those are quite sincere. * The ones who have set up housekeeping and faith before them should love anyone who has migrated to them; they should not find any need in their breasts for anything that has been given them and prefer them ahead of themselves, even though some privation exists among them. Those who are shielded from their own avarice will be prosperous. ** The ones who came after them say:

Refugees

10

"Our Lord, forgive us and our brethren who have preceded us in faith, and do not place any rancor in our hearts concerning those who believe. Our Lord, You are Compassionate, Merciful!"

(II) * Have you not considered those who act hypocritically? They tell their brethren among the People of the Book who disbelieve: "If you are expelled, we will leave along with you. We shall never obey anyone concerning you. If you are attacked, we will support you."

God will show them up as liars! * If they ever are expelled, they will not leave with them, while if they are attacked, they will never support them. Even if they should support them, they will still turn their backs [on them]; then they will not be supported. * They are more in dread of you (all) than anything they feel in their breasts towards God. That is because they are a folk who do not comprehend [anything]. * They will not fight you as a group except from inside fortified towns or from behind walls. Their violence towards one another is serious; you would reckon they would stick together, while their hearts are so at odds. That is because they are a folk who do not use their reason.

** Just as the ones shortly before them tasted the consequence of their own action, even so they will have painful torment. * It is just as Satan does when he tells a man: "Disbelieve," and then once he does disbelieve, says: "I am innocent of you; I fear God, Lord of the Universe." * The outcome for them both is that they [will land] in the Fire, to remain there for ever. Such will be the reward for wrongdoers.

11

Hypocrites Again

Satan's Victims

(III) * You who believe, heed God! Let every soul watch out for whatever it has prepared for the morrow, and heed God; God is Informed about anything you do. * Do not be like those who have forgotten about God, so He lets them forget about their own souls. Such people are immoral! ** The inmates of the Fire are not equal to the inhabitants of the Garden; the inhabitants of the Garden will achieve [whatever they want].

18

20

* If We had sent this Qurɔān down on a mountain, you would have seen it solemnly splitting open out of awe for God. These are the parables We make up for mankind so that they may meditate.

The Qurɔān on a Mountain

A Hymn
to God

* He is God,
besides Whom there is no [other] deity;
Knowing the Unseen and the Visible,
He is the Mercy-giving, the Merciful!

   * He is God [Alone]
besides Whom there is no [other] god,
the Sovereign, the Holy, the [Source of] Peace,
the Secure, the Preserver, the Powerful,
the Compeller, the Magnificent:
glory be to God ahead of anything
they may associate [with Him]!

   * He is God,
the Creator, the Maker, the Shaper.
His are the Finest Names.
Whatever is in Heaven and Earth
celebrates Him. He is
the Powerful, the Wise.

60
Examining Her

THIS CHAPTER was revealed after **The Coalition** 33 and before **Women** 4. Its 13 verses in two sections, which are noticeably longer than the succeeding Meccan ones, date from the Madīna period.

The chapter begins with Abraham's prayer (I) before it deals with women converts (II). This chiefly concerns woman's role as Islamic society was developing; at the end it gives the woman's profession of faith.

In the name of God, the Mercy-giving, the Merciful!

(I) * You who believe, do not take My enemy and your own enemy as friends, offering them affection while they disbelieve in any Truth that has come to you; they exile the Messenger as well as you yourselves just because you believe in God, your Lord. If you have gone forth to strive for My sake, seeking to please Me, would you secretly show them your affection? I am quite Aware of what you hide and what you show. Any of you who does so will stray from the Level Path. * If they should encounter you, they would act as enemies of yours and stretch out their hands as well as their tongues to injure you. They would love to make you disbelieve!

* Not even your blood relations nor your children will benefit you on Resurrection Day; He will sort you out. God is Observant of anything you do. * You have a fine model in Abraham and those with him when they told their folk: "We are innocent of you and anything you serve instead of God. We disown you, and hostility and hatred have set in between us for ever, unless you believe in God Alone (except for Abraham's statement to his father: 'I'll seek forgiveness for you, even though I do not control anything at all with God for you ')."

Our Lord, on You do we rely,
to You do we refer,
and towards You lies the goal!
** Our Lord, do not make us a trial
for those who disbelieve,
and forgive us! Our Lord,
you are the Powerful, the Wise!

Abraham's
Prayer

* You had a fine model in them for anyone who has been hoping [to meet] God and the Last Day. Yet anyone who turns away [will find] God is the Transcendent, the Praiseworthy.

7

*Choosing
One's
Friends*

10

*Women
Converts*

*Their
Remarriage*

*The Women's
Oath* OR
*Profession
of Faith*

(II) * Yet God may still plant affection between you and those of them you felt were enemies. God is Capable, and God is Forgiving, Merciful. * God does not forbid you to act considerately towards those who have never fought you over religion nor evicted you from your homes, nor [forbid you] to act fairly towards them. God loves the fairminded. * God only forbids you to be friendly with the ones who have fought you over [your] religion and evicted you from your homes, and have abetted others in your eviction. Those who befriend them are wrongdoers.

** You who believe, whenever believing women come to you as refugees, **examine** them. God is quite Aware of their faith, so if you recognize them to be believing women, do not send them back to the disbelievers; such women are not lawful for them nor are such men lawful for such women. Give [their former husbands] whatever they may have spent [on them]. There is no objection if you marry such women off, once you give them their allotments. Do not hold on to any ties with disbelievers; ask for whatever you may have spent and let them ask for what they have spent. Such is God's discretion; He will settle things between you. God is Aware, Wise. * Yet if anything of your spouses has slipped over to the disbelievers and you chance to acquire something else [in return], give those whose spouses have gone away the equivalent of whatever they may have spent. Heed God in Whom you (all) believe.

* O Prophet, whenever any believing women come to swear allegiance to you, saying they will not associate anything with God, nor steal, nor misbehave sexually, nor kill their children, nor give any [cause for] scandal that they may invent between either their hands or legs, nor to disobey you in any decent matter; then accept their allegiance and seek forgiveness from God for them. God is Forgiving, Merciful.

* You who believe, do not patronize any folk whom God has become angry with; they despair of the Hereafter just as disbelievers despair of the inhabitants of tombs.

61
Battle Array

THIS TWO-SECTION chapter is arranged in 14 verses which date from
Madīna. It was revealed after **Haggling** 64 and before the next one on
Friday (OR Congregation) 62.

The chapter begins with the refrain: "Whatever is in Heaven / and
whatever is on Earth / celebrates God ...", the same refrain as with **Iron** 57
and **Banishment** 59, four and two chapters preceding, and in the one
immediately following, **Friday (OR Congregation)** 62. It also contains the
famous prediction by Jesus that another messenger would follow him. The
shorter chapters in the Qurʾān begin here.

In the name of God, the Mercy-giving, the Merciful!

(I) * Whatever is in Heaven
and whatever is on Earth
celebrates God. He is
the Powerful, the Wise!

* You who believe, why do you preach something you are not
practising? * God feels a strong distaste for you to preach something you
do not practise. * God loves those who fight for His sake in **[battle] ranks** as
if they were a solid structure.

** Thus Moses told his folk: "My folk, why do you annoy me? You
know I am God's messenger to you." When they wavered, God let their
hearts waver too; God does not guide immoral folk.

* So Jesus the son of Mary said: "Children of Israel, I am God's
messenger to you, confirming whatever came before me in the Old
Testament and announcing a messenger coming after me whose name
will be Aḥmad." Yet when he brought them explanations, they said:
"This is sheer magic!"

*A New
Messenger
Predicted
in the
Gospel*

* Who is more in the wrong than someone who invents a lie about God
while he is being invited to [embrace] Islam? God does not guide such
wrongdoing folk. * They want to blow God's light out with their mouths
while He is Perfecting His light no matter how disbelievers may dislike
it. * He is the One Who has sent His messenger with guidance and the
True Religion, so He may have it prevail over every other religion no
matter how those who associate [others with God] may hate it.

The Pagans

10

*The
Spiritual
Struggle*

(II)** You who believe, shall I lead you to a bargain that will save you from painful torment? * You should believe in God and His messenger, and **strive in God's way with your property and your persons;** that will be better for you if you only knew. * He will forgive you your offences and show you into gardens through which rivers flow, and wholesome dwellings in the gardens of Eden. That will be the supreme Achievement! * And something else you will love to have: support from God and a victory close at hand. Proclaim such to believers!

* You who believe, act as God's supporters just as Jesus the son of Mary told the disciples: "Who will be my supporters [along the way] towards God?" The disciples said: "We are God's supporters." A faction from the Children of Israel believed, while another faction disbelieved. We assisted the ones who believed against their enemy, till they held the upper hand.

62

Friday (OR *Congregation*)

T HIS CHAPTER containing 11 verses from the Madinese period was revealed after the previous one on **Battle Array** 61 and before **Victory** 48. It describes the Prophet's increasing troubles with his Jewish neighbors in and around Madīna, and contains the famous parable on "The Donkey Carrying Books" (I), concerning those who do not practise what they preach, nor profit from what they can learn.

In the name of God, the Mercy-giving, the Merciful!

(I) * Whatever is in Heaven
and whatever is on Earth
celebrates God the Sovereign
[Who is] the Holy, the Powerful, the Wise!

* He is the One Who has despatched a messenger from the Unlettered [people] among themselves, to recite His verses to them and purify them and teach them the Book and wisdom, even though previously they were in obvious error; * as well as others of them who have not yet joined them.

He is the Powerful, the Wise!
* Such is God's bounty which He gives
to anyone He wishes.
God possesses splendid bounty!

** Those who are laden with the Old Testament, yet do not carry it out may be compared to **a donkey who is carrying scriptures**. It is such a dreadful way to have to compare people who reject God's signs! God does not guide such wrongdoing folk.

The Donkey Carrying Books

* SAY: "You who are Jews, if you claim to be God's adherents ahead of [other] people, then long for death if you are so truthful." * They will never long for it because of what their hands have already done. God is Aware as to who are wrongdoers.
    * SAY: "If it is death that you flee, it will still overtake you. Then you will be sent back to the Knower of the Unseen and the Visible; He will notify you about whatever you have been doing."

(II) * You who believe, when [the call to] prayer is announced on the day of **Congregation**, hasten to remember God and close your [place of] business. That will be better for you if you only realized it.

9
Friday Prayers

10   ** Once prayer has been performed, then disperse throughout the land and seek God's bounty. Remember God frequently so that you may prosper. * Yet whenever they see some business or some sport they flock towards it and leave you standing there [alone].

SAY: "Whatever God has is better
than any sport or business.
God is the Best Provider!"

63
Hypocrites

THIS CHAPTER like the previous one on **Friday** 62 contains 11 verses from Madīna. It was revealed after **Pilgrimage** 22 and before **The Pleading Woman** 58. This places it following the battle of Uḥud which occurred near Madīna in the third year of the Hijra or 625 A.D. Its description of hypocrisy is very telling.

In the name of God, the Mercy-giving, the Merciful!

(I) * Whenever **hypocrites** come to you, they say: "We admit that you are God's messenger." God already knows that you are His messenger, while God testifies that the **hypocrites** are liars. * They use their faith as a disguise and obstruct God's way; they are evil because of what they have been doing. * That is because they have believed, then disbelieved; so their hearts are sealed off and they do not comprehend a thing.

* Whenever you see them, their physical appearance may attract you, while if they speak, you will listen to what they say as if they were just sticks of kindling all stacked up. They reckon every shout is [directed] against them. They are the [real] enemy, so beware of them! May God assail them! How they shrug things off!

** Whenever they are told: "Come, God's messenger will seek forgiveness for you," they twist their heads around and you will see them trying to slip away, while they act so haughty. * It is the same for them whether you seek forgiveness for them or do not seek forgiveness for them; God will never forgive them! God does not guide such immoral folk.

* They are the ones who say: "Do not spend anything on anyone who is with God's messenger until they desert [him]." God holds the treasures of Heaven and Earth, yet **hypocrites** do not comprehend this. * They say: "If we should ever return to the City, the grandees there would expel the lower [classes]." Yet influence belongs to God, His messenger and believers, even though **hypocrites** do not realize it.

(II) * You who believe, let neither your wealth nor your children distract you from remembering God. Those who do so will be the losers. ** Spend something from whatever We have provided you with before death comes to one of you and he says: "My Lord, if You would only delay things for me for a short while, then I will act charitably and become honorable!"

* God will never postpone things for any soul once its deadline has arrived. God is Informed about anything you do!

9
10
On Paying Taxes

Eleventh Hour Repentance

64
Haggling

THIS CHAPTER of 18 verses dates from the transition between the late period in Mecca and the first year in Madīna. It was revealed after **Prohibition** 66 and before **Battle Array** 61.

The haggling will occur on the day when God gathers everyone in and we all shall have to account for our actions. The chapter is full of suggestion when it is read attentively.

In the name of God, the Mercy-giving, the Merciful!

(I) * Whatever is in Heaven
and whatever is on Earth
celebrates God. Control is His
and praise is (also) His.
He is Capable of everything!

Free Choice

* He is the One Who created you so that while one of you may be a disbeliever another of you is still a believer. God is Observant of anything you do. * He created Heaven and Earth in [all] Truth, and shaped you and even improved on your shapes. Towards Him lies the Goal! * He

God's Omniscience

knows whatever is in Heaven and Earth, and knows anything you conceal as well as anything you disclose; God is Aware of what is on one's mind.

** Has not news come to you (all) about those who have disbelieved previously? They tasted the effect of their action and [experienced] painful torment. * That was because their messengers had brought them explanations and yet they said: "Will human beings ever guide us?" So they disbelieved and turned away. God has no need of such [people]; God is Transcendent, Praiseworthy.

* The ones who disbelieve claim they will never be raised up again. SAY: "Indeed, by my Lord, you will be raised again! Then you will be notified about whatever you have been doing. That will be easy for God to do!"

* Believe in God and His messenger, and the Light which We have sent down. God is Informed about anything you do. * Some day He will gather you (all) in on the Day of Gathering; that will be the day for **haggling**! He will remit the misdeeds of anyone who believes in God and has acted honorably, and show him into gardens through which rivers flow, to live there for ever. That will be the supreme Achievement!

10

** Those who disbelieve and reject Our signs will become inhabitants of the Fire, to remain there. What an awful goal it is!

(II) * No disaster has ever struck anyone unless it was with God's consent. Anyone who believes in God, has Him to guide his own heart. God is Aware of everything. * Obey God and obey the Messenger; for if you should turn away, Our messenger needs only to proclaim things clearly.

* God, there is no deity except Him;
so on God [Alone] let believers rely!

* You who believe, some of your spouses and children may be your own enemies, so beware of them! Yet if you pardon, condone and forgive [them], God will (likewise) be Forgiving, Merciful. ** Your wealth and your children are simply a [means of] testing [you]. Yet God holds a splendid fee. * Heed God however you can manage to; hear, obey and spend money on one another. Those who feel secure from their own soul's grasping, will be successful. * If you will advance God a handsome loan, He will compound it for you and forgive you.

God is Appreciative, Lenient;
* Knowing the Unseen and the Visible,
[He is] the Powerful, the Wise!

65
Divorce

THIS CHAPTER of 12 Madinese verses was revealed after **Everyman** 76 and before **Evidence** 98. As shown by the title, it contains legislation on domestic matters.

In the name of God, the Mercy-giving, the Merciful!

(1) * O Prophet, whenever you [and other Muslims] **divorce** women, send them away according to their [legal] number and count up the amount [of months carefully], and heed God your Lord. Do not turn them out of their homes, nor should they be forced to leave except when they have committed some flagrant act of sexual misconduct. Such are God's limits, and anyone who oversteps God's limits thereby harms himself. You do not know whether God may let some matter happen later on!

* Thus whenever women reach their deadline, hold on to them in decency, or part from them in decency. Have two impartial persons from among you act as witnesses, and set up a way to witness their testimony before God. That is what anyone who believes in God and the Last Day is instructed to do. God will grant a way out for anyone who heeds Him, * and provide for him in a manner he could never anticipate. God suffices for anyone who relies on Him; God will accomplish His purpose. God has granted everything in due proportion.

* If you have any doubt concerning those women of yours who have finished with menstruation, then their count is three months; as it is with the ones who are still not menstruating. With those who are pregnant, their term will be whenever they give birth. God makes His matter easy for anyone who heeds Him. ** Such is God's command which He sends down to you (all). Anyone who heeds God will have his evil deeds remitted while He will pile up [his] earnings for him.

* House women wherever you reside, according to your circumstances, and do not harass them in order to make life difficult for them. If they are pregnant, then provide for them until they give birth; while if they are nursing [any babies] for you, then give them their allowances. Discuss things among yourselves in all decency, while if you are hard on one another, then seek another wetnurse for [the father to pay]. * A man of means should spend out of his means, while anyone whose income must be budgeted more carefully, should spend some of whatever God has granted him.

God only holds a person responsible for something He has given him. God will grant **ease, following hardship!**

Personal Responsibility

(II) * How many towns have acted insolently towards both their Lord's and His messengers' command, so We summoned them to a stern accounting and punished them with unheard-of torment. * They tasted the effect of their action and the outcome of their conduct was perdition. ** God has prepared severe torment for them, so heed God, you prudent persons who believe; God has sent you down a Reminder * through a messenger reciting God's clear verses, so He may remove those who believe and perform honorable deeds from darkness into Light. God will show anyone who believes in Him and acts honorably into gardens through which rivers flow, to live there for ever. What a handsome provision God has granted him!

    * God is the One Who created seven heavens, and the same [number of planets] which are like the earth. The Command prevails among them so you (all) may know that God is Capable of everything. God comprises everything in knowledge!

8

10

Salvation

Divine Law

66
Prohibition

THIS CHAPTER containing 12 more verses from Madīna was revealed after **The [Inner] Apartments** 49 and before **Haggling** 64. It forms the last of twelve Madinese chapters that are found in this portion of the Qurʾān.

The subject matter concerns the Prophet's own family life and disputes with his wives Ḥafṣa and ʿĀ'isha over Mary the Egyptian (I), the mother of his shortlived son Ibrāhīm or Abraham. The light given to believers is pictured in section II; and then a parable on both "Bad and Good Wives", which includes a final statement on Mary, Jesus' saintly mother.

In the name of God, the Mercy-giving, the Merciful!

*Handling
Impossible
Oaths*

(I) * O Prophet, why do you **prohibit** something that God has permitted you? You seek to please your wives while God is Forgiving, Merciful. * God has stipulated that you (all) should disregard such oaths of yours. God is your Patron; He is the Aware, the Wise.

*The
Prophet's
Family
Life*

* Thus the Prophet confided a story to one of his wives and when she spread it around, God disclosed the matter to him. He let some of it be known, and overlooked part [of it]. However when he informed her about it, she said: "Who told you about this?", he said: "The Aware, the Informed One told me so."

* If both of you will turn to God (in repentance), then let your hearts be so inclined; while if you back each other up against him, then God will be his Patron as well as Gabriel, plus any honorable believer. The angels furthermore are [his] backers. ** Perhaps, should he divorce you, his Lord would grant him even better wives than you are in exchange, ones committed to (live in) peace, who are believers, devoted, repentant, worshipful, serving as social workers, both matrons and virgins.

* You who believe, shield yourselves and your families from a fire whose fuel will be men and stones: over it there [lurk] fierce, stern angels who do not disobey God in anything He commands them [to do]. They do whatever they are ordered to. * You who disbelieve, do not make up any excuses today; you are merely being rewarded for whatever you have been doing.

8

*Believers'
Light*

(II) * You who believe, turn to God in frank repentance. Perhaps your Lord will remit your evil deeds for you and show you into gardens through which rivers flow, on a day when God will not let the Prophet be humiliated. Those who believe will stand alongside him, their light streaming on ahead of them and to their right. They will say: "Our Lord, perfect our light for us, and forgive us! You are Capable of everything!"

* O Prophet, strive against disbelievers and hypocrites; act stern with them! Their refuge will be Hell and it is such a wretched goal.

** God has made up a parable for those who disbelieve: Noah's wife and Lot's wife were both married to two of Our honorable servants, yet they betrayed them both. Neither received any help at all for them so far as God was concerned. They were told: "Enter the Fire along with [the rest of] those who are entering it."

* God has (also) made up a parable for those who believe, concerning Pharaoh's wife when she said: "My Lord, build a house for me in the Garden alongside You, and save me from Pharaoh and his action. Save me from such wrongdoing folk!"

* And [concerning] Mary, the descendant of ʿImrān, who preserved her chastity; We breathed some of Our spirit into [her womb], and she (thereby) confirmed her Lord's words and books. She was so prayerful!

10
Bad and Good Wives

Mary the Chaste

67
Control

THIS CHAPTER of 30 Meccan verses was revealed after **The Mount** 52 and before **Reality** 69. The next two Parts of the Qurʾān (XXIX and XXX) are Meccan again, except for the short chapter called **[Divine] Support** 110, and they comprise two-score lyric gems. The present chapter gives us a picture of how the Universe was formed, as well as another of the final Blaze which will mark the end of the world (1).

The title *Al-Mulk* gives some difficulty in translation from the Arabic. In a so-called republican or pseudo-democratic age, I prefer the word 'control' instead of monarchical terms such as 'dominion' or 'sovereignty', since control here refers to the ultimate power of the Divinity, while actual political power was being slowly forged in Arabia through a confederation of Arab tribes, the Islamic commonwealth or *Umma* which the Prophet tried to achieve. 'Control' also gives us an easier verb form to use. God is here addressed as the Mercy-giving or *ar-Raḥmān*.

PART TWENTY-NINE

In the name of God, the Mercy-giving, the Merciful!

Cosmogony (OR Creation)

(1) * Blessed is He in Whose hands there rests **control**; He is Capable of [doing] everything, * the One Who created death and life, so He may test which of you is finest in action. He is the Powerful, the Forgiving, * Who created seven matching heavens. You do not see any discrepancy in the Mercy-giving's creation. Look once again; do you see any flaws?

The Blaze

* Then look still another time: (your) gaze will come back to you bewildered, and feel exhausted. ** We have decorated the nearest sky with lamps. We have placed them as missiles directed towards the devils and prepared torment from the Blaze for them.

* Those who disbelieve in their Lord will have Hell's torment; it is such a wretched goal! * As they are flung into it, they will hear it gasping as it seethes, * almost burning with rage. Each time a group is cast into it, its keepers will ask them: "Did no warner come to you?"

10

* They will say: "Of course a warner came to us, and we rejected [him] and said: 'God has not sent down anything; you (all) are merely in gross error.'" ** They will further say: "If we had only listened and reasoned things out, we would not have become inmates of the Blaze." * They will acknowledge their offence, so away with the inmates of the Blaze!

* The ones who live in awe of their Lord even though [He is] Unseen will have forgiveness and a large payment. * Hide anything you say or else

shout it out: He is still Aware of whatever is on your minds. * Does He not know anyone He has created? He is the Gracious, the Informed!

(II) ** He is the One Who has placed the earth to be developed by you, so walk along its byways and eat some of what He provides you with, for with Him lies reviving it again. * Do you feel confident that Whoever is in Heaven will not let the earth swallow you up? How it will sway! * Or do you feel secure that Whoever is in Heaven will not send a hailstorm against you, so that you shall find out how [true] My warning was? * Their predecessors denied it, and how [great] was My disgust!

    * Have they not watched the birds flapping [their wings] in rows above them? What holds them up except the Mercy-giving? He is Observant of everything. ** Who is there [to act] as an army for you in order to support you, besides the Mercy-giving? Disbelievers are merely suffering from delusion. * Who is there to provide for you if He should stop providing [for you]? Rather they persist in insolence and disdain. * And is someone who walks along with his face bent down better guided than someone who walks properly along a Straight Road?

    * SAY: "He is the One Who has produced you and granted you hearing, eyesight and vital organs. Yet how seldom are you grateful!"

      * SAY: "He is the One Who has scattered you all over the earth, and to Him will you be summoned." ** They say: "When will this promise [come to be] if you are so truthful?"

    * SAY: "Knowledge rests only with God; I am merely a plain warner."

* Yet when they see it close at hand, the faces of those who disbelieve will look wretched and someone will say: "This is what you were appealing for!" * SAY: "Have you (all) considered whether God will wipe me out, as well as anyone who is with me, or whether He will show us mercy? Still who will shelter disbelievers from painful torment?" * SAY: "It will be the Mercy-giving. We believe in Him and on Him do we rely. You will know anyone who is in plain error."

    ** SAY: "Have you considered who, if your water should sink into the ground, will bring you any water from a spring?"

(margin notes) 15   20   *God*   *Doomsday*   30

68
The Pen
(OR *The Letter N*)

THIS CHAPTER contains 52 very early Meccan verses, all except for vv. 17-23, which form a graphic parable of "The Arrogant Orchardmen", (OR "The Blighted Garden" as it is sometimes called). These farmers committed the sin of arrogation and ended up by losing their crops (I). Another later story in vv. 48-50 concerns the prophet Jonah (II). Both of these tales date from Madīna. The main body however was revealed after **The Clot** 96 (with which it should be compared), and before **Bundled Up** 73.

This chapter brought comfort to the Prophet, and it is sometimes called the "Second Revelation". Its initial statement shows his growing preoccupation concerning literacy.

In the name of God, the Mercy-giving, the Merciful!

(I) * N.

Muḥammad Not Deranged

By the **pen** and whatever they record, * you, by your Lord's favor, are no madman! * You will receive payment which will never be withheld. * You have been [formed] with tremendous character, ** so you will observe even as they observe, * which of you is being tested.

* Your Lord is quite Aware as to who has strayed from His path, just as He is quite Aware as to who are guided. * Do not obey rejectors; * they would love to have you shift about so they too may shift around. ** Do not obey every contemptible oathmonger, * any faultfinder who goes around spreading gossip, * hindering good, defiant, vicious, * brawling, and a bastard besides that * even though he possesses both money and children. ** Whenever Our verses are recited to him, he says: "Legends by primitive people!"

10

* We shall brand him on the snout!

The Arrogant Orchardmen

20

* We shall test them just as We tested the owners of the orchard when they swore they would pick its fruit next morning * and did not make any reservation about having a second chance; * so a calamity from your Lord came round to them while they were sleeping ** and one morning it lay as if it had been already harvested!

* Thus they called out to one another next morning: * "Get out early to your crop if you [want to] harvest it!" * They hurried off muttering to one another: * "Dont admit any needy person in on you today!"

** So they went off early, grumbling yet ready for work, * and when they saw it, they said: "We must be lost! * In fact, we feel destitute."

   * Someone more considerate among them said: "Did I not tell you: 'Why do you not glorify [God]?'" * They said: "Glory be to our Lord; we have been doing (something) wrong."

   ** Still some of them pounced on others, blaming one another; * they said: "It's too bad for us; we have been so arrogant. * Perhaps our Lord will exchange it for something even better than what we already have. We will plead with our Lord!"   30

* Such is torment, although torment in the Hereafter will be even greater if they only realized it.

(II) * The heedful will have gardens of bliss alongside their Lord. ** Are   34
We to treat Muslims as if they were criminals? * What is wrong with you? How do you decide matters? * Or do you have some book to study from? * Do you have whatever you select from it? * Or do you have some pledge binding on Us until Resurrection Day that you shall have whatever you decide upon?" ** Ask them which of them will lay claim to   40
that. * Or do they have associates [along with God]? Well, let them bring on their associates if they are so truthful.

   * Some day when their shinbone will be laid bare and they will be called upon to bow down on their knees, and they will not manage to; * with their eyes cast down, disgrace will overwhelm them. They had been called upon to bow down on their knees while they still felt safe.

   * Leave Me Alone as well as anyone who rejects this account: We will lead them on gradually by means they do not recognize. ** I shall even put up with them for a while; for My plan is certain.

* Or are you asking them for some fee while they are weighted down with   *Jonah*
debt? * Or do they hold the Unseen which they are writing down? * Be patient with your Lord's decision and not like the Whale's Companion when he called out as he felt stifled. * If favor from his Lord had not reached him, he would have been flung upon the empty beach while he was still to blame. ** His Lord picked him out and placed him with honorable   50
people.

   * The ones who disbelieve almost trip you up by glaring at you whenever they hear the Reminder, and they say: "He's deranged!" * Yet it is merely a Reminder to [everybody in] the Universe.

69
Reality

THESE 52 EARLY Meccan verses were revealed after **Control** 67 and before **Staircases Upward** 70, the next chapter in sequence. The apocalyptic vision is superb and now becoming clearer, for this chapter offers us a vivid idea of how the Last Trumpet will sound on Judgment Day. It also talks about the ancient peoples of Arabia called Thamūd and ʿĀd, as well as about Pharaoh and Noah.

In the name of God, the Mercy-giving, the Merciful!

(I) * **Reality!**
* What is **reality?**
* What will make you recognize
what **reality** is like?

Thamūd
and ʿĀd

* Thamūd and ʿĀd denied [they would face] disaster. ** As for Thamūd, they were wiped out by the Thunderbolt. * As for ʿĀd, they were wiped out by a furiously howling gale. * He loosed it on them for seven grueling nights and eight days. You would see folk collapsing in it as if they were hollow palm trunks. * Do you see any survivors from them?

Pharaoh

10

* Pharaoh came, as well as those before him, and the places Overthrown through [their own] misdeeds; ** they defied their Lord's messenger, so He seized them with a tightening grip. * When the water

Noah

overflowed, We loaded you on the vessel, * so We might set it up as a Reminder for you and so (your) attentive ears might retain it.

*The Last
Trumpet*

* When a single blast is blown on the Trumpet * and the earth is lifted up along with the mountains and they are both flattened by a single blow, ** the Event will take place on that day! * The sky will split open and seem flimsy that day; * while angels [will stand] along its edges. Eight [in all] will bear your Lord's throne above them on that day.

*The Final
Judgment*

20

* On that day you will (all) be arraigned; no secret of yours will remain hidden. * Anyone who is given his book in his right hand will say: "Here, read my book! ** I always thought I would face my reckoning!" * He will be in pleasant living * in a lofty garden * whose clusters [of fruit] will hang within easy reach. * "Eat and drink to your heart's content because of what you sent on ahead in bygone days."

** However anyone who is given his book in his left hand will say: "It's too bad for me; if only my book had not been given me, * I would not have known my reckoning! * If it had only been the Sentence [once and for all]! * My money has not helped me out; * my authority has been wiped out on me."

** "Take him off and handcuff him! * Then let Hades roast him! * Then padlock him to a chain gang seventy yards long. * He did not believe in God Almighty * nor ever urge [others] to feed the needy. ** He has no close friend here today, * nor any food except for some garbage * which only sinners eat."

(II) * Yet I swear by whatever you observe * and what you do not observe, ** that it is a statement [made] by a noble messenger. * It is no poet's statement; how little do you believe! * Nor is it some fortune teller's statement; how little do you think things over! * [It is] something sent down by the Lord of the Universe.

* If he had mouthed some [false] statements about Us, ** We would have seized him by the right hand; * then cut off his main artery. * Not one of you would have prevented it!

       * It is a Reminder for the heedful:
       * We know too that some of you will reject it.
       ** It means despair for disbelievers;
       * yet it is the absolute Truth!
       * So hymn your Lord's almighty name!

30

38
40

50

70
Staircases Upward
(OR *A Skeptic Asking*)

THIS CHAPTER containing 44 early to middle Meccan verses was revealed after the previous one called **Reality** 69 and before **The Announcement** 78. The Arabic word *al-Maᶜārij*, meaning staircases or ladders, is the plural of *Miᶜraj*, which appears as the title of Chapter 17, where it is translated as **The Night Journey** that was made on one of them.

The chapter deals mainly with what one can expect to find in the Hereafter. Morals and proper conduct are also discussed. The rhymes in the Arabic add to the effect of the theme, although they are unfortunately lost through translation.

In the name of God, the Mercy-giving, the Merciful!

(1) * **A skeptic** was **asking** about torment that is bound to happen * to disbelievers; there will be no defence against it * [since it comes] from God Who owns the **staircases** leading **upward**. * The angels and the Spirit will climb up to Him on a day whose range is fifty thousand years. ** So **act patient with a handsome patience!**

* They consider it is far away * while We see it as nearby * on a day when the sky will be like molten brass * and the mountains like tufts of yarn. ** No close friend will question any [other] friend; * they will merely give each other a knowing look. A criminal might like to ransom himself from that day's torment through his children, * his wife, a brother of his, * his family circle which has sheltered him, * and everyone who is on earth if [such action] might then save him.

** Of course not; it would flare up * tugging at his scalp, * claiming anyone who tries to escape and turns away, * through saving (things) up and hoarding (them).

* Man has been created restless, ** so he panics whenever any evil touches him, * and withdraws when some good touches him;

* except for the prayerful * who are constant at their prayers * and whose wealth comprises an acknowledged responsibility ** towards the beggar and the destitute;

* and the ones who accept the Day for Repayment, * and those who are apprehensive about their Lord's torment— * (their Lord's torment is nothing to feel too safe from!)— * and the ones who preserve their chastity, ** except with their own spouses or those living under their control; with such they are blameless.

10

20

Man's Character

Morals; Conduct

30

* Those who desire [to go] beyond that, will be going too far—
* and the ones who preserve their trusts and oaths, * and the ones who stand by their testimony, * and the ones who attend to their prayer— ** those will be honored in gardens.

(II) * Yet what is wrong with those who disbelieve, that they should try to dash on ahead of you * in batches to the right and on the left? * Does every man among them aspire to enter the Garden of Bliss?

* Of course not! We created them out of something they well know. ** And I do swear by the Lord of the Eastern places and the Western places that We are Able * to replace them with someone better than they are. We shall never be overruled!

* Leave them speculating and playing around until they face their day which they have been promised, * the day when they will hasten forth from their graves as if they were rushing towards some objective, * their eyesight cast down, disgrace overshadowing them on that day which they have been threatened with!

36

The Fate of Disbelievers

40

7'1
Noah

T HESE 28 LATER Meccan verses were revealed after **Bees** 16 and before
Abraham 14. The chapter concerns Noah's mission.

The end of the first section tells how the Universe was formed; this
section really consists of a short sermon. As usual in these shorter, early
chapters in this part of the Qur'ān, this one also has a rhyme.

In the name of God, the Mercy-giving, the Merciful!

(1) * We sent **Noah** to his people: "Warn your people before some painful
torment comes to them!"

   * He said: "My folk, I am a plain warner for you: * serve God and
heed Him, and obey me! * He will forgive some of your offences for you
and postpone things for you until a specific deadline. God's deadline will
never be postponed once it comes, if you only realized it."

   ** He said: "My Lord, I have appealed to my people night and
day * and my appeal has only made them flee farther away from
me. * Each time I appeal to them to ask You to forgive them, they stick
their fingers in their ears and try to wrap themselves up in their clothing.
They persist in that and have become so overbearing!

10   * "Next I appealed to them publicly; * then I broadcast it to them,
and confided with them privately ** and said: 'Seek forgiveness from your
Lord; He has been so Forgiving. * He causes the sky to send torrents down
upon you * and He supplies you with wealth and children, and grants you
gardens and even grants you rivers.

   * "'What is wrong that you do not expect God to have any
dignity * while He has created you over and over again? ** Have you not
Cosmogony   (all) considered how God created seven matching Heavens? * He has set
the moon as a light among them, and set the sun up as a source of
light. * God makes you grow out of the earth like plants; * later He will
return you to it, and bring you forth once more.

20   * "'God has laid the earth out as a carpet for you, ** so you may
travel around on highways which lead through mountain passes.'"

21   (II) * **Noah** said: "My Lord, they have defied me and followed after
someone whose money and children will only increase [their chance of]
losing. * They have hatched a great plot * and said: 'Do not forsake your
gods: do not leave Wadd, nor Suwāʿ, nor Yaghūth, nor Yaʿūq, nor
Nasr!' * They have led so many astray; just let wrongdoers go even farther
astray!"

** Because of their mistakes, they were drowned and despatched into the Fire. They did not find they had any supporters apart from God.

* **Noah** said: "My Lord, do not leave any disbelievers with homes upon the earth. * If You should leave them any, they will lead Your servants astray and will only breed loose-living disbelievers. * My Lord, forgive me and my parents, as well as anyone who enters my house as a believer, plus believing men and believing women! Do not increase wrongdoers in anything except destruction."

72
Sprites

THIS GRAPHIC chapter was revealed after **The Heights** 7 and following the Prophet's apparently unsuccessful mission to the mountain town of Ṭāʾif (OR Ṭayif) 50 miles to the southeast of Mecca. This event took place in 620 A.D., or two years before the *Hijra* or his Transfer to Madīna. It, like the previous chapter, contains 28 Meccan verses arranged in two sections. Its style resembles that of Chapter 18 on **The Cave**, for it relates similar allegories.

The terms *jinn* or 'genie' (which forms the usual rendering for the title) are confusing, and when employed they tend to give an undesirable "Arabian Nights" atmosphere to this sacred text. The *jinn* (which is a plural in Arabic) are intelligent yet immaterial beings created from fire. If the cognate word 'spirits' is used in English, it can be confused with the Holy Spirit (or *Rūḥ*—who in Islamic theology is the archangel Gabriel); thus I prefer the more popular term 'sprites', which somewhat makes them resemble the gremlins, elves or the so-called 'little people' in Western folklore, especially in Celtic areas. Professor Fārūqī calls them: 'spiritual beings between man and angels" (in referring to 51:III).

We can also remember the evil spirits which Jesus cast out in **Matthew** 8:16 and **Mark** 5. Some commentators consider these sprites to be opponents of the Prophet's mission, because of those associated with Solomon.

In the name of God, the Mercy-giving, the Merciful!

(1) * SAY: "It has been revealed to me that a band of **sprites** sat listening, and then said: 'We have heard a wonderful Reading * guiding [people] to normal behavior, so we have believed in it. Not one of us will ever associate anyone else with our Lord. * Our Lord's excellence must be exalted! He has taken no consort nor any son. * Some fool among us has been saying outrageous things about God. ** We thought that no human being nor any **sprite** would ever tell a lie about God!'

* "Once human men used to take refuge with men from the **sprites** and it made them even more pretentious. * They thought, just as you have supposed, that God will never send anyone up again.

* "We reached out for Heaven and found it staffed with stern guards and shooting stars. * We used to squat in some of its seats to listen, though anyone who eavesdrops now finds a shooting star lurking there for him. ** We do not know whether evil is intended for anyone on earth, or their Lord wants integrity for them. * Some of us are honorable while others of us are quite the opposite of that: we [travel] along such diverse routes.

10

* "We supposed we would never escape God on earth, and we shall never escape Him by fleeing. * When we heard about guidance, we trusted it. Anyone who trusts in his Lord needs not fear about being undersold nor caught short. * Some of us are Muslims while others of us are [still] holding back. Those who have committed themselves to (live in) peace are dedicated to integrity; ** while those who hold back will become kindling for Hell."

* If they would only keep straight along the highway, We will let them drink plenty of water * so We may test them by means of it; while it will lead anyone away to mounting torment who avoids mentioning his Lord. * Mosques belong to God, so do not appeal to anyone besides God (in them). * Yet whenever **God's servant** stood up to appeal to Him, they almost crowded in upon him!

Association Forbidden

(II)** SAY: "I appeal only to my Lord and never associate anyone else [in my worship of] Him." * SAY: "I do not control any harm for you nor any integrity." * SAY: "No one grants protection from God nor will I ever find any sanctuary besides that in Him * except through a decree from God, and in His message. Anyone who defies God and His messenger will have Hell fire to live in for ever * until once they see what they have been promised, they will realize who has the weakest supporter and are fewest in numbers."

20

** SAY: "If I only knew whether what you are promised is near, or whether my Lord has set a grace period for it; * Knowing the Unseen, He never discloses his Unseen [secrets] to anyone * except for some messenger whom He approves of. He leads him off with an escort both before him and behind him * so He may know that they have delivered their Lord's messages. He embraces anything that lies in their presence, and calculates everything by means of numbers."

73
Bundled Up

THESE 20 VERSES arranged in two sections all date from Mecca, except for vv. 10, 11 and 20, which are from Madīna; the short crisp Meccan verses are thus followed by a longer passage from Madīna. The chapter was revealed after **The Pen** 68, and it refers to the Prophet's worries as he initially accepts his mission and searches for Truth. It gives us an excellent picture of his concern at this period as well as his care in attempting to fulfil his prophetic mission.

In the name of God, the Mercy-giving, the Merciful!

(I) * You who are **bundled up**,
* stay up all night,
except for a little while: * half of it
or a trifle less than that,
* or [even] add some to it,
and chant the Qurʾān distinctly
as it should be chanted. ** We will cast
a weighty statement on you!

* The onset of night is more serious for impressions, as well as more effective for speaking in. * You have lengthy employment during daylight. * Mention your Lord's name and devote yourself to Him utterly! * Lord of the East and the West, there is no deity except Him, so accept him as your Defender. ** Be patient about anything they may say, and steer clear of them in a polite manner. * Let Me deal with rejectors who are enjoying their leisure; put up with them for a while. * Before us there lie fetters and Hades, * plus food which will make one choke, and painful torment.

    * Some day the earth and mountains will rumble, and the mountains spill over as if they had been turned into sand. ** We have sent a messenger to you (all) to act as a witness concerning you, just as We sent Pharaoh a messenger. * Yet Pharaoh defied the messenger, so We seized him mercilessly!

    * So how will you do your duty if you already disbelieve in the day which will turn children into greybeards? * The sky will crack open from it; His promise will be fulfilled. * This is a Reminder, so let anyone who so wishes, adopt a way unto his Lord.

10

(II)** Your Lord knows how you stay up close to two thirds of the night [in prayer], half of it, and even a third of it; and [so do] a group of those who are with you. God measures out both night and daylight; He knows that you (all) will never count them up, so He has relented towards you.

20
Prayer
at Night;
Vigil

Read whatever seems feasible from the Qurɔān. He knows that some of you may be ill while others are out travelling around the earth seeking God's bounty, and still others are fighting for God's sake. So read any of it that seems feasible, and keep up prayer and pay the welfare tax, and advance God a handsome loan. Anything good you send on ahead for yourselves, you will find [later on] with God; it is better and more important as earnings.

Charity
and
Taxes

> Seek forgiveness from God;
> God will be Forgiving, Merciful.

74
The Man Wearing a Cloak

T HIS CHAPTER is commonly considered to be the second one revealed to Muḥammad, six months after his very first one called **The Clot** 96, and even before **The Opening** 1, which formally introduces the Qurˀān. Its 56 Meccan verses were revealed as a complete chapter in two sections. They have a short, rapid style which is difficult to copy in English, although I have attempted to imitate some of this by means of free verse.

The Interval or gap between the Prophet's first call and his second is referred to as the *Fatra*. This chapter contains some striking pictures of the Last Trumpet; the Proud Man; and Hell Fire. The last section (II) lays down conditions for individual responsibility. It all requires thought and explanation. SEE also **Extinguished**! 81 for a similar apocalyptic mood.

In the name of God, the Mercy-giving, the Merciful!

Muhammad's Second Call

(I) * You who are **wrapped in a cloak,**
* stand up and warn!
* Magnify your Lord,
* purify your clothing
** and steer clear of filth.
* Do not give so much away
that you must ask for more;
* act patiently towards your Lord!

10

The Last Trumpet

* When the bugle is sounded on that day, * it will be such a harsh day, ** anything but easy on disbelievers! * Leave Me Alone with anyone I have created to be lonely, * to whom I have granted ample wealth * and some standing before him, * and for whom I have smoothed things over. ** Still he aspires for Me to add even more [to it]!

20

* Of course not; he has acted stubbornly towards Our signs. * I shall weigh him down with mounting trouble. * Let him think things over and measure them out. * Yet he still will be damned just as he has measured; ** once again, he will be killed just as he has measured things out!

The Proud Man

* Then he looked; * next
he frowned and scowled;
* then he stepped back,
glanced around haughtily

* and said: "This is just some magic
which has been handed down;
** this is merely a statement
made by some human being!"
    * I'll roast him by scorching!
* What will make you realize
what scorching is? * It spares nothing
nor leaves anything over
* as it shrivels human [flesh].

Hell Fire

** Over it there are Nineteen; * We have placed none but angels as
guardians of the Fire. We have placed such a number merely as a test for
those who disbelieve, to convince the ones who have been given the Book,
while those who believe may be increased in [their] faith; and so the ones
who have been given the Book as well as believers may not doubt, while
the ones in whose hearts there lurks malice, as well as disbelievers will say:
"What does God want to compare this to?"

    Thus God lets anyone He wishes go astray while He guides whomever
He wishes. No one knows your Lord's armies except He Himself. It is only
a Reminder for humanity.

30

Predestination

(II) * Indeed not; by the moon,
* and night as it retreats
* and morning when it shines forth,
** it is one of the greatest [signs],
* [given] as a warning for humanity,
* for anyone of you who wishes
to advance or lag behind!

32

* Each soul is [held] as a pledge for anything he has earned, * except for
the companions on the Right ** who will be in gardens enquiring
* about the criminals: * "Whatever induced you to be scorched?"

    * They will say: "We were not among the prayerful * nor did we
feed the needy. ** We speculated along with the speculators * and kept
denying [about appearing on] the Day for Repayment * until [its]
certainty came home to us."

    * No intercession by any mediators will benefit them. * What is
wrong with them that they avoid remembering [God] ** as if they were
startled donkeys * who have just fled from a lioness? * Yet every last man
among them wants to be handed scriptures all spread out!

    * Of course, it is rather because they do not fear the Here-
after. * Indeed, it is a Reminder; ** so let anyone who wishes to,
remember it. * Yet they will not remember except however God may
wish.

Responsibility

40

Meditation is Futile

50

He is Entitled to be heeded,
as well as entitled to grant forgiveness!

75
Resurrection

T HIS SPLENDID chapter of 40 very early Meccan verses was revealed after **The Stunning [Blow]** 101 and before **The Gossipmonger** 104. It tells us how we should read the Qur›ān (I) and describes man's stages as he is reproduced or created (II), just as his spiritual stages are suggested at the very beginning (I). The last section moves very graphically.

In the name of God, the Mercy-giving, the Merciful!

(I) * I do swear by **Resurrection** Day,
* as I swear by the rebuking soul,
* does man reckon We shall never
gather his bones together [again]?

* Of course We are Capable of reshaping even his fingertips. ** Yet man wants to carouse right out in the open. * He asks: "When will **Resurrection** Day be?"

* When one's sight is dazzled,
* and the moon is eclipsed,
* as the sun and moon are brought together,
10   ** on that day (every)man will say:
"Where is there any escape?"

* Of course there will be no sanctuary; * recourse will be only with your Lord on that day. * Man will be notified that day about anything he has sent on ahead or else held back. * Indeed man holds evidence even against himself ** although he may proffer his excuses.

How to Read the Qur›ān

* Do not try to hurry it up with your tongue; * it is up to Us to collect it, as well as [to know how] to recite it. * So whenever We do read it, follow in its reading; * **it is then We Who must explain it!**

20   ** Indeed how you (all) love the fleeting present * while you neglect the Hereafter! * Some faces will be radiant on that day, * looking toward their Lord; * while other faces will be scowling on that day, ** thinking that some impoverishing blow will be dealt them. * Indeed when it reaches as high as one's collarbone * and someone says: "Who is such a wizard?", * he will suppose that it means leave-taking * while one shin
30   will twist around the other shin [to keep it from moving]; ** towards your Lord will the Drive be on that day!

(II) * He was not trusting and did not pray,
* but said: "No!" and turned away.
* Then he stalked off haughtily
to his family, * [though] closer to you
and even closer! ** Then closer
to you [lies your doom]
and still closer!

   * Does man reckon
he'll be left forlorn?
* Was he not once a drop
of ejected semen? * Then he became
a clot, so [God]
created and fashioned [him]
* and made him into two sexes,
male and female. ** Is such a Being
not Able to revive the dead?

31
*The
Atheist*

Man's Stages
OR
Development

40

76
Everyman (OR *This [Day and] Age*)

THIS CHAPTER of 31 early Meccan verses was revealed after **The Mercy-giving** 55 and before **Divorce** 65. Both alternate titles of **(Every)man** (OR *Al-Insān*) and **This (Day and) Age** (OR *Ad-Dahr*) are contained in the first verse. The name *Insān* is also inferred in Chapter 36, **Yā-Sin.**

The chapter deals with the subject of eschatology or how we shall spend our afterlife. It also speaks of freewill. We are told how to attain perfection or, as some phrase it, how to progress into sinlessness.

In the name of God, the Mercy-giving, the Merciful!

(1) * Has a period in **[this] age** not come over **(every) man** when he was nothing worth mentioning? * We have created man from a drop of semen [forming] cells so We might test him; thus We made him alert, observant. * **We have guided him along the [right] path, whether he is thankful or thankless.** * We have prepared chains, shackles and a Blaze for disbelievers!

Man's Freewill

The Virtuous in Paradise

** The virtuous will drink from a cup which will be mixed with camphor, * a freely gushing spring where God's servants will drink. * They [always] keep their word, and fear a day whose evil tends to spread around. * They offer food to the needy, the orphan and the captive out of love for Him: * "We are only feeding you for God's sake. We want no reward from you nor any thanks. ** We fear a gloomy, dismal day from our Lord."

10

* God will shield them from that day's evil, and procure them splendor and happiness. * Their compensation for being patient will be a garden and silk [clothing], * relaxing on couches there where they will see neither sun nor any frost. * Close over them will hang its awnings, while its clusters of fruit will droop low. ** Silver pitchers will be passed around them, and glasses made from crystal, * crystal [set] with silver, which they will measure out just as they please, * and be allowed to drink from them a cup flavored with ginger, * [from] a spring there that is called Nectar.

* Immortal youths will stroll around them; whenever you see them, you will reckon they are scattered pearls. ** Wherever you look, you will see bliss and vast control. * They will wear clothing made from green brocade and cloth of gold, and will be dressed up with silver bracelets,

20

while their Lord will offer them a pure drink: * "This is your reward, for your effort has been appreciated."

(II) * It is We Who have sent the Qur[>]ān down to you as a revelation * so **23** be patient concerning your Lord's decision and do not obey any wicked or ungrateful person among them. ** Remember your Lord's name both in the early morning and late afternoon, * and during the night; bow down on your knees before Him and glorify Him all night long. * Those people love a fleeting show, and leave a heavy day behind them. * We too have created them and strengthened their sinews. Whenever We wish, We will replace them with others like them in exchange.

Times of
Prayer

* This is merely a Reminder; **anyone who wishes, may**
adopt a way to [meet] his Lord. ** Anything   **30**
you (all) wish is only if God so wishes
too; God is Aware, Wise! * He
will admit anyone He wishes into
His mercy, while He has prepared painful torment
for wrongdoers.

77
[Winds] Sent Forth

THIS EARLY chapter was revealed after **The Gossipmonger** 104 and **(The Letter) Qāf** 50 (compare it also with Chapter 51 called **Winnowing [Winds]** and **The Chargers** 100). It consists of 50 Meccan verses, although v. 48 dates from Madīna.

This chapter has another refrain running through it: "[It will be] too bad for rejectors on that day!" and begins with a series of oaths. The whole expresses a poetic mood which is extremely difficult to capture in translation. Compare this manner with the one in **The Chargers** 100.

In the name of God, the Mercy-giving, the Merciful!

(I) * By **the [winds] sent forth** for a purpose
* and gales that rage on and on,
* scattering things around;
* then dividing them all up,
** and delivering a Reminder
* either as a plea or a warning,
* you (all) are surely promised
something inevitable.

* When the stars fade away,
* when the sky splits open,
** when mountains are pulverized
* and when messengers' time is set,
* till which day will they be put off?

10

* Till the day for Sorting [things] out!
* What will make you realize
what the day for Sorting is?
** It will be too bad
for rejectors on that day!

The Day for Sorting Things Out

* Did We not wipe out ancient men?
* Then We followed them up with later ones.
* Thus We deal with criminals!
* It will be too bad
for rejectors on that day!

20

** Do We not create you (all)
from a despised fluid?
* We place it in a firm resting-place

* for a known period. * We measure it out
and how favored are Those Who measure it!
    * It will be too bad
    for rejectors on that day!

** Have We not placed the earth as a round-up
* for the living and the dead?
* We have planted lofty headlands on it
and offered you (all) fresh water to drink.
    * It will be too bad
    for rejectors on that day!

* Hurry off to whatever you have been rejecting!
** Hurry away to shade which has three sections,   30
* which is not shady nor any help against flame.
* It throws off sparks like a palace [on fire],
* [bright] as a yellow camel herd.
    * It will be too bad
    for rejectors on that day!

** This will be a day when they will not
utter [a sound]; * nor will they
be permitted to offer any excuse.
    * It will be too bad
    for rejectors on that day!

* This is a day for Sorting [things] out;
We shall bring you (all) together
with the original men. * If you have any scheme,
then scheme against me.
    ** It will be too bad   40
    for rejectors on that day!

(II) * The heedful will be in shady nooks by springs   41
* and have whatever fruit they may hanker for: *Those who*
* "Eat and drink at leisure   *Do their*
because of what you have been doing."   *Duty*
* Thus We reward those who act kindly.
    ** It will be too bad
    for rejectors on that day.

* Eat and enjoy yourselves
for a little while,
since you are criminals.
    * It will be too bad
    for rejectors on that day.

* When someone told them: "Bow your heads!",
they would not bow their heads [in prayer].
    * It will be too bad
    for rejectors on that day.

** Yet what report will they believe in later on?   50

78
The Announcement

T HIS CHAPTER containing 40 short, early Meccan verses was revealed after **Staircases Upward** 70. It deals with cosmogony or the subject of how the world was created in section I; still in the first section we hear the Last Trumpet announcing the final judgment, which continues in II. It achieves this message with a stirring yet quiet dignity, especially towards the end. Again the mood is assisted by rhyme or assonance.

Chapter 78 also marks the beginning of Part XXX, the final and most lyric part of the Qurɔān. This follows the traditional manner of dividing the sacred text into equal divisions for the purpose of continuous reading or recitation, especially during Ramaḍān, the month of Fasting.

In the name of God, the Mercy-giving, the Merciful!

**PART
THIRTY**

(I) * What are they questioning one another about? * About an important **announcement** * which they are disagreeing over. * However they soon will know! ** Then indeed they shall know!

* Have We not laid the earth out as a cradle
* and [set] the mountains up as kingpins?
* We have created you in pairs
* and granted your sleeping for repose

10   ** and granted night as a garment,
* and granted daytime for [you to earn your] living in.

Cosmogony   * We have built seven firmaments above you * and set a blazing lamp there. * We send down water in torrents wrung from rainclouds ** so We may produce grain and plants with it, * as well as luxuriant gardens.

*The Last
Trumpet*   * The day for Sorting has been appointed,
* the day when the Trumpet shall be blown
so you will come in droves,
* and the sky will open up
as if it had gates,

20   ** and the mountains will travel along
as if they were a mirage.

* Hell will lurk in ambush * to receive home the arrogant, * who will
linger there for ages. * They will taste nothing cool in it nor any
drink ** except hot scalding water and slops, * [which are such] a fitting
compensation * since they have never expected [to meet with] any reckoning * and have wittingly rejected Our signs. * Everything have We calculated in writing: ** "So taste! Yet We shall only increase torment for
you!"

Hell

30

(II) * The heedful will have their scene of triumph * with parks and
vineyards, * as well as buxom maidens their own age * and a brimming
cup. ** They will hear no idle talk nor any lying [gossip] there, * as a
compensation from your Lord, a calculated gift.

31
*The
Heedful
in
Paradise*

* Lord of Heaven and Earth as well as whatever is in between them,
[He is] the Mercy-giving! They control no means of addressing
Him; * on the day when the Spirit and the angels will stand there in
ranks, only someone the Mercy-giving grants permission to shall speak,
and he will speak straight to the point.

*The Mercy-
giving*

* That day will seem too real! Anyone who wishes to, may adopt his
recourse to [reach] the Lord. ** We have warned you (all) how
punishment lies close-at-hand, on a day when any man will see whatever
his own hands have sent on ahead, and the disbeliever will say: "If I were
only dust!"

40

79
[Soul-]Snatchers

T HIS CHAPTER of 46 early Meccan verses was revealed after **Prophets**
21 and before **Bursting Apart** 82. Its soaring message is mystic in
content and poetic in form. Moses and Pharaoh are discussed in section I,
while II concerns creation and the final Hour.

In the name of God, the Mercy-giving, the Merciful!

(1) * By those who **snatch** [men's souls] away
at their last gasp * and others
who act more nimbly
* as well as those floating by,
* and still others racing past
** to regulate some matter!

* Some day a rumbling will be felt;
* another will follow on its heels!
* Hearts will be pounding on that day;
* their sight will be downcast.

10

** They will say: "Will we be restored
to our original state
* once we are crumbled bones?"

* They say: "That would then be a losing proposition!" * There would
only be a single rebuke * and then they would never be able to sleep
again!

Moses
and
Pharaoh

** Has Moses' story ever come to you, * when his Lord called to him by
the sacred valley of Ṭuwà? * "Go off to Pharaoh; he has acted
arrogantly. * SAY: 'Would you care to be purified * and for me to guide
you to your Lord so you may [learn to] dread [Him]?'"

20

** He showed him the greatest sign. * Yet he denied and defied
it; * then he turned away to try his best. * He summoned, and called
out, * and said: "I am your supreme lord!" ** God seized him as an
example in (both) the Hereafter and from the First [life]. * In that there
lies a lesson for anyone who dreads [retribution].

27

(II) * Were you harder to create or the sky He has raised? * He has lifted

30

its canopy up and smoothed it off. * He darkens its night and brings forth
its morning glow; ** and the earth has He spread out besides, * and
produced its water and its pasturage from it. * The mountains has He
anchored * as an enjoyment for you and for your livestock.

* When the greatest calamity comes along, ** on the day when everyman will remember whatever he has tried to accomplish, * and Hades will loom forth for anyone to see, * anyone who has acted arrogantly * and preferred worldly life * will have Hades for a dwelling place. ** Anyone who has been afraid to stand before his Lord and restrained himself from passion, * will have the Garden for a dwelling place.

40

* They will ask you about the Hour: "When will it come to pass? * Why are you reminding us about it?" * It lies up to your Lord to set it. ** You are merely a warner for anyone who dreads it; * just as some day they shall see they have hung around for only an evening, or its morning glow.

The Final Hour

80
He Frowned!

THIS CHAPTER containing 42 very early Meccan verses was revealed after **The Star** 53 and before **Power** 97. It refers to an incident when the Prophet was conferring with some of the leading citizens of Mecca, and a blind man, ʿAbdullāh ibn-Umm-Maktūm, interrupted their conversation to ask him some questions of his own. Muḥammad is here cautioned against being overbearing and is reminded about how he must provide instruction for everybody.

The chapters from this point on have no sections; previously the sections have been indicated by means of small Roman numerals—I, II, III, IV etc.

In the name of God, the Mercy-giving, the Merciful!

* **He frowned** and turned away
* because the blind man came to him!

* What will make you realize that he may [yet] be purified (of disbelief) * or even reminded, and the Reminder may benefit him? ** However anyone who seems indifferent, * you will attend to. * It is not your concern whether he will purify himself (or not)!

10

* Yet with someone who comes to you eagerly * and anxiously, ** you act so distracted! * Indeed, it serves as a Reminder! * Anyone who wishes should remember how it * [exists] on honored pages * which are held aloft [for display], cleansed ** by the hands of noble, * virtuous scribes.

Man's Stages

20

* Let man be damned! What makes him act ungrateful? * From what sort of thing did He create him? * From a drop of semen has He created him and proportioned him. ** Then He made the Way easy for him; * next He will let him die and bury him. * Then [later on] He will raise him up again whenever He may wish.

God's Bounty

30

* Of course he does not accomplish what He orders him to. * So let man look at his own food! ** We let water pour down abundantly; * then We split the earth right open * and cause grain to sprout from it, * and grapes and fodder, * olive trees, datepalms ** and dense woodlots * and fruit[-trees] and pastures * as an enjoyment for both you and your livestock.

Doomsday

* When the uproar comes * on a day when man will flee from his brother, ** his mother and his father, * his mate and his children,

* every last man among them will have enough concern that day to keep him occupied. * Some faces will be beaming on that day, * laughing, rejoicing; ** while other faces will be covered with grime on that day, * soot will overshadow them. * Those will be the shameless disbelievers.

40

8 I
Extinguished! (OR
Wrapping Things Up)

T HESE 29 EARLY Meccan verses were revealed after **The Flame** (OR **Palm Fibre**) 111 and before **Glory to Your Lord in the Highest** 87. The chapter is quite poetic, and rhymed throughout; it concerns the Last Judgment, and in this aspect resembles Chapter 74 **The Man Wearing a Cloak**. Its graphic quality conveys vivid dreams or visions to us, while the prophetic message moves swiftly.

In the name of God, the Mercy-giving, the Merciful!

Doomsday

* When the sun has been **extinguished**,
* when the stars slip out of place,
* when the mountains travel along,
* when ten-month pregnant camels are neglected,
** when wild beasts are herded together,
* when the seas overflow,
* when souls are reunited,
* when the buried girl is asked
* for what offence she has been killed,

10

** when scriptures are unrolled,
* when the sky is stripped bare,
* when Hades is set blazing,
* when the Garden is brought close,
* each soul shall know
what it has prepared!

** So I swear by the planets
* moving, sweeping along,
* and night as it draws on,
* and morn when it breathes again,
* it is a statement by a generous messenger

20

** possessing strength established
by the One Enthroned * Who is
to be Obeyed and more than that
is Trustworthy. * Your companion
is not crazy! * He saw him
on the clear horizon;

* nor was he grudging about the Unseen.
** Nor is it a statement [made]
by some outcast Satan.

  * So where are you (all) heading for?
* It is merely a Reminder
to [everyone in] the Universe.
* So anyone of you who wishes
may go straight. * Yet you will only wish
whatever God, Lord of the Universe,
may wish.

*The
Universal
Message*

82
Bursting Apart

THESE 19 EARLY Meccan verses were revealed after **[Soul-]Snatchers** 79 and before **Splitting Open** 84. Like the previous chapter, this one also deals with Doomsday. The late Professor Nicholson observes on p. 167 (n. 2) in his *Literary History of the Arabs* that this passage is written in "true prophetic style". Zamakhshari tells how it brings God's abundant mercy whenever it is recited.

In the name of God, the Mercy-giving, the Merciful!

Doomsday

* When the sky **bursts apart**
* when planets are strewn around,
* when the seas spill forth,
* when graves are overturned,
** [each] soul will know what it sent on ahead
and has left behind.

* O man, what has lured you away from your generous Lord * Who created you, fashioned you and proportioned you * in whatever shape He wished? He has put your frame together.

10

   * Nevertheless you still reject religion! ** Yet over you (all) there stand * some noble guardians, writing it all down; * they know anything you do.

   * The virtuous shall be in bliss, * while the loose-living will be in Hades; ** they shall roast there on the Day for Repayment, * they will never be led out of it.

   * What will make you realize what the Day for Repayment is? * Again, what will make you realize what the Day for Repayment will be like?

* [It is] a day when no soul
will control anything in favor
of any other soul; God [Alone]
will hold command on that day!

83
The Cheats
(OR *Cheating*)

THESE 36 LATE Meccan verses come after **The Spider** 29, and were the last to be revealed in Mecca before the *Hijra* or Transfer to the new Islamic capital of Yathrib or Madīna in 622 A.D., the Zero year A.H.

The chapter gives us a hint as to our future life and its rewards. Again it is rhymed throughout. The beginning is a condemnation of fraudulent practices.

In the name of God, the Mercy-giving, the Merciful!

* It will be too bad for **cheats** * who insist on receiving everything when they have people measure something out for them; * yet whenever they measure or weigh things for others, they give (them) less than their due. * Do not such persons suppose they will be raised up again ** [to render accounts] on a tremendous day, * a day when mankind will stand before the Lord of the Universe?

* Indeed not, the loose-livers' book will be [kept] in a vault. * What will make you realize what such a dungeon is like? * An annotated book! ** It will be too bad for rejectors on that day, * those who deny the Day for Repayment! * Each vicious transgressor will plainly reject it; * when Our signs are recited to him, he will say: "[These are] legends by primitive men!"   10

* Of course not; rather whatever they used to do lies like rust on their hearts. ** Indeed they will be screened off from their Lord on that day; * next they will roast in Hades. * Then someone will say: "This is what you have been rejecting."

* Of course the book for the virtuous will rest in the Highest [Heavens]. * What will make you realize what the Highest [Heavens] are? ** An annotated book * which those closest [to God] will bear   20 witness to. * The virtuous will [dwell] in Bliss, * on couches watching. * You will recognize a blissful splendor on their faces. ** They will be offered a sealed potion to drink * whose seal will be musk. For that let rivals compete! * It will be blended with a beverage * from a spring where those close [to God] will drink.

* Those who commit crimes used to laugh at those who believe. ** Whenever they pass by them, they nod to one another. * Then when   30 they go back to their own people, they return exultant. * Whenever they see them, they say: "Those (men) are far astray!"

* They have not been sent as overseers (to be) set up over them, * so today those who believe will laugh at disbelievers, ** from couches where they [lie] watching. * Are not disbelievers being compensated for just what they have been doing?

84
Splitting Open

THESE 25 EARLY Meccan verses were revealed after **Bursting Apart** 82 and before **The [East] Romans** 30. This is one of the earlier pictures of Doomsday, but the message is not esoteric or hidden. The language in fact is clear and simple even for an apocalyptic vision.

In the name of God, the Mercy-giving, the Merciful!

* When the sky will **split open**
* and listen to its Lord as it ought to,
* suddenly the earth will flatten out,
* and throw up whatever it contains,
and fall back empty; ** and (also) listen
to its Lord as it ought to!

Doomsday

* Everyman, you are toiling constantly for your Lord, and you will meet Him! * Anyone who is given his book in his right hand * will be called to account with an easy reckoning, * and return joyfully to his family; ** while anyone who is given his book behind his back * will appeal to be blotted out * and will roast in the Blaze.

10

* He used to be happy with his own people; * he supposed he would never revert [to God]. ** Nevertheless his Lord had still been Observing him!

* So I swear by the gloaming,
* and night and whatever it enshrouds,
* and the moon when it blossoms full,
* you shall ride along stage by stage.

** What is wrong with them that they do not believe? * When the Qurʾān is read to them, why do they not **bow down** on their knees? * Instead, those who disbelieve keep on rejecting * while God is quite Aware of how they are holding back.

20

BOW DOWN HERE (Except for Those In Authority)

* Give them news of painful torment, ** except for those who believe and perform honorable deeds; they will have payment which will never be withheld.

85
Constellations

THESE 22 MECCAN verses were revealed after **The Sun** 91 and before **The Figtree** 95. The chapter is named from the starry 'mansions' in the sky called the signs of the zodiac. It is rhymed, generally in -*d*.

The chapter concerns the Christians who lived in the Najrān highlands to the south of the Ḥijaz, north of Yaman and east of the Red Sea before Islam; they were massacred by Dhū-Nuwās, a Jewish king of Yaman, by being burned alive in the year 570 A.D., when the Prophet had just been born.

In the name of God, the Mercy-giving, the Merciful!

* By the sky holding **constellations**
* and the promised day,
* and a witness plus his evidence,
* the diggers of the Trench
    will be slain!

** The fire was full of fuel * as they were crouching over it, * and themselves were witnesses of what they were doing to believers. * They persecuted them merely because they believed in God, the Powerful, the Praiseworthy, * Who holds control over Heaven and Earth. God is a Witness for everything!

10   ** Those who harass believing men and women, then do not repent, will have Hell's torment; they will have the torment of burning. * The ones who believe and perform honorable deeds will have gardens through which rivers flow; that will be the great Achievement.

* Nevertheless your Lord's onslaught will be severe; * He is the One Who originates [matters], then repeats them all over again. * He is the Forgiving, the Affectionate, ** Possessor of the Majestic Throne, * Doer of anything He wants.

* Has the report on the armies ever come to you, * about Pharaoh
20   and Thamūd? * Rather those who disbelieve [persist] in denial ** while God comes sweeping in behind them.

* Still it is a majestic Reading
* [preserved] on a guarded tablet!

86
The Nightcomer
(OR *The Morning Star*)

THIS CHAPTER of 17 early Meccan verses was revealed after **This Countryside** 90 and before **The Moon** 54. The title Ţāriq is a popular man's name today, as it was with the conquerer of Spain in 711 A.D.

The translation should evoke some mystery, yet not confuse us; here the name clearly means the morning star that announces dawn. This shows the dramatic symbolism found in many Arabic names.

In the name of God, the Mercy-giving, the Merciful!

* By the sky and the **Nightcomer!**
* What will make you realize
what the **Nightcomer** is?
* The star shining [before dawn]!

* Each soul has a guardian [set up] over it,
** so let everyman notice
what he has been created from.
* He was created from a fluid ejected
✦ from between his backbone and his ribs.
* He is Able to revive him
* on a day when secrets will be tested;
** so he will have no strength [left]
nor any supporter.

10

* By the sky with its cycle,
* by the earth cracking open,
* it is a decisive statement!
* It is no joke.

** They are hatching some plot
* while I too am hatching a plot;
* so put up with disbelievers;
put up with them as long as you can!

87

Glory to Your Lord in the Highest!

T HESE 19 EARLY Meccan verses form the chapter following **Extinguished!** (OR **Wrapping Things Up**) 81 and preceding **Night** 92. It forms a long doxology or hymn in praise of the Deity; reading it over or attending its recital bears a handsome reward.

In the name of God, the Mercy-giving, the Merciful!

* **Glorify** the name of your Lord,
the All-Highest,
* Who has created and fashioned,
* Who has proportioned and guided,
* Who brings forth pasturage,
** then turns it into weather-beaten stubble.

* We shall make you recite,
so do not forget [anything]
* except whatever God may wish;
He knows the obvious and what is hidden.
* We will make it easy for you
to take the easy way, * so remind [men],
if reminding will benefit [anyone].

10   ** Anyone who feels afraid will be reminded * while the unluckiest,
* the one who will roast in the greatest Fire, shunts it aside; * then he will neither die in it, nor yet live there.

* Anyone who purifies himself,
** mentions his Lord's name
and prays, will prosper.
* Instead you prefer worldly life
* whereas the Hereafter is better
and more enduring. * This has been [written]
on the earliest scrolls,
* the scriptures of Abraham and Moses.

88
The Pall

T HESE 26 EARLY Meccan verses were revealed after **Winnowing**
[**Winds**] 51 and before **The Cave** 18. Here Muḥammad's divine charge
or prophetic commission is announced. The chapter gives a clear picture of
the final Judgment and its ultimate reward. It ends somewhat like the
passage "to the hills around do I lift up my longing eyes" found in Psalm 121.

In the name of God, the Mercy-giving, the Merciful!

* Has the story of the **Pall** ever reached you?

* Some faces will be downcast on that day,
* laboring, toiling. * They will roast
in a scorching fire; ** offered
a boiling spring to drink from,
* they will have no food except some cactus
* which will neither fatten (them)
nor satisfy their hunger.

*The Last
Day*

  * Other faces will be blissful on that day,
* pleased with their effort,
** (dwelling) in a lofty garden. * No loose talk
will be heard in it. * There will be
a flowing spring there; * by it
couches will be raised up,
* glasses set in place, ** cushions lined up
* and carpets spread around.

10

Paradise

  * Do they not consider
how camels have been created?
* Nor how the sky has been lifted up?
* Nor how the mountains have been erected?
** Nor even how the earth
has been flattened out?

20

* **So remind: you need only to remind!**
* You are no taskmaster set up over them,
* except for someone who turns away and disbelieves;
* God will punish him with the worst torment.

  ** Toward Us lies their retreat;
* then their reckoning will fall on Us.

89
Daybreak

THESE 30 VERY early Meccan verses were revealed after **Night** 92 and before **Morning Bright!** 93. Its title of 'Daybreak' or *Al-Fajr* should be compared with that of *Al-Falaq* or 'Dawn' 113 (and also with the last line in Chapter 97).

This chapter ends with a short but moving passage on "The Tranquil Soul" which finally has found rest.

In the name of God, the Mercy-giving, the Merciful!

* By the **Daybreak** * and ten nights
* and the even and the odd,
* and night as it journeys on,
** does that not contain an oath
for someone who is mindful?

* Have you not seen how your Lord
dealt with ʿĀd, * [the people of] Iram,
possessing columns * whose like
had never been created in the land?
* And Thamūd who carved rock out of the valley;
10 ** and Pharaoh wielding kingpins
* who were (all) so arrogant in the land
* and increased corruption there?
* Your Lord unleashed the scourge of torment on them.

* Your Lord is ever on the lookout! ** Yet everyman says, whenever his Lord tests him by honoring and favoring him: "My Lord has honored me!"; * while whenever He tests him by rationing His sustenance for him, he says: "My Lord has disgraced me."

Charity
20 * Rather you are not generous with the orphan * nor do you promote feeding the needy, * and greedily use up anything you inherit. ** You love money till it's brimming over!

* Indeed when the earth has been completely flattened out * and your Lord comes with the angels, row upon row, * and brings up Hell on that day; on that day everyman will remember, as if remembrance even matters to him! * He will say: "It's too bad for me! What did I send on ahead during my lifetime?"

** On that day, no one will torment [anyone] with torment like His, * and no one will hold to any agreement as he will hold to His!

* O Tranquil Soul,
* return to your Lord
  well pleased and pleasing [Him]!
* Enter among My servants,
** and enter My garden.

30

90
[This] Countryside

THESE 20 EARLY Meccan verses were revealed after **(The Letter) Qāf** **(OR Q)** 50 and before **The Nightcomer** 86; they are composed in rhymed prose. A clear statement concerning free will or the choice which is offered Muslims is made here. Reciting it brings us spiritual blessings, especially on Fridays.

The term *Al-Balad* contained in the title is difficult to translate, for its meaning ranges from the idea of 'city' to 'country', and includes that of district, home town, municipality, community, or land. Various versions use most of these English terms. It here means the sacred surroundings of Mecca.

In the name of God, the Mercy-giving, the Merciful!

* I swear by **[this] countryside,**
* you are a native settled on **this land**
* as well as any parent and whatever he may father.

   * We have created man under stress.
   ** Does he reckon that no one
can do anything against him? * He says:
"I have used up piles of money!"
   * Does he consider that no one sees him?

Free Choice

   * **Have We not granted him both eyes,**
* **a tongue and two lips,**
   ** **and guided him along both highroads**?

10

* Yet he does not tackle the Obstacle!
* What will make you realize
what the Obstacle is?

   * [It means] redeeming the captive,
* or feeding ** some orphaned relative
on a day of famine * or some needy person
in distress.

* Then he will act like someone who believes,
recommends patience and encourages mercifulness.
* Those will be the companions on the right-hand side,
* while the ones who disbelieve in Our signs
will be companions on the sinister side:

20

** above them a fire will hem them in.

91
The Sun

THIS CHAPTER of 15 early Meccan verses was revealed after **Power** 97 and before **Constellations** 85. The chapters are becoming increasingly lyric at this point, and the poetic mood in this message is carried along by a continuous and pronounced rhyme in the Arabic.

This chapter deals with Ṣāliḥ or Methusaleh, the messenger who was sent to the early Arabian nation of Thamūd, and the punishment which the latter people received. It brings out the fact that most persons must strive hard in order to remain pure.

In the name of God, the Mercy-giving, the Merciful!

* By the **Sun** and its radiance,
* and the moon as it trails after it,
* and daylight which shines resplendent from it,
* and night when it covers things up,
** and the sky and whatever built it,
* and the earth and what has stretched it out,
* and any soul and whatever has fashioned it
* and filled it with both its debauchery

and its sense of duty!

* Anyone who purifies himself will prosper
** while whoever neglects to do so will be disappointed.

10

* Thamūd rejected it through their arrogance
* when their meanest wretch was delegated
* and God's messenger told them:
"[Here is] God's she-camel; give her
her day to drink."

Thamūd's Camel

* They rejected him and mistreated her,
so their Lord snarled at them
because of their offence
and levelled things off.
** He does not fear its outcome!

92
Night

THESE 21 EARLY Meccan verses were revealed after **Glory to your Lord in the Highest!** 87 and before **Daybreak** 89. It is a poetic chapter which is often recited in public ceremonies, because its recital brings merit.

In the name of God, the Mercy-giving, the Merciful!

* By **night** as it broods,
* and daylight when things seem radiant,
* and whatever has created
the male and the female,
* your effort has been too diffuse.

** For anyone who gives [generously], performs his duty
* and acts charitably in the finest manner
* We shall facilitate an easy way for him;
* while anyone who acts miserably,
and feels he is self-sufficient
* and rejects the finest [things in life]
** We shall make it easy for him
[to go] the hard way. * His money
will not help him out as he stumbles along.

* Guidance is Our concern:
* to Us belongs the Hereafter
and the very First [of life];
* so I have warned you (all)
about a raging fire.

** Only the most wretched will roast in it,
* the one who rejects [the Message]
and turns away; * while the most heedful
will keep away from it,
* the one who gives his money away
and (thereby) purifies himself.

* No one is awarded any favor by Him
** except through seeking the countenance
of his Lord, the All-Highest.
* [Such a man] shall meet approval.

93
Morning Bright!

THESE 11 EARLY Meccan verses were revealed after **Daybreak** 89 and before the next chapter which is called **Consolation** (OR **Relief**) 94. The first two paragraphs deal with the sense of history, while the third and fourth concern some of the Prophet's personal experience and spiritual striving. Here we glimpse Muḥammad's childhood; one should bear in mind that the Prophet had once been a poor orphan boy, protected only by his extended family.

The passage shows the intimate manner in which God comforted him during the Prophet's deep anxiety. Nicholson has a beautifully rhymed paraphrase of this chapter on pp. 152-3 of his *Literary History of the Arabs*.

In the name of God, the Mercy-giving, the Merciful!

* By the **morning bright,**
* and at night when all is still
* your Lord has not forsaken you
nor is He annoyed.

* The Hereafter will be even better for you
than the first [life] was. ** Your Lord
will soon give you something
which will leave you satisfied.

* Did He not find you an orphan
and sheltered [you]? * He found you lost
and guided [you]. * He found you destitute
and made you rich!

* Thus the orphan must not be exploited;
** and the beggar should not be brushed aside.
* Still tell about your Lord's favor.

10

94
Consolation
(OR *Relief*)

THESE 8 EARLY Meccan verses were revealed after the previous chapter called **Morning Bright!** 93, and before **Eventide** 103. The chapter marks divine confirmation of the Prophet's mission, and it brings him further comfort. During any depressed mood we can find much solace by repeating it.

In the name of God, the Mercy-giving, the Merciful!

* Did We not **relieve** your breast for you,
* and remove your burden from you
* that pressed down upon your back?
* We have even raised up renown of you!

** Yet hardship will bring ease.
* Indeed, hardship must bring ease!
* So whenever you have finished,
still toil on! * Towards your Lord
          direct your longing!

95
The Figtree

THIS SHORT chapter of 8 very early Meccan verses was revealed after **Constellations** 85, and before **Quraysh** 106. Its message of moral guidance is borne along on homely figures like the two useful sub-tropical fruits, the fig and the olive.

In the name of God, the Mercy-giving, the Merciful!

* By the **Figtree** and the Olive,
* Mount Sinai * and this safe countryside,
* We have created man with the finest stature;
** then reduced him to the dregs
on the bottom, * except for those who believe
and perform honorable deeds—their earnings
shall never be withheld from them.

* What would make you reject religion later on?
* Is God not the Wisest
of those who judge?

96
The Clot
(OR *Read!*)

THESE 19 MECCAN verses form what is traditionally considered to be one of the very earliest portions of the Qur'ān that was revealed to Muḥammad. They are thrilling words through which God spoke directly to mankind. It is calculated that this incident occurred about the year 610 of the Christian era, or over a decade before the *Hijra* or eventual Transfer to Madīna.

This chapter was revealed before **The Pen** 68 with which it is connected in mood and message, and after **The Man Wearing a Cloak** 74 (which SEE). These chapters recognize the fact that the art of reading or literacy forms the basis for civilized life and culture. The Muslims' respect for it helped to build up the Islamic commonwealth later on which held off the West European middle ages from much of Africa and Asia.

The latter half of this chapter shows a subtle though quite apparent change in mood which is directed against the Meccans' opposition to the Prophet's public prayers.

In the name of God, the Mercy-giving, the Merciful!

Muḥammad's First Call

* **READ** in the name of your Lord Who creates,
* creates man from **a clot!**
* **READ**, for your Lord is most Generous;
* [it is He] Who teaches
by means of the pen,
** teaches man what he does not know.

* However man acts so arrogant,
* for he considers he is self-sufficient.
* Yet to your Lord will be the Return!

10 ·

A Plea for Tolerance

* Have you seen someone who stops ** a worshipper as he prays? * Have you considered whether he is [looking] for guidance * or ordering heedfulness? * Have you seen whether he has rejected [the message] and turned away?

BOW DOWN HERE (Except for those in Authority)

* Does he not know that God sees [everything]? ** Of course not! Yet if he does not stop, We shall catch him by his forelock! * Such a lying, sinful forelock!

* Let him appeal to his henchmen: * We shall appeal to the avenging [angels]. * Of course, do not obey him; **bow down** on your knees, and come closer!

97
Power (OR *Fate*)

THESE 5 MECCAN verses were revealed after **He Frowned!** 80 and before **The Sun** 91. This chapter is thus one of the first to be revealed.

The 'Night of Power' refers to one of the last ten days during the month of Ramaḍān, when the Qurʾān was first sent down to Muḥammad. This passage might be compared with 24:v for a similar hymn to God's power or glory, as this is manifested in His light.

In the name of God, the Mercy-giving, the Merciful!

* We have sent it down on the Night of **Power**!
* What will make you realize
what the Night of **Power** is like?

* The Night of **Power** is better
than a thousand months. * Angels and the Spirit
descend on it on every errand
with their Lord's permission; ** [it means]
peace till the approach of daybreak.

98
Evidence

THIS CHAPTER of 8 verses was revealed after **Divorce** 65 and before **Banishment** 59. Since it dates from the late Meccan or early Madinese periods, the verses here are somewhat longer. It distinguishes the true believer from those who merely play with belief and good behavior.

In the name of God, the Mercy-giving, the Merciful!

* Those People of the Book who have disbelieved, plus the associators [of others with God] did not give up until **evidence** came to them,

> * [through] **a messenger from God**
> **reciting purified pages**
> * which comprise changeless books.

* Nor did those who were given the Book disagree (about it) until after **evidence** had come to them.

** Yet they have merely been ordered to worship God sincerely—[reserving] religion for Him [Alone], as righteous seekers [after Truth]—and to keep up prayer and pay the welfare tax. That is the religion for an established [community].

Hell and Paradise

* Those People of the Book who disbelieve as well as the associators will remain in Hell fire; those are the worst creatures. * Those who believe and perform honorable deeds are the best creatures; * their reward from their Lord will be gardens of Eden through which rivers flow, to live in for ever. God is pleased with them while they feel pleased with Him. That is [reserved] for anyone who dreads his Lord.

99
The Earthquake

T HESE 8 EARLY Meccan (OR possibly Madinese) verses were revealed after **Women** 4, about the same time as **The Stunning [Blow]** 101 and **Eventide** 103 but before **Iron** 57. One should also SEE 22:(i) about this earthquake which will announce Doomsday, and 7:(x) for how this happened with Thamūd. The apocalyptic mood is conveyed through the use of assonance.

In the name of God, the Mercy-giving, the Merciful!

* When earth is shaken
in her [final] **quaking,**
* and earth throws forth her burdens,
* and everyman says: "What is [happening] to her?"

* on that day she will report her news
** which your Lord has inspired her with.
* On that day men will appear in droves
to be shown their actions;

* and whoever has done an atom's weight
of good will see it; * while whoever
has done an atom's weight of evil
will see it.

IOO
The Chargers

THIS CHAPTER containing 11 early Meccan verses was revealed after **Eventide** 103 and before **Plenty** 108. Its panting racehorses (which are mares) make a vivid picture, but they also give a keen sense of foreboding, somewhat as in **Winnowing [Winds]** 51 and **[Winds] Sent Forth** 77. The final syllables -$\bar{a}(n)$, -$\bar{\imath}d$, and $\bar{u}r$ carry the rhymes.

In the name of God, the Mercy-giving, the Merciful!

* By the snorting **chargers**
* striking sparks [with their hooves]
* and racing [home] by morning,
* so they leave a trail of dust
** as they dash into the middle
of the troops with it; * everyman
is grudging towards his Lord!

   * He himself [acts] as a witness to that;
* and is quite passionate
in his love of wealth.

   * Does he not realize that when whatever
[lies] in graves is tumbled out,
** and whatever is on [people's] minds
is checked up on, * their Lord
will be Informed about them
      on that day?

IOI
The Stunning [Blow]
(OR *The Disaster*)

T HESE 11 EARLY Meccan verses were revealed along with **The Earthquake** 99 and before **Resurrection** 75. Its theme is apocalyptic and also composed in "true prophetic style", to quote Nicholson in his *Literary History of the Arabs*, p. 167.

In the name of God, the Mercy-giving, the Merciful!

* **The stunning [blow]**!
* What is a **disaster**?
* What will make you realize
something is going to **stun** [you]?

  * Some day mankind will act like scattered moths
** and the mountains seem like tufts of yarn!   *Doomsday*
* So anyone whose scales are weighted down
* [will land] in pleasant living;
* while whoever's scales are light
* will have a Pit to mother him.

  ** What will make you realize   IO
what this will be like?
     * Scorching fire!

102
Competition

THESE 8 MECCAN verses were revealed after **Plenty** 108 and before **Almsgiving** 107. They describe the race to get ahead or for worldly gain which distracts too many people. Its recital brings us blessings.

In the name of God, the Mercy-giving, the Merciful!

* **Competition** has distracted you
* until you visit graveyards.
* Nevertheless you soon will know;
* once more, you soon shall know!

** Of course, if you realized
with absolute certainty
* how you will (all) see Hades,
* then you would see it
with the [very] eye of certainty;
* next you will be questioned
concerning bliss on that day.

103
Eventide
(OR *The Epoch*)

THESE 3 MECCAN verses were revealed after **Consolation** 94, but before **Jonah** 10 and **The Chargers** 100, and about the same time as **The Earthquake** 99. It offers us a consoling prayer which is recited frequently, since it brings home to us how all things change, and we must learn patiently to face the inevitable. A final consonant in *-r* carries the rhyme.

In the name of God, the Mercy-giving, the Merciful!

* By **eventide**, everyman
* [is indeed] at a loss
* except for those who believe,
  perform honorable deeds,
  encourage Truth, and recommend patience.

I04

The Gossipmonger

T HESE 9 EARLY Meccan verses were revealed after **Resurrection** 75 and before **[Winds] Sent Forth** 77. As its name implies, the chapter deals with slander of the Prophet, which hurt him deeply. The punishment predicted is dire, yet natural. and to be expected.

In the name of God, the Mercy-giving, the Merciful!

* How awful [will it be]
for every backbiting **slanderer**
* who hoards wealth and keeps on adding to it!
* He reckons that his money
will make him immortal.
* Nevertheless he will be flung
into the Bonecrusher!

** What will make you realize
what the Bonecrusher is?
* [It is] God's kindled fire which leaps up
* to clutch at one's vitals.
* It will be vaulted over them
* in outstretched columns.

105
The Elephant

T HIS CHAPTER of 5 Meccan verses was revealed after **Disbelievers** (OR **Atheists**) 109 and before **Dawn** 113. It has a rhyme in -*īl* to parallel the title word of *fīl* or 'elephant'.

The historic reference is to the time when the Abyssinians ruled Yaman in southern Arabia. In the year 570 of the Christian era, the very year when the Prophet was born, they invaded the territory of Mecca under their King Abraha. Fortunately they were repulsed, as this chapter shows, but the campaign became legendary as the Year of the Elephant.

In the name of God, the Mercy-giving, the Merciful!

* Have you not considered how your Lord dealt
with the owners of the **Elephant**?
* Did He not cause their plan to miscarry,
* and sent birds in flocks against them
* which threw stamped clay pellets at them?
** It left them just like chewed-up chaff.

106
Quraysh
(OR *Winter*)

THESE 4 MECCAN verses were revealed after **The Figtree** 95. An alternate title is **Winter**, taken from v. 2. This message shows us that God is the Source of our relative security and commercial prosperity.

The Quraysh were the Prophet's own clan, who at first opposed his mission and felt they were the only aristocrats fit to live in Mecca. Later members of this family became his successors or caliphs in the great cities of Damascus and Baghdad.

In the name of God, the Mercy-giving, the Merciful!

* In dealing with the **Quraysh**,
* for their preparations to travel
in **winter** and in summer;
* let them worship the Lord of this House
* Who feeds them against famine
and secures them from fear.

107
Almsgiving
(OR *Have You Seen...?*)

T HE FIRST three of these 7 verses are early Meccan, while the rest date from Madīna. The chapter was revealed after **Competition** 102 and before **Disbelievers** (OR **Atheists**) 109. It explains that one should be ready to offer charity (for which recommendation SEE also 9:(XIII) & 58:(II).

In the name of God, the Mercy-giving, the Merciful!

* **Have you seen** someone who rejects religion?
* That is the person who pushes the orphan aside
* and does not promote feeding the needy.

  * It will be too bad for the prayerful
** who are absent-minded as they pray,
* who aim to be noticed
* while they hold back **contributions**.

108
Plenty

THIS IS the shortest chapter in the Qurɔān, consisting of only three
verses, like **[Divine] Support** 110; however in this case the message is
expressed in fewer words. These 3 Meccan verses were revealed after **The
Chargers** 100 and before **Competition** 102.

The title is the name of a legendary river which flows through Paradise;
its water is reserved exclusively for God-fearing Muslims. It is sweeter than
honey, whiter than milk and smoother than cream. This lyric chapter gives
added consolation to the Prophet during his early persecution.

In the name of God, the Mercy-giving, the Merciful!

* We have given you **plenty**,
* so pray to your Lord and sacrifice
* since your opponent is the one
who will be lopped off.

109
Disbelievers
(OR *Atheists*)

THESE 6 EARLY Meccan verses were revealed after **Almsgiving** 107 and before **The Elephant** 105. They implicitly teach us to practise tolerance even with atheists, and tell us to treat non-Muslims with respect yet firm disavowal. This chapter forms the traditional Islamic answer to any suggestion of compromise.

In the name of God, the Mercy-giving, the Merciful!

    * SAY: "O **disbelievers!**
    * I do not serve what you serve
    * nor are you serving what I serve!
    * I will not worship what you have worshipped,
    ** neither will you worship what I worship.
        * You have your religion
        while I have my religion."

110
[Divine] Support

THESE 3 VERSES were revealed at Minà on the eastern outskirts of Mecca during the Farewell Pilgrimage, and they, as well as v. 281 in **The Cow** 2 and v. 3 in **The Table** 5, are dated after the chapter on **Repentance** 9. They might thus be considered to date chronologically from the late Madinese period, even though the geographical location is the vicinity of Mecca. These verses thus form the very last chapter to be revealed to the Prophet. It is one of the shortest chapters (along with **Plenty** 108, which likewise consists of three verses).

The message assures Muḥammad that Islam will ultimately be successful. The word 'support' exists as both a noun and verb and is thus more effective in rendering such meanings or situations, so I use it in preference to 'victory' (which I have retained for the word *fath* as in Chapter 48).

In the name of God, the Mercy-giving, the Merciful!

> * When God's **support** comes
> as well as victory, * and you see
> mankind entering God's religion in droves;
> * then hymn your Lord's praise
> and beg Him for forgiveness,
> since He is so Relenting!

III
The Flame
(OR *Palm-Fiber*)

THESE 5 VERY early Meccan verses were revealed shortly after **The Opening** 1 and before **Extinguished!** (OR **Wrapping Things Up**) 81. The mood is graphic as Muhammad's fanatic and "unreconstructed" uncle ʿAbd-al-ʿUzzà is denounced, and thus nicknamed for ever.

In the name of God, the Mercy-giving, the Merciful!

* May Abū-Lahab's both hands waste away
and may he waste away [as well]!
* His wealth and what he's earned
will never profit him:
* he'll roast in a fire with a **flame**;
* while his wife who carries kindling around
** will have a **palm-fiber** rope
around her neck.

112
Sincerity
(OR [*God's*] *Oneness*)

THESE 4 MECCAN verses were revealed after the last chapter in the Book, **Mankind** 114, and before **The Star** 53. The doctrine of God's pure Unity or the Divine **Oneness** is stated clearly here; in fact, it is a strong declaration against the Godhead being looked upon as consisting of more than one person or God's having any son. The title *Al-Ikhlāṣ*, one of the divine attributes, is the direct opposite to *shirk* or the sin of 'association', and involves freeing oneself from such impure worship through pure faith.

This chapter is sometimes called the "Third" of the Qurɔān, since it explains one of the three essential dogmas in Islam, but its stark simplicity is not always appreciated by non-Muslims, nor translated clearly. It forms an answer to a previous rhetorical question implied in the first word, which is "SAY:"

It may be said in cemeteries, (and generally is recited there eleven times), and in memory of deceased loved ones. Through it awareness of God's Omnipresence reaches us. The rhyme is in *-ad*.

In the name of God, the Mercy-giving, the Merciful!

* SAY: "God is **Unique!**
* God is the Source [for everything];
* He has not fathered anyone
nor was He fathered, * and there
is nothing comparable to Him!"

113
Dawn

THESE 5 MECCAN verses were revealed after **The Elephant** 105 and before the next and final chapter on **Mankind** 114. The theme of the title is similar to that of **Daybreak** 89.

This and the next chapter are called *Al-Muᶜawwidhatān* or 'Two Entreaties' OR else *Al-Mudanniyyatān*, 'the Pair that bring one close [to God]', which are invoked in times of anxiety. This short chapter thus forms a true prayer which may be used to dispel superstitious doubt since it shows that something we think of as being evil may actually have another purpose, especially if we can consider it from some fresh aspect or point of view.

In the name of God, the Mercy-giving, the Merciful!

    * SAY: "I take refuge with the Lord of **Dawn**
    * from the mischief of whatever He has created,
    * and from the evil of dusk
    as it settles down, * and from the mischief
    of women spitting on knots ** and from
    the evil of some envier when he envies."

114
Mankind

THESE 6 MECCAN verses were revealed after the previous chapter on **Dawn** 113 and before its preceding one, **Sincerity** (OR **[God's] Oneness**) 112. This chapter likewise forms a prayer for times of anxiety, bringing God's presence to us in our trials.

NOTE the haunting rhyme in the Arabic, contrasted with the assonance in -a- in the previous chapter; the gossiping sound of the recurring "*-ās*" rhyme here is not easily reproduced in English.

In the name of God, the Mercy-giving, the Merciful!

* SAY: "I take refuge with the Lord of **Mankind**,
* the King of **Mankind**,
* the God of **Mankind**,
* from the evil of the stealthy Whisperer
** who whispers in the breasts of **Mankind**,
* whether among sprites or **Mankind**.

THE END

Ṣadaqa Allāh al-ʿAḍhīm!
"Almighty God has spoken the Truth!"

The following longer prayer is usually said whenever one completes reading
the Qurɔān all the way through:

> O God, calm my desolation in my grave!
> O God, grant me mercy through the Mighty Qurɔān
> and place it before me as a token
> and as a Light and guidance,
>   and a mercy.
>
> O God, make me remember
> whatever I may forget of it,
> teach me what I may ignore of it,
> and sustain me while it is being recited
> in the small hours of the night
> and the early hours of the day.
>
> Make it an instrument to [protect] me,
> O Lord of the Universe!

OutReach (Da'wah) Coordinator
**Central Illinois Mosque and
Islamic Center (CIMIC)**
106 S. Lincoln, Urbana, IL 61801
Ph: 217-344-1555
Cimic@prairienet.org
http://www.prairienet.org/cimic/